Discrimination in   world

Discrimination in an Unequal World

EDITED BY
Miguel Angel Centeno
Katherine S. Newman

OXFORD
UNIVERSITY PRESS

2010

OXFORD
UNIVERSITY PRESS

Oxford University Press, Inc., publishes works that further
Oxford University's objective of excellence
in research, scholarship, and education.

Oxford   New York
Auckland   Cape Town   Dar es Salaam   Hong Kong   Karachi
Kuala Lumpur   Madrid   Melbourne   Mexico City   Nairobi
New Delhi   Shanghai   Taipei   Toronto

With offices in
Argentina   Austria   Brazil   Chile   Czech Republic   France   Greece
Guatemala   Hungary   Italy   Japan   Poland   Portugal   Singapore
South Korea   Switzerland   Thailand   Turkey   Ukraine   Vietnam

Copyright © 2010 by Oxford University Press, Inc.

Published by Oxford University Press, Inc.
198 Madison Avenue, New York, New York 10016

www.oup.com

Oxford is a registered trademark of Oxford University Press.

Library of Congress Cataloging-in-Publication Data
Discrimination in an unequal world / edited by Miguel Angel Centeno, Katherine S. Newman.
     p.   cm.
Includes bibliographical references and index.
ISBN 978-0-19-973216-6 (hbk. : alk. paper)—ISBN 978-0-19-973217-3 (pbk. : alk. paper)
1. Discrimination.   2. Racism.   3. Equality.   I. Centeno, Miguel Angel, 1957–
II. Newman, Katherine S., 1953–
HM821.D57 2009
305.09—dc22   2009038282

9 8 7 6 5 4 3 2 1

Printed in the United States of America
on acid-free paper

Preface: The Global Network on Inequality

This volume grew out of an annual conference sponsored by Princeton University's Global Network on Inequality, a group of 25 research institutions around the world that are actively engaged in research on the causes, consequences, and remedies for inequality. Now spanning universities and research institutes in Latin America (Brazil and Chile), Africa (South Africa), Asia (China, Korea, India, Japan), the Middle East (Israel), South Asia (India), and Europe (Ireland, England, Spain, Italy, France, Finland, Denmark, Germany, and Poland), the network has been in existence since 2004 and continues to grow to incorporate new countries and new fields of study.

Inequality is growing rapidly both in postindustrial societies and in the high-growth economies of the developing world. The symptoms can be measured in Gini coefficients and gated communities, in unequal access to institutions of social mobility and the emergence of stark health disparities, in the flows of international migration and the local patterns of segregation. The consequences are visible in unequal patterns of educational attainment, lopsided engagement in elections, and earlier mortality for some groups than for others. Indeed, few problems of interest to sociologists, political scientists, labor economists, and social psychologists are unrelated to the broad patterns of inequality sweeping the modern world.

The forces leading to increased inequality are not completely understood and generate animated controversy in the academic world and the popular press. Some have suggested that globalization is the culprit, permitting the movement of jobs out of the center and into the periphery, where wages are low, setting off high growth rates in countries like China and India that accelerate the advantages of education in those countries. Others have fingered technological change, emphasizing the ways in which the computer revolution created a demand for a well-educated workforce and casting the poorly prepared into an abyss of poverty, the "gray economy," and criminal occupations. The declining strength of unions—itself a response to global pressures and runaway firms—has diminished the clout of labor, now far less able to halt the downward pressures on wages. Shaky welfare states are diminishing the protections provided to workers, exposing young entrants to labor markets to a regime of contingent work where lifetime employment was once the norm.

What is the relationship between these patterns of inequality and discrimination? Is discrimination integral to inequality or an optional by-product? What is the relationship between the organization of the market, the hierarchies that result, and the subjective dimensions of social experience that result in outcomes that appear to privilege groups defined by ascriptive characteristics like race, ethnicity, gender, or citizenship status? These are the questions that animate this volume and indeed, the Global Network on Inequality itself.

The present volume is a collaborative effort among scholars from a variety of social science disciplines, across many continents, aided by our able editor at Oxford, James Cook, our expert editorial consultant, Jill Fraser, and our organizational assistant, Nancy Turco. I am particularly grateful to my colleague Miguel Centeno for serving as coeditor, as his commitment to comparative research on questions like discrimination was central to seeing this volume to completion. Together we express our gratitude for the financial support of Princeton's Institute for International and Regional Studies, without which this project would have been impossible.

Katherine Newman
Director of the Global Network on Inequality and
The Princeton Institute of International and Regional Studies

Contents

Contributors

Paul Attewell is a Professor of Sociology who teaches in the doctoral programs in sociology and in urban education at the Graduate Center of the City University of New York. His research interests include the sociology of education, social inequality and stratification, and the sociology of technology. His most recent book, coauthored with David Lavin, was *Passing the Torch: Does Higher Education for the Disadvantaged Pay Off Across the Generations?* It won the 2009 Grawemeyer Award in Education and also the American Education Research Association's Outstanding Book Award for 2009. His current research focuses on government policy and student careers among nonelite undergraduates and inequality within systems of mass higher education.

Justine Burns is an Associate Professor in the School of Economics at the University of Cape Town, South Africa. She is a behavioral economist whose work focuses on issues of inequality, discrimination, and labor market dynamics. Her recent work examines the impact of racial identity on trust, altruism, and the resolution of collective action problems among South African youth. She has also collaborated on projects examining the impact of income inequality on the provision of local public goods, as well as the role of social networks in improving employment outcomes.

Miguel Angel Centeno is a Professor of Sociology and International Affairs at Princeton University. From 2003 to 2007, he served as the founding director of the Princeton Institute for International and Regional Studies. He has published many books and articles on Latin America, globalization, and state development. (http://www.princeton.edu/~cenmiga)

Michael Cosser is a Chief Research Specialist in the Education, Science and Skills Development research program at the Human Sciences Research Council (HSRC), South Africa. Most of his work at the HSRC has been in the field of human resources development, specifically on learning pathways through the education system and into the labor market. His monographs in this area are: with Jacques du Toit, *From School to Higher Education? Factors Affecting the Choices of Grade 12 Learners* (2002); with Simon McGrath, Azeem Badroodien, and Botshabelo Maja (coeditors), *Technical College Responsiveness: Learner Destinations and Labour Market Environments in South Africa* (2003); with Jacques du Toit and Mariette Visser, *Settling for Less: Student Aspirations and Higher Education Realities* (2004); *Studying Ambitions: Pathways from Grade 12 and the Factors That Shape Them* (2009); and with Sekinah Sehlola, *Ambitions Revised: Grade 12 Learner Destinations One Year On* (2009). Cosser's current research is on the impact of social capital on human capital development and on the valorization of human capital.

Carlos Antonio Costa Ribeiro is a Professor of Sociology and Director of Graduate Studies at Instituto Universitário de Pesquisas do Rio de Janeiro (IUPERJ) and a Professor of Sociology at Universidade Estadual do Rio de Janeiro (UERJ). During the 2007–2008 academic year, he was a fellow at the Center for Advanced Studies in the Behavioral Sciences (CASBS) at Stanford University. Costa Ribeiro is the author of three books and many articles on topics related to social mobility, economic inequality, and race relations. He was also responsible for the Pesquisa Dimensões Sociais das Desigualdades (Social Dimensions of Inequality Household Survey), a national survey collecting information on social stratification within 8,048 households in Brazil. His research focuses on the determinants of economic opportunity within and across generations.

Ashwini Deshpande is a Professor of Economics at the Delhi School of Economics, University of Delhi, India. Her PhD and early publications study the international debt crisis of the 1980s. Subsequently, she has worked on the economics of discrimination and affirmative action issues, with a focus on caste and gender in India, as well as on aspects of the Chinese economy: the role of FDI in the reform process, regional disparities, and gender discrimination. She has recently been selected as a Fellow of the India China Institute at the New School, New York. She has published several articles in leading international journals. She is the editor of *Boundaries of Clan and Color: Transnational Studies of Inter-group Disparity* (with William Darity Jr., 2003) and *Globalization and Development: A Handbook of New Perspectives* (2007).

Surinder S. Jodhka is a Professor of Sociology at the Centre for the Study of Social System in the School of Social Sciences, Jawaharlal Nehru University, New Delhi. He earlier taught at the University of Hyderabad and Panjab University. He is currently the director of the Indian Institute of Dalit Studies,

New Delhi, and country coordinator of the University of Birmingham-sponsored research program on Religions and Development (RaD). He has been actively engaged in research and teaching broadly in the field of development studies. He also works on subjects of castes and communities in contemporary India and has published extensively, including an edited book, *Community and Identities: Contemporary Discourses on Culture and Politics in India* (2001).

Kunihiro Kimura is a Professor of Behavioral Science and Member of the Center for the Study of Social Stratification and Inequality (CSSI) at Tohoku University, Japan. Kimura is the author of eight academic articles written in English on topics ranging from social dilemmas, collective action, measurement of inequality, gender role attitudes, and sex discrimination. Some of these articles were published in international journals such as *Journal of Mathematical Sociology* and *Quality and Quantity*. His current research focuses on the process and the outcomes of statistical discrimination, with special reference to gender. Kimura's most recent work in English is "Education, Employment and Gender Ideology," in *Gender and Career in Japan*, edited by Atsuko Suzuki (2007).

S. Madheswaran is a Professor in the Centre for Economic Studies and Policy at the Institute for Social and Economic Change, Bangalore. He has been working on economics of human resources with special emphasis on the economics of labor and the economics of education. He has completed eight projects related to labor issues in India. His current research focuses on rates of return on education, labor market discrimination, inequality, social security for unorganized workers, and child labor issues. He has published 50 research articles in both international and national journals in the field of labor economics. Apart from research, he has been teaching applied econometrics for the past 13 years for postgraduate and PhD students.

Koyo Miyoshi is a researcher in the Global Center of Excellence Program at the Graduate School of Economics, Keio University. Miyoshi is the author of several chapters in the series, *Dynamism of Household Behavior in Japan*. His current research focuses on gender roles in the Japanese labor market. A recently published article is "Male-Female Wage Differentials in Japan" in *Japan and the World Economy*.

Katherine S. Newman is the Malcolm Forbes Class of 1941 Professor of Sociology and Public Affairs and the director of the Institute for International and Regional Studies at Princeton University. Newman is the author of nine books on topics ranging from urban poverty to middle-class economic insecurity to school violence. Her current research focuses on the increasingly delayed departure of young adults from the family home in Western Europe and Japan, on the experience of democratic rule among the first generation of young people in postapartheid South Africa, and on the impact of affirmative action policy in India and Brazil. Newman's most recent books include *The Missing Class: Portraits of the Near Poor in America* (2007) and *Laid Off, Laid Low: The Social and Political Consequences of Employment Instability* (2008). Her forthcoming book, *Brothers' Keepers? The Limits of Solidarity from the New Deal to the Era of Inequality*, was coauthored with Elisabeth Jacobs.

Devah Pager is an Associate Professor of Sociology and Faculty Associate of the Office of Population Research at Princeton University. Her research focuses on institutions affecting racial stratification, including education, labor markets, and the criminal justice system. Pager's current research has involved a series of field experiments studying discrimination against minorities and ex-offenders in the low-wage labor market. Her book, *Marked: Race, Crime, and Finding Work in an Era of Mass Incarceration* (2007) investigates the racial and economic consequences of large-scale imprisonment for contemporary U.S. labor markets. A recent article (with Bruce Western and Bart Bonikowski), "Race at Work: Results from a Field Experiment of Discrimination in Low Wage Labor Markets" (*American Sociological Review*, 2009) investigates racial and ethnic discrimination in the low-wage labor markets of New York City.

Jeremy Seekings is a Professor of Political Studies and Sociology at the University of Cape Town and has been a Visiting Professor at Yale and Princeton. His books include *The UDF: A History of the United Democratic Front in South Africa, 1983–1991* (2000) and *Class, Race and Inequality in South Africa* (coauthored with Nicoli Nattrass, 2005). He is coeditor of the *International Journal of Urban and Regional Research*. He is codirector of the Cape Area Panel Study (a panel study of adolescents) and director of the Cape Area Study (a series of cross-sectional surveys of adults' attitudes and behavior). His current research concerns the politics of welfare state-building in developing countries, and the reproduction of inequalities in South Africa and elsewhere.

Sukhadeo Thorat is Chairman of the University Grants Commission, New Delhi, and Professor at Jawaharlal Nehru University, New Delhi. He was the founding director of Indian Institute of Dalit Studies and has been a Visiting Professor at Iowa State University. He has written twenty-one books and eighty-four papers on such topics as agricultural development, problems of marginalized groups, caste discrimination and poverty, and human rights. In recognition of his contribution to the upliftment of the downtrodden in the field of higher education, he was honored with various awards, honorary degrees, and the Padma Shree of the Government of India. His recent books include *Dalits in India: Search for Common Destiny* (2008) and *B.R. Ambedkar: Perspectives on Social Exclusion and Inclusive Policies* (2008).

Thomas E. Weisskopf taught at the Indian Statistical Institute and at Harvard University before joining the faculty of the University of Michigan, where he is a Professor of Economics. Weisskopf has coauthored nine books, including (with Samuel Bowles and David M. Gordon) *After the Waste Land: A Democratic Economics for the Year 2000* (1991). He has also published more than 100 articles in a wide range of journals in the fields of economic development, macroeconomics, comparative economic systems, political economy, and public policy. In recent years his research has focused on the analysis of affirmative action policies in theory and in practice, especially in the sphere of higher education. This is the subject of his latest book, *Affirmative Action in the United States and India: A Comparative Perspective* (2004), and a series of related articles.

PART I

STUDYING GLOBAL DISCRIMINATION

1

Discrimination in an Unequal World

Miguel Angel Centeno

Over the past decade, the challenge of inequality has become central to the discussion of the costs and benefits of globalization. Most readers of the relevant media know that the world is an extremely unequal place and that globalization might just be making it more so, even as it appears to reduce levels of poverty.

Defenders of globalization tend not to deny this trend.[1] Yet they also assert that globalization brings about a freeing of human potential and the elimination of traditional barriers. The argument is the classic one from both classic economics and liberal ideology: in a competitive world, no one can afford to discriminate except on the basis of skills. As used to be said about Atlanta, the world is too busy making money to hate (or it was until 2008). This claim does make logical sense and is supported by some historical readings. Certainly the battle for civil rights in the American South was abetted by the process of industrialization as well as the migration to the North. Progress in gender equity has often accompanied moments of labor shortage when skills are too valuable for traditional prejudice to stand in the way of women's movement into male-dominated occupations. The "city air" of capitalism does make those fleeing the countryside freer.

Opponents of globalization counter these claims by pointing out that the new emphasis on human resources only serves to mask prior inequities by rewarding education and skills only the already wealthy could attain. From this perspective, globalization does nothing but provide a meritocratic patina on a consistently unequal distribution of opportunity. This stance is also reasonable given that many measures of global inequality have increased over the past 20 years.

Despite the often deafening volume of the debate, surprisingly little empirical work is available on the extent to which the process of globalization over the past quarter century has had any effect on discrimination as opposed to general inequality. There are quite a few journalistic anecdotes celebrating the rise of members of low castes, women, or non-Europeans in corporate hierarchies and in the global market in general. It is true that even a single one of these cases would have been unimaginable a few decades ago. Globalization has changed many things, and for the better. It has provided unforeseeable opportunities. The question is how and how much. That is the central question behind the chapters of this book.

We need to begin by making a critical distinction between inequality and discrimination—one that is too often forgotten in the salient debates. Inequality is a static measure of a condition. It involves a disparity with respect to resources. When it involves actions, it has to do with inequity in what the *Oxford English Dictionary* parsimoniously calls "dignity, rank, or circumstance." In and of itself, few would argue for the elimination of all forms of inequality; it would appear that practically all forms of social life involve some form of hierarchy. The argument is about how unequal a society may be and how and where the inequity originates.

Condemnations of inequality come in two forms. Some assert that a distribution of resources may be so skewed as to challenge any notion of fairness. Others focus more on whether this unequal distribution was created by what the OED calls "unequal treatment of others; unfair dealing, unfairness, partiality." The former quality involves both an empirical measure and a philosophical judgment—how much does anyone deserve? The latter is less open to ethical debates: has someone been treated differently from others?

This last question is the aspect of inequality that has to do with discrimination. Note that not all discrimination may be bad. In a somewhat anachronistic sense of the term, it can mean establishing differences on the basis of some criteria, not too dissimilar from the Bourdieuan concept of distinction. In the more common or modern usage, it involves the act of noting some characteristic of an individual and then using it as a guide for behavior with that person. Even here, there is room for ethical wiggling. Elite universities apply distinctions by discriminating in favor of some intellectual talent. But to what extent are these distinctions really based on a discrimination against racial or class backgrounds? Almost universally, humans distinguish between the beautiful and the ugly (indeed, this may be the most powerful form of distinction and discrimination). Is such favoritism or bias more legitimate if based on some form of genetic signal? What if patterns of valued facial features parallel historical aesthetic domination by particular groups with the preferred phenotypes?

The selection of categories on which to focus the analysis of discrimination is somewhat arbitrary. As social observers, we identify forms of discrimination and order them into a hierarchy of unjustifiable inequities. For example, despite some recent work, discrimination against the obese or the scarred does not warrant the same attention as that against those who have darker skin. The privileging of the beautiful, the intelligent, or the charming usually does not take into account prior injustices that may have led to inherited advantages (although as medicine progresses, the link between income and chromosomes will become a much more debated topic). Perhaps the most disturbing aspect of the legitimation of discrimination is what we may call the issue of prejudice familiarity; distinctions will be considered less legitimate if they make no intuitive sense to the observer. In short, we are biased about our biases. Thus, hatred of *burakus* in Japan can seem absurd to those who cannot tell the difference between them and other Japanese, hatred between Protestant and Catholic or Shia and Sunni may puzzle those unfamiliar with the respective theological and historical knowledge, and individuals who fail to understand how caste could ever make a difference may still be able to make fine distinctions by hair texture and skin color.

Is there a logic in the manner in which we regard some discriminations as pernicious and others that we ignore? Yes. Some forms of discrimination appear universal (e.g., against those with some indication of physical or mental handicap) and we tend to largely disregard these or consider them unavoidable. Our collective critiques tend to focus on those distinctions that are geographically or socially isolated or relatively rare, are somehow "foreign," or against which it has become progressively easier to rail. So, for example, the opposition to South African apartheid increased as de jure racial segregation declined in the rest of the developed world. The biases of the non-Western societies are habitually scolded as being irrational, harmful, and ingrained, while those of the more "modern" are either natural or even functional: "They are biased; we are selective."

We also focus attention on those differences that are most closely linked to historical patterns of domination, as opposed to those that might appear "natural." We can easily trace the imperial path toward discrimination by skin color. The creation of a caste system (despite the historical mists into which it seems to recede) is obviously a product of some process of conquest. The millennia-old burden of gender is clearly linked to subordination within the family and the workplace that varies by levels of economic development. These forms of discrimination fascinate in part because they can be easily measured, but also because they tend to be supported by elaborate institutions, norms, and rituals.

To what extent has globalization destabilized these? And where do they persist? Have some traditional forms of discrimination endured while others have gone by the wayside? Have new forms of illegitimate distinctions reared their heads?

The greatest difficulty in the comparative study of discrimination, and in particular in determining policies to combat it, is defining and locating what we may call the moment of agency or when it actually occurs. In the simplest situations, such discrimination is part of the law as was most explicitly established in apartheid South Africa. In de jure more open societies, one may still find "smoking memos" where institutions explicitly discuss creating barriers for individuals with a certain identity (as was the case, for example, with "Jewish quotas" in Ivy League schools until the 1960s). There are always the individual instances of gatekeepers making clear their wish to exclude. But the study of discrimination cannot rely on finding such evidence in every single suspected case.

There remains the difficulty of assigning intention. Do we need to prove that at particular gates the keepers are consciously practicing discrimination? To do so would be to equate individual aspirations or beliefs with social facts. To cite one obvious example, an overrepresentation of black male drivers being stopped by the police on the road does not necessarily imply that the majority of police personnel are racist, but it does indicate that there is a systemic discrimination against such persons compared to others who have chosen to take a leisurely Sunday drive. From the point of view of the young African American continually stopped, however, it matters little how the process of tagging him might work. Moreover, even those who might express discriminatory beliefs will often do so in language that either proclaims benign intent ("They wouldn't fit in") or is hidden behind a patina of meritocracy ("They just can't do the job").

These issues bring out the sometimes uncomfortable and complex relationship between inequality as a condition, inequality as a history, and discrimination as a practice. In the simplest cases we can link current inequalities to similar historical asymmetries supported by discriminatory practices. Thus we may find group X is vastly underrepresented in the top percentiles of a measure (income, education, power), has always been near the bottom on these scales, and has consistently suffered from restricted access due to discrimination against individuals who possesses the qualities used to identify them as members of group X. The long and tragic history of the Roma fits this pattern.

A somewhat more complex situation arises when the current inequality exists due to historical exclusion, but is no longer accompanied by overt discrimination (or at least the level of discrimination observed would not in and of itself account for the level of inequality). This is arguably the situation for women and racial minorities in many countries in which the struggles for civil and human rights have created legal and cultural safeguards against discrimination, if not necessarily eliminated it. In most cases, the underrepresentation of the group previously discriminated against is expected to decline as the biographical consequences of historical practices move down the demographic curve. So the numbers of women in the business hierarchy slowly crawl up across the years. In yet another variant, discrimination persists, but is blamed on some distant past injustice, the consequences of which appear to be too difficult to fight: "We would like to hire more, but the pipeline is empty." This process can turn into an eternal wait for the historical shift in the provision of equal merits. Sadly, this seems the case with African Americans in the American professoriate.

In order to address this type of concern, a reverse form of discrimination or distinction has been instituted in some cases in order to attempt to address the historical legacies of exclusion. This, in turn, is often viewed as discriminatory by those with the previously advantaged identity. While some of these arguments appear to be no more than pining for an earlier era of domination, in other cases the complaints are harder to dismiss. So, for example, poorer members of the previously advantaged group may reasonably resent policies that provide special opportunities for those of the previously stigmatized population, regardless of their current class position. The politically charged debate in the United States on university admissions criteria is a perfect example. (But note how choices are made about which discrimination is "worse": more lawsuits are filed about ethnic preferences than about legacies or athletic recruitment.)

It is also critical to keep in mind that inequality may exist (or even become more pronounced) after discriminatory practices are eliminated. Again, this is because unequal possession of valued characteristics (e.g., education, athleticism) produces its own forms of distinction. Simply because we do not label such differences and their subsequent differential rewards as discriminatory does not make the resulting social structure any less unequal. In some cases, historical legacies of discrimination in one field (say military service) may produce an overrepresentation of a group in another socioeconomic area (e.g., commerce). Social and political changes altering the differential rewards associated with one or the other area could lead to a reversal of group fortune. The diasporic commercial elites of Chinese, Bengalis, Lebanese, and Jews are classic examples. Such populations are often in turn accused of discriminatory policies against the majority and then subject to new forms of exclusion, exile, or violence.

Such dilemmas pose a difficult challenge to the liberal ideology of much of globalization. One of the most explicit ideological foundations of globalization is the celebration of individual aspiration and achievement. For such reasons, globalizing forces are usually arrayed against customs and practices that result in discrimination. But cheerleaders for the greater freedom brought about by the global meritocracy need to be cautious. There is first the obvious danger of groups using the supposedly bias-free criteria to merely perpetuate or strengthen unequal access. This does not have to necessarily involve opportunistic duplicity; discrimination may be unconscious or more institutionalized. Perhaps more troubling is that as globalization increases the relative rewards of performance, it may produce greater barriers and broaden social gulfs. Thus, taking down the barriers that prevent individual merit from its just rewards may be a good in and of itself, but it is not a panacea for the ongoing problems of inequality. It is important to face the possibility that because of such trends, inequality might actually increase in a society, even after (or even because) of the elimination of discriminatory practices. Should we be more comfortable with higher Gini indices simply because they are based on forms of distinction we find more palatable than skin color or ethnic heritage?

The relationship between discrimination and unequal outcomes should therefore be understood in the appropriate geographical and historical context. Each society tends to see its particular version of discrimination as universal and obvious, but if we are to draw any generalizable conclusions we must expand the set of cases to include the broad variety of social relations and practices that may be observed. The simple collection of cases will not do as methods will differ and often will be designed for particular national circumstances. Our task in this book is to establish a base with which we can begin comparing different forms of discrimination across the world. Do humans distinguish in different ways or merely in the definition of salient characteristics? Are these systemic forms of bias reeling in the face of globalization? How do they play out in and interact with new global market logics?

Readers will no doubt find many areas that we have neglected. Anti-Semitism is an obvious example, as is, sadly, the treatment of Arabs in contemporary Israel. The history and contemporary experience of the Roma in Europe also deserve much more attention. Ethnic distinctions in sub-Saharan Africa and religious differences in the Middle East have also produced complex systems of exclusion and discrimination. Closer to home, the barriers faced by the descendants of the pre-Columbian populations have already seen much study and again deserve to be better integrated into the broader literature on discrimination. As the world becomes more closely linked and as the demographic changes in these countries continue, the percentage of immigrants in the richer societies will no doubt increase, as well as the social problem of managing relations between new arrivals and "natives." At the very least, we hope that this volume will encourage more comparative work in these and other areas.

In the next section, I begin with a broad view of how globalization and discrimination may be interconnected. I then move to a discussion on how we could ever measure something as particularistic as discrimination in any meaningful comparative way. Following this introductory material I then move to a summary of the major cases. This is followed by a discussion of what general principles we may gather from the studies.

FINDINGS

How much does globalization matter in discrimination? Weisskopf, in chapter 2, reminds us that this not the first time the world has been globalized, and the previous two global epochs were largely disastrous for non-Europeans. The experience of those earlier eras should, if nothing else, make us question any semifunctionalist accounts of global hierarchy by simple recourse to claims that the "West is the best." The fact that global capitalism was born in such violence should also challenge our expectations that global interconnections consist solely of trucking and bartering. Weisskopf analyzes both how globalization may affect discrimination and how it will help or hinder perhaps the best-known policy solution to current and historical discrimination, affirmative action. He answers this question by separating these effects into those in the center and those in the periphery.

In the center, Weisskopf notes the oft-cited cost of globalization to low-skilled workers now competing either domestically or internationally with previously peripheral labor. This fosters discrimination in two forms: indirectly by the fact that when the lower income levels are disproportionably filled by minority ethnics in the center countries, the globalization of labor hurts a specific racial group disproportionably. More directly, and as we have seen in the past few years of nativist backlash, it creates demands for anti-immigrant policies and taints anyone suspected of being nonnative. He finds that globalization should not deter affirmative action policies meant to abet these consequences. However, to the extent that globalization leads to those on the bottom being perceived as invaders, it will reduce support for any positive state action to ameliorate their conditions.

On the periphery, Weisskopf notes that the growth of capitalist institutions and ideas will tend to reduce "the salience of ethnicity-based discrimination while giving rise to other forms of inequality." From the point of view of discrimination (as opposed to a broader social inequity), the question becomes whether members of a particular ethnic group are systematically prevented from accessing the skills or contacts necessary to succeed in the brave new globalized world. If elite universities remain closed to members of group X, or if they find their access to tourism-related jobs obstructed, or if they are unable to immigrate with the same ease (thereby reducing the aggregate remittances sent home to their base ethnic group), then the process of globalization will not represent an exit strategy, but yet another circle of exclusion.[2]

What I find particularly useful about Weisskopf's chapter is that it demonstrates that the effects of globalization on the racial dynamics of a society are not determined solely by international flows, but in how these interact with domestic institutions. Countries are therefore not doomed or blessed to suffer or benefit from globalization dynamics, but can help determine how these will penetrate their societies.

In order to determine the relationship between discrimination and globalization, we need a metric. Most would agree that discrimination exists, that we can sometimes recognize it (often in or against ourselves) and that it makes a difference in a variety of life outcomes. The point is, how much of a difference? How much salience should we give to deeply embedded inequities? For every person believing that discrimination has determined an important aspect of his life, there is arguably another who minimizes the consequences and thinks of most discrimination as nothing more than bad manners or bad taste. Obviously these two opposing views tend to be highly correlated with the relevant category of the observer: the dominant are often unaware of the nature of their dominance. Arriving at an agreed-on form of counting and defining behavior is always important in policy debates, but perhaps nowhere as critical as in the study of discrimination. This is even more critical when one is trying to do comparisons across cases, as we hope this volume will encourage others to do. So, if we are to understand the nature and consequences of racism in the United States, Brazil, and South Africa, then coming up with a single common measure and a means to count it has been the first step.

Chapter 3 provides a base for that discussion. In it, Devah Pager analyzes the various difficulties associated with measuring discrimination. First, there is the problem with the point of view of the victim. Some may feel that random acts are actually part of a systemic pattern of exclusion, while others may have so internalized prejudice as to be unaware of discrimination. When is it perfectly rational for a member of a categorized group to be paranoid? Similarly, the views of those doing the discriminating are also difficult to measure. Efforts to create a politically correct society may distort the information respondents provide, or they may be blissfully unaware of the cognitive connections in their minds. Bias against a particular group shades into prejudice against certain associated characteristics. Moreover, any measurement of perceptions still leaves the question of linking this to behavior and social consequences.

One way of remedying this is to bypass the social interaction altogether and focus on the statistical evidence of over- or underrepresentation of a group in a desired status. Thus, consistent underrepresentation in leadership positions across a broad array of institutions would seem to indicate some measure of discrimination. Yet here it is often difficult to control for other variables that may better explain the relationship between identity and attainment. This is particularly important for discussions of globalization when access to a dominant language, a critical skill, or a valued certificate both increases the likelihood of success in a globalized world and is highly correlated with membership in a certain category. The problem for comparative work here is that few countries outside of the Organisation for Economic Co-operation and Development (OECD) have the databases necessary to complete this kind of work. Fortunately, as we see in the chapters on India, Brazil, and South Africa, this does not apply to arguably the most interesting cases.

A very different methodological turn takes us away from the social reality and emphasizes laboratory experiments. These are particularly well suited for analyzing the psychological or microlevels of discrimination: for example, how we process identity signals and then decide to act or not act on them. Precisely because of their artificial nature, such studies may be ideally suited to cross-national comparison as the specific conditions can be easily controlled or explicitly adjusted to meet local standards. Such an effort might allow us to define a universal model of discrimination.

Pager is most excited by methods that take insights from all of the above and seek to measure the extent of discrimination in specific exchanges. Audit studies essentially create parallel sets of individuals, divided by some form of identity marker but identical in every other possible way. These groups are then sent into social situations where the response to these differences can be easily gauged, callbacks from real estate or employment ads being the most common. The results in the United States have demonstrated much higher levels of discrimination against African Americans, for example, than even many experts would have guessed. The appeal of this method for comparative work is obvious and some of the chapters on India demonstrate its potential. The drawbacks for comparative work, however, are significant. First, there is the serious, if plebian, constraint of money; these studies cost a great deal and such resources are not often available to local scholars in the relevant countries. Second, given the variance in the national processes of finding a home, a school, or a job, there are clear limits on how much a single methodological design can be applied across borders. Where jobs are routinely not advertised, for example, such methods will obviously be of more limited utility. The key here seems to be to very explicitly deal with these issues on a case-by-case basis.

Our identifying obvious and critical arenas of discrimination determined the selection of case studies. The cases of Brazil and South Africa seemed particularly fruitful as they involved large multiracial democracies only recently beginning to grapple with the historical legacies of massive systemic discrimination. We considered including chapters on the United States, but soon realized that size limitations would make it impossible to provide even an uneven reflection of the scholarly work in that area. Many of the methodologies used in the studies, will, however, be quite familiar to students of race in America. The sheer size of the exclusionary system in India and the relative lack of work on it by Western academics made the inclusion of these chapters also obvious. The Japan chapters originated in our interest in focusing on gender exclusion in an otherwise fairly homogenous society, one that has led the world in the globalization of its economy. Each of these cases had something to teach us, but in surprising ways, they told similar stories.

Especially in the contemporary era, discrimination is often less based on automatic assignment of lower status to a particular identity than on a perceived correlation between that identity and some disagreeable or disapproved behavior. Thus, it is no longer considered legitimate to say that "People X should be on the bottom," but more acceptable to say, "People X are lazy and don't work, so of course they are on the bottom." In many of the case studies, we find evidence of gatekeepers explicitly rejecting traditional prejudices while legitimating their discriminatory practices by references to the expected behavior of the relevant group. This process is particularly important in South Africa, where previously sanctioned distinctions are now taboo, yet where mobility has been frustratingly slow.

Chapter 4 explores how South African respondents distinguish between what we might call the deserving and undeserving poor. Using a series of vignettes in a survey instrument, Jeremy Seekings first finds that respondents make an important overall distinction between the unfortunate who should be helped (the sick or those providing care) as opposed to those who do not deserve any such assistance (e.g., drinkers). In itself this is an important finding as it indicates that efforts to fight against discrimination must first deal with often vague notions of worth, disadvantage, and justification. Over and above detailing discrimination, policies must also meet some sense of deservedness.

In many of the vignettes, Seekings's team provides information on the race of the subject in question. Based on this data, Seekings establishes several key points: African respondents seem most willing to accept the deserving status of someone in dire circumstances while whites were the least. Yet when asked how much money someone would receive, whites were the most generous. All of the racial categories were least likely to define a white subject in dire circumstances as deserving. Overall, however, Seekings finds that neither African nor white respondents significantly discriminate against any group in their response to vignettes.

When the respondents are asked about specific policies (as opposed to abstract grants of money), the pattern becomes more complicated. Specific questions regarding affirmative action elicit much more negative responses from both coloured and white respondents. This finding leaves in question whether a rejection of such policies has to do with a racialized judgment or with ideological opposition. This chapter again underlines the importance of convincing a population of the legitimacy of a historical claim to having being discriminated against.

Chapter 5 further explores the interaction between race and behavioral expectations. Justine Burns reports results from two experiments with college and high school students in South Africa. In the first "dictator game," respondents are given an endowment of money and asked how much they would like to give to another participant. In the control cases, the race of the possible recipient is hidden. In others it is indicated by either surname or a photograph. In a second variant of such games, this time with a strategic element added, the initial gift is tripled and the recipient then asked how much she would like to give back to the initiating respondent. If the first set of games measures some element of generosity or altruism, the second emphasizes strategic trust.

The results indicate that both socioeconomic context and racial identity matter. In all settings black initiators give away less money than their white counterparts. This reflects the much lower economic resources common in the black community (and thus the relative higher value of each monetary unit). This is an important finding as it indicates that those on the bottom of a social ladder may be less generous to their counterparts, even if these share a common identity. This is not an indication of racially defined meanness but a reflection of the value of a rand for different classes. Both races shared a set of expectations regarding black behavior with consistent reports of lower expected gifts from black recipients. The racial identity of the recipient does not appear to be significant in the simpler altruistic game. While there is a bias toward those with the same identity (e.g., white to white or black to black), it is only in the strategic game that this bias becomes important. Thus, while members of a multiracial society may be as generous to a member of a different group as to one of their own, the level of trust in outsiders is significantly lower.

The evidence presented in Michael Cosser's chapter indicates that it will take much longer than many would suspect to dismantle the legacies of a system such as apartheid. There remains a huge gap in educational participation across the races, almost exactly reflecting the status of the various groups under the pre-1994 regime. Thus whites are vastly overrepresented not only in higher education and in the locales with most prestige, while blacks are vastly underrepresented in both, with coloureds and Indian Asians somewhere in between.

There is room for hope, however, as the more recent enrollment figures are significantly better in terms of race than their equivalents in 2001. While whites are still vastly overrepresented (with a quarter of higher education enrollments as opposed to less than 7% of the relevant age group nationally) and again blacks are underrepresented (58–83% respectively), this is better than in 2001 and a vast improvement over 1993 when blacks only accounted for 9% of higher education enrollment.

That the difference in racial enrollment can continue despite the transition to majority rule, with the explicit encouragement of black university education by practically all relevant institutions, and within an economy globalized enough to make it clear that education is the path to take, indicates how entrenched the legacies of discrimination may be. In order to explore the reasons for this continuity, Cosser analyzes the class background of participants in a survey of 12th graders (unfortunately, we appear not to have data on the class composition of current university cohorts). The vast majority of black South Africans in this age cohort (76.3%) come from low socio-economic status (SES) families while only 10.3% of whites do so (and nearly half come from high-SES households). (These figures are consistent with the concentration of whites in rich households, blacks in poor ones, and coloureds throughout the income spectrum, as found by Seekings in his study of Cape Town.) Yet again, there is some hope as these numbers represent a significant improvement over 2001 (not to speak of 1993), and by 2006 nearly 10% of black students in 12th grade came from high-SES households.

For many years, Brazil was said to represent a remarkable model of racial democracy. While no one denied the vast inequalities of the country (it is arguably the most unequal society on earth), a distinguished list of Brazilian and foreign observers remarked that racial discrimination was not significant in Brazil and that social barriers were largely along regional and class lines. Beginning in the 1960s, this benign image was consistently challenged by increasingly sophisticated studies of Brazilian reality, and the role of race came to be more and more appreciated. The real question became not so much whether there was racial prejudice in Brazil (there was—even if in a different form than that found in the United States or South Africa), but what the relative roles of race and class were in defining the Brazilian social hierarchy.

Chapter 7 provides a systemic analysis of the composition of inequality in Brazil and demonstrates that racial discrimination still pervades the society, but in surprising ways and places. For the purposes of this book, Costa Ribeiro accurately focuses not just on the comparative social position of different groups (evidence of inequity), but also on the barriers to mobility (more related to discrimination per se). He finds that discrimination needs to be contextualized by level; that depending on what social level gatekeepers are providing access to, their proclivities or abilities to hinder passage will be quite different. This is a vital observation in and of itself since its shifts the question from whether discrimination exists to a much more empirically analyzable question of where it exists and specifically against whom.

In his first set of findings, Costa Ribeiro shows that racial discrimination is much more relevant the higher one climbs in the social ladder. This goes against the far too easily adopted stereotypes of discrimination as practiced by the poor and ignorant, while the rich and educated behave in cosmopolitan ways. Costa Ribeiro demonstrates that in the first rungs of the occupational ladder, race does not matter, controlling for parents' class background. In the higher levels, however, whites have a much higher chance of being able to pass on their status generationally while nonwhites have a lower chance of climbing and a higher chance of falling. In other words, for whites, a parent's class position can be much more of a guarantee for the progeny. For nonwhites, a higher class position is much less easily inherited.

The next stage of Costa Ribeiro's analysis concerns access to education. It is now well established that in a globalized world, access to education is the key to social position. By analyzing the probabilities of obtaining the next educational level within the ranks of the Brazilian educational system, Costa Ribeiro demonstrates that class has a major effect. One optimistic sign is that the effect of class decreases as we progress up the educational pyramid. That is, once children achieve a certain level of education, the probability of their being able to escape their parents' class position increases. Less happily, the effect of race functions in the opposite direction. As one climbs the educational ladder, race appears to become more and more of a factor, again controlling for class origins.

This pattern becomes even clearer when Costa Ribeiro combines the various models and seeks to predict class position based on both class origin and educational position. For those in the lower part of the occupational and class structure, the racial differences appear to be nil. That is, at the bottom, Brazil is relatively democratic racially. But, as the social funnel becomes smaller, race becomes increasingly salient. The well-educated children of the black professional class will face racial discrimination. While this finding goes against certain widely held prejudices regarding racial attitudes among the working class, it makes a great deal of sense. As one climbs up the labor market the level of discretion and the importance of nonformal selectivity increases. Thus the opportunity to close access based on particularistic identity preferences also increases.

If Brazil has often been sold as a racial democracy, Japan enjoys fame for its social equity. Yet the stereotypical image of working life in Japan has a male face, the ubiquitous salary man. When women do appear to be working, they tend to be the equally ubiquitous hostesses at apparently every hotel lobby or large department store. Chapters 8 and 9, by Kimura and

Miyoshi, give us a much deeper understanding of the barriers faced by female workers in Japan.

Both Kimura and Miyoshi analyze the effect of entry level on subsequent wages. Kimura begins by providing an optimistic view of the male-female income gap from 1965 to 2000. As we would expect, given the increasing globalization of the economy, the increasing pressure on performance, the demographic decline, and the internal and external pressures to address gender inequity, the gap shrinks significantly across this time period and is consistently smaller for younger workers. A Japanese woman younger than age 30 in 2000 could expect to make roughly 80% that of a male equivalent—not equal, but certainly an improvement on the less than half made by her older female counterparts or in 1965. Kimura argues that the declining gap has largely to do with the increasing female participation in higher education. This would fit well with the standard economistic reading of globalization, as norms make exclusion of women even more difficult, and education provides a greater net benefit.

Much less optimistic is the analysis of the "marriage bar" involving discrimination among employers against married women. While the number of married women working outside the home has increased since 1965, there remains a huge gap in labor force participation between married and unmarried women. According to Kimura, the discrimination is ensconced in employers' concerns that female married employees cannot or will not devote the same energy to their careers, particularly after childbirth. This leads them to provide fewer opportunities for promotion or job enhancement, thus leading to some voluntary dropout from the labor market by women. Interestingly, Kimura argues against analyses that see gender stereotypes as leading to internalization of values, but believes that women want the same opportunities and believe that they are capable of meeting these challenges.

Koyo Miyoshi seeks to explore gender inequities by analyzing wage differentials. He does so by taking into account not only remuneration, but also participation in the more regularized work force. He begins by confirming the widely held belief that women in Japan do suffer from a larger wage gap than in other OECD nations (67% of male salaries as opposed to 79% in the United States).

Miyoshi seeks to disaggregate this gap by first looking at the likelihood of participating in the regular workforce (full-time and long service). Using household survey data, he finds that male workers are much more likely to be working as regulars and to have had previous experience as such. Not surprisingly, this is associated with an astounding gap in university education (40.8% for males as compared to 14.8% for females in his sample). As in most discriminatory institutions, the effect of these biases is additive:

previous experience as a regular worker increases the likelihood of having such a position and seniority in such jobs is also positively correlated with currently holding them. The returns on human resource characteristics are also biased as experience and seniority in the regular sector (associated with males) produces more income, but the same in the irregular labor force has little effect. Even when possessing the same set of educational and professional experiences, females seem to enjoy much less of a human resource benefit than their male counterparts. The resulting analysis leads to the inevitable conclusion that there are significant wage differences between men and women that cannot be explained by differences in the professionally relevant characteristics of the individuals.

The persistence of such gender inequality in Japan (arguably the first country to demonstrate the economic benefits of globalizing the economy) would indicate that economic modernization in and of itself does not necessarily lead to significant challenges to traditional discrimination. Social life can consistently be bifurcated into a modern or cosmopolitan sphere and one in which all barriers retain their salience. This is perhaps best illustrated by Miyoshi's findings regarding the motivation to enter the labor force. For women, this appears to be closely linked to the number and age of children and the income of the spouse (both negatively related to likelihood of participating in the labor force). For men, neither factor seems to matter. In short, women in Japan are only allowed to work when they can (no young children) or when they have to (low household income).

The caste system is perhaps the one thing that most people know about the Indian subcontinent. This partly reflects the exoticized nature of the hierarchies, and partly the very clear and real inequities that it produces. In my observation, people who much more readily accept similar gulfs in human well-being across and within societies appear particularly horrified with the example of caste barriers. This is partly a product of "Orientalist" views of India and its social divisions, but also reflects the sheer numbers involved: nearly 200 million Dalits and perhaps over half a billion total lower castes. Caste is perhaps the largest functioning national scheme of systemic exclusion by identity on the planet (other than gender).

Despite the huge literature on the caste system and the well-known discrimination it produces, we possesses relatively little empirical data on how much caste matters in India. The last four chapters are part of an ongoing collaboration between a group of American scholars seeking new arenas in which to use and explore their methodologies and Indian counterparts looking to more exactly document the inequities they know are there. In part because the costs of the caste system are so obvious in many settings, especially rural ones, these authors sought to focus on caste in those areas of Indian life where it is supposed to matter the least. Celebratory stories of globalization's impact on Indian poverty and society have become quite common in the past decade.[3] These scholars sought to measure the impact of caste in precisely the space where modernization is supposed to render it irrelevant: the educational and corporate heights of the formal sector in India.

That education in and of itself is not an automatic leveler of the playing field is the conclusion reached by Newman and Deshpande in their replication of the pioneering study made by Deirdre Royster (2003) in the United States. Rather than focusing on statistical methods or field studies, chapter 10 follows 172 graduates or soon-to-be graduates of some of India's most prestigious universities as they enter the job market. Despite some differences in the skills with which they entered university (reflecting historical patterns of discrimination and differential familial resources), the qualifications possessed by the two categories of caste (essentially reflecting Dalits vs. non-Dalits) do not explain the very different postgraduate experiences.

First, Dalit students expect much less. They expect to make less money and have less prestigious jobs, and do not expect to be hired in the generally more dynamic and remunerative private sector. This form of employment autocensure would in itself cause a significant difference in the professional outcomes of the two groups even in the absence of discrimination. But accounts of job interviews clearly demonstrate that these students are facing a considerable barrier of expectations having to do with family background and the like. Yet students from the more advantaged category do not see that they may enjoy advantages and, in fact, consider that the system is rigged in favor of the lower castes. While this early stage of the study does not allow an analysis of job outcomes, all indications are that the Indian environment is replicating that found in the United States by Royster and others. Not only does the "in" group enjoy significant advantages, but also a rhetoric of individual meritocracy has developed that allows the privileged to see any efforts to level the playing field as illegitimate.

The expectation that the job market will present significant barriers to graduates with identity markers of "out" groups is verified in chapter 11, by Newman and Jodhka. Based on interviews with 25 individuals with significant hiring power in successful Indian private firms, these authors find a set of attitudes explicitly claiming to be bias free, but also supporting discriminatory judgments.

All of the interviewees expressed explicit commitments to a meritocratic hiring system and all expressed their disdain for what they perceived as outdated norms of favoritism and prejudice. To be modern is to hire by merit. But as observed in a variety of other arenas, the definitions of merit are hardly socially neutral.

The social construction of merit is perhaps clearest in the employers' discussion of the importance of family background. From their more specific comments, it is clear that these gatekeepers are looking to hire people who come from situations similar to their own. Interestingly, they express the well-established bias against both ends of the social hierarchy, claiming that neither the very poor nor the very rich will fit into their firms. These same biases are also expressed in terms of regional preferences with various locales associated with the relevant values sought by the firm.

Despite holding these views, the employers are practically unanimous in their rejection of any affirmative action policies that, they argue, will not only be unjust but will also hinder Indian development. In the powerful closed circle of their meritocratic ideology, they see their standards as not only fair but also efficient, while those imposed by the state are neither.

In a pioneering replication of the audit studies discussed in chapter 3, Attewell and Thorat seek the document the extent to which signals of membership in a religious minority or a Dalit group cost potential job applicants. By replicating professional and educational experiences, but differentiating some identity signal, such studies seek to control for any and all of the endowment characteristics that may reflect historical barriers rather than contemporary discrimination. These authors discuss that the type of discrimination they are studying does not have to be accompanied by the Indian version of stereotypical racialist perceptions and behaviors, but can be embedded in more subtle cultural hierarchies.

The authors focus on a search for employees that already neglects critical forms of discrimination. By looking at only open employment notices, the authors are excluding the arguably much more exclusive hiring practices that go on behind public view. The results of these experiments have already been the subject of considerable media and political attention in India. When applying for these professional jobs, applicants with a Dalit name had .67 of the odds of an equivalently qualified applicant with a high-caste Hindu name. For those with a Muslim name, the figure was .33. Perhaps even more astoundingly, for jobs that nominally required post-BA degrees, applicants with high-caste names, but without such qualifications, had the same chance of contact as those with Dalit names but with advanced degrees.[4]

Chapter 13, by Attewell and Madheswaran, demonstrates the effect of all of these discriminatory practices by providing a statistical bird's-eye view of the wage hierarchy in what they call liberal India. They find that, as expected, education pays a significant premium and that, over time, the return on ever-higher qualifications has increased. Predictably this has produced more inequality across classes in India. But this is not coming at the expense of more traditional forms of discrimination: in a fascinating if depressing finding, they show that returns on education vary by caste and that those on the bottom of the hierarchy benefit less from their educational investment than those above.

They then break down the data further to establish how much of the caste-based gap has to do with educational attainment (largely reflecting historical discrimination) and how much can only be explained by contemporary exclusion. Operating through a series of mechanisms (including occupational segregation), they find that simple discrimination against lower castes accounts for 30% of the wage gap (and again, this is in the formal urban sector, not in the rural villages where caste penalties are expressed in even more ferocious terms). Of greater concern to those who see the globalization of the capitalist ethic as bringing greater equity, the wage gap is much greater in the private sector than in the public one where some affirmative action policies have existed since Independence.

GLOBAL FORMS OF DISCRIMINATION

The analyses of discrimination in these chapters indicate that the patterns of exclusion may be more universal than we might first believe. Certainly the markers and the categories are different from society to society. But all the cases seem to share the same mechanisms: marking off a group as unable to perform (at best) or inhuman (at worst). These attributes are often expressed in the same breath as protestations wishing it were another way and claims not to be biased. Meritocratic language has been globalized, but the underlying reality remains the same.

What are the underlying patterns?

The first and most obvious is a form of discrimination that requires little sociological analysis (at least as a social phenomenon): simple refusal to allow those possessing a certain characteristic to have access to a position or an opportunity. In much of the world the explicit ideology that used to be openly expressed against members of the disadvantaged group has disappeared, except in some marginal cases. But the real effects of such sentiments are still clearly visible. Among the cases studied in this volume, the best evidence seems to come from the studies by Attewell, Thorat, and Madheswaran. Whether as measured by the differential return to education across castes or the astounding results of the job audit study, it is clear that Dalits, Muslims, and members of lower castes still confront the age-old challenges of signs that stipulate "none of you wanted here."

A more subtle form of discrimination does not operate on the exclusion of categories, but rather ascribes qualities to members of a certain group and then denies them access on the basis of these supposed negative characteristics. Such practices claim to judge individuals on the "content of their character" but then assume certain content based on external signals. An obvious example is found in the work of Newman, Deshpande, and Jodhka where employers speak of the problems with the family background of lower caste applicants that would supposedly interfere with their professional effectiveness. Issues of "deservedness" among the poor or of trust among coworkers, as discussed in chapters 4 and 5, are also critical in this regard. Assumptions of likely actions (even if not associated with a character issue) hamper groups such as women, whose devotion to the employer may be questioned (chapter 8). These kinds of expectations can easily be internalized and in the case studies we see several examples of the relevant populations asking for and expecting less than their due.

The most significant form of discrimination found in the cases involves denial of access to critical gateways. In both chapters 8 and 9, for example, we see that women find their access to the first step in remunerative employment effectively blocked. This then facilitates later blockage as these women of course do not subsequently possess the skills, training, or experience to obtain the best jobs. In chapters 6 and 7 we find that some of this denial of access is of course a historical legacy. But at least in the case of Brazil, we also note that even when provided with some of the tools necessary to succeed by their relatively successful parents, children and young adults of color will find significant obstacles.

Despite these patterns, the cases reveal an apparently universal aversion to affirmative action policies by those whose privileged position is being challenged. Some of this has to do with a simple defense of self-interest. Some stems from a continued refusal to accept that past (and current) practices deserve some policy response. The most complex responses use the very language of meritocracy to deny the possibility of any active policy intervention in education and employment. This latter response makes rigorous work on discrimination ever more important as only with clear evidence of the results of discrimination can policies to remedy it be defended politically.

Perhaps the most important lesson from comparing all of these papers is that education is the new means by which the world creates social hierarchies. Access to schooling is obviously critical, not just because in any case education is closely tied to future SES, but also because all experts recognize that globalization is making education the new standard for the definition of inequality. If one finds, for example, that particular groups are unable to lay their hands on this "currency of the global realm," then there is little chance that the democratizing forces of globalization can play a positive role and a very good chance that they will simply confirm and support more of the same.

In this way, education may be seen as the new form of landed property. To an extent, but one not analyzed in these chapters, education may even "whiten." This would be consistent with claims from defenders of globalization that the liberalization of the global economy is democratizing inequality and getting rid of traditional categories. There remains the interesting question of whether skill-defined class fissures will actually reduce levels of inequality from those maintained by ethnic or racial barriers. But the studies also clearly demonstrate that the educational world is far from flat and that traditional distinctions are being supported through privileged access to education. Whether in South Africa, Brazil, Japan, or India, access to education is highly correlated with membership in previously privileged categories.

All of the studies were carried out at the apex of the latest globalizing boom. Given the findings in fairly positive settings, we fully expect that the crisis that began in 2007 will have exacerbated the discriminatory policies discussed in this book. We hope that the models serve as a guide for continuing work that, unfortunately, is ever more likely to remain salient.

Fortunately for the future of comparative studies of these phenomena, the studies reveal that while requiring a great deal of local sensitivity, methodologies can be carried across borders. The data sets increasingly exist outside of the OECD, allowing for sophisticated statistical techniques. Local colleagues can design the signaling marks needed for audit studies. Experiments can be carried out in locales far removed from American psychology laboratories. The editors hope that this volume will encourage the geographical and methodological expansion of scholarship on discrimination and that such comparative work will provide new clues for policies needed to ameliorate practices of exclusion.

Notes

1. But the methodological finer points of measurement receive a great deal of attention.

2. The last two processes are very much in play in Cuba, for example. The majority black population is underrepresented in both the tourist industry and in the exile community, thereby creating a form of dollar apartheid.

3. This is not to deny these stories. Indian participants in the project are themselves proof of the changes. The question is not whether anything has changed, but how much and how fast.

4. This eerily parallels findings in the United States that white men with prison records fared as well as black men without them in the market for low-skill jobs.

2

Reflections on Globalization, Discrimination, and Affirmative Action

Thomas E. Weisskopf

In this essay I take the opportunity to reflect in a speculative manner about the ways in which the process of globalization might affect the extent of discrimination against people on account of their (broadly defined) ethnic group identity, as well as the extent of efforts to combat such discrimination via affirmative action. I begin by offering definitions of the key terms contained in the title of the chapter. These terms can be and have been interpreted in many different ways, so it is important to make clear what I have in mind. In section 2 I address the question: how does globalization influence the propensity for ethnicity-based discrimination? In section 3 I consider how globalization might impinge on the propensity to counter such discrimination with policies of affirmative action. In the final section I offer a brief conclusion.

1. DEFINITIONS

Globalization

Globalization refers to the process whereby regions and countries of the world, as well as their peoples and economies, become more and more closely connected to one another. It involves the reduction of impediments to the movement of goods, people, information, and finance across societal or national boundaries, with resulting increases in connections among— and mixing between—peoples throughout the world.

Globalization is a long-term trend in human history, but an uneven one. At various times—for example, from the beginning of World War I through the end of World War II—it was interrupted or even reversed. It can be useful to distinguish three phases of globalization, since European explorers sailed the oceans in the late 15th century to Asia and to the Americas and began to chart the geography of a world recognized to be round:[1]

- A first phase, from the late 15th to the late 18th centuries, characterized by European explorations and conquests of territories throughout the rest of the world
- A second phase, from the end of the Napoleonic era (1815) to the beginning of World War I (1914), which featured European colonization of much of Asia and Africa as well as U.S. neocolonization of much of South and Central America
- A third phase, from roughly 1950 to the present, marked by an accelerated spread of capitalist institutions—markets, private property, and so on—across the world, at the expense of both precapitalist and socialist economic formations

Discrimination

Discrimination involves making distinctions. There are many ways in which people can discriminate—some benign, others malign. The kind of discrimination that has greatest salience as a social problem is discrimination by members of a relatively well-off and powerful group in a given society against members of a relatively poorly off and weaker group within that society. This involves the meting out of less favorable treatment to members of the weaker group, simply by virtue of their group identity—as distinct from their capabilities, their actions, or their achievements. "Less favorable" can range across a spectrum running from the imposition of a slight disadvantage in access to some valued opportunity, to second-class citizenship, to outright enslavement. Group identity is based on characteristics that are physical or cultural and rarely alterable—such as race, caste, gender, and sexual preference. Discriminatory behavior by members of more powerful identity groups at the expense of members of weaker identity groups is best characterized as "negative discrimination," to distinguish it from discrimination in favor of weaker groups; but I will drop the adjective except when the possibility of positive discrimination is also at issue.

In this chapter I limit discussion to discrimination of the kind that is rooted in identity groups based on ethnicity, as opposed to gender or sexual preference. I define the term *ethnicity* in a broad sense to encompass any one—or any combination—of the following potentially identifying characteristics: race, caste, tribe, region of origin, mother tongue, and cultural tradition. I do not consider the important subject of discrimination against groups identified by gender or sexual preference, because the issues surrounding these groups are of a qualitatively different kind and deserve separate analysis.

It is important to recognize that discrimination by one group against others is only one of several basic possible sources of intergroup inequality. In principle, members of a group A can be better off (on average) than members of another group B for a variety of reasons, including (1) having greater per capita resource endowments, (2) expending greater per capita effort in work activities, (3) having devoted a larger share of available resources to investment (as opposed to consumption), and (4) benefiting from discrimination against members of group B.[2] Current discrimination may not loom as a very important source of current intergroup inequality, at least in the contemporary era when the extent and impact of intergroup discrimination has significantly diminished as compared to past eras. However, past discrimination remains an important source of current intergroup inequality, because it is generally a very important source of current intergroup differentials in resource endowments, which in turn can also result in current intergroup differentials in the propensity to invest rather than consume.

Adding to the salience of discrimination as a source of intergroup inequality is the fact that it is likely to play a much larger role in generating intrasociety inequality as distinct from intersociety inequality—and for that reason it generates also more significant political challenges. Inequalities between members of societies that are distant from one another and largely separate are plausibly explained primarily by differential initial endowments and other factors independent of intergroup discrimination; they are consequently likely to be accepted as in the more or less natural order of things. By contrast, inequalities between members of different groups within the same society are likely to be explained to a much greater extent—and (even more so) to be seen as explained—by discrimination against members of less-well-off groups. As a consequence, intrasociety intergroup inequalities are far more likely to evoke strong feelings about the unfairness of the social order, and they are much more likely to lead to social and political tensions and divisions. Even where current discrimination has largely been curbed, ongoing intergroup inequalities can reasonably be seen as attributable in some considerable part to past discrimination; and the failure to address the unequal consequences of past discrimination can pose a continuing challenge to social and political stability.

Affirmative Action

Affirmative action has arisen as a policy response to the deleterious effects of past as well as present discrimination. A great variety of affirmative action policies have been proposed or implemented in various parts of the world.

It will be useful to distinguish between the following two principal forms of affirmative action, which have qualitatively different objectives:

Elimination of ongoing discriminatory practices. The aim of this kind of affirmative action is to ensure that access to valued positions or benefits in a society be influenced not arbitrarily by a person's membership in any particular identity group, but only by qualifications and considerations relevant to the position or opportunity in question. It includes efforts to provide all potential applicants with equal access to information about available opportunities as well as efforts to ensure that selection processes are procedurally nondiscriminatory—that is, oriented solely to a candidate's capacity to perform successfully.[3] To ensure in this way a level playing field requires not only strong antidiscrimination laws but also thorough monitoring and vigorous enforcement of the laws. This kind of affirmative action can be defended in terms of the efficient allocation of resources as well as social justice; and its desirability is not a matter of controversy.

Positive discrimination in favor of identity groups underrepresented in desirable positions or in the distribution of scarce opportunities. This means the opposite of negative discrimination: more favorable treatment of people belonging to less-well-off identity groups than of people belonging to better-off identity groups. The advocates of positive discrimination argue that the procedural fairness ensured by antidiscrimination policies does not produce enough substantive fairness, because it fails to offset the adverse long-term effects of past negative discrimination.[4]

Affirmative action in the form of positive discrimination involves the provision of some amount of preference, in processes of selection for access to scarce and desirable opportunities or benefits, to members of groups that are on average relatively poorly off and underrepresented (in proportion to their population) in society's desirable positions. The preference may be provided in various ways—for example, reserving a significant proportion of the available opportunities or benefits for members of a less-well-off group, or by providing a preferential boost to members of such a group in an open competition with others for access to the benefit or opportunity; but it always has the effect of increasing the number of members of an underrepresented group selected.

Most of the direct beneficiaries of positive discrimination policies are likely to be relatively well-off members of their marginalized groups, because among group members they are the ones best able to compete for access to the opportunities or benefits made more accessible. Such policies cannot therefore be expected to do much to reduce overall socioeconomic inequalities in a society, but they can contribute significantly to a reduction in intergroup inequalities. In particular, positive discrimination policies can do much to integrate and diversify the upper strata of a society, with benefits extending well beyond the improved well-being of the direct beneficiaries. It can improve the well-being of many other members of the beneficiaries' communities, by improving their access to resources and to jobs and by providing greater motivation for young community members to work hard to better their future prospects. Ethnic diversification of the upper strata can also generate such society-wide benefits as greater legitimacy for the political system and better performance of jobs requiring a good understanding of disadvantaged communities.[5]

Unlike efforts to eliminate discriminatory practices, the application of positive discrimination policies is highly controversial, because these policies do treat people differently depending on their identity group membership. They are therefore in tension with the fundamental liberal principle that people should be treated as autonomous individuals rather than as members of a community to which they happen to belong, independently of their own will or action. But positive discrimination policies are often defended on grounds of egalitarianism or social justice: to ensure truly equal opportunity for all individuals, one must compensate for the disequalizing effects of past as well as present negative discrimination, and this cannot adequately be accomplished without taking account of the group identity of members of groups targeted by negative discrimination. This is precisely what was meant by U.S. Supreme Court Justice Harry Blackmun in stating: "In order to get beyond racism, we must first take account of race...and in order to treat some persons equally, we must treat them differently."[6]

2. THE EFFECTS OF GLOBALIZATION ON DISCRIMINATION

Discrimination against particular ethnic groups is of course an age-old phenomenon, which predates globalization in any meaningful sense of the term. The prerequisite for such discrimination is simply the mingling within the same geographic and social space of ethnic groups with unequal power. As soon as members of a stronger ethnic group begin to take advantage of their greater power to systematically limit the opportunities available to members of a weaker group, discrimination is under way.

The question at hand, however, is whether globalization has served to exacerbate or to mitigate the phenomenon of discrimination that has been in evidence for millennia. By definition globalization brings into closer contact people of different ethnicities, and with different degrees of power, so it stands to reason that it increases the potential for ethnicity-based discrimination. But a useful assessment of whether or not globalization actually generates greater discrimination must move from such a high level of abstraction to examine particular historical circumstances. My primary interest is in the contemporary phase of globalization; but I will first address the question briefly in the context of each of the other two phases of globalization distinguished above.

Past Phases of Globalization

The first phase of globalization—beginning in the late 15th century and continuing through the late 18th century—was characterized by voyages, discoveries, and conquests around the globe on the part of European explorers. This phase saw first the establishment of outposts of European powers in geopolitically or economically strategic areas and, later, the establishment of settler colonies in regions that were sparsely populated or where indigenous groups could be driven off some of their land (e.g., in the Americas and in Australasia). The forcible expansion of European power across the globe entailed in quantitative terms only a limited amount of migration from Europe to the rest of the world; by 1800, even in the areas of white settlement, the populations of European origin were relatively small compared with what was to come (Held et al. 1999: 291). Far more significant in terms of long-distance human migration was the development of the transatlantic slave trade, which forcibly removed huge numbers of Africans from their continent of origin to regions in the Western Hemisphere where their slave labor was instrumental in the development of plantation-based agricultural economies. Estimates of the total number of Africans transported to the Americas range widely but center around 10–12 million, and the lion's share—about 80%—took place before the end of the 18th century (Held et al. 1999: 292–93).[7]

The calamity visited by European conquerors upon indigenous peoples throughout the non-European world cannot be exaggerated; among many other things, European guns and germs decimated much of the original population of the Western hemisphere. The term *discrimination*, however, applies not to the interaction of ethnic groups across societal or national borders but to relations between ethnic groups that live side by side and form parts of the same society. It follows that the first phase of globalization generated discrimination in those places where it brought European settlers together with indigenous peoples within a common economic arena. This was most importantly the case with plantation and mining activities, where European settlers commanded large numbers of indigenous or enslaved workers. On a smaller scale, European military, missionary, and trading outposts were likely arenas of discriminatory practice.

The second phase of globalization spanned the century from the final defeat of Napoleon in 1815 to the outbreak of World War I in 1914. This was the period in which the dominant European powers, whose explorers had established outposts around the world, took possession of much of the lands of Asia and Africa and established direct colonial rule over the territories they conquered. It was also the period of mass European migration to the Americas and—on a much smaller scale—to other areas of significant white settlement such as Australia, New Zealand, and South Africa. It is estimated that roughly 45 million Europeans migrated to the Americas during this period, of which about two-thirds arrived in the last two decades of the 19th century and the first decade and a half of the 20th century.[8] As the slave trade declined in the 19th century, it was superseded by another significant wave of global migration involving not Africans but Asians, transported to work as coolie laborers under exploitative contracts for very low pay. The great bulk of such laborers came from India (then including what is now Pakistan and Bangladesh) and from China, to work in British and other European colonies and in the United States. Many of these laborers ultimately returned to their home countries, but the number of permanent migrants is estimated at around 12 million (Held et al. 1999: 293–94, 311). During the second phase of globalization, most of the erstwhile colonies of Spain and Portugal in Central and South America became independent nations in which people of various ethnicities were ruled by an elite of predominantly European origin. By the end of the period, the United States had become a colonial power in its own right, ruling over the Philippines as well as some Caribbean and Pacific island territories; and it exercised neocolonial dominance over many nations in Central and South America.

The conquest of overseas territories obviously involved a great deal of violence perpetrated by the strong against the weak, but it was the subsequent establishment of colonial rule that created the conditions for discrimination on a massive scale. Second-class citizenship—at best—was of course the rule for indigenous populations in every colony; and even upper-class or Western-educated indigenous elites faced discrimination. During the 19th century there was very little immigration of natives from the colonized periphery to the colonial center, and hence little scope for discrimination against colonized peoples within the colonizing nations. But where important native or slave populations had earlier been incorporated into settler economies—as in the United States and many Central and South American countries—discrimination against these peoples remained rampant, if somewhat less violent in purely physical terms after slavery was finally abolished.

It is clear from the above account that each of the first two phases of globalization contributed very significantly to the growth of ethnicity-based discrimination across the world. Yet any account of the impact of globalization on discrimination must also take account of a countervailing force that became significant during the second phase and gained much greater strength during the 20th century. Against the violence and discrimination associated with European and American colonial conquest and enslavement there arose movements to abolish slavery, to end colonialism, and to reduce—if not eradicate—discrimination. These resistance movements developed not only among victims of the violent and discriminatory practices, but also among an enlightened segment of the populations of powerful nations who were the main perpetrators. The growth in communications and transport associated with globalization enabled ideas of freedom, equality, and human rights to spread ever more quickly and comprehensively across the globe, providing encouragement and useful lessons in resistance that helped to sustain and support the resisters. Having contributed for centuries to the rise of discrimination around the world, globalization ultimately contributed also to the significant reduction in violence and discrimination associated with the abolition of slavery (in the 19th century) and the end of colonial rule in most of the world (in the 20th century).

Contemporary Globalization

Consider now the case of the latest phase of globalization, beginning after World War II and gaining strength in the latter part of the 20th century and the beginning of the 21st century. Quantitatively speaking, this phase—like the others—has involved rapidly expanding economic links between national and regional economies; and it has now created a global economic system far more interconnected than ever before. Qualitatively, however, it has had a rather different impact on the (previously colonized) periphery than on the (previously colonizing) center.[9] Capitalism was already dominant in the center nations by the middle of the 20th century; and the latest era of globalization has merely strengthened the capitalist nature of their economies. In many parts of the periphery, however, noncapitalist economic formations remained quite significant at the beginning of the contemporary phase of globalization. This phase has therefore brought about more fundamental change in the periphery, as it has greatly reduced the significance of noncapitalist formations and transformed peripheral economies into capitalist formations that fit much more closely into the global capitalist system.

The contemporary phase of globalization differs from the earlier ones in a number of important respects. The migration of people from the rich countries of the capitalist center to the poorer countries and territories of the periphery is much less significant than in the past. It is true that capital flows from center to periphery have been accompanied by the movement of highly educated businesspeople and professionals; but they are most often only on temporary assignment. What has become far more important is the migration in the opposite direction, as impoverished people from the periphery seek better economic opportunities in the nations of the center. This flow of labor to the center constitutes the most powerful force currently bringing people of different ethnic identities—with highly unequal power—together. And it is tellingly captured by the remark of a black man in the U.K.: "I am here because you were there."[10]

The magnitude of the migratory flow characteristic of contemporary globalization is far greater in numbers of people than that of any previous era; and as a proportion of the population of recipient countries, it is comparable to the mass migration of Europeans to the Americas in the late 19th and early 20th centuries. It is estimated that in the 50 years from the end of World War II to the mid-1990s, some 35 million immigrants—primarily from Latin America and Asia—entered the United States, and roughly 80 million—primarily from Africa and Asia—entered the nations of Western Europe, Australia, and Canada (Held et al. 1999: 311–12). The proportion of foreign nationals living in the United States rose from 6% in the 1960s to at least 10% in the 1990s; comparable estimates for the major Western European nations show sharp increases to 8% in Germany, to 6% in France, and to 3% in the U.K.; and if citizens of foreign origin were included, the percentages would be considerably higher in the United States, France, and the U.K. (Held et al. 1999: 315–16). Some of the migrants into the center countries eventually return to their countries of origin, but most stay on; and the migratory inflow from the periphery to the center has been at least as great in the years since 1995. According to a report from the U.S. Council of Economic Advisors (2007), foreign-born workers accounted for 15% of the U.S. labor force in 2006.

A second development that has become far more significant in the contemporary phase of globalization is the worldwide spread of information. As a result of the rapid development of communications technology and the expansion of transport networks in recent decades, people across the world are becoming much more aware of what is going on in other parts of the world than in any previous era. Exposure of inhabitants of poor societies to lifestyles in the rich societies—through television, the Internet, visiting tourists, and so on—sets in motion powerful demonstration effects. This leads to growth in aspirations (especially among the middle and upper classes most exposed to the center) that are difficult to satisfy in the periphery, and it has intensified the flow of migrants from the periphery to the center.

A third characteristic of contemporary globalization worthy of mention here is a sharply intensified degree of international competition, as capital and labor markets have become much more closely interlinked across the world and technology has become much more widely diffused. Reductions in the costs of transport and communications, as well as reduction of tariffs and other barriers to trade, have led to greater international competition in each of the phases of globalization. What is qualitatively different in the contemporary phase, however, is the extent to which enterprises and workers in the richer countries find themselves in competition with enterprises and workers not only in other rich countries but also in poorer countries. Many countries in Latin America, Asia, and Africa, which used to export primarily raw materials to the rich countries, are now increasingly capable of producing and exporting industrial goods as well as services that used to be produced mainly in the rich countries. And the collapse of the communist regimes of the "second world"—the former Soviet Union and its allied Eastern European nations—has opened up their economies to the rest of the world, bringing large numbers of new workers and substantial new productive potential into the global market system.

How may these developments have affected discriminatory practices around the world? The answer to this question is likely to be very different between the center and the periphery of the new global system, since the two poles are very differently affected by the trends just delineated.

In the Center

First of all, the nations of the center have experienced—and continue to experience—substantial inflows of migrants from the poorer countries to the richer countries. Those of the migrants who enter legally obtain typically a second-class status as resident aliens, at best; while the large numbers of undocumented migrants who enter illegally have no meaningful status at all. Some of the (legal) migrants are highly educated and gain access to good jobs, but the great majority of all migrants are relatively unskilled and find jobs at the lowest level of the occupation wage hierarchy; many others (especially in continental Europe) simply join the ranks of the unemployed. The addition of large numbers of relatively unskilled migrants to the supply of labor puts pressure on the job opportunities and the wages of the least-well-off national workers (who are often members of ethnic groups whose past victimization by discrimination accounts in part for their low socioeconomic status).

Not only the least skilled workers, but also many moderately skilled workers of the center have been confronting significant increases in the supply of their kind of labor. In this case the additions to the labor supply stem not so much from an inflow of migrant labor as from increased international competition in many sectors of the economy, as companies of the center find it ever easier—and more profitable—to move operations overseas in order to tap cheaper supplies of capable industrial or service workers in the periphery. The increasingly intense competition between lower-wage workers in poorer countries and higher-wage workers in richer countries puts great downward pressure on the wages, working conditions, and job security of the latter (who are predominantly—but by no means exclusively—members of ethnic groups that have faced little discrimination in the past).

Contemporary globalization has of course also added to the effective supply of highly educated and well-paid workers to the center nations. However, the "analytical workers" (to use Robert Reich's term) of the center do not suffer the kind of downward pressure on their economic status faced by less skilled workers, because—unlike the others—they are highly mobile. Their mobility makes them employable anywhere in the world, so the demand for their labor is not limited to companies and organizations operating in the center but is effectively worldwide.

In increasing the effective supply of low-skilled and semiskilled labor to the center, and especially in enabling firms more easily to shift their operations from one country to another, contemporary globalization has strengthened the hand of capital in the center nations vis-à-vis all but highly skilled labor. This has contributed significantly to the ongoing decline in bargaining power of trade unions in the center, which tend to represent primarily semiskilled and—to a lesser extent—low-skilled workers (see Choi 2006). The reduction in trade union bargaining power has not only limited unions' ability to obtain wage and benefit increases for workers; it has also weakened their ability to fight in the political arena for social and economic programs benefiting workers. Furthermore, by easing the movement of highly skilled and well-remunerated workers across national frontiers, contemporary globalization has constrained the ability of national governments to tax these beneficiaries of globalization in order to compensate their compatriots who find themselves losing ground (see Bowles 2006).

All of the developments just described contribute to increasing economic inequalities within the center nations. But what is likely to be their overall impact on the incidence of ethnicity-based discrimination in the center? First of all, migrant workers themselves typically constitute a group that is discriminated against—as temporary residents at best, and as illegal workers at worst. Even to the extent that they become permanent residents or citizens, they are often afflicted by discriminatory treatment similar to that directed at temporary and illegal workers, because of their shared ethnic identity. Others—for example, members of ethnic groups that are stronger within the national context—often lack the knowledge or the will to distinguish between different categories and legal statuses among members of ethnic groups that figure prominently in current migratory flows.

Adding significantly to the tendency toward discrimination against prominent immigrant ethnic groups is the worsening life chances of wage workers belonging to the dominant ethnic groups of the center nations. At the same time that these workers face intensified competition with workers of other ethnic identities, they find their unions less able to protect them and their governments less able to provide them with social and economic support. It is hardly surprising that worker insecurity generates suspicion and resentment of members of other ethnic groups, thereby aggravating tendencies toward discrimination.[11]

Contemporary globalization tends to exacerbate socioeconomic inequalities within center nations in a context in which the ranks of the poor disproportionately include members of those ethnic groups originating in the periphery that have historically been the most discriminated against—not only groups whose members have migrated to the center within the latest phase of globalization, but also groups whose origins in the periphery go back much further in time. The relegation of disproportionate numbers of people from such ethnic groups to low socioeconomic status often leads to the segregation of many of their members into ghetto-like residential conditions, which exacerbates social pathologies such as delinquency and thereby reinforces perceptions of these ethnic groups as undeserving of equal treatment.

Of course enlightened social policy in center nations can reduce—and perhaps even offset or reverse—the inequalities generated by globalization, thereby arresting the negative consequences that tend to exacerbate ethnicity-based discrimination. But the constraints on government revenue raising noted above make it more difficult for the needed social policies to be financed.[12]

In the Periphery

The effects of contemporary globalization on the countries of the periphery are in important respects quite different than its effects on the center. In greatly increasing the sway of capitalist economic formations in the periphery, globalization has also strengthened institutions and ideas closely associated with capitalism—such as markets and private property, and the importance of the autonomous individual as opposed to the community or the state. At a very general level one would expect that the penetration of these institutions and ideas would tend to undermine the salience of ethnicity, thus weakening ethnicity-based discrimination, at the same time as they tend to increase inequalities linked to socioeconomic class.

A critical difference between the contemporary and the previous phase of globalization is that the flow of migrant labor is now predominantly in the opposite direction, out of the periphery rather than into it. And it is composed not primarily of people of the very lowest socioeconomic status, but of people from the lower middle or middle classes (who have sufficient personal and financial resources to be able to manage the generally challenging and expensive process of emigration) and—to a much lesser extent—the highly educated upper classes (whose emigration is often facilitated by having pursued higher education in the center). While the adventure of emigration from the periphery to the center can turn tragic for the poorest of the migrants, it does enable most of them to improve their material—if not their spiritual—well-being. It also contributes to greater economic well-being in their countries of origin, reducing rates of unemployment and increasing remittances from migrants to family members back home.[13] Such remittances have become a more and more significant form of financial transfer from rich to poor countries; they are estimated to have amounted to more than three times the total value of world foreign aid in 2006 (DeParle 2007).

Contemporary globalization facilitates and encourages increased flows of physical and financial capital, as well as technological know-how, from the center to the periphery. This has led in many countries to stepped-up economic activity and the creation of new employment opportunities (Bardhan 2006). It is true that, in a process characteristic of capitalist creative destruction, the expansion of new jobs is often accompanied by the destruction of old ones. And it is true that wages and working conditions in the new jobs are significantly inferior to those of comparable jobs in the center. However, the net employment effect of this process is more often positive than negative; and the comparatively low wages and poor working conditions generally prove to be rather more attractive to workers in the periphery than the alternatives available to them.

Finally, by requiring greater communication and engagement of individuals across national frontiers and—in particular—between the periphery and the center, contemporary globalization confers a premium on cosmopolitanism on the part of periphery workers. Those who can speak a language of the center, and whose education provides them with some understanding of the social, cultural, and economic environment of the center, are in a far better position to take advantage of the new opportunities generated by the flow of capital and technology from center to periphery. As Newman and Deshpande (chapter 10, this volume) have found, social and cultural capital play a huge role in Indian formal labor markets, favoring upper-class and upper-caste graduates who are comfortable speaking English. In parallel with its disequalizing effects in the center, globalization is thus likely to generate significant cleavages in the periphery between "cosmopolitans," whose skills enable them to adapt easily to the global capitalist economy, and "provincials," who are far less able to adapt (Bowles and Pagano 2006). This helps to explain the finding by Attewell and Madheswaran (chapter 13,this volume) that the returns on education are significantly greater for higher-caste than for lower-caste Indians.

The expanded flow of capital and technology from center to periphery clearly creates significant opportunities for improving the material welfare of people in the poorer countries of the world—including, in particular, some the most disadvantaged of them. Yet given the extent of the poverty and the excess labor supply that still characterize much of the periphery, these improvements are unlikely in the foreseeable future to significantly stem the incentives for emigration—especially as demonstration effects become ever more powerful. The premium on cosmopolitanism tends to increase the social and economic distance between cosmopolitans and provincials, thereby strengthening the political power of the former (which is usually relatively strong to begin with). This reinforces preexisting tendencies for governments to show much greater concern for those who already have better opportunities to become cosmopolitan than for those who are mired in provincialism. And of course this contributes to widening economic inequalities within peripheral nations.

What is likely to be the overall impact of these trends on the incidence of ethnicity-based discrimination in the periphery? I have already suggested that the growing dominance of capitalist economic institutions and ideas, by displacing traditional and more group-oriented social and economic patterns, tends to reduce the salience of ethnicity-based discrimination (while giving rise to other forms of inequality). More specifically, transnational corporations based in the center—and new domestic firms linked to them—are less likely to practice ethnicity-based discrimination than domestic firms entrenched in long-standing discriminatory patterns;[14] and they may also help reduce discrimination by increasing the degree of competition for consumers and workers. But contemporary globalization has many other effects that also need to be taken into account.

In the periphery, as in the center, members of discriminated-against groups are disproportionately found among the lower socioeconomic classes. But the effect of contemporary globalization on economic opportunities for the poor and lower-middle classes is on the whole favorable in the periphery (the opposite of its effect in the center), and globalization can therefore be expected to reduce incentives for outright discrimination on behalf of people competing for jobs with members of marginalized communities in the periphery (unlike in the center). Moreover, the fact that upper-class cosmopolitans—and upper-middle-class potential cosmopolitans—in the periphery are advantaged by globalization is likely to make these groups less worried about competition from more provincial folks further down the socioeconomic ladder and hence perhaps less likely to rely on discriminatory practices to protect their interests.[15]

One should, however, distinguish between two quite different segments of the lower classes in the periphery that are differentially affected by globalization. On the one hand, there are the people who can hope and expect to benefit from improved employment opportunities either at home (via capital inflows, etc.) or abroad (via emigration); on the other hand, there are those who are most likely to be victimized by the creative destruction associated with capitalist development. The former tend to be of the urban lower-middle and perhaps lower classes; the latter tend to be of the rural or tribal lower classes, whose ties to and assets in land and natural resources are threatened by expansion of the global capitalist economy. There is likely to be intensified conflict between the predominantly lower-middle-class workers who see their interest in the growth of employment opportunities in capitalist enterprise, and the more provincial and generally poorer people clinging to subsistence on the land. Since these cleavages are often also ethnic—for example, potential industrial and service workers tend to be ethnically distinct from tribal groups close to the land—the potential is great for increased ethnicity-based discrimination against the former.

3. THE EFFECTS OF GLOBALIZATION ON AFFIRMATIVE ACTION

Discrimination against members of particular groups on the basis of their ethnic identity naturally generates resentment and, sooner or later, organized resistance on the part of the victims. In societies without a formal commitment to individual rights independent of group identity, the first step in the struggle against negative discrimination usually takes the form of demands for legal recognition of equal rights for all individuals irrespective of their ethnicity. Nowadays most nations around the world are indeed legally committed to equal rights for all of their citizens, so efforts to end discriminatory practices generally include demands for enactment and vigorous enforcement of antidiscrimination laws. In many countries, however, the difficulty of ensuring that antidiscrimination laws will be respected, and the fact that such laws cannot alone do much to offset huge intergroup inequalities attributable in considerable part to past discrimination, have led to demands for positive discrimination in favor of marginalized ethnic groups. I focus here on this strong form of affirmative action, which has proven to be far more contentious than the enactment and enforcement of antidiscrimination laws.

The history of positive discrimination policies goes back no further than 100 years; the earliest examples of such policies are to be found in British-ruled India in the first half of the 20th century. It is during the last 50 years, however, that positive discrimination policies have spread across many countries of the world—including several other South Asian nations, Malaysia, the United States, and (more recently) South Africa and Brazil. In examining the possible effects of globalization on the propensity to pursue such policies, we can therefore confine ourselves to the contemporary phase of globalization, whose key characteristics are discussed in the previous section. In view of the differential impact of contemporary globalization on the center and on the periphery of the global system, I address its impact on positive discrimination separately for the center and the periphery—just as I did earlier for its impact on negative discrimination.

In the Center

The contemporary phase of globalization, in greatly increasing the interconnectedness of national economies within a global market system, has made every national economy more sensitive to developments elsewhere in the global system. It has also greatly increased the mobility of various forms of capital and of highly skilled labor, which can respond rapidly to differential opportunities between home and abroad. All of this tends to limit the scope for independent national economic policymaking—for example, by reducing the extent to which national macroeconomic policy actions affect aggregate demand for domestic products, and by constraining governments' ability to tax mobile factors of production. Under these circumstances, policy interventions that seek to serve social goals inconsistent with market logic tend to become more difficult and more costly to carry out. To the extent that they impose additional costs on businesses operating within national borders, for example, they risk causing business firms to look for alternative settings beyond those borders.

Globalization can thus be a serious deterrent to national social policies that involve real trade-offs between economic efficiency and social desirability. Policies of positive discrimination, however, are not necessarily of this nature. First of all, they are not very costly. (Indeed, opportunity-shifting positive discrimination policies often appeal to lawmakers more than resource-redistributing social programs, because their implementation requires much less in government outlays.) Second, policies of positive discrimination can, under certain circumstances, significantly improve the allocation of labor and increase economic efficiency. For example, the performance of organizations or enterprises that must interact with representative samples of the population as a whole—or disproportionately with marginalized groups therein—may well be improved if its upper ranks become ethnically more diverse. When and where it can be shown that integrating members of marginalized ethnic communities more proportionately into the middle or upper echelons of the society will boost productivity, political leaders even in the most individualistic and capitalist of societies may be persuaded to adopt policies of positive discrimination.

This latter possibility can explain why a conservative Supreme Court in the United States—one of the most individualistic and market-oriented nations of the world—ruled in 2003 that affirmative action on behalf of African Americans, Hispanic Americans, and Native Americans in admissions to elite higher educational institutions can be justified, even though it appears inconsistent with the liberal tenets of the U.S. Constitution.[16] In statements to the Court, a wide-ranging coalition of U.S. corporate and military leaders argued forcefully that greater ethnic diversity at all levels of their institutions—achievable only via positive discrimination in education, if not in employment—was essential to the efficient achievement of their institutional missions. Indeed, U.S.-based companies and institutions may well find it difficult to prevail in an era of heightened competition across an increasingly multicultural world if their leadership ranks are populated predominantly by people of European American identity.

There are, however, other forces at work that suggest that contemporary trends in globalization may not be so hospitable to positive discrimination. In general people are more likely to be willing to support policies that help others who are like themselves, only poorer, than people who are of different ethnicity. Substantial flows of immigrants from poorer into richer nations increase the ethnic diversity of the latter, and may well therefore erode the sense of common community that sustains the willingness of the well-off to help those who are not well-off (Soroka et al. 2006). This is all the more the case when the prospective beneficiaries are exclusively from minority ethnic communities; so ethnicity-based positive discrimination is particularly vulnerable to reduced public support as societies become ethnically more diverse.

The fact that contemporary globalization has been heightening the economic insecurity of wage workers in the center further undermines support for positive discrimination. First of all, when many people are suffering economically, it becomes much harder to makes the case—and gain political support—for helping a particular group of people. Heightened economic insecurity on the part of many wage workers from longtime resident communities tends to generate increasing suspicion and resentment against immigrant workers and members of their ethnic communities. In many of the richer nations this has increased the power of right-wing populist ethnocentric political forces, stiffening political opposition to immigration and raising tensions more generally between the various ethnic groups whose economic fortunes are at risk. In an overall climate of increased economic insecurity, one would expect a decline in support for policies designed to aid members of marginalized ethnic groups—and not only those linked to recent waves of immigration from the periphery.

Polling data on attitudes toward affirmative action are often difficult to interpret, but there is evidence of declining public support for race- or ethnicity-based positive discrimination from the 1970s into the 1990s in the United States (Steeh and Krysan 1996). There are many possible reasons for this trend in public opinion, which is consistent with the concurrent rightward drift of public discourse and political life in the country. The visible success of a significant number of African Americans and Hispanic Americans in entering the middle class—and even the upper strata—of American society has led some to conclude that affirmative action policies are no longer needed to ensure that members of such groups have sufficient opportunities to improve their lot. It stands to reason, however, that the increased economic insecurity of American wage workers, in the context of accelerated globalization in recent decades, has also contributed to the diminishing public support for positive discrimination.

In the Periphery

As peripheral societies are integrated into the contemporary global system, capitalist institutions and principles increasingly displace noncapitalist ones, and as a general rule this tends to weaken the salience of community membership and group identity and shift the focus to the individual. In this context positive, as well as negative, ethnicity-based discrimination becomes harder to sustain. Ethnicity-based identity politics can certainly prolong and even intensify ethnic consciousness as well as support for ethnicity-based positive discrimination; but in the long run the spread of capitalism, with its underlying liberal individualist tenets, tends to undermine support for it.

Second, just as in the case of the center, and for the same reasons, contemporary globalization tends to limit the scope for independent national economic policymaking in the periphery. Indeed, in many ways the poorer countries of the periphery are even more dependent on external economic forces than are the rich countries of the center; so their scope for pursuing policies that seek to serve social goals inconsistent with market logic is even narrower. And there appear to be fewer prospects in the periphery that political decision makers can be persuaded that policies aiding members of marginalized communities will enhance overall economic efficiency and well-being. This is because globalization strengthens the economic salience of highly skilled cosmopolitans in the periphery; and it is these cosmopolitans who are the key to the success of a peripheral country in capitalizing on the opportunities—and avoiding the pitfalls—associated with tighter integration into the global economic system. Government policymakers are therefore likely to be much more concerned with sustaining and promoting relatively elite individuals and groups, rather than catering to the needs of the most marginalized communities in their societies. By strengthening the political power of cosmopolitan forces in the periphery, globalization contributes to a political climate in which there is little inclination to intervene in favor of marginalized and discriminated-against groups.[17]

This helps to explain an interesting contrast in attitudes toward affirmative action as between Indian and U.S. business, military, and educational leaders. In the United States, as noted above, many such leaders support affirmative action even in the form of positive discrimination. In India, however, such leaders—especially those representing the most elite institutions—line up firmly against positive discrimination policies (Weisskopf, 2004a, chapter 2). They argue that these policies weaken India's ability to compete in a globalized world, because they provide opportunities to typically underprepared and culturally deprived members of marginal groups, who are likely to perform poorly, at the expense of well-prepared and culturally sophisticated members of mainstream groups, who are primed for success on the world stage. Indeed, Newman and Jodhka (chapter 11, this volume) found that all 25 of the human resource managers they interviewed in a study of contemporary Indian corporate employers firmly opposed positive discrimination policies in hiring—on the grounds that it would hinder Indian economic development.[18] Globalization puts a high premium on the capacity to speak fluent and articulate English, so it is from the uppermost echelons of Indian society that effective players on the world stage are indeed most likely to be recruited. Moreover, India does not need to look for members of underrepresented racial or ethnic groups in order to show the world an assemblage of leaders who reflect the diversity of the world's population, rather than looking like members of a privileged club, and who can therefore be expected to inspire more confidence and less suspicion around the globe.

Support for positive discrimination in education and employment has remained strong among Indians from the lower classes and castes who are its potential beneficiaries; but for several decades now such support has been waning on the part of India's English-speaking upper classes and castes (Weisskopf, 2004a, chapter 2). Elite opinion is not always so hostile to the long-standing affirmative action policies in place for Scheduled Castes and Tribes, but it is strongly opposed to continuing popular demands for the expansion of groups eligible for positive discrimination and for its extension from the public to the private sector. Moreover, as two scholars of India's positive discrimination policies have observed, "new elites from the middle order of castes along with the high castes have become more stridently opposed to reservations (quotas) in education and employment" (Patwardhan and Palshikar 1992: 3).

The tendency for globalization to diminish the propensity to adopt affirmative action policies in the periphery will not be sufficient to prevent them from being introduced or expanded in situations where there are other forces strongly at work to promote such policies. This is most obviously the case in nations like South Africa and Malaysia, where the traditional elite is drawn from a small minority community and the great majority of the population consists of members of a previously marginalized community. When leaders representing the majority community come to power in such circumstances, they will surely have strong feelings of solidarity with the disadvantaged members of their community. They will also have substantial political interest in pursuing policies that increase access of members of the majority community to opportunities and positions previously dominated by a privileged minority community. In this and other situations where ethnic identity provides a strong basis for political mobilization, positive discrimination in favor of members of marginalized communities can be expected to have a great deal of staying power, in spite of the contrary influence of contemporary globalization.

4. CONCLUSION

Adopting an approach to globalization that distinguishes three different phases of its modern history, I have addressed the changing ways in which successive phases of globalization have influenced the extent of negative ethnicity-based discrimination. I have focused particular attention on the different patterns of long-distance migration that have characterized the different phases of globalization, for these migratory patterns have major repercussions for the propensity of stronger ethnic groups to discriminate against weaker ones. Here I briefly summarize my conclusions regarding the impact of the contemporary phase of globalization on negative discrimination, as well as efforts to counter it via positive discrimination, in the center and in the periphery of the global system.

Contemporary globalization is characterized by major migratory flows of people from the periphery to the center, reversing the direction of migration most characteristic of the previous phase. Although globalization tends to exacerbate socioeconomic inequalities within nations of both the center and the periphery, it seems far more likely to exacerbate negative ethnicity-based discrimination in nations of the center than in those of the periphery. I have identified several major ways in which contemporary globalization tends to intensify such discrimination in central nations, and no major way in which it is likely to reduce it. In the case of peripheral nations, however, several elements of globalization now tend to reduce negative discrimination, and only one seems likely to work in the other direction.

The effects of contemporary globalization on the pursuit of policies of positive discrimination in favor of marginalized ethnic groups are more complex and less predictable than its effects on negative discrimination against such groups. In the center, globalization can be expected to strengthen support for positive discrimination among elites, but it seems more likely to weaken such support among the general public. In the periphery, globalization seems most likely to reduce support for positive discrimination among elites, if not also among the general public. Where a marginalized and under-represented group constitutes a substantial majority of the population, however, positive discrimination policies in its favor are likely to be pursued when representatives of the group gain political power.

Notes

The initial version of this chapter was prepared for presentation at the conference Global Studies of Discrimination, sponsored by the Princeton Institute for International and Regional Studies, held at Princeton University on May 18–19, 2007. I am grateful to numerous conference participants—especially Miguel Centeno—for helpful comments on the version I presented at the conference.

1. Many scholars have distinguished three phases of globalization along the lines that I do here; see, for example, Papastergiadis (2000) and Cohen (2005). Held et al. (1999) also identify a prior phase of "premodern globalization."

2. Another basic possible source of intergroup inequality is differential average innate abilities; but I reject this possibility for lack of any persuasive empirical support.

3. Note that there are circumstances when one's group identity is in fact relevant to a candidate's capacity to perform a job successfully—for example, when policing or medical care can be better carried out by a person with the same group identity as the great majority of the community to be policed or provided with medical care. Under these circumstances, group identity becomes a relevant rather than an arbitrary characteristic of a candidate and can be taken into account without violating procedural fairness.

4. See Loury (2002), especially chapters 3 and 4, for a highly persuasive exposition of this argument. The distinction between the two forms of affirmative action highlighted here is actually not quite as sharp as I am suggesting. As Fryer and Loury (2005) have argued (in discussing what they label Myth #1), efforts to eliminate negative discrimination may unavoidably entail some degree of positive discrimination.

5. This paragraph summarizes arguments I have made in greater detail in Weisskopf (2006).

6. The quotation is from Blackmun's opinion in *University of California Regents v. Bakke*, 438 U.S. 265 (1978).

7. Manning (2005: 146) estimates that roughly two-thirds of the transported slaves were headed for North America and the Caribbean and roughly one-third to South America.

8. Manning (2005: 146) estimates that almost 80% of the transatlantic European migrants were headed for North America and the Caribbean; the bulk of them settled in the United States. Manning also indicates that some 7 million Europeans migrated to Asia; many of them were Russians spreading into Siberia.

9. The broad dichotomization of the world into a dominant center (consisting of relatively wealthy nations whose populations are predominantly white) and a subordinate periphery (consisting of relatively poor nations and territories whose populations are predominantly nonwhite) is a framework commonly adopted by globally oriented social scientists, but of course it abstracts from a considerably more complex reality. Some parts of the world do not fit easily into the dichotomy—for example, wealthy Japan, the oil-rich countries of the Middle East, and the much less prosperous countries of the Southern Cone. My analysis in this paper applies most clearly and forcefully to a center defined to include the nations of Western Europe and North America with a history of colonial rule (and/or neocolonial domination) and a periphery defined to include the nations and territories of Asia, Africa, and Latin America with a history of colonization (and/or neocolonial subordination) by center powers.

10. Quoted by Papastergiadas (2000: 196), at the beginning of his concluding chapter, "Clusters in the Diaspora."

11. I do not want to suggest that economic insecurity is paramount in generating anti-immigrant feeling among workers of the dominant ethnicity in center nations. Certainly perceptions of cultural differences, and possible threats to the majority culture, also play a significant role.

12. However, as Miguel Centeno has pointed out (at the conference), the worldwide spread of information associated with contemporary globalization shines more light on practices within any given country; and growing worldwide determination to eradicate racial and ethnic discrimination may well put pressure on governments in laggard countries to take action to reduce it.

13. In any overall evaluation of the economic impact on a peripheral nation of migration to center nations, the gains from the emigration of relatively poor citizens must be balanced against the losses resulting from the "brain drain" associated with the loss of highly skilled workers.

14. This is not to say that the more modern firms are free from discriminatory practices; as Attewell and Thorat (chapter 12, this volume) have shown, in India even modern firms posting open employment notices discriminate against low-caste and Muslim minority applicants.

15. However, Miguel Centeno has suggested (at the conference) that the growth in numbers of successful cosmopolitans—who tend to be relatively light skinned—could increase the signaling salience of skin color in peripheral nations, thereby reinforcing tendencies for color-based discrimination against members of marginalized communities—who are typically darker skinned.

16. This paragraph draws on Weisskopf (2003).

17. Yet the same kind of demonstration effect described above may operate also on governments of peripheral nations, pressuring them to take stronger measures against discrimination. The globalization of information encourages increasing cross-fertilization of resistance movements against racism and other forms of discrimination; and governments late to undertake affirmative action policies can draw on examples of affirmative action policies undertaken elsewhere.

18. India's affirmative action policies currently apply only to public sector enterprises and institutions, but there has recently been much discussion of the possibility of extending them to private enterprises and institutions as well.

3

Measuring Discrimination

Devah Pager

Discrimination has long been a fascinating and frustrating subject for social scientists. Fascinating because it is a powerful mechanism underlying many historical and contemporary patterns of inequality; frustrating because it is elusive and difficult to measure. Over a century of social science interest in the question of discrimination has resulted in numerous techniques aimed to isolate and identify its presence, and to document its effects. Perhaps more than any other issue in mainstream inequality research, the focus on discrimination has been as much preoccupied with method as it has with substance. In this chapter, I talk about the dominant methods that have been used to study discrimination in the United States, including studies of perceptions, attitude surveys, statistical analyses, laboratory experiments, and field experiments. Much of the discussion in this chapter focuses on the case of racial discrimination, as this substantive application has received the most attention in the research literature. A very similar set of priorities and concerns applies to the measurement of a vast array of topics, including the study of criminal stigma and other important forms of social differentiation.

Each of the approaches discussed in this chapter has unique advantages and limitations. Each method grapples with the trade-off between internal validity (the assurance that what we are measuring is really discrimination) and external validity (that our measures are relevant to real-world settings). For example, interview-based studies or large-scale statistical analyses often do a good job representing the broader population, but leave some uncertainty as to whether they provide accurate measures of discrimination. Conversely, experimental methods offer a means of isolating the effects of discrimination, though their research designs are often far removed from the real social contexts in which discrimination takes place. Field experiments offer one solution that bridges these competing priorities, adopting experimental designs within the context of real-world settings. In the following discussion, I provide a brief overview of the varying approaches, examining their unique strengths and limitations. In thinking about each of these methods, the primary question we seek to answer is: How do we really know when or where discrimination is at work?

"I KNOW IT WHEN I SEE IT": PERCEPTIONS OF DISCRIMINATION IN EVERYDAY SETTINGS

To some, discrimination is as easy to spot as a train wreck in daylight. We notice subtle cues in the ways others around us are treated, or in the ways we ourselves are treated. The curt exchange with the shop clerk, the security guard who keeps a watchful eye, the cab driver who doesn't stop. Whether due to age, gender, race, disability, sexual orientation, or any other stigmatized identity, most of us can think of at least one instance in which we, or someone close to us, was treated unfairly on the basis of a single status distinction. In these instances, it doesn't take a social scientist to certify the case as discrimination.

Social scientists have capitalized on the insights and interpretations individuals have of their own lived experiences by asking people about their own encounters with discrimination. Studies have documented perceptions of discrimination among women, the mentally ill, gays and lesbians, and the overweight, among others (Corrigan et al. 2003; Carr and Friedman 2004). Not surprisingly, the most common use of research on perceptions of discrimination applies to the experiences of racial minorities (Smith 2001; Schuman et al. 1997). Numerous surveys have asked African Americans and other racial minorities about their experiences with discrimination in the workplace, in their search for housing, and in other everyday social settings. One startling conclusion from this line of research is the frequency with which discrimination is reported. A 2001 Gallup poll, for example, found that nearly half of all black respondents reported having experienced discrimination at least once in one of five common situations in the past month.[1] Further, the frequency with which discrimination is reported does not decline among blacks higher in the social hierarchy; in fact, middle-class blacks are as likely to perceive discrimination as are working-class blacks, if not more (Feagin and Sikes 1994; Kessler et al. 1990).

What can we make of these findings? One important conclusion is that African Americans—and other stigmatized groups—perceive discrimination to be pervasive in their lives. This is an important finding in its own right. Research shows that those who perceive high levels of discrimination are more likely to experience depression, anxiety, and other negative health outcomes (Kessler et al. 1990). But what we don't know from this line of research is to what extent these trends represent merely perceptions versus an accurate depiction of reality. While some instances of discrimination leave little room for doubt, many others can be subject to misinterpretation or distortion. A curt shop clerk might have been having a bad day; the security guard may be vigilant with all passersby; the cab driver may simply not have seen the pedestrian waving him down. What may be blatant evidence of discrimination from one vantage point could be a simple misunderstanding from another.

The problem with relying on perceptions for our measure of discrimination is not only that some cases may be blown out of proportion. The opposite can be just as much of an issue—acts of discrimination are often imperceptible to the victim. Due to social norms and legal sanctions, contemporary forms of discrimination are rarely overt, leaving countless instances of discriminatory action entirely invisible to the very individuals who have been targeted.[2] While highly relevant to the concrete lived experiences of individuals (external validity), the use of perceptions can only provide one incomplete account of the prevalence of discrimination (internal validity). In order to get closer to the source of discriminatory action, researchers have turned their attention to the potential discriminators themselves.

"I'M NOT RACIST, BUT...": SELF-REPORTS AND ATTITUDE RESEARCH ON DISCRIMINATION

Rather than relying on the perceptions of victims, another line of social science research focuses on the general attitudes and actions of dominant groups for insights into when and how racial considerations come into play. The most well-developed line of work in this area is the long tradition of survey research on racial attitudes. Similar questions have been asked for several decades on national polls such as Gallup and the General Social Survey, among others, gauging white Americans' views on issues of race relations and racial inequality. Because the same questions have been asked over many years, we are able to chart changes in the expressed racial attitudes of Americans over time. And indeed, according to these items, much has changed in race relations since the times of Jim Crow. In the 1940s and 1950s, for example, fewer than half of whites on surveys believed that white students should go to school with black students or that black and white job applicants should have an equal chance at getting a job. By the 1990s, by contrast, more than 90% of white survey respondents would endorse the principle that white and black students and job applicants should be treated equally by schools and employers (Schuman et al. 2001). These changes in attitudes over time indeed suggest a substantial decline in prejudice, and imply that overt forms of racial hostility and discrimination are no longer acceptable among the majority of the American public.[3]

Some critics, however, question the interpretation of these trends as indicative of meaningful change in underlying racial attitudes. Pointing to the lack of support for policies aimed to achieve the widely supported principles of equality—such as busing programs to achieve racial integration in schools or affirmative action programs to support diversity in higher education and the workplace—these researchers question the endorsement of principles of equality as superficial.[4] If not linked to support for meaningful social change, what exactly do these attitudes tell us about the state of race relations today?

One of the main criticisms of attitude research is of its vulnerability to social desirability bias, or the pressure for respondents to give politically correct responses to questions even if this means distorting or lying about their true beliefs. In charting trends in racial attitudes over time, it is hard to separate the changing beliefs of respondents from the increasing pressures to provide socially appropriate (nondiscriminatory) responses. Of course this is a problem to which social scientists have given a lot of thought. Parallel to traditional public opinion questions, researchers have developed a number of innovative approaches to measuring attitudes using techniques thought less vulnerable to distortion from social pressure. Two that stand out as especially promising include experimental survey designs and in-depth interview procedures.[5]

Experimental survey techniques have been developed to study sensitive topics such as racial attitudes by providing the opportunity to gauge differences in the evaluations of various groups without requiring any direct comparisons between groups.

Instead, randomly chosen subsamples of respondents are primed with one of several variants of a survey question to assess responses to a particular group or condition.[6] For instance, a study by Howard Schuman and Lawrence Bobo (1988) used a split-ballot design in which half the sample was asked whether they "would mind a lot, a little, or not at all" if a Japanese American family moved into their neighborhood, while another half was asked the same question with reference to a black family moving into their neighborhood. Where this study found significantly more negative reactions to the black family, had each respondent been asked about both a black and a Japanese family on the same survey, they may have biased their responses toward similar evaluations of the two groups, consistent with norms of equal treatment. Through statistical comparisons across the two groups, split-ballot studies are thought to produce valid population-level estimates of the importance of race for the question of interest, while reducing concerns about social desirability bias that arise from direct racial comparisons.[7] Experimental survey designs have clear advantages for measuring sensitive topics, and their results have indeed revealed greater incidence of prejudice relative to traditional survey designs.

Nevertheless, the problems of social desirability bias are not completely absent in the case of experimental survey designs. Even if respondents are not asked to make direct racial comparisons within individual surveys, respondents may well be aware—consciously or not—that the issue of race has been raised (see Pager and Quillian, 2005). When asked about a black neighbor then, for example, a white respondent may artificially boost his approval rating, even without direct comparisons to a white or Asian neighbor. Race is such a charged subject in this country that individuals can react—and react to their reaction—at its slightest mention. Experimental survey techniques then are not immune to threats to internal validity, though they certainly can offer substantial improvement over conventional survey research.

Perhaps a larger concern about the use of survey items as proxies for discrimination is the uncertainty with which self-reported attitudes correspond to any meaningful patterns of expected behavior. While it is commonly assumed that there is a close link between attitudes and behaviors, existing research—particularly on questions of racial prejudice and discrimination—has found surprisingly little correspondence between the two (LaPiere 1934; Kutner et al. 1952; Saenger and Gilbert 1950; Pager and Quillian 2005). This research cautions us that it is in fact difficult to anticipate how any individual, including oneself, may react to a situation previously encountered only in hypothetical terms. While sophisticated survey designs may successfully detect racial bias, it is not readily apparent what the implications may be for actual expressions of discrimination. The external validity of survey designs—at least for predicting behavior—thus remains in question.

Experimental survey techniques attempt to increase the precision of responses by presenting key stimuli through highly controlled protocols; these techniques move survey research toward greater complexity and precision. Moving in the opposite direction, interviews conducted in less formal settings with lower levels of structure have also proven effective in gauging respondents' views on sensitive topics. In particular, in-depth, in-person interviews have been shown to be highly effective in eliciting candid discussions about sensitive hiring issues (Kirshenman and Neckerman 1991; Wilson 1996; Moss and Tilly 1996; Newman 1999). In these interview settings, researchers typically arrange a place to meet that is comfortable and convenient for the respondent, and interviews typically follow a semistructured format that allows respondents to emphasize those issues they feel are most important. Interviews often last for up to two hours per respondent and are sometimes carried out over multiple sessions. The opportunity for rapport building in the in-person interview context is thought to reduce social desirability pressures, making respondents feel at greater ease in expressing counternormative beliefs. Likewise, these open-ended interviews offer the opportunity for respondents to discuss the complexities and, at times, inconsistencies in their views of various groups, thereby going beyond the more generalized assessments expressed on traditional survey items. Indeed, researchers using this approach have typically found respondents willing to express much higher levels of prejudice and to endorse racial stereotypes more overtly, than is typically found using survey techniques. Joleen Kirshenman and Kathryn Neckerman, for example, describe employers' blatant admission of their avoidance of young, inner-city black men in their search for workers. Attributing characteristics such as "lazy" and "unreliable" to this group, the employers included in their study make little pretense of the fact that they appear to be actively engaging in discriminatory hiring practices (Kirschenman and Neckerman 1991: 213; see also Wilson 1996; Moss and Tilly 1996).

These in-depth studies have been invaluable in providing detailed accounts of what goes through the minds of employers—at least consciously—as they evaluate members of different groups. The primary limitation of research of this kind is its reliance on employers' willingness to express their true attitudes and beliefs. We tend to believe the results of these studies because they produce greater than expected reports of prejudice. But if this is our only measure of validity we are left with some rather circular reasoning, where our evaluation of the method depends on the content of its results. If employer interviews reveal racial bias, they must be accurate; but what if they reveal little bias—in this case would we believe employers are telling the truth?[8]

"EVERYTHING BUT THE KITCHEN SINK": STATISTICAL ANALYSES OF LARGE-SCALE DATA SETS

Perhaps the most common approach to studying discrimination is to investigate inequality in outcomes between groups. Rather than focusing on the attitudes or perceptions of actors that may be correlated with acts of discrimination, this approach looks to the possible consequences of discrimination in the unequal distribution of employment or other social and economic resources. Using large-scale data sets from the U.S. Census or other large samples of the population, researchers can apply statistical techniques to assess differences in employment patterns or income by race for individuals with otherwise equivalent levels of schooling, work experience, and other related characteristics. For example, an analysis by Cancio and colleagues (1996) shows that, after controlling for education, work experience, job tenure, region of residence, marital status, parental status, and family background, black men earn approximately 74 cents for every dollar earned by similar white men. The implication from this research is that the remaining 26%, not accounted for by relevant labor market variables measured on the survey, is likely the result of racial discrimination. If blacks (or ex-offenders) with equal qualifications are being paid less than equally qualified whites (or nonoffenders), what else could it be? As critics have been quick to point out, any number of alternate explanations could be at work. Differences in verbal ability, interpersonal skills, motivation, or work habits could explain some of the observed employment disparities; differences in access to transportation, social networks, and other information resources likewise account for some of the gap (Moss and Tilly 1996; Farkas 2003; Fernandez and Su 2004). It is difficult to directly measure the influence of many of these possibilities (survey measures of punctuality, for example, are nonexistent), but it would likewise be impossible to conclusively rule them out. Just as discrimination represents one possible explanation for some or all of the measured inequality between groups, so too do many other factors. Indeed, the Achilles' heel of survey research is its inability to effectively account for the many possible sources of spuriousness (or unmeasured causes), thus compromising our ability to make strong causal claims. Thus while the strength of this line of research is the strong statistical power to detect differences between groups (e.g., U.S. Census data contain over a million respondents) in the context of real labor market outcomes (e.g., employment and wages), its limitation is in the ability to conclusively explain them.

LABORATORY EXPERIMENTS ON DISCRIMINATION

Social psychological experiments on racial stereotypes and discrimination excel in exactly those areas where statistical analyses flounder. Laboratory experiments conducted in highly controlled environments provide insights into the mechanisms by which racial biases are triggered, processed, and expressed. Experiments typically begin with clearly defined treatment and control conditions, to which subjects are randomly assigned.[9] All other environmental influences are carefully controlled. A specific outcome variable is then recorded to test for differences between groups. Often subjects are not told the purpose of the experiment to ensure a naïve or natural reaction to the experimental condition.

In one study, for example, subjects were led to believe they would be having a discussion with two other students, either on a race-related topic (e.g., racial profiling) or a race-neutral topic (e.g., romantic relationships). Half of the subjects were led to believe their conversation partners would be black (treatment group); half believed their partners would be white (control group). While waiting for the fictitious conversation partners to arrive, the subject was asked to set up the three chairs lined up in the corner of the room so that the three of them could "have a comfortable conversation." Unbeknownst to the subject, the arranging of the chairs was the very focus of the experiment. Researchers measured how far apart the subject placed the chairs from one another (outcome variable), depending on the race of the expected other students and on the proposed subject of discussion. The findings indicate that race has a substantial effect on the distance placed between seats—but only when the subject expects to be discussing a controversial topic like racial profiling (Goff 2005). These results suggest that anxieties about interracial interaction are not uniform. Rather, certain interactions (or anticipated interactions) trigger high levels of anxiety and corresponding acts of social distance. Creative research designs such as these allow researchers to investigate the subtle ways in which behavior is influenced by racial considerations, even when these influences remain entirely unconscious to the individual himself.

Laboratory experiments have been extremely useful in identifying the mechanisms by which racial stereotypes exert their influence. The above example documents the influence of race on subtle behaviors; others have demonstrated the impact of racial stereotypes on selective or distorted memory for stereotype-consistent information (Bodenhausen 1988; Sagar and Schofield 1980). Understanding the cognitive and interpretive processes that occur when racial information is being processed helps us to understand how stereotypes exert their influence and how discrimination comes into being.

The clear strength of laboratory experiments is in identifying causal effects; we can isolate the influence of race on behavior without the interference of confounding factors. The primary limitation of experiments, however, relates to their ability to generalize to real-world settings. Because these studies are typically conducted in laboratory settings under somewhat contrived conditions, it is difficult to know to what extent the findings would apply in a more everyday social context. Likewise, the reliance on undergraduate psychology students for the subject pool of most experiments further limits their generalizability. How can we be sure that the processing of race among 19-year-old psychology majors is the same as that among 50-year-old employers, or among the population more generally? Indeed, some research suggests that research findings differ simply varying the college major of the subject pool, let alone other key demographic variables (Marwell and Ames 1981). While laboratory experiments offer some of the strongest evidence of causal relationships, we have little way of knowing to what extent their findings relate to the kinds of actual decisions made in their social contexts—to hire, to rent, to move, for example—that are most relevant to understanding the forms of discrimination that produce meaningful social disparities. Seeking to bring more realism to the investigation, researchers have moved experiments out of the laboratory and into the field.

CLEAR AND CONVINCING EVIDENCE: FIELD EXPERIMENTS OF DISCRIMINATION

Field experiments blend experimental methods with field-based research, relaxing certain controls over environmental influences in order to better simulate real-world interactions. While retaining the key experimental features of matching and random assignment important for inferences of causality, this approach relies on real contexts (e.g., actual employment searches, real estate markets, consumer transactions, etc.) for its staged measurement techniques. For example, rather than asking undergraduate subjects to rate hypothetical job applicants in a lab experiment, a field experiment would present two equally qualified job applicants to real employers in the context of real job searches.

Field experiments designed specifically for the measurement of discrimination are typically referred to as audit studies. The audit methodology was first pioneered in the 1970s with a series of audits conducted by the Department of Housing and Urban Development to test for racial discrimination in real estate markets (Yinger 1995; Wienk et al. 1979; Hakken 1979). The approach has since been adopted by numerous government agencies, nonprofit organizations, and university researchers to test for discrimination by race, age, gender, and other protected characteristics. The audit methodology has been applied to numerous settings, including mortgage applications, housing markets, negotiations at a car dealership, and hailing a taxi.[10] In the case of employment discrimination, three main types of audit studies offer useful approaches: correspondence tests, in-person audits, and the mediated audit approach.

Correspondence Tests

The correspondence test approach, so named for its simulation of the communication (correspondence) between job applicants and employers, relies on fictitious matched résumés submitted to employers by mail or fax. In these studies, two or more résumés are prepared reflecting equal levels of education and experience. The race (or other group characteristic) of the fictitious applicant is then signaled through one or more cues, with race randomly assigned to résumé type across employers (i.e., minority status is assigned to one résumé for half the employers, the other résumé for the other half; this is to ensure that any differences between résumés will not be correlated with the measured effects of race).[11] Reactions from employers are then typically measured by written responses (to constructed mailing addresses) or callbacks (to voice mail boxes) for each applicant. An exemplary study of this kind, for example, was conducted by Marianne Bertrand and Sendhil Mullainathan (2004). In this study, the researchers prepared two sets of matched resumes reflecting applicant pools of two skill levels. Using racially distinctive names to signal the race of applicants, the researchers mailed out résumés to roughly 1,300 employers in Chicago and Boston. The results of their study indicate that white-sounding names were 50% more likely to elicit positive responses from employers relative to equally qualified applicants with "black" names. Moreover, applicants with white names received a significant payoff to additional qualifications, while those with black names did not. The racial gap among job applicants was thus higher among the more highly skilled applicant pairs than among those with fewer qualifications.

The advantage of the correspondence test approach is that it requires no actual job applicants (only fictitious paper applicants). This is desirable for both methodological and practical reasons. Methodologically, the use of fictitious paper applicants allows researchers to create carefully matched applicant pairs without needing to accommodate the complexities of real people. The researcher thus has far more control over the precise content of treatment and control conditions. Practically, the reliance on paper applicants is also desirable in terms of the logistical ease with which the application process can be carried out. Rather than coordinating job visits by real people (e.g., creating opportunities for applicants to get lost, to contact the employer under differing circumstances such as when the employer is out to lunch, busy with a customer, etc.), the correspondence test approach simply requires that résumés are sent out at specified intervals. Additionally, the small cost of postage or fax charges is trivial relative to the cost involved in hiring individuals to pose as job applicants. At the same time, there are several limitations of correspondence tests: first, the signaling of key characteristics is not always feasible with names alone. For example, in the United States, distinctively African American names often signal class background as well as race. Clarifying the nature of discrimination thus becomes difficult in these cases (see Fryer and Levitt 2004). Second, correspondence tests can be used only for jobs for which mailing or faxing a résumé is an appropriate method of application. While common in white-collar positions, low-wage jobs typically require in-person applications. Thus, while correspondence tests do have many attractive features, there are also certain limitations of this design that have led many researchers to prefer the in-person audit approach.

In-Person Audits

The use of in-person audits, as opposed to mail-in résumés, represents a more elaborate simulation of the hiring process.[12] In-person employment audits involve the use of matched pairs of individuals (called testers) who pose as job applicants in real job searches. Applicants are carefully matched on the basis of age, race, physical attractiveness, interpersonal style, and any other employment-relevant characteristics to which employers may respond in making hiring decisions. As with correspondence tests, résumés are constructed for each applicant that reflect equal levels of schooling and work experience. In addition, the in-person presentation of confederate job seekers must be carefully controlled. Testers typically pass through an intensive training period during which they learn the details of their fictitious profile and run through many mock interviews to practice the comparability of their interview style. Tester pairs (or triplets) typically visit each employer within a 24-hour period, randomly varying the order in which testers apply. Testers then record their experiences of the application process immediately after leaving each employer, typically filling out an extensive response form containing closed-ended questions (about company size, composition, features of the application and interview, etc.) and space for an extended narrative describing the interaction or interview with the employer.

Though in-person audits are time-consuming and require intensive supervision, the approach offers several advantages over correspondence studies. In-person audits provide a clear method for signaling race (through the physical presentation of job applicants); they allow for a wide sample of entry-level job types (which often require in-person applications); and they provide the opportunity to gather both quantitative and qualitative data, with information on whether or not the applicant receives the job as well as how he or she is treated during the interview process. Though the audit approach is not without its critics (cf. Heckman 1998), it does offer a direct approach to measuring discrimination in realistic settings.

The Mediated Audit Approach

In many national contexts, particularly in parts of the developing world, the vast majority of jobs are located in the information labor market, not included in formal classified listings, and not available for systematic sampling procedures used for correspondence tests or audit studies. In these cases, traditional audit approaches to measuring discrimination are inadequate because they can reach only a small fraction of employers. The "mediated audit" approach represents a strategy for adapting elements of the field experiment to measure discrimination in a broader range of settings, including informal labor markets.[13]

The basic design of the mediated audit approach involves the use of a single tester. In this case, rather than posing as a job applicant, the tester poses as an employment intermediary (an individual who connects job seekers with employers). The basic elements of this approach are as follows:

1. A researcher poses as an employment counselor from a vocational training program (or a university placement service, or a job development service, or some other mediating organization, depending on context) seeking to establish links with employers, to assess their hiring needs and priorities, and to obtain their feedback on the employability of selected graduating members of the program.
2. Two to three employment files are constructed containing materials appropriate for the job level under evaluation (e.g., résumé, transcript, letters of reference). The files should not be identical (to avoid suspicion) but should vary in quality and types of background experience.
3. Names signaling race (or gender, religion, ethnicity, caste, etc.) are randomly assigned to the résumés. Names should be counterbalanced, so that each resume (high and low quality) is associated with each name in an equal number of cases.
4. Other application materials can also be included (presented as part of the placement service's screening process). This may include information about the applicant's criminal background, results from skills tests or personality tests, a letter of evaluation from the program director, and so on.
5. A sampling strategy is devised based on the local labor market context. The research may target a particular set of neighborhoods, sampling every third employer. If available, a list of eligible employers may be generated from employer registries, phone books, or any appropriate comprehensive listing. All employers should be included who fit the appropriate sampling criteria (within a specified geographic area, within a specified range of occupations, etc.).

6. A random sample of employers should be drawn from the complete list. This random sample should be several times larger than the desired final sample size.

7. The researcher then begins contacting employers (or the relevant human resource personnel) to set up an interview (see no. 1 above). Large employers may first require a letter explaining the nature of the appointment. For smaller employers, a phone call or even a walk-in visit may be sufficient. A strong effort should be made to draw selected employers into the sample. The researcher should be willing to accommodate the employer's schedule in any way necessary, and efforts should be made to convert refusals by repeated contact and incentives (e.g., cash payment, a gift, gift certificate, etc.).

8. Employers are first asked a series of general questions about their hiring practices and experiences (9) and then asked to evaluate two candidate files for individuals seeking employment (10). In total, interviews should last no more than half an hour. If possible, interviews should be tape recorded.

9. Interviews begin with a short series of general questions. Relevant topics include:

   a. Composition of current workforce
   b. Typical recruitment strategy
   c. Education and skill requirements for target job
   d. Characteristics of last worker hired for target job

10. Employers should then be asked to offer their opinion on two individuals who are currently looking for work (about to finish the program, etc.). Questions about the candidates can include:

    a. How would you rank this individual relative to your current employees (average, above average, etc.)?
    b. How likely would you be to hire this individual for job x in your company?
    c. What concerns might you have about this individual?
    d. How would you rank this individual on the following scales: competence, commitment, intelligence, language ability, ability to integrate with coworkers, etc. (Likert scales)?

11. If an employer expresses interest in hiring one or more of the candidates, he or she should be notified as soon as possible that this individual is considering (or has just recently accepted) another position. Effort should be made to put the employer in touch with an alternate source of eligible workers.

12. Analyses focus on both qualitative (employers' comments as they read through the application materials) and quantitative outcomes (ratings of likelihood of hiring, evaluations of competence, etc.) based on scales and other formalized ranking systems.

The mediated audit approach restores several elements of the traditional laboratory experiment design. As described above, in lab experiments of discrimination, subjects (typically undergraduate psychology majors) are often asked to evaluate the suitability of bogus job applicants for a specified position. This approach offers a high degree of internal validity because all elements of the job applicant materials are carefully controlled, but it is limited in its external validity because of its reliance on subjects that have no direct connection to the employment world. The mediated audit approach, by contrast, seeks to bring the lab experiment into the field. Instead of asking undergraduate students to rate the candidacy of bogus job applicants, these files are presented to actual employers or human resource personnel who make hiring decisions for real jobs. Further, subjects are made to believe that the job candidates are real (and available for hire), and that, even if the employer does not wish to consider the candidate for a position in his or her own company, the evaluation will provide valuable feedback both to the candidate and to the mediating agency.

The advantage of this approach over standard correspondence or audit approaches is twofold: first, this approach does not require that employers advertise a job opening for inclusion in the sample. Employers can be selected for participation even if they are not actively hiring or even if they recruit applicants through means other than formal job postings. In this sense the approach works well in labor markets that rely on informal networks for filling positions and informal labor markets in which jobs are not officially on the books.

Second, this approach does not rely on a single dependent variable (e.g., the callback). Instead, employers will be asked to rate applicants on multiple dimensions, including their interest in hiring the candidate for current or future positions, as well as their evaluation of the candidate according to a range of specific criteria. This design feature has the advantage of increasing the power of the analyses (i.e., response rates will be high, variation wide), and will further illuminate the specific dimensions according to which members of marginalized groups are seen as undesirable relative to those from majority groups (e.g., whether differences in overall ratings are explained by differences in specific assumptions about competence, reliability, criminality, etc.). While this approach is one step removed from the realistic simulation of the hiring process represented by the traditional audit approach, it does retain a fairly high level of realism (as the role of intermediaries has been increasing in many labor markets) and allows researchers to enter labor markets that traditional audit studies would not reach.

CONCLUSION

Despite its various complexities, field experiments remain the most effective approach to measuring discrimination in real-world settings. By interacting with real employers, and by simulating the process of actual job applicants or intermediaries, we can get as close as possible to the interactions that produce discrimination in contemporary labor markets. While no research method is without flaws, careful consideration of the range of methods available helps to match one's research question with the appropriate empirical strategy. Although the field experiment cannot address all relevant aspects of labor market disadvantage, it can provide strong and direct measures of discrimination at the point of hire, a powerful mechanism regulating the employment opportunity.

Notes

1. These situations include shopping, at work, dining out, using public transportation, and with police.

2. Likewise, research suggests that individuals may underestimate or suppress the incidence of discrimination in their own lives, even when conscious of high levels of discrimination against their group (Crosby 1984; Taylor et al. 1990).

3. Some contemporary attitude scales, however, do show large amounts of racial bias. Smith (1991) reports findings from a series of scales asking respondents to rate various racial and ethnic groups according to polar characteristics (e.g., violence-prone/not violence-prone, hardworking/lazy, unintelligent/intelligent, etc.), according to which blacks are consistently rated more negatively than whites and other ethnic groups. These scales are not part of a time series, however, and it is thus impossible to know to what degree these group ratings may have changed over time.

4. Kinder and Sears (1981); Bobo et al. (1997). Some researchers have formally integrated views on policy and politics into their battery of items gauging racial attitudes. The Modern Racism Scale, for example, includes clusters of items intended to measure traditional forms of racial prejudice along with more subtle "modern" forms of racism (McConahay 1986). Measures of modern racism include believing, for example, that blacks have gotten more economically than they deserve, that the government and the media give blacks more respect than they deserve, that discrimination is no longer a problem, and that blacks are too demanding (National Research Council 2004: 176).

5. An alternative approach more common in psychology involves the study of unconscious or implicit attitudes, with subliminal primes used to trigger racial associations across a number of contexts (cf. Fazio and Olson 2003; Banaji et al.

1993). These measures show strong and pervasive indications of racial bias, though their interpretation remains somewhat controversial (e.g., Mitchell and Tetlock 2006).

6. See Sniderman and Grob (1996) for a review.

7. Indeed, the results of this survey indicate significantly more opposition to a black family moving next door (19.6%) relative to a Japanese American family (10.4%). A subsequent version of the survey item including the phrase "of the same income and education" does not reduce racial disparities (18.6% vs. 2.7% said they would mind, for a black and Japanese American family of equal education and income, respectively). See also Schuman (1995).

8. A second limitation of in-depth interview studies results from the extraordinary investments of time and resources required to complete these interviews, often resulting in relatively small sample sizes. Though some projects using in-person interviews have achieved substantially larger samples (Wilson 1996: 179; Moss and Tilly 1996: 174), the scale of these studies nevertheless pales relative to the numbers achieved by more traditional survey techniques.

9. Random assignment helps to remove the influence of any respondent characteristics that may affect their outcomes by breaking the link between respondent characteristics and selection into treatment conditions.

10. Turner and Skidmore (1999); Ayres and Siegelman (1995); Ridley et al. (1989); Yinger (1995); Massey and Lundy (2001); Cross et al. (1990); Turner et al. (1991); Bendick et al. (1994); Neumark (1996). For a review of experimental field experiments in international contexts, see Riach and Rich (2002).

11. The present discussion focuses on the case of racial discrimination, but these methods can be readily applied to studies of discrimination on the basis of gender, age, neighborhood, and numerous other social categories.

12. For an in-between approach using telephone contact (with voice signaling race, class, and gender), see Massey and Lundy (2001).

13. Schwartz and Skolnick (1962) use a similar approach to study employers' willingness to hire individuals with criminal records, though in their study they presented each employer with only a single applicant file.

PART II

CASE STUDIES

4

Racial and Class Discrimination in Assessments of Desert in Postapartheid Cape Town

Jeremy Seekings

RACE, CLASS, AND DISTRIBUTIVE JUSTICE

In multiracial or otherwise multicultural societies, people may discriminate in the allocation of scarce resources against members of particular racial or cultural groups. This chapter examines how people in postapartheid South Africa assess the desert of others in terms of access to social assistance from the state and employment opportunities. The chapter uses attitudinal survey data from Cape Town—a city characterized by both inequality and cultural diversity—to examine who is viewed as deserving and undeserving of public assistance. In particular, it explores whether perceptions of desert reflect racial discrimination. I find that there are clear perceptions of what kinds of poor people are considered deserving of public assistance and who is considered undeserving, that these perceptions are shared widely across the population, and that explicit racial consideration makes little or no differences to these perceptions. These patterns contrast with those in some other areas of public life—including, notably, employment decisions— where racial differences are evident. One lesson from the chapter is that there are some areas of public policy that are likely to be relatively amenable to building cross-racial support for interracial redistribution.

Contemporary South Africa—like the United States—stands at the intersection of two traditions that are likely to shape attitudes toward desert. First, it is firmly rooted in the British poor law tradition, which distinguishes sharply between deserving and undeserving poor, primarily around the capacity of someone to work. The South African welfare state developed along lines similar to other English-speaking societies, providing for people who were unable to work on the grounds (primarily) of age or infirmity, and excluding able-bodied adults of working age (Seekings 2007a, 2008a, 2008b). Second, South Africa faces the legacy of centuries of state-sanctioned and even state-driven racism. Apartheid entailed a system of institutionalized racial segregation and discrimination that exceeded even that of the American South in the era of Jim Crow. In both direct and (especially) indirect ways, public policy both exacerbated inequality and allocated places in the hierarchy on the basis of race (Seekings and Nattrass 2005).

It would not be surprising if attitudes toward distributive justice in postapartheid South Africa were shaped or even determined by these traditions. South Africans might be expected to distinguish between deserving and undeserving poor on the bases of race and willingness or capacity to work. In the United States, attitudes toward the poor are bound up with race: "welfare" for the poor is unpopular (among white Americans) because it is seen as benefiting undeserving lazy black Americans; many white Americans think that their black compatriots should make more of an effort and not "depend" on the state (Sniderman and Piazza 1993; Gilens 1999). Such attitudes are surely even more likely to be found in South Africa than in the United States, where there is a long tradition of white people denouncing "idle" or "work-shy" African people (see Seekings and Nattrass 2005: chapter 5), and where today African people might be expected to view tax-financed social assistance as appropriate (partial) compensation for past racial inequity and continuing racial disadvantage.

Some survey data suggest that there are some sharp racial differences in attitudes toward government policy in postapartheid South Africa. African and white people differ starkly in their views on the redistribution of land and affirmative action (i.e., racial discrimination in favor of people in the same racial categories as people who were discriminated against under apartheid; Roberts 2004). In previous research, I began to investigate this in innovative but preliminary ways. Using data from a small survey ($n = 588$) conducted in Cape Town in 2003, I showed that attitudes toward distributive justice were mutable; that is, they were contingent on the precise specification of the problem (with some poor people apparently seen as more deserving than others) and the costs of any intervention. (Would taxes have to be increased?) Many respondents could be persuaded to change their minds when provided with additional information. For example, the perceived desert of an unemployed person described in a vignette fell sharply when it was suggested that the unemployed person might be a heavy drinker (Seekings 2008d). I also showed that there was little evidence of any racial dimension to assessments of desert in one specific (albeit abstract) context. When respondents were presented with a vignette in which (inter alia) the race of an unemployed person was specified, neither the race of the respondent nor the race of the described subject was significant in respondents' assessments of the desert of the subject. In fact, white respondents proved to be much more generous than African or coloured respondents in terms of the absolute sums that they suggested should be paid (by the government) as social assistance to the unemployed subject in the vignette. The explanation of this is in part but not entirely because richer respondents are more generous (in absolute terms, not relative to their incomes). White respondents appear more generous even controlling for their income, which I attribute to a sense of guilt about enduring racial inequalities and the hope that redistribution will reduce the chances of racial retribution (Seekings 2008d).

Attitudinal data from a survey may not correspond to actual behavior. Pager and Quillian (2005) remind us of a classic American 1930s study of racial discrimination, in which hotel and restaurant proprietors reported in a survey much higher levels of prejudice against Chinese customers than they exhibited in actual practice. Pager and Quillian suggest that this reflects the proprietors' desire to avoid difficult or even confrontational interpersonal situations. In the contemporary United States, where racial prejudice is generally frowned upon, it is more likely that surveys tend to underestimate discrimination because racial prejudice is socially undesirable, or because people are not aware of their own prejudice, or because it is more observable in real settings or interpersonal interactions than in the abstract. One response to these problems is to try to observe actual behavior in controlled settings, either through audit studies (e.g., Pager and Quillian 2005), through studies in laboratory settings (such as psychologists' Implicit Association Test), or through experimental research into behavior in "real" but nonetheless contrived conditions (Quillian 2006; for examples in South Africa, see Burns 2006, 2008). An alternative response is to endeavor to improve survey methodology, most notably through the use of vignettes in which the racial dimension is disguised. This essay uses more detailed data from vignettes, from a second survey conducted in Cape Town, in 2005.

CAPE TOWN

Cape Town is a multicultural and highly unequal city with a population of almost 3 million people. Like all South African cities, Cape Town bears the obvious scars of apartheid: persisting racial residential segregation, very high unemployment, and a highly unequal distribution of income and wealth. It also shows some of the positive changes that have occurred since the transition to democracy, notably the rapid improvement of municipal infrastructure and public services in poorer areas.

But the population of Cape Town is unlike those of other South African cities. At the time of European settlement and expansion between the 17th and 19th centuries, there were no African (i.e., Bantu language speakers) in the Western Cape. The indigenous Khoi and San groups were incorporated into the racial category of "coloured," along with slaves from the Dutch East Indies and elsewhere and the offspring of mixed-race relationships. In Cape Town itself, there were still more white than coloured people as late as 1946 (see figure 4.1), although the coloured population rose rapidly thereafter. The apartheid state sought to prevent immigration into Cape Town by African people from the Eastern Cape. But the erosion, then collapse, of "influx control" resulted in a very rapid growth of the African population from the 1970s. By 2001, only 19% of Cape Town's population was white, compared to 48% coloured and 32% African.

Postapartheid Cape Town is a city characterized by both multicultural diversity and deep socioeconomic inequality. Diversity and inequality are linked in that some racial divisions are also cultural divisions; there is a close relationship between race and class; and there remains a high level of segregation by both race and class. Cape Town's population is divided between white and coloured people speaking either Afrikaans (41% of the total population) or English (28%), and Xhosa-speaking African people (29%). Most people are Christian, divided between many denominations, with no single church claiming more than 10% of the population as adherents. A minority (about one-sixth) of the coloured population is Muslim. Besides language, a second strong cultural divide between coloured and African residents is length of residence in the city. Survey data from 2002 suggest that as many as 84% of coloured adults were born in Cape Town, with another 11% born elsewhere in the Western Cape.[1] Among African adults, however, only 22% were born in Cape Town and another 2% elsewhere in the province. As many as 71% of African adults in Cape Town were born in the Eastern Cape, almost all in rural areas. Only two in five

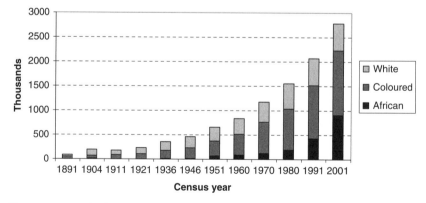

Figure 4.1 Growth of Cape Town's population, by race.

white Capetonians were born in Cape Town, but almost all white Capetonians were born in an urban area. In many cultural respects, the city's white and coloured populations are broadly similar to each other, and distinct from the city's African population.

In Cape Town, as in South Africa as a whole, the end of apartheid did not mean an end to inequality. The Gini coefficient for the distribution of household income in Cape Town in 2002 was about 0.58, which is slightly lower than for the country as a whole but is nonetheless very high. The top decile of households in Cape Town, by household income, receive about 45% of all income in the city, or about 50 times as much as the poorest decile of Cape Town households. By standard international measures, about 10% of households in the city live in severe poverty; two-thirds of these are African and one-third coloured. Another 15% live in mild poverty; just over one-half of these are African and just under one-half are coloured. Inequality reflects, especially, the combination of high (and rising) unemployment with high (and rising) real earnings for a wide range of middle- and working-class people who have jobs.

Table 4.1 shows the relationship between race (or population group) and household income in Cape Town in 2002. African households are concentrated in the poorest third of the city's population and white households in the richest third, with coloured households spread across the income distribution. The mean household income for African households in 2002 was about R2,000 (US$300) per month; the mean household income among coloured households was more than double this, and the mean household income among white households about five times this.[2]

These economic inequalities are a major reason why patterns of residential segregation have not broken down to any great extent since the transition to democracy. Cape Town was segregated racially with brutal and devastating force under apartheid (Western 1991; Bickford-Smith et al.,

Table 4.1 Household Income by Race, Cape Town, 2002

Household Income (Rands Per Month)	African (%)	Coloured (%)	White (%)	Total (%)
0–1,999	20	12	1	33
2,000–5,999	10	23	4	37
6,000+	2	12	17	31
Total	32	47	22	100

Source: Cape Area Panel Study household survey, 2002. At the time, R2,000 was approximately US$300.

1999). Like other South African towns and cities, it began to desegregate in the 1990s, but "the vast majority of the urban population continues to live in highly segregated suburbs" (Christopher 2005: 267). Segregation is as thorough in residential areas built since the end of apartheid as in those that were populated earlier under segregationist legislation. There is some desegregation in middle-class residential areas, and more in schools in those areas (in part because many African and coloured children from other neighborhoods choose to commute to the better schools in formerly white neighborhoods). There is also considerable racial interaction within many workplaces, especially among white and coloured employees; this interaction is no longer entirely hierarchical. Overall, however, race has proved highly resilient in social and cultural terms (see Seekings 2008b).

The 2005 Cape Area Study was designed to shed new light on aspects of inequality and diversity in Cape Town. The survey sought to gather data on how Capetonians see themselves and others, in terms of both diversity and inequality, and how this affects or is affected by their social interactions with each other and their political engagement with the local state.

DATA

The realized sample for the 2005 Cape Area Study comprised 1,200 adults spread across metropolitan Cape Town (see further Seekings et al., 2005). We used a two-stage cluster sample design. First, a sample of 70 enumerator areas (EAs) was selected. Second, a sample of about 1,820 households was selected in these EAs, using a combination of aerial photographs and on-site visits. We anticipated different response rates in different kinds of area, and therefore oversampled in some kinds of area relative to others (rather than allow substitutions in the field). Within each household that was contacted successfully, an adult was randomly selected.

Inevitably, the actual sample was flawed. Poor, shack settlements posed minor problems for our sampling, and rich gated neighborhoods posed a major problem. We were unable to work in one selected EA because of an outbreak of violence locally, and one other—comprising a converted hostel for migrant workers—posed insuperable practical difficulties. In 7 of our 70 selected EAs, we collected no or a negligible number of interviews. In African and coloured residential areas, our response rates were excellent. But in white areas our response rates were so low overall that we were compelled to supplement our sample with a convenience sample. We suspect that it is impossible to conduct a survey among a truly representative sample of white South Africans or of the population of white areas. Overall, our response rate was between 60% and 64%, excluding the supplementary interviews in white areas. Overall, our realized sample comprised too many members of the kind of people more readily found at home by interviewers—that is, women and older people—but did not neglect working people and was not substantially out of line in terms of race. Weights are used to adjust for gender, age, and race.

Fieldwork was conducted between April and June 2005. Xhosa-speaking African respondents were interviewed by Xhosa-speaking African fieldworkers, while English- and Afrikaans-speaking respondents, mostly white and coloured, were interviewed by English- and Afrikaans-speaking fieldworkers, mostly coloured.

The Cape Area Study 2005 questionnaire included a series of vignette-based questions. Respondents were presented with a vignette describing a situation, followed by a question or series of questions related to the situation. What distinguishes the technique is that the description of the situation can be varied between questionnaires, allowing analysis of the effects of variation on responses. The use of vignettes to probe racial attitudes in Cape Town was inspired by Sniderman and Piazza's (1993) study of the nuances of American attitudes. Sniderman and Piazza used vignettes in part because they wanted to test the hypothesis that modern forms of racism disguise racism behind other, more innocuous attitudes. Conservatives might discriminate against black people not because they are explicitly racist, but because (they say) black people do not adhere to the mainstream American values that conservatives hold sacrosanct. Sniderman and Piazza used a laid-off worker experiment in which respondents were presented with a scenario in which a person (or subject) was retrenched, and were then invited to suggest how much (if any) financial assistance that person should receive from the government while looking for work. The scenario varies insofar as the subject (or retrenched person) is given different characteristics: white or black, male or female, younger or older, single or married, with or without children, and dependable or not dependable. Experimental vignettes have been used in South Africa by Gibson and Gouws in their studies of tolerance (Gibson and Gouws 2003) and reconciliation (Gibson 2004). Our 2003 survey included a variant of Sniderman and Piazza's laid-off worker experiment to probe the effects of race on distributive justice (see Seekings 2008d).

The core vignette in our 2005 survey expanded on the vignette we used in 2003. We did not limit the vignette to a scenario in which the subject was said to have lost his or her job, but included also a wider range of circumstances in which a subject might be considered deserving of financial assistance. Respondents were first told: "The government provides grants to some people in need, for example old-age pensions to elderly people. I am going to describe a situation, and then ask you what the government should do to help the person involved." The government's noncontributory old-age pension system is long established and well known. In 2005, it cost more than 1% of GDP and reached more than 2 million pensioners, that is, excluding only rich elderly people. The pension system enjoys general legitimacy. In surveys, almost everyone supports raising the benefits.

A specific subject was then described. For example: "Eddie is sick. He is a coloured man, aged 55, and is not married and has no children." The respondent is then asked: "Should the government provide a monthly grant or financial assistance to Eddie?" This is what we call henceforth the "assessment of desert." If the respondent said yes, he or she was then asked: "How much financial assistance should the government give Eddie per month?" This is what we call henceforth the "assessment of award." The inclusion of the second question allows us to put a value on the assessment and to interrogate the consistency with which the respondent responds to the vignette.

The subjects varied between interviews. First, the general circumstances of the subject varied. Some subjects were described as retrenched workers, others as people who were sick; some were disabled and others abandoned by husbands; and so on. Other characteristics of the subject were also varied: race, gender, age, and family status (single, with or without dependents, or married). In some cases, the subjects were said to be in some way responsible for their situation (e.g., a worker might have been retrenched because he or she was always late for work). Names were changed as appropriate. A total of about 200 variations were described. We endeavored to use each in a wide range of neighborhoods. Each respondent was presented with two substantially different vignettes, so that we have data on a total of about 2,400 assessments of desert. After the second vignette, respondents were presented with further information to see if they could be persuaded to change their minds.

The vignette probed desert with respect to public support, not private charity or generosity. The respondents are not being asked to make any direct sacrifice themselves. The vignette thus probes something rather different than experiments that entail respondents playing with real resources (see e.g., Burns 2008). Given that massive resources are transferred through the state, however, the vignette probes a crucial dimension of desert.

DESERVING AND UNDESERVING POOR

People in postapartheid Cape Town clearly distinguish between the deserving and undeserving poor. In 2003 we found quite high levels of support for financial assistance to the unemployed. The 2005 data show even higher levels of popular approval of government financial assistance to the sick and disabled, especially. Between 80% and 90% of respondents assessed that subjects who were "sick with AIDS and unable to work," or "disabled and unable to work," or just "disabled" should receive financial assistance from the government. More than 70% of respondents said the same for subjects who were "sick and unable to work," "sick with AIDS," or just "sick." By comparison, only just over one-half of our respondents supported financial assistance to subjects who "could not find work" or who had been "retrenched because their employer closed." In assessing desert, incapacity due to health or disability seems to be far more important than unemployment per se. The mean desert of subjects according to their circumstances is shown in figure 4.2.

It is striking that the assessment of desert for subjects described as sick with AIDS is the same as when there is no mention of AIDS. AIDS might be understood as a health condition for which people are themselves responsible (as smokers may be deemed responsible in part for smoking-related illness). But there is no indication of AIDS-related stigma that detracts from the desert of AIDS-sick subjects.

Subjects with dependents attracted support. About 75% supported assistance to women who had been abandoned by their husbands and had children to look after, and about two-thirds supported assistance to women who were looking after sick and elderly parents. Almost as many supported assistance to women who could not find work, having been abandoned by their husbands.

Our respondents were least supportive of the subjects whose behavior was questionable. Less than 20% supported financial assistance to subjects who

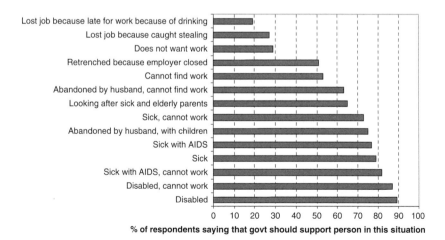

Figure 4.2 Assessment of desert, according to situation (percentage of respondents saying that government should support person in this situation).

had "lost their jobs because they were late for work because they had been drinking," and only slightly more supported assistance to subjects who "lost their job because they were caught stealing" or who "do not want work." Some of this residual support is likely to reflect either fieldworker error or respondent disinterest in the question, so this 20% support should probably be regarded as a baseline against which more deserving cases can be compared.

The various circumstances can be bundled into four broad categories of desert, as shown in table 4.2. The second column reports the assessment of desert, that is, whether or not the respondent considered the described subject as deserving of financial assistance from the government. There are clear and statistically significant differences between the assessment of desert of the "least deserving" subjects (i.e., subjects in some way responsible for their predicament), those who "cannot find work," "caregivers," and the "sick or disabled." The mean assessment of the desert of subjects in these categories rises from 28% for the "least deserving" to 54% (cannot find

Table 4.2 Assessments of Desert and Award, by Circumstances of Subject

Circumstances of Subject	Assessment of Desert: % Saying Yes	Assessment of Award: Mean Award (Rands/Month)	
		Only if Initial Assessment of Desert Was Yes	Including Values of o if Initial Assessment of Desert Was No
The least deserving: Retrenched because late for work because drinking; lost job because caught stealing; or does not want work	28 (24–31) n = 577	717 (656–779) n = 157	206 (174–238) n = 568
Cannot find work (including also retrenched because employer closed and abandoned by husband, cannot find work)	55 (52–59) n = 777	830 (771–888) n = 386	447 (403–490) n = 734
Caregivers Looking after sick and elderly parents or abandoned by husband, looking after children	69 (63–75) n = 229	776 (716–836) n = 149	523 (459–586) n = 216
Sick or disabled (including due to AIDS)	81 (78–84) n = 810	948 (882–1,016) n = 578	765 (705–825) n = 744

Note: Figures in parentheses show range within 95% confidence intervals. Data are weighted.

work), 69% (caregivers), and 81% (sick or disabled). The 95% confidence intervals for these different categories do not overlap.

The third and fourth columns of table 4.2 show the assessment of award, that is, what respondents suggested was the appropriate amount of financial assistance that should be paid to the described subject in the vignette. The third column reports only the actual assessed awards, that is, when the subject was considered deserving.

While smaller mean awards were made to the least deserving subjects and larger awards to the most deserving, the overall variation in the suggested awards is muted in comparison to the initial assessment of desert. The distribution of awards made is shown in figure 4.3. If a respondent assessed a subject to be deserving, he or she then assessed the award at a level a little higher than the then-value of the government's noncontributory old-age pension (which had just been increased from R740 to R770 per month at the time of the survey; this is approximately US$100–110 per month, but worth more than this in terms of real purchasing power), with only limited regard for the circumstances of the deserving subject. The South African old-age pension is unusually generous in comparison with tax-financed social assistance in other countries in the global South. It is set at about the minimum wage for domestic workers, and well below the minimum wages covering workers in formal employment in industrial or other service sectors. The typical award suggested by the respondents in our survey is generous by some criteria, but entails an income replacement rate of perhaps one-third to one-half for most unskilled or semiskilled workers.

The final column in table 4.2 includes values of zero (i.e., awards of R0 per month) if the respondent did not support any financial assistance to the subject, that is, did not consider the subject deserving. This column thus

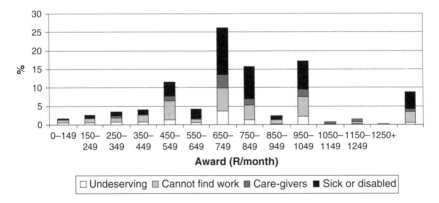

Figure 4.3 Assessment of award, by circumstances of subject

Table 4.3 Assessments of Desert and Award, by Circumstances of Subject

Circumstances of Subject		Assessment of Desert: % Saying Yes	Assessment of Award: Mean Award (Rands/Month)	
			Only if Initial Assessment of Desert Was Yes	Including Values of 0 if Initial Assessment of Desert Was No
Gender	Male	54 (51–58) n = 918	876 (819–932) n = 461	466 (424–507) n = 867
	Female	60 (58–63) n = 1,475	834 (793–876) n = 829	496 (463–528) n = 1,395
Age	25	55 (52–58) n = 945	873 (815–931) n = 484	472 (439–515) n = 895
	55	69 (66–72) n = 841	808 (769–847) n = 523	543 (506–581) n = 779
Family status	Single, no children	52 (49–55) n = 1,020	787 (743–871) n = 490	398 (365–432) n = 968
	Married with children	62 (59–65) n = 924	906 (842–969) n = 529	553 (504–601) n = 867
	Single parent: single, with children	66 (61–72) n = 288	822 (792–951) n = 179	569 (498–641) n = 274

Note: Figures in parentheses show range within 95% confidence intervals. This table uses unweighted data.

combines the effects of discrimination in the initial assessment of desert and of the subsequent conditional assessment of award. The table shows that the mean awards to sick or disabled subjects were substantially higher than to subjects who could not find work or were caregivers, and they were substantially higher than to the least deserving subjects.

Respondents assessed women as more deserving than men, and older subjects as more deserving than younger ones. Married people and especially single parents were assessed as more deserving than single, childless subjects (see table 4.3). As with the circumstances considered above, the gender, age, or family status of the subject makes only a little difference in the awards assessed for deserving subjects. If the discrimination in assessment of desert and in assessment of award are combined, as in the final column, then women, older subjects, and subjects with families are all again seen to be more deserving.

Multivariate probit regressions show strong conditional correlations between the situation and the assessment of desert, and weaker conditional correlations between age or family status and the assessment of desert, but almost none between gender and the assessment of desert (see table 4.4). Subjects who could not find work were 27 percentage points more likely to be considered deserving than subjects in the least deserving category. Caregivers were 35 percentage points more likely to be considered deserving, and the sick or disabled 50 percentage points more likely. Controlling for the gender, age, or family status of the subject makes almost no difference

Table 4.4 Multivariate Regression Models on Assessment of Desert

	Model A	Model B	Model C
Cannot find work	.27 (.02) ***	.26 (.02)***	.27 (.02)***
Caregivers	.35 (.02)***	.34 (.02)***	.38 (.02)***
Sick or disabled	.50 (.02)***	.50 (.02)***	.48 (.02)***
Female		.05 (.02)**	.03 (.02)
Older			.12 (.02)***
Married with children			.13 (.02)***
Single parent			.22 (.03)***
Pseudo r^2	.14	.13	.16
N	2393	2393	2393

Notes: Coefficients are for marginal effects (dF/dx). Standard errors are in parentheses. Significance shown at 1% level (***), 5% level (**), or 10% level (*). All independent variables are dummy variables. This table uses unweighted data. Coefficients refer to assessments relative to the least deserving subjects, i.e., undeserving, young, white men without children.

to these coefficients. Older subjects are 12 percentage points more likely to be considered deserving than younger subjects, while subjects with families and single parents were 13 and 22 percentage points respectively more likely to be considered deserving than an unmarried, childless subject.

Capetonians' construction of desert falls firmly within the poor law tradition of supporting those who are unable to work but not those (of working age and in good health) who are unwilling to do so. But the pattern of support entails the extension of welfare to cover a wider range of caregivers and even unemployed. The South African social assistance system currently provides for the elderly and the certified disabled or chronically sick, as well as modest grants to poor families with children. There is also contributory health insurance, retirement provision, and very limited unemployment insurance for most workers in formal employment (Seekings 2008b). Support for the category of caregivers in table 4.2 entails an extension beyond present modest levels of support (and also to adults looking after elderly parents as well as those looking after children). Support for the category of sick and disabled entails the endorsement of the present system. Given the limits to unemployment insurance, support for the category of subjects who cannot find work would entail an entirely new program of social assistance.[3]

THE EFFECTS OF RACE

Race can be brought into the analysis through specifying both the race of the respondent and the race of the subject. Table 4.5 sets out the assessments of first desert and then award by the various racial combinations. These trivariate data suggest that white respondents assess desert most negatively, and African respondents most positively. African and coloured respondents may assess the desert of same-race subjects more positively than that of other-race subjects. Coloured and white respondents clearly, and African respondents possibly, assess the desert of white respondents least positively. In terms of the assessment of awards, white respondents are clearly far and away the most generous, especially to African and perhaps to coloured subjects. The confidence intervals are too wide to be certain of the other comparisons, but it is possible that coloured respondents are more generous than African respondents, and it is possible that both African and coloured respondents are more generous to same-race subjects.

The findings are broadly similar to those from the prior and preliminary 2003 survey (Seekings, 2008d). There are minor differences. The 2003 data hinted that diverse respondents were more generous in their assessment of awards to white subjects. Here the opposite seems to be the case. There is

Table 4.5 Assessment of Desert (%) and Mean Award (R) (with 95% Confidence Intervals)

		Race of Subject or Beneficiary		
		African	Coloured	White
Race of respondent	African	71% (65–77) *n* = 236	65% (59–71) *n* = 269	63% (57–68) *n* = 300
		R758 (695–820) *n* = 161	R720 (684–756) *n* = 173	R729 (691–767) *n* = 185
	Coloured	62% (56–67) *n* = 307	65% (60–70) *n* = 322	48% (42–53) *n* = 326
		R841 (740–942) *n* = 171	R873 (790–957) *n* = 194	R800 (717–882) *n* = 141
	White	50% (43–57) *n* = 178	53% (45–61) *n* = 143	42% (34–49) *n* = 183
		R1,345 (1,041–1,649) *n* = 78	R1,136 (908–1,364) *n* = 64	R1,019 (875–1,163) *n* = 62

Note: Race of respondent uses data on reported racial classification under apartheid. This table uses unweighted data.

some evidence of racial discrimination among African and coloured respondents. The 2005 data indicate more emphatically that white respondents are not only more generous in their assessment of awards (in absolute terms, although not relative to their own much higher incomes), but also discriminate against white subjects and in favor of African and coloured subjects in their assessment of awards.

These findings can be interrogated more fully in a multivariate framework. The second column in table 4.6 shows the results of regressing the assessment of desert against the characteristics of the beneficiary (or subject) and the race of the respondent. The coefficients are marginal effects, relative to a young white unmarried and childless man in the least deserving category of subjects, and to a white respondent. Thus, overall, there is weak discrimination in favor of coloured subjects and women, and stronger discrimination in favor of older subjects and those who have families or are single parents. African respondents are the most positive in their assessments, coloured respondents in the middle, and white respondents the least positive. The strongest coefficients remain on the circumstances of the subject, with strong discrimination in favor of caregivers and (especially) the sick.

The final three columns of table 4.6 report the results of separate regressions for African, coloured, and white respondents. African and white

Table 4.6 Multivariate Probit Regression Models on Assessment of Desert

	All	African Respondents	Coloured Respondents	White Respondents
Beneficiary/subject:				
African	.04 (.03)	.06 (.04)	.05 (.04)	.01 (.05)
Coloured	.06 (.03)**	−.03 (.04)	.13 (.04)***	.06 (.06)
Cannot find work	.29 (.03)***	.14 (.04)***	.33 (.04)***	.49 (.06)***
Caregiver	.36 (.02)***	.27 (.03)***	.35 (.04)***	.57 (.03)***
Sick or disabled	.49 (.02)***	.43 (.03)***	.53 (.03)***	.55 (.06)***
Female	.05 (.03)**	.09 (.04)**	.08 (.04)*	−.10 (.06)*
Older	.12 (.02)***	.15 (.03)***	.15 (.04)***	.01 (.06)
Married with children	.13 (.02)***	.21 (.03)***	.05 (.04)	.15 (.05)***
Single parent	.20 (.03)***	.18 (.04)***	.14 (.06)**	.35 (.07)***
Respondent				
African	.20 (.03)***			
Coloured	.11 (.03)***			
Pseudo r^2	.18	.21	.20	.16
N	2264	805	955	504

Notes: Coefficients are for marginal effects (dF/dx). Standard errors are in parenthese. Significance shown at 1% level (***), 5% level (*). All independent variables are dummy variables. This table uses unweighted data.

respondents appear not to discriminate at all on the basis of the race of the subject, contrary to what was suggested in table 4.5 (and presumably because the multivariate analysis controls for other, more important factors). But coloured respondents do seem to discriminate in favor of coloured subjects. African respondents assess the desert of subjects who cannot find work less positively (relative to the least deserving) than do coloured and white respondents. This might reflect the higher rates of unemployment in African neighborhoods, and perhaps also higher levels of ambivalence about how hard all unemployed adults try to find work.

The analysis of the assessment of award requires the use of a procedure to account for selection bias. Table 4.7 reports the results of analysis using a Heckman two-step regression procedure. The Heckman procedure takes into account the selection bias arising (in this context) from the fact that there are missing data on the dependent variable (the award) for the nonrandom set of cases where the subject was not considered deserving in the first place (see Winship and Mare 1992; Breen 1996). The first step, selection, reported in the bottom half of the table, regresses the assessment of desert on the key characteristics identified in table 4.6. The second step, reported in the top half of the table, regresses the assessment of award conditional on the prior positive assessment of desert. The second step uses the logged value of the award to approximate a more normal distribution. The final row shows that the use of a Heckman two-step procedure is warranted (albeit less emphatically with respect to coloured respondents), with a very low probability that the two equations (i.e., in each of the two steps) are not independent of each other. Table 4.7 reports first the results for the total sample, then separate results for the subsamples of African, coloured, and white respondents.

Overall, as we can see in the second column, coloured and especially African respondents are more positive in their assessments of desert, but less generous in their assessments of awards. The multivariate two-stage analysis reported in table 4.7 that, in aggregate, respondents discriminate in favor of African and coloured beneficiaries in the assessment of desert (more strongly so than was suggested in table 4.6), but there is no significant discrimination in their assessment of awards. Turning to the regressions for the racial subsamples (in the final three columns), we can see that there is very little evidence of racial discrimination. Only coloured respondents appear to discriminate—in their case, in favour of coloured beneficiaries.[4] There is no evidence of racial discrimination in the assessment of award. Table 4.7 suggests that discrimination is overwhelmingly on the circumstances of the beneficiary—that is, whether they are in a more deserving situation and have dependents—and entails weak race effects.

Table 4.7 Heckman Two-Step Regression Models on Assessments of Desert and Award				
	All	African Respondents	Colored Respondents	White Respondents
Assessment of award (logged):				
Respondent is African	−.41*** (−.57 −.27)			
Respondent is colored	−.31*** (−.44 − −.18)			
Beneficiary is African	Negligible and insignificant (with CI from<0 to >0)		(See cell below)	Negligible and insignificant (with CI from <0 to >0)
Beneficiary is colored		Negligible and insignificant (with CI from <0 to >0)		
Beneficiary is white			Negligible and insignificant (with CI from <0 to >0)	
Respondent's neighborhood income (per R 10,000)	(See cell above)	.01**		(See cell above)
Constant	7.1***	6.7***	Irrelevant	Irrelevant
N uncensored observations	1,228	519	449	204
Selecting on assessment of desert:				
Respondent is African	.61*** (.45−.76)			
Respondent is coloured	.29*** (.15−.43)			
Beneficiary is African	.16** (.03−.29)	.15 (−.05−+.36)		
Beneficiary is coloured	.16** (.03−.29)		.24*** (.07−.43)	
Beneficiary is older	.14** (.03−.25)	.21** (.04−.37)	.22** (.04−.4)	−.1 (−.33−+.14)
Beneficiary has family	.31*** (.19−.43)	.44*** (.26−.62)	.08 (−.1−+.27)	.62*** (.37−.86)
Beneficiary is single parent	.47*** (.29−.65)	.37*** (.12−.62)	.27* (−.01−+.55)	.76*** (.39−1.13)
Beneficiary cannot find work	.64*** (.49−.78)	.15 (−.07−+.31)	.82*** (.6−1.05)	1.06*** (.7−1.42)
Beneficiary is care-giver	.96*** (.75−1.17)	.77*** (.49−1.06)	.9*** (.58−1.21)	1.4*** (.85−1.95)
Beneficiary is sick or disabled	1.15*** (1.0−1.31)	.77*** (.54−1.01)	1.26*** (1.02−1.49)	1.44*** (1.09−1.79)
Constant	−1.21***	−.31***	−.91***	−1.5***
N (censored plus uncensored observations)	2,264	806	954	504
Probability of two equations not being independent of each other	0.000***	0.0000***	0.06*	0.000***

Notes: 95% confidence intervals are in parentheses. Significance shown at 1% level (***), 5% level (**), or 10% level (*). All independent variables except respondent's neighborhood income are dummy variables. Note that the regression on assessment of desert is not a probit. Data are weighted.

THE (UN)DESERVING (NON)POOR

Perceptions of what is a socially desirable response might well color respondents' assessments of both desert and award, especially among white respondents faced with African subjects. It is possible that white respondents, for example, tailored their responses when faced with African subjects to avoid the impression of discrimination. Other questions in the questionnaire can shed some, albeit indirect, light on this.

The survey also presented respondents with a minivignette involving the justice of possible discrimination in employment. Affirmative action in employment is one of the major mechanisms by which the postapartheid state has sought to accelerate improved opportunities for black, and especially African, people. The Employment Equity Act requires employers to report on the racial composition of their personnel, and to have plans for transforming these so that they reflect more closely the racial demographics of the country. The basic vignette was as follows:

Two young men apply for the same job at a bank. They both graduated from the University of Cape Town with the [qualifications and marks]. One of the men is [race] and the other is [race]. At the interview the men are told that the job is an affirmative action position. The [race] man gets the job. Do you approve of this outcome?

Variation is introduced into this vignette by specifying whether they have the same or different qualifications, changing their racial categorization, and changing the outcome (i.e., who gets the job). Only six different variations were used in the survey, and three of these are difficult to interpret because they specified that the candidates had different qualifications without specifying which was more qualified. Also, some important possible manipulations were unfortunately omitted. We did not ask about the fairness of outcomes when the white applicant got the job, or when a coloured applicant got the job in preference to an African candidate. Including these would have expanded the scope of analysis.

Table 4.8 reports the results of the three variations in which the candidates were said to have the same qualifications and marks from university. In each case, African respondents are much more favorable to the outcome in which the African candidate is successful than are coloured or white respondents. In this affirmative action vignette, coloured and white respondents are happy to express deep ambivalence or even hostility. This is in keeping with the findings of other surveys which show that white and other non-African people are ambivalent or opposed to affirmative action policies. Ambivalence to or hostility to apparent affirmative action need not indicate racial prejudice, or collective self-interest (given that affirmative action imposes much more direct costs on nonpoor, non-African Capetonians

Table 4.8 Manipulations of Affirmative Action Vignette

Version	Who Gets the Job	Who Does Not Get the Job	African Respondents	Coloured Respondents	White Respondents
1	African	White	45% (37–53) $n = 120$	36% (28–43) $n = 128$	25% (14–36) $n = 46$
2	Coloured	White	56% (48–64) $n = 124$	41% (33–48) $n = 148$	29% (18–40) $n = 48$
3	African	Coloured	49% (41–57) $n = 130$	15% (10–21) $n = 146$	24% (14–33) $n = 60$

Note: % are percentage saying that the outcome was fair; the response "maybe/it depends" counts as 0.5. Data are weighted.

than social assistance payments to the poor). It could equally be the product of a principled opposition to racial discrimination in any form (as Sniderman and Piazza [1993] suggested with respect to the United States). Whatever its cause, the fact that there appears to be an element of racial discrimination in assessments of the desert of affirmative action when there is no such observable element with respect to assessments of the desert of a candidate for social assistance, lends some credibility to the latter.

Much of the criticism leveled at attitudinal data focuses on the difference between what people say they would do and what they actually do in practice, that is, between self-reported attitudes and actual behavior. Pager and Quillian (2005), for example, show that there is no correlation between a self-reported willingness to employ black workers or workers with criminal records and the observed practices of the same employers in terms of calling job applicants in for interviews. The core vignettes in the 2005 Cape Area Study did not ask respondents to say what they would do, however. Rather, they were focused on the perceived desert of the description in the vignette. Insofar as any behavior is implied, it is on the part of the government—which pays social assistance, or legislates affirmative action—not on the part of the individual respondent. The absence of racial discrimination in attitudes toward the desert of the poor—but, for non-African people, not the nonpoor—does not mean that respondents practice nonracism in every dimension of everyday life. It suggests, instead, that there are limits to the racialization of thought—and, perhaps, practice also.

CLASS AND POPULAR PERCEPTIONS OF DESERT

To what extent is race simply a proxy for class? Given the relationship between race and class, it is not easy to disentangle the effects of each. By comparing regression models with and without race or class variables, however, we can begin to identify discrete effects. Unfortunately, the 2005 survey data on occupational class are not sufficiently clean to use, and data on household incomes are incomplete and of uncertain quality. The easiest proxy for class is a measure of mean household income in the neighborhood, taken from the 2001 census.

Neighborhood income certainly correlates with the assessment of awards, with respondents in richer neighborhoods making more generous awards. The generosity of white respondents relative to their African and coloured counterparts is in part due to income. Figure 4.4 shows that the actual award made rises slightly with neighborhood income. Figure 4.5 shows the actual award made as a fraction of the mean household income in the neighborhood. Respondents in rich neighborhoods might propose larger awards, but

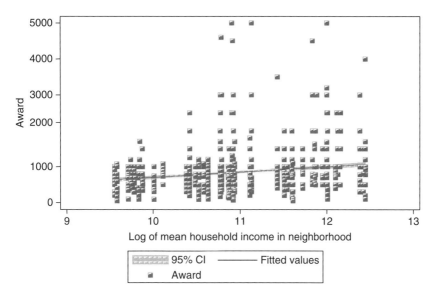

Figure 4.4 Awards by income in neighborhood

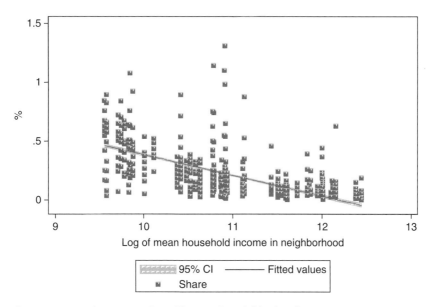

Figure 4.5 Awards as proportion of income in neighborhood

these are smaller in proportion to neighborhood income than their counterparts in poorer neighborhoods.

The median award, measured as a share of neighborhood income, is 0.18; that is, the value of the recommended award is one-sixth of the mean household income in the neighborhood. Table 4.9 shows the value of awards

Table 4.9 Awards as Share of Neighborhood Income, by Neighborhood Income Quintile

Neighbourhood Income Quintile	Mean Award (Rands Per Month)	Mean Share	95% Confidence Interval	n
1	713	.43	.41–.45	375
2	811	.22	.21–.23	263
3	811	.18	.16–.2	259
4	914	.11	.07–.12	208
5	1,097	.08	.07–.09	191
Total	842	.23	.22–.24	1,296

Note: Data are weighted.

made in each neighborhood income quintile, as a share of the mean household income in the neighborhood. Unsurprisingly, respondents in poor neighborhoods recommend awards that are larger as a share of local incomes than respondents in rich neighborhoods, even though the latter recommend awards that are much larger in absolute terms.

Table 4.10 reports the results of three multivariate regressions on the award. The first includes the variable for logged mean household income in

Table 4.10 Multivariate Regression Models on Assessment of Award

	Model A	Model B	Model C
Respondent:			
African		−394*** (45)	−314*** (70)
Coloured		−306*** (44)	−259*** (54)
Mean household income in neighborhood (logged)	145*** (19)		47 (31)
Beneficiary/subject:			
Cannot find work	79 (50)	81 (52)	78 (51)
Caregiver	95 (63)	118* (65)	110* (65)
Sick or disabled	153*** (48)	170*** (49)	163*** (49)
Married with children	106*** (34)	113*** (35)	108*** (35)
Single parent	55 (45)	56 (45)	54 (46)
Constant	−890	973	417
R^2	.06	.08	.08
N	1,286	1,226	1,225

Notes: Standard errors are in parentheses. Significance shown at 1% level (***), 5% level (**), or 10% level (*). All independent variables except for mean household income in neighborhood are dummy variables. This table uses weighted data.

the neighborhood but not the race of the respondent; the second excludes the income variable but includes the race variables; and the third includes both income and race variables. All three models control for the most important circumstances of the subject. This is not a Heckman, and takes no account of the selection bias arising from the prior assessment of desert. The important finding is that neighborhood income appears to be statistically significant when race is not controlled for (model A), but it ceases to be statistically significant when race is controlled for (model C). The race variables retain significance even when neighborhood income is controlled for (although the coefficients do decrease). It appears to be race, rather than class, that drives differential assessments of award.

The prior assessment of desert is also shaped by class, or at least by neighborhood income. Including the measure of neighborhood income in the probit regression reported in table 4.6 (or in the first step of the Heckman procedure reported in table 4.7) has the effect of eliminating the significance of the race of the respondent. This is shown in table 4.11. Neighborhood income has a clear and negative effect on assessments of desert, even when race is controlled for, in contrast to its ambiguous (because conditional on race) and positive effects on assessments of award.

Table 4.11 Multivariate Probit Regression Models on Assessment of Desert

	Model A	Model B	Model C
Respondent:			
African		.2*** (.02)	.05 (.05)
Coloured		.1*** (.03)	.01 (.03)
Mean household income in neighborhood (logged)	−.1*** (.01)		−.09*** (.02)
Beneficiary/subject:			
Cannot find work	.29*** (.02)	.29*** (.03)	.3*** (.03)
Caregiver	.36*** (.02)	.35*** (.02)	.35*** (.02)
Sick or disabled	.48*** (.02)	.48*** (.02)	.49*** (.02)
Married with children	.13*** (.02)	.12*** (.02)	.13*** (.02)
Single parent	.22*** (.03)	.21*** (.03)	.2*** (.03)
Female	.05** (.02)	.06** (.03)	.06** (.03)
Older	.1*** (.02)	.13*** (.02)	.12*** (.02)
Pseudo r^2	.18	.18	.18
N	2,391	2,264	2,262

Notes: Standard errors are in parentheses. Significance shown at 1% level (***), 5% level (**), or 10% level (*). All independent variables except for mean household income in neighborhood are dummy variables. This table uses weighted data.

CONCLUSION: BEYOND THE RACIAL CONSTRUCTION OF DESERT?

The evidence from these vignettes suggests that there is a widespread perception, cutting across all racial groups and classes, that there are deserving and undeserving poor and that this perceived desert relates strongly to perceived capacity and willingness to work. People in need who are unable to work, due to illness, disability, age, or commitment to caregiving, are considered relatively deserving. This assessment is largely, although not entirely, independent of race. Coloured people may discriminate weakly in favor of coloured subjects, while African people may do so in favor of African subjects, in the initial assessment of desert. People who are white or live in richer neighborhoods—which are strongly overlapping categories—are more negative in the initial assessment of desert generally, but insofar as they discriminate by race they do so in favor of African subjects. White people are more generous in their assessments of the financial award but there is no evidence of racial discrimination among them or any other respondents with respect to the awards.

South African society remains highly racialized, for at least three reasons (see further Seekings 2008c). First, disadvantage remains correlated with race: the poor, who lack social and human capital, employment, and land, are overwhelmingly African, while almost all white people are rich (notwithstanding the growth of a huge African elite and middle class). Second, South Africans are culturally diverse, and many dimensions of culture vary by race. Third, there no doubt remain vestiges of racial prejudice and discrimination between members of different racial categories. It is unclear how far affirmative action, that is, racial discrimination in favor of black (or at least African) people has actually transformed the landscape (although it is clear that it prompts polarized political attitudes). Questions in the survey about affirmative action prompted responses that were clearly differentiated by race, showing that there certainly are some issues of distributive justice that remain racialized. Insofar as there is continuing racial discrimination with respect to distributive justice, however, it does not appear to be expressed in popular perceptions of the desert of the poor. Attitudes toward the poor are dominated by other considerations besides race.

In South Africa, as elsewhere, norms of distributive justice may vary between contexts. Norms concerning equity might be more important in the workplace or employment, while norms concerning equality might be applied more to public policy. South Africans might share generally positive attitudes toward public policy around pro-poor social assistance programs, favoring public support for the deserving poor, and do so independently of racial difference or distinction. With respect to affirmative action, however, attitudes are more racialized. And in their everyday personal interactions with other people, racial differentiation is likely to persist, whether consciously or subconsciously.

While the survey data cannot alone explain these patterns, some explanations seem more plausible than others. By and large, white South Africans endorse equality of individual opportunity. They endorse strongly educational programs aimed at improving the quality of schooling for children from poorer backgrounds. They endorse welfare programs that provide assistance to people who—for reasons such as age and infirmity—face evident disadvantage in terms of opportunities to provide for themselves. At the same time, most white South Africans are strongly opposed to programs including affirmative action in employment that appear to provide some people with markedly improved opportunities on the basis of racial classification. Among African South Africans, in contrast, there is more willingness to endorse racial discrimination in favor of African people as members of a previously disadvantaged group. To some extent this might reflect an emphasis on equality of outcomes rather than of opportunity. This contrast should not be overstated, however. Survey data suggest that, even with respect to affirmative action, attitudes are more nuanced and less polarized than might be expected, while with respect to social programs, there is no evidence that African respondents feel that white subjects should be excluded from benefits on the basis of historical advantage.

A supposedly meritocratic ideology is commonplace among the beneficiaries of past advantage, whether among white South Africans, upper-caste Indians, light-skinned and wealthy Brazilians, or their counterparts in many other societies, as other chapters in this volume show. The coincident endorsement of pro-poor welfare spending across racial lines in South Africa is more curious—and encouraging. If, in South Africa, broad political support can be built for pro-poor and racially redistributive social programs, then are there similar possibilities in India or Brazil?

Notes

1. These data are also from the 2002 household survey component of the Cape Area Panel Study. See Cape Area Panel Study (2005). www.caps.uct.ac.za.

2. Ibid.

3. There is some evidence that the disability grant serves as a disguised form of social assistance for some unemployed people (see Nattrass 2006). A modest basic income grant or universal social assistance has been proposed (see Standing and Samson 2003).

4. There is a hint that African respondents may discriminate weakly in favor of African beneficiaries. The coefficient of .15 is significant at the 15% level, although the 95% confidence interval does extend from <0 to >0.

5

Race and Social Interactions in Postapartheid South Africa

Justine Burns

In 1994, South Africa experienced a remarkably peaceful transition to democracy despite being one of the most unequal countries in the world, with a history of legislated discrimination based on race. A key challenge for government in the postapartheid era was to undo the economic legacy of a political system based on racial identity, in which black South Africans were systematically marginalized in every sphere of life. It was hoped that the transition would usher in a new era of higher economic growth that could be shared by all, and ease the task of redressing past racial injustices. However, since 1994, the economy has experienced lower than expected economic growth and an unambiguous increase in income poverty, with black South Africans, on average, remaining the most disadvantaged in socioeconomic terms, with limited opportunities for upward mobility. Unemployment is high, irrespective of whether one adopts a broad or a narrow definition, and has increased during the postapartheid era, from 15.6% in 1995 to 30.3% in 2002 (Banerjee et al. 2006).[1] Income inequality has also increased, with the Gini coefficient rising from 0.68 in 1996 to 0.73 in 2001, a level comparable only to Brazil (Leibbrandt et al. 2006). Importantly, this increase has been characterized by declining interracial inequality and increasing intraracial inequality (Leibbrandt et al. 2006). On a more positive note, there have been significant improvements in service delivery, and while the daily circumstances for rural households and those in poverty remain dire, they have benefited significantly from government transfers.

Thus, the hopes for an economic miracle that would allow the society to rid itself of large socioeconomic disparities so closely tied to racial identity have not been fully realized. However, significant social and institutional changes have occurred, with the extension of voting rights to all, the introduction of affirmative action policies in labor markets and efforts toward greater school integration. These changes provide a unique backdrop against which to examine whether racial identity impacts on individual willingness to redistribute resources or to engage in mutually profitable exchange opportunities with fellow South Africans from different race groups. While a large number of empirical techniques are available to social scientists interested in trying to quantify the existence and persistence of discrimination, including, inter alia, audit and correspondence studies (Daniel 1968; Jowell and Prescott-Clarke 1970; Riach and Rich 1991; Brown and Gay 1985; Bertrand and Mullainathan 2004), Oaxaca-Blinder (1973) wage and employment decompositions, or even observing the outcomes of discrimination lawsuits (Darity and Mason 1998), this chapter reports evidence from experimental games, adapted to explicitly observe whether racial identity has any impact on social interactions among black and white South Africans.

IDENTITY AND SOCIAL INTERACTIONS

A well-established social psychology literature demonstrates that group identity or affiliation matters for outcomes in society, particularly since individuals tend to favor members of their own group over outsiders. Simple categorization of individuals into groups, on the basis of some trivial criteria, such as the outcome of a coin toss or the tendency to over- or underestimate the number of dots on a screen, may be sufficient to induce a favorable in-group bias in behavior (Tajfel 1970). Experimental games that mimic social dilemmas confirm that individuals are more likely to cooperate with an in-group member than an outsider (Orbell et al. 1988; Brewer and Kramer 1986; Kollock 1997; Kramer and Brewer 1994; Wit and Wilke 1992).

While in-group members may be identified as such on the basis of any number of different characteristics, an individual's race or gender are two cues typically accorded much salience, especially in segmented societies where such characteristics may be highly correlated with other traits regarded as significant in some way. For example, Akerlof (1970) argues that employers, in their quest to maximize profits, might rely on race as a proxy for employee quality through its correlation with educational background, while Arrow (1973, 1988) argues that race may be used to proxy productivity. Since race and gender are costlessly observable, they may even be privileged over other categorizations, such as class or educational background, even when the latter might be more relevant (Chandra 2003; Cornell and Welch 1996).

This chapter reviews some available experimental evidence from dictator games and trust games played in South Africa, adapted to examine the extent to which racial identity affects social interactions between black and white South Africans. Considering evidence from both games is useful, since it allows the opportunity to explore whether racial identity affects interactions uniformly in different social contexts as imposed by the differing game structures. The dictator game is a *nonstrategic interaction* between two individuals and provides a measure of individual generosity or altruism toward another individual. In contrast, the trust game involves a *strategic interaction* between two individuals, who stand to benefit substantially through mutual cooperation with one another.

RACIAL IDENTITY AND ALTRUISM

The dictator game (Forsythe et al. 1994) is a commonly used experimental tool that provides a behavioral measure of generosity or altruism toward others. In this nonstrategic interaction between two individuals, the proposer is given a fixed endowment and asked whether he would like to transfer any amount to his partner in a one-way split. Any amount transferred by the proposer is deducted from the initial endowment, and hence, entails material sacrifice on his part. Since the proposer stands only to gain the "warm glow" (Eckel and Grossman 1996) effect of having been generous toward another individual, positive offers in this game reflect nonselfish behavior and are ascribed to generosity or altruism.

The outcome of this game is very sensitive to the framing of the context, and to what is known about the recipient. Table 5.1 provides a brief overview of some of the key studies in this regard. Average offers made by dictators are significantly lower when the game is conducted in a double-blind setting with complete anonymity than compared to a setting where the experimenter is able to observe the actions of the proposer (Hoffman et al. 1996), or where something is known about the recipient in this game (Eckel and Grossman 1996). Eckel and Grossman (1996) demonstrate that if the proposer is made aware of the "deservingness of the recipient," this can dramatically and positively affect the size of the offers made.[2] This finding is confirmed by Bohnet and Frey (1999), who find that if the identity of the recipient is revealed to the dictator, along with some personal information about the recipient, this results in significantly higher levels of altruism than in an anonymous treatment. This is even further enhanced if the identity of both partners is publicly revealed in a two-way identification process.

Experimentalists have only relatively recently begun to focus attention on the ways in which personal attributes such as race and gender affect outcomes in a dictator game setting. The majority of experimental work that has been done has focused almost exclusively on studying the effect that the personal characteristics of the proposer, gender in particular, has

Table 5.1 Overview of Key Findings from Dictator Games

Authors	Treatment	Stratification	Mean Offer (%)
Hofmann et al. (2004) (USA)	Anonymous (double blind)	None	9.00
Forsythe et al. (1994) (USA)	Single blind	None	23.00
Eckel and Grossman (1996) (USA)	Anonymous (double blind)	None	10.00
	Recipient deservedness (Red Cross)	None	30.00
Bohnet and Frey (1999) (Switzerland)	Anonymous	None	26.00
	One-way identification	None	35.00
	One-way identification with information	None	52.00
	Two-way identification	None	50.00
Bolton and Katok (1995) (USA)	Gender of dictator	None	No gender effect
Eckel and Grossman (1996, 1998) (USA)	Gender of dictator	None	Female dictators make higher offers
Selten and Ockenfels (1998) (USA)	Gender of dictator	None	Female dictators make higher offers
Fershtman et al. (2002) Israel	Ethnicity	Male Eastern to Ashkenazi	25.00
		Male Ashkenazi to Ashkenazi	25.00
		Male Israeli to Ashkenazi	26.00
		Male Eastern to Eastern	29.00
		Male Ashkenazi to Eastern	26.00
		Male Israeli to Eastern	29.00

(Continued)

Table 5.1 Continued

Authors	Treatment	Stratification	Mean Offer (%)
Carter and Castillo (2003) (South Africa)	Anonymous		42.00
Ashraf et al. (2004) (South Africa)	Race	Offer by white	25.00
		Offer by nonwhite	25.00
	Race (DG where offers were tripled)	Offer by white	30.00
		Offer by nonwhite	26.00
Harbaugh et al. (2003) (USA)	Age	All	12.00
		9th–12th grade only	16.50

Note: With the exception of Harbaugh et al. (2003) and Carter and Castillo (2003), all studies cited use university students as their subject pool. Harbaugh et al. (2003) sampled children from grades 2–12, while Carter and Castillo sampled nonuniversity adults.

on the offers made.[3] Evidence regarding the impact of the proposer's gender on offers made in an experimental setting is at best mixed (Aranoff and Tedeschi 1968; Ortmann and Tichy 1999; Stockard et al. 1988; Orbell et al 1994), although there is evidence that men and women play the game differently depending on the gender of the person they are paired with (Moely and Skarin 1979; Nowell and Tinkler 1994; Buss 1999). In the dictator game specifically, Eckel and Grossman (1996, 1998) and Selten and Ockenfels (1998) find evidence that women are more generous than men, while Bolton and Katok (1995) find no significant gender differences in giving. However, Dufwenberg and Muren (2002) find that when the gender of the partner in the dictator game is revealed to the proposer, women receive higher offers than men, particularly from other men.

Evidence concerning the impact of racial identity on the propensity of proposers to be generous in this setting is scant. In a series of dictator game experiments run in South Africa, the United States, and Russia, Ashraf et al. (2004) do not find significant differences in the mean offers made by white and nonwhite participants on average, nor do they find significant differences in the mean offers made by white and nonwhite South Africans.[4] Arguably, the race of the recipient might also affect generosity in this setting, particularly in segmented societies with institutionalized prejudice, or in settings where race is correlated with socioeconomic differences between groups. Fershtman and Gneezy (2001) examined this possibility in a dictator game played between Eastern Jews and Ashkenazi Jews in Israel, where ethnicity was revealed through participants' surnames, and did not find any significant differences in the average offers made in a dictator game to members of different ethnic groups.[5] In other words, ethnicity of the recipient among this sample of Israelis does not significantly affect the size of the offers made by proposers in this nonstrategic setting.

South African Evidence on Race and Altruism

Given South Africa's unique history of legislated discrimination and ongoing efforts to redress the legacies of apartheid, understanding the extent to which racial identity might affect individual willingness to voluntarily transfer resources toward others is important. This question has been examined among two different samples of South Africans, using a dictator game, which effectively tests the extent to which the voluntary transfer of resources from the proposer to the recipient is affected once racial identity is known.

The first set of evidence comes from Van der Merwe and Burns (2008), who present results from dictator games run among a sample of 240 university students, ranging in age from 18 to 22, with females slightly outnumbering males. Participants were randomly allocated to one of two treatments in a standard dictator game: an anonymous treatment in which the proposer and recipient knew nothing about each other, and a race treatment in which proposers were told the surnames of the recipients with whom they were paired. Only students with typically black or typically white-sounding surnames were recruited to participate in these games. Importantly, in a postgame questionnaire, the overwhelming majority of proposers indicated that the surname of their partner revealed information about the recipient's ethnic or racial background and most participants correctly specified the race of the recipient with whom they were paired when asked (Van der Merwe and Burns 2008).[6] Each participant was given a participation fee of 20 rands and the proposer was given an endowment of 50 rands with which to make their decision.[7]

The results from these games are presented in panel A of table 5.2. Proposers make significantly higher offers when they know the racial identity of their partner than when identity is anonymous. This accords with the international literature in this regard (Eckel and Grossman 1996; Bohnet and Frey 1999). Proposers offered 15% of their endowment on average in the anonymous treatment compared to 25% in the race treatment, a mean difference that is significant at the 1% level. Second, black proposers make significantly lower offers than their white counterparts. In the anonymous treatment, white proposers offer 17% of their endowment compared to 13% for black proposers, while in the race treatment, white proposers offer 29% of their endowment on average compared to 19% for black proposers. These differences are statistically significant.

In line with the findings of Fershtman and Gneezy (2001), the race of the recipient does not appear to have any significant impact on the offers made on average; that is, the offers made to black recipients are not significantly different than those made to white recipients on average. However, a more nuanced picture emerges once one begins to look at specific race pairings. White proposers exhibit an insider bias in their offers, making significantly higher offers to partners with white-sounding surnames, than compared to partners with black-sounding surnames. This same pattern does not characterize the offers made by black proposers, with median offers in black-black pairings being identical to those in black-white pairings, and very small (and insignificant) differences in mean offers. The net result is that while on average it appears that there are no significant differences in the offers made by black and white proposers to black recipients, white proposers in this sample do, in fact, make significantly lower offers to black partners, even in this nonstrategic setting.

The second set of evidence comes from Burns (2008), in which photographs were used to reveal the racial identity of partners in a dictator game. The results reported in panel B of table 5.2 refer only to the interactions

Table 5.2 Offers Made in Dictator Games among South African Subjects

Study	Mean (Rands)	% of Endowment	Median (Rands)	% of Endowment	Number of Pairs (*n*)
A: Van der Merwe and Burns (2008) Endowment: R50 Show-up fee: R20					
Anonymous treatment					
Offers by white proposer	8.21	17%	2.50	5%	14
Offers by black proposer	6.42	13%	0.00	0%	14
Combined offers	7.32	15%	0.00	0%	28
Race treatment					
Offers by white proposer	14.50	29%	15.00	30%	44
Offers by black proposer	9.53	19%	10.00	20%	43
Combined offers	12.60	25%	10.00	20%	87
White to white	17.00	34%	20.00	40%	21
White to black	12.30	25%	10.00	20%	23
Black to white	9.13	18%	10.00	20%	20
Black to black	10.00	20%	10.00	20%	23
B: Burns (2008) Endowment: R30 Show-up fee: R30					
Race treatment					
Offers by black proposer	5.37	18%	5.00	17%	45.00
Offers by white proposer	11.19	37%	10.00	33%	29.00
Offers to black recipient	8.01	27%	10.00	33%	43.00
Offers to white recipient	6.89	23%	5.00	17%	31.00
Black to black	6.23	21%	5.00	17%	26.00
Black to white	4.95	16%	5.00	17%	19.00
White to black	10.12	34%	10.00	33%	17.00
White to white	12.25	41%	12.50	42%	12.00

between the 148 white and black high school students who participated in these games.[8] The behavior of these subjects is particularly interesting since these high school students form part of the first generation of South African students who have not only had the opportunity to participate in a more integrated schooling environment,[9] but have also spent much of their lives living in the "new" South Africa, where attempts to redress the devastating effects of racial segregation under apartheid have been made. Each participant was paid a show-up fee of 30 rands, and each dictator was allocated a 30-rand endowment.[10]

Similar results to those of the Van der Merwe and Burns (2008) study emerge in the study by Burns (2008). While proposers offer just over a quarter of their endowment to their partner, white proposers make significantly higher (at 1% level) offers than black proposers. Similarly, the race of the recipient does not appear to significantly affect the average offers made by proposers in these games either. Black recipients are not treated significantly differently than white recipients, although black proposers favor black partners while white proposers do not.

Considering the evidence from these two games together, in both cases, black proposers make significantly lower offers than their white counterparts. This is similar to the findings by Seekings (chapter 4, this volume) in his work using vignettes to assess desert and award. The higher offers in these games, and the higher assessments of award by whites in the Seekings study, are arguably attributable to the ongoing stark socioeconomic disparities between these two groups, since there is no a priori reason to expect altruism or generosity to differ by race. In relation to the experimental games reported here, the argument is simply that the postgame consumption value of the endowment monies provided for the experiments may vary sufficiently between black and white participants that black students may prefer to retain their endowment for use outside of the experimental setting rather than allocate it to their partner. Evidence from postgame questionnaires tends to support this argument. In the Van der Merwe and Burns (2008) study, a third of black participants classified their families as poor compared to only 1% of white participants, while in the Burns (2008) study, 24% of black participants self-classified their families as poor compared to only 2% of whites. In both studies, white participants were more than twice as likely to report that their families were better off than most South Africans than black participants were. Employment rates among parents were also considerably higher among white participants.

Second, the results also suggest that while proposers may respond to the racial identity of their partner and favor insiders over outsiders, this effect is not statistically significant. This is similar to the results of Seekings (chapter 4, this volume), who finds that race does not appear to influence the assessment of award or desert by survey participants who are presented with vignettes, but rather that the "deservingness" of the recipient as judged by some other characteristics is more important. The lack of statistical significance in the experimental games may, of course, simply reflect small sample sizes. In both experimental studies, white proposers exhibit a stronger insider bias in their allocation behavior, preferring white partners to black partners, than compared with the insider bias demonstrated by black proposers. If this kind of behavior is evident in the nonstrategic stetting of the dictator game, this begs the question of whether these effects persist, disappear, or are strengthened in a strategic setting as characterized by the trust game.

RACIAL IDENTITY AND TRUST

The trust game (Berg et al. 1995) represents social exchange in a context characterized by contractual incompleteness and asymmetric information. In the trust game, the proposer is given an endowment and asked what portion (if any) of this endowment he would like to pass on to his partner (the responder), who is at a separate location. The offer by the proposer is tripled before being passed on to the responder, who must then decide how much, if anything, to send back to the proposer. Within this context, offers by proposers in the trust game reflect an expectation on their part that they will not be exploited by their trading partner, even though the incentive structure facing the latter suggests otherwise (Harvey 2001), while return offers made by the responder reflect reciprocity. These behaviors are typically termed *trust* and *trustworthiness* respectively in the literature.[11] While the efficient outcome in this strategic interaction implies that the proposer should send his entire endowment to the responder, the subgame perfect equilibrium prediction is that no transfer of resources will occur at all. Yet there is now a substantial body of evidence indicating that proposers do in fact send non-negligible amounts to their partners, who return at least as much as the initial endowment sent (Berg et al. 1995; Fehr et al. 1993; Fehr and Kirchsteiger 1997; Scharleman et al. 2001; Glaeser et al. 2000; Croson and Buchan 1999). An overview of some of the key findings from trust games is presented in table 5.3.

Available evidence to date suggests that real attributes such as race (Glaeser et al. 2000; Eckel and Wilson 2003), gender (Scharleman et al. 2001; Chaudhuri and Gangadharan 2002; Croson and Buchan 1999), and ethnicity (Fershtman and Gneezy 2001; Bouckaert and Dhaene 2004) do affect behavior in the trust game, although the direction of this effect is not uniform. In their work on the impact of linguistic segmentation in Belgium,

Table 5.3 Overview of Key Findings from Trust Games

Authors	Sample	Treatment	Stratification	Mean Offer by Proposer (%)	Mean Remitted by Responder (%)
Ashraf et al. (2004) (South Africa)	University students	Single blind	All	42.80	27.34
			By white student	52.18	28.67
			By nonwhite student	33.43	26.00
Croson and Buchan (1999) (China, Korea, Japan, USA)	University students	Gender	By men	0.70	28.60
			By women	0.63	37.40
Fershtman et al. (2002) (Belgium)	University students	Language	Flemish to Flemish	50.50	19.00
			Flemish to Walloon	26.80	54.00
			Walloon to Walloon	60.00	48.00
			Walloon to Flemish	37.25	17.00
Fershtman et al. (2002) (Israel)	University students	Religion	Ultraorthodox to ultraorthodox	66.60	40.00
			Ultraorthodox to secular	47.10	29.00

Study	Subjects	Category	Subgroup		
Fershtman and Gneezy (2001) (Israel)	University students	Ethnicity	Offer to Ashkenazi male	75.60	39.35
			Offer to Eastern male	40.30	37.80
			Eastern male to Eastern male	26.40	
			Ashkenazi male to Eastern male	30.20	
			Israeli male to Eastern male	27.10	
			Eastern male to Ashkenazi male	87.00	
			Ashkenazi male to Ashkenazi male	92.20	
			Israeli male to Ashkenazi male	80.50	
Bouckaert and Dhaene (2004) (Belgium)	Male entrepreneurs	Ethnicity	Belgian to Belgian	67.70	
			Belgian to Turkish	60.90	
			Turkish to Turkish	60.70	
			Turkish to Belgian	56.00	
Glaeser et al. (2000) (USA)	University students	Race	By white	60.50	
			If partner of different race	54.40	
			If partner different sex	42.10	
Harbaugh et al. (2002) (USA)	School children (2nd–12th grade)	Anonymous	All	33.00	
			9th–12th grade	37.00	
Carter and Castillo (2003) (South Africa)	Adults	Anonymous	All	53.00	38.00

and religious segmentation in Israel, Fershtman et al. (2002) find evidence of insider favoritism, with individuals tending to favor players from their own linguistic or religious group. In their work on ethnic affiliation in Israel, Fershtman and Gneezy (2001) find that significantly lower offers are made to Jews of Eastern origin, particularly men. Most surprising about this pattern of distrust toward Eastern Jewish males is that it is perpetuated by Eastern Jewish males themselves. In contrast, Bouckaert and Dhaene (2004) do not find any evidence of discrimination in the levels of trust or reciprocity in a trust game in which male small business owners of Turkish and Belgian ethnic backgrounds were matched with each other and names were used to reveal ethnic identity. They attribute this to the fact that the small business owners shared other common characteristics (namely, gender, socioprofessional status, and place of residence) sufficient to reduce the salience of ethnic differences.

Other studies have allowed participants to see each other face to face before the experiment begins (Glaeser et al. 2000) or have made use of photographs to transmit information about the race of players (Eckel and Wilson 2003). Again, the results here are mixed. Glaeser et al. (2000) find that trustworthiness (as measured by return offers) is significantly higher in same-race pairs than mixed-race pairs, and while proposers in same-race pairs made higher offers in the trust game than if their partner was from a different race group, this effect was not statistically significant. In contrast, Eckel and Wilson (2003) find that the trustworthiness of responders was unaffected by the race of the proposer.[12] Rather, proposers were significantly less likely to make an offer (i.e., display trusting behavior) if they were paired with members of minority race groups.[13]

South African Evidence on Race and Trust

Given the legacy of entrenched discrimination in South Africa, the interesting question that arises is what salience racial identity might hold for behavior of South Africans who find themselves in this strategic setting. This was examined by Burns (2006), who used photographs to reveal the racial identity of partners in trust games played among a group of South African high school students. Table 5.4 reports the results from these strategic interactions between black and white high school students who were recruited to participate in a trust game.[14] The endowment in the trust game was 30 rands and all payments were made in cash at the end of the experimental session.[15]

On average, proposers offered a third of their endowment. While this is low in comparison with other international studies in which proposers send 50% of their endowment on average (Camerer 2002), it is similar to results

Table 5.4 Summary Statistics of Mean Offers and Returns in Trust Game among South African Students

Categorization	Mean Offer as Proportion of Endowment	Proportion of Tripled Offer Proposer Expects to Be Returned	Actual Proportion of Tripled Offer Returned to Proposer
Panel A: By race of proposer			
Proposer is black	0.24 (0.19)	0.43 (0.26)	0.21 (0.23)
	46.00	39.00	39.00
Proposer is white	0.43 (0.31)	0.37 (0.13)	0.24 (0.23)
	46.00	37.00	35.00
Total	0.33 (0.26)	0.39 (0.22)	0.23 (0.21)
	92.00	100.00	74.00
Panel B: By race of responder			
Responder is black	0.27 (0.28)	0.35 (0.22)	0.28 (0.25)
	48.00	36.00	35.00
Responder is white	0.36 (0.24)	0.40 (0.16)	0.25 (0.19)
	44.00	40.00	39.00
Total	0.33 (0.26)	0.39 (0.22)	0.23 (0.21)
	92.00	76.00	74.00
Panel C: By race pairing			
Black to black	0.16 (0.14)	0.39 (0.29)	0.26 (0.30)
	23.00	18.00	18.00
Black to white	0.28 (0.20)	0.41 (0.20)	0.25 (0.18)
	23.00	21.00	20.00
White to black	0.41 (0.36)	0.31 (0.13)	0.22 (0.26)
	25.00	18.00	17.00
White to white	0.47 (0.26)	0.44 (0.09)	0.28 (0.20)
	21.00	19.00	18.00

found among an age-comparable sample of school children in grades 9–12 in the United States, where average offers were 37%.

Black proposers make significantly lower (at 1% level using Mann-Whitney) offers than white proposers in the trust game, offering 24% of their endowment on average, compared with 43% offered by white proposers. Moreover, it does not appear to be the case that black proposers make lower offers because they expect to receive significantly lower return offers.[16] Black proposers expected on average to receive 43% of the tripled endowment back compared to an expected return of 37% for white proposers. These expectations held by black proposers concerning return offers are not statistically different than those held by white proposers, nor do they vary significantly with the race of the person they are paired with.

An important focal point in these experiments is, of course, the extent to which the race of the recipient affects the offers made by proposers. On average, offers made to black responders are significantly lower (at the 1% level of significance using the Mann-Whitney test) than offers made to white responders. Black responders are offered 27% of the proposer's endowment on average, compared with offers of 36% for white responders. These lower offers to black responders are partially attributable to an expectation that black responders would remit less than white responders on average. Black responders are expected to return 35% of the tripled offer compared with expected returns of 40% from white responders. These differences are statistically significant at the 5% level using Mann-Whitney. However, any expectation that black responders would remit significantly lower amounts is mistaken. There are no significant differences in the amounts returned by black and white responders, who return an average of 28% and 25% respectively.

Perhaps surprisingly, this lack of trust toward black partners is exhibited by black proposers themselves. Offers in black-black pairings are significantly lower (5% level using Mann-Whitney) than black-white pairings. Moreover, while it is the case that black proposers expected to receive lower return offers from black responders, the difference in expected returns from white and black partners is marginal and not statistically significant. Interestingly, this lack of trust in black partners exhibited by black proposers is not sufficient to prevent black proposers from making any offer at all to a black partner. The simple statistics presented in table 5.4 treat an offer of zero in the trust game as part of a continuum of offers, when arguably a zero offer indicates the proposer's unwillingness to engage in an interaction at all. If making a zero offer is a qualitatively different response than making a positive offer, in that it signals an unwillingness or refusal to trust at all, as opposed to a decision to trust a little, then examining behavior in terms of the decision to make an offer or not, as separate from the decision of how large an offer to make once the participation hurdle has been crossed, may be instructive. This analysis is expanded upon in Burns (2006), which utilizes Cragg's (1971) econometric specification, which provides a means of testing whether the probability of a zero offer is determined apart from the level of the nonlimit outcome as a variant of the Tobit model, using a likelihood ratio test. The results suggest that for black proposers, being paired with a black partner has no impact on the decision to make an offer or not. Rather, it impacts (negatively and significantly) only the size of the offer that is made.

White proposers also exhibit lower trust in black partners, although the difference in mean offers made by white proposers to black and white responders is not statistically significant. However, given the very large and significant differences in expected returns held by white proposers, one might expect the difference in offers made by white proposers to white and black partners respectively to be much larger than it is. The fact that the gap is not larger may suggest the confounding influence of altruism on trusting behavior (Carter and Castillo 2003; Cox 2002; Ashraf et al. 2004), since even though white proposers expect black responders to return significantly less,[17] they do not make significantly lower offers to black partners relative to white partners. However, a more nuanced picture emerges when one separates out the decision to make an offer or not in this game from the decision of how large an offer to make once the participation hurdle has been crossed. White proposers with black partners are significantly less likely to make an offer at all, preferring to opt out of any interaction. In contrast, those white proposers who do decide to engage in an interaction with a black partner do not treat black responders significantly differently than white responders (Burns 2006).

PREJUDICE OR PROGRESS?

Having considered these different sets of experimental evidence from South Africa, it is tempting to draw broad-ranging conclusions concerning the ongoing influence of racial identity on social interactions, and what this might mean for efforts to dismantle discrimination and promote affirmative action in a country that is now firmly part of the global village. However, concerns over external validity must obviously temper any inclinations to make strong statements in this regard, since the sample sizes are small, with very specific demographic features, not the least being that participants are students, many of whom live in Cape Town. However, it is encouraging that some of the findings in this work corroborate the results reported by Seekings, whose sample sizes are large and whose demographics profiles are different albeit also specific to Cape Town, perhaps suggesting that making comments on some broad themes that emerge might not be wholly inappropriate.

It is undoubtedly true that globalization has had an influence on changing racial attitudes in South Africa. The imposition of sanctions by the international community against the apartheid state sent a clear signal that these kinds of racial intolerances were unacceptable and must inevitably change if South Africa were to have any hope of joining the global village as a productive partner. During the postapartheid era, as the economy has liberalized, the exchange and flow of information and new ideas as well as popular culture has surely had an impact on old attitudes and stereotypes, particularly among the youth. As Weisskopf argues (chapter 2, this volume), globalization should reduce (although not necessarily eliminate) the salience of ethnicity as a basis for discrimination, and arguably, the experimental evidence presented in this chapter provides some conditional support for this.

Bearing in mind the obvious caveats concerning external validity, the results from the experiments suggest that pure racial prejudice as a driver of behavior is substantially weakened. Taking the dictator game and trust game results together, if racial prejudice were a strong motivating factor, one would expect to see black partners being systematically and significantly discriminated against by white partners in both games (and vice versa). However, in the dictator game, whose simple structure reflects a voluntary redistribution of resources from one individual to another, the racial identity of the partner does not appear to be a statistically significant feature in the decision-making process. This is not to say that race is not economically important. However, if racial prejudice were driving behavior in these games, one would expect stronger results in terms of the statistical significance of lower offers between members of different race groups compared to offers in same-race pairs. It is only in the trust game that black partners are systematically discriminated against. The point here is simply that proposers do not appear to respond to racial cues in some uniform manner devoid of social context. Rather, response to the racial identity of the individuals one is interacting with depends crucially on the nature of the interaction at hand and the socioeconomic status of those involved and may also be intricately bound to notions of which groups have gained and lost the most in the new South Africa, and hence are worthy of redistributive redress.

In both the dictator game and trust game, black South Africans make significantly lower offers than white South Africans. Similarly, Seekings (chapter 4) finds that white South Africans are more generous in their assessment of reward. Since there is no a priori reason to expect altruism, generosity, or trust to vary according to ascriptive characteristics such as race, these differences may arguably reflect the ongoing stark socioeconomic disparities between these two groups. Simply put, race and socioeconomic status are highly correlated, and this affects the way that participants approach their decisions in these games. If the postgame consumption value of the experimental endowment given in the game is higher for black participants relative to their white counterparts, the former may rationally choose to make lower offers to their partners to ensure that they are able to take as much money away with them after the game as possible.

The confounding effect of the correlation between race and socioeconomic status is also evident in the mistaken stereotypes that appear to be held by proposers in the trust game, with both white and black proposers expressing an expectation that they would receive lower return offers from black partners. It is not surprising, given the existing socioeconomic differences between these groups, that proposers in this game might rationally expect lower return offers from black partners, whom they expect, on average, to be poorer, and thus, due to need, to be less likely to return any of the transferred amount. These stereotypes were shown to be mistaken in light of the actual return offers by black partners in the trust game. Thus, to the extent that individuals used racial identity as a proxy for socioeconomic status, thereby making inferences about the likely behavior of a black partner relative to a white partner in this strategic setting, some proposers missed out on potentially profitable exchange opportunities. If such behavior also characterizes mutually beneficial exchange opportunities in the everyday workings of the economy, this would be cause for concern.

More important, the effect of these stereotypes resulted in the outcome that black participants, on average, fared worse in terms of monetary payoffs in the trust game than their white counterparts, since not only did they receive lower offers, but fewer proposers (white proposers in particular) made any positive offers to them in the first place. This hearkens to the "circle of exclusion" described by Weisskopf (chapter 2, this volume), in which some groups or individuals are systematically denied access to beneficial opportunities, not because of their race per se, but because of a perceived correlation between race and some other characteristics, in this case, socioeconomic need, which holds some negative connotation for expected behavior. In a globalized world, this circle of exclusion may be exacerbated by the fact that economically powerful local elites are now able to exploit trading opportunities with individuals in other nations, and no longer need rely on domestic opportunities alone. Hence, over time, the stereotypes may become entrenched, thereby making it increasingly difficult for black South Africans to escape their marginalized economic position. The fact that in the trust games reported here even black proposers preferred white partners over black partners suggests just how pervasive these stereotypes might be in serving to entrench existing inequalities of opportunity (for trade and exchange) as well as socioeconomic differences.

At the same time, the experimental results also do not suggest any strong support for racially based redistributive policies. While prejudice may not be rampant in the dictator game, it is also not the case that black recipients receive significantly higher offers, even from white proposers, which is what one might expect if white proposers were actively trying to redress any perceived inequalities between themselves and their black partners. Plausibly, the lack of response to racial cues in the dictator game setting may reflect that racial identity on its own is no longer sufficient to convey information about the deservingness of the recipient, which, in a nonstrategic setting eliciting an altruistic response, may be a far more important consideration. Alternatively, it could simply reflect that youth in postapartheid South Africa no longer believe race to be an important signal of circumstance, given that the new South Africa is purportedly a place of equal opportunity for all. Regardless, one would not, on the basis of these results, argue that there is evidence in favor of redistributive mechanisms based on race alone. To the extent that these results generalize, this holds implications for attitudes toward affirmative action policies. Efforts to fight discrimination will certainly require policies that signal deservingness, perhaps by highlighting the intergenerational legacy of past discrimination.

Notes

1. Nattrass (2006) reviews the official labor statistics and argues that these increases appear to be credible and are not an artifact of mismeasurement.

2. In this study, when proposers were told the recipient of their donation would be the Red Cross, offers were significantly higher than in the anonymous treatment.

3. Other factors, such as class, age, race, income, or even political affiliation, may affect outcomes too. Frolich and Oppenheimer (1984) find a significant relationship between the type of choice made in a modified dictator game and self-identification by the participants with a political party. Hook and Cook (1979) find that behaviors consistent with notions of justice or equity increase with age.

4. For the sample as a whole, the mean offer by whites is 26.21 experimental dollars compared with 23.02 experimental dollars for nonwhites. White South Africans offer 25.5 experimental dollars compared with 24.98 for nonwhite South Africans. The racial gap is larger for participants in the United States, where white participants offer 27.08 on average, compared with nonwhites, who offer 19.93.

5. However, differences in the distribution of offers made to members of the respective groups are marginally and significantly different. Eastern Jews were more likely to receive an offer of 5, while Ashkenazi Jews were more likely to receive offers of zero or 10.

6. Eighty percent of white proposers indicated that the surname of their partner indicated the racial or ethnic group that their partner belonged to, compared to 90% of black proposers.

7. Payment of a participation fee is fairly standard in experimental games, and is given to cover the opportunity cost of participants' time. At the time of the experiments in 2002, the exchange rate was approximately US$1 = ZAR10.

8. In the full study, 294 high school students were recruited. Half of the students were black, and just less than a third were colored, with whites making up the remainder. However, since the focus of this chapter is on interactions between black and white subjects only, the results relevant to colored students are excluded. For the full set of results, see Burns (2008).

9. The Schools Act of 1996 mandates compulsory schooling for all children aged 7 to 15, and prohibits exclusion of students from schools on the basis of admissions tests or inability to pay fees. This effectively paved the way for greater integration by expanding school choice options, especially for children from disadvantaged communities. However, integration efforts are far from complete, and it would appear that significant socioeconomic barriers remain in the form of uniform and transport costs as well as information flows about schools and admission requirements.

10. At the time of the experiments in 2002, the exchange rate was approximately US$1 = ZAR10.

11. There is some debate concerning whether the trust game measures trust at all, since it is devoid of the kinds of social sanctions or contractual arrangements that characterize many trust relationships in real-world interactions. Camerer (2002) thus argues that the trust game measures "pure trust," that is, trust between strangers, where agents may be able to observe each other but may not necessarily interact in the future.

12. Trustworthiness was measured as the probability that the responder returned the full amount of the loan (before being doubled) made to them by the proposer.

13. Specifically, African American and Asian responders were significantly less likely to receive an offer.

14. In the full study, 337 high school students, ranging in age from 14 to 19, with an almost equal gender split, were recruited to participate. Just over two-fifths of the students were black, with white and colored (of mixed-race descent) students making up the remainder in roughly equal proportions. However, since the focus of this chapter is on interactions between black and white students, the data pertaining to colored participants are excluded. For the full set of results, see Burns (2006).

15. At the time of the experiments in 2002, the exchange rate was approximately US$1 = ZAR10. Students were also paid a show-up fee of 30 rands.

16. Hoff and Pandey (2003) argue that members of historically disadvantaged groups may not take advantage of economic opportunities because they expect to be poorly rewarded for their efforts.

17. White proposers expect black responders to remit significantly less than white responders. Mean expectations in white-black are significantly lower than for white-white pairings, at the 1% level using Mann-Whitney.

6

Race and Opportunity in the Transition from School to Higher Education in South Africa

Michael Cosser

INTRODUCTION

From within and outside its borders, South Africa is perceived to have achieved a miraculous transformation from apartheid rule to a democratic order. In many ways this perception is accurate: South Africa has a constitution and bill of rights that entrench rights for all, and the lot of many of its citizens has been improved in the 15 years since the transition to democracy. In the educational arena, the new dispensation has seen the establishment, among other things, of a single, coordinated schooling system (Republic of South Africa 1996, 1998), the restructuring of the further education and training and higher education systems (Republic of South Africa 1997, 2006), and the passing of legislation that paves the way for the transformation of the Adult Basic Education and Training system (Republic of South Africa 2000). The South African Qualifications Authority Act objectives of "creat[ing] an integrated national framework for learning achievements" and of "accelerat[ing] the redress of past unfair *discrimination* in education, training and employment opportunities" (Republic of South Africa 1995, clause 2; emphasis added) appear indeed to have been realized.

While the framework for educational transformation is clearly in place, however, the extent to which transformation has been achieved in practice is questionable. One way of assessing whether transformation has occurred is to ascertain whether the various pieces of legislation that have been enacted, both separately and in combination, translate into enhanced educational opportunity, particularly in the context of the "redress of past unfair discrimination," as quoted above. Can learners of all races pursue, with equal opportunity, educational pathways of their choice in their pursuit of qualifications?

Against this backdrop, this chapter examines the school-to-higher education transition to ascertain the extent to which grade 12 learners of all races have been able to fulfill their aspirations of proceeding to higher education.

The chapter begins by setting out the parameters within which the notion of discrimination in learning pathways can be considered. It proceeds to compare the findings of a 2001 baseline study of the higher education aspirations of grade 12 learners, across all nine provinces of South Africa, with the higher education enrollment profile for 2002. This comparison is then juxtaposed against a second one, derived from the findings of another baseline study. In that case, the higher education aspirations of grade 12 learners in a 2005 cohort are compared with the higher education enrollment profile for 2006. An exploration of the determinants of discrimination in learning pathways follows this analysis. The chapter concludes with a consideration of the effect of racial classification on the perpetuation of discrimination.

DISCRIMINATION IN THE DIVERGENCE OF LEARNING PATHWAYS

While 1994 cannot be held up as the year in which all structural racism in South Africa ceased, it is undeniable that, with the formal demise of the apartheid state in that year, institutions of higher learning in South Africa increasingly began opening their doors to students of all races (Bunting 2002a). The participation rate of black African (henceforth, black) students in higher education in 1993 was 9% (as against 75% black representation in the general population), while that of white students was 70% (as against 13% white representation in the general population) (Bunting 2002b). These percentages reflect directly the state policy of promoting white student access to higher education rather than access for black students.

The Mutation of Discrimination

It is common knowledge that during the apartheid era (1948–1993) in South Africa and before the civil rights movement in the United States, laws separated various population groups in both nations (Aguero 2005). In South Africa, indeed, clear distinctions were drawn, and actual geophysical divisions were created, between four major races: blacks, coloureds, Indians, and whites. In the United States, many racial groups (now officially delineated as black or black Americans, American Indians or Alaskan Natives,

Asians, Native Hawaiians or other Pacific Islanders, and whites) as well as the ethnic group Hispanics (who may be of any race) have historically faced severe discrimination: pervasive and open denial of civil, social, political, educational, and economic opportunities (Blank et al. 2004). The practice of the apartheid and pre–civil rights movement eras was to discriminate on the basis of race: a practice well-epitomized by the employment advertisements that appeared in the United States during this period (Darity and Mason 1998).

The apparent disappearance of such direct evidence of discrimination hardly implies that discrimination has ended, however; rather, its historical effects are now seen in the differential opportunities open to different race groups. Large differences in outcomes among racial and ethnic groups continue to exist in employment, income and wealth, housing, education, criminal justice, health, and other areas. Although many factors may contribute to such differences, their size and extent, as Blank et al. (2004) asseverate, suggest that various forms of discriminatory treatment persist in U.S. society and serve to undercut the achievement of equal opportunity.

The same is true of South African society, where the systematic implementation of apartheid policies over a 45-year period (1948–1993) entrenched differential opportunity. The legacy of this is felt 15 years into democratic rule.

From this perspective, discrimination is not a phenomenon that occurs at one point in time in a particular process or stage of a particular domain, which would represent an episodic interpretation. Rather, it is a dynamic process that functions throughout the stages within a domain, across domains, across individual lifetimes, and even across generations (Blank et al. 2004). Discrimination against prior generations, accordingly, may diminish opportunities for present generations, even in the absence of current discriminatory practices.

Institutional Racism

Discrimination is perpetrated, among other ways, through institutional racism. First used in the American literature (Carmichael and Hamilton 1967; Knowles and Prewitt 1969; Blauner 1972), the term *institutional racism* refers to the effects of institutional operations that "systematically reflect and produce racial inequalities" (Jones 1972: 131). Most definitions of institutional racism, such as the one proffered here by Jones, subsume the notion of unintentional discrimination, emphasizing instead the discriminatory effects of institutional practice. On this reading, racial inequalities are simply the unintended consequences of normal institutional practices (Scarman 1981).

In the education sphere, racism manifests itself in the persistence of "significant inequalities of opportunity" (Gillborn 1999: 90). It is this thesis which this chapter seeks to confirm.

MEASURING DISCRIMINATION

In the context of learning pathways, discrimination has to do with the ways in which differential opportunities for progression are available to different race groups. Accordingly, this chapter compares two transitional junctures (the transition of grade 12 learners to higher education, first, between 2001 and 2002, and then, between 2005 and 2006). The goal is to measure the extent to which racial transformation of higher learning opportunity has taken hold in South Africa, more specifically, between the first and second decades of democratic rule in the country (between 1994 and 2003, and from 2004 onward). The unit of measurement is the percentage of students of the four major race groups enrolled in higher education institutions, set against the aspirations for higher education of the grade 12 learner cohort.

In 2001, a team of researchers at the Human Sciences Research Council undertook a study of grade 12 learner aspiration to enter higher education. A predominantly closed-end survey was distributed to a random sample of learners, stratified by province and by school pass rate in the 2000 Senior Certificate Examination.[1] The representativeness of the response profile allowed for generalization of the findings to the entire grade 12 learner population. In the year following the aspiration survey, an analysis of Higher Education Management Information System (HEMIS) data was undertaken to establish the enrollment profile of students in higher education institutions and in the programs they offer.[2]

In 2005 the research team was again afforded the opportunity to mount a similar study. This time 20,659 survey returns were obtained. In 2007, analysis of HEMIS data on student enrollments during 2006 afforded the research team the opportunity to establish the first-time entry profile of students who were in grade 12 the previous year.

Since race is a variable that features prominently in both transition studies, it is possible, both separately (for each transition study) and in relation to each other, to compare black, coloured, Indian, and white learner responses to questions about the aspiration to proceed to higher education to the higher-education aspiration and enrollment profiles of the four race groups. Both types of comparison are made in the analysis that follows.

Table 6.1 Aspiration to Enter Higher Education in 2002, Enrollments in 2002 of Students Who Were in Grade 12 in 2001, and Representation in the General Population Aged 15–24 in 2002, by Race

Category	BA	C	I/A	W	Total
Aspiration to enter higher education in 2002	83.5	5.5	3.8	7.2	**100.0**
Enrollment in higher education in 2002	53.2	7.7	8.6	30.5	**100.0**
General population aged 15–24 in 2002	82.0	8.3	2.3	7.4	**100.0**

Key: BA = black African; C = coloured; I/A = Indian/Asian; W = white.

Notes: Figures are percentages. The ages of students entering higher education in South Africa vary. Despite a small proportion of white students who take "gap years" prior to registration, whites tend for the most part to enter higher education earlier than their black counterparts, many of whom enter employment first in order to support their families and to save sufficient money for higher education registration fees. Therefore, the age categories 15–19 and 20–24 are combined in this and subsequent analyses. For a discussion of similar findings in the United States, see Morgan (2005).

Source: Author's own table, derived from Cosser with du Toit (2002), South African Department of Education (2002a, 2002b), and Statistics South Africa (2006).

LEARNER ASPIRATION AND STUDENT ENROLLMENT: A STUDY
IN BLACK AND WHITE

In this section, I present the pertinent findings of these two surveys, along with the concomitant analyses of the higher-education enrollment profiles for the years immediately following the surveys. The presentation takes the form of a comparison of these two transitional junctures.

The 2001–2002 Transition Study

The percentage of learners in the 2001 aspiration survey who intended to enter higher education within three years of the survey date (i.e., in 2002, 2003, or 2004) was 84%, if we factor out those 14% who were unsure. A disaggregation of these data by race shows that 86% of blacks, 70% of coloureds, 92% of Indians, and 81% of whites planned to proceed to higher education within three years of the survey date.

Table 6.1 compares grade 12 learner aspirations to enter higher education in 2002 to the actual first-time entering student enrollments in 2002 (among those students who had been in grade 12 the previous year).

As the table shows, there is a strong correlation between the percentages of learners of the four race groups who aspired to enter higher education in 2002 and the distribution of 15- to 24-year-olds within these race groups in the general population. This indicates, if nothing else, the representivity of the higher education aspiration response profile. So, for example, while 84% of learners who aspired to enter higher education in 2002 were black, blacks made up 82% of the population of the country aged 15 to 24 in 2002.

However, the enrollment profile is profoundly out of step with this correlation. Thus only 53% of first-time enrollments in higher education institutions in 2002 were black, in relation to blacks' 82% representation in the general population of 15- to 24-year-olds. And at the other end of the spectrum, 31% of first-time enrollments in higher education institutions in 2002 were white, in relation to whites' 7% representation in the general population of 15- to 24-year-olds.

The 2005–2006 Transition Study

The percentage of learners in the 2005 aspiration survey who intended to enter higher education (whether in 2006 or at some future date) was 54%. This contrasts with a figure of 84% in the 2001 aspiration survey.

A disaggregation by race of those who indicated that they planned to proceed to higher education (whether in 2006 or later) reveals that 54% of blacks, 44% of coloureds, 65% of Indians, and 59% of whites wanted to do so. A comparison with the 2001 profile, where 86% of blacks, 70% of coloureds, 92% of Indians, and 81% of whites aspired to enter higher education, shows that there has been a significant tapering off in interest in higher education among all four race groups. The percentage change can be indicated as shown in table 6.2.

As table 6.2 reveals, in total there was a 36% decline in aspiration to enter higher education from 2001 to 2005. The greatest decline was among blacks, the smallest among whites. The racial profile, in fact, follows a continuum stereotype common in disaggregations by race in South Africa, which places black and white learners at opposite ends of a continuum of response, with coloured and Indian learners between the two poles.

An analysis of the Department of Education HEMIS database of enrollments for 2006 (South African Department of Education 2007b) reveals that 63,149 of the 508,363 learners who sat for the Senior Certificate Examination in 2005 enrolled in a higher education institution in 2006: that is, 12% of the cohort. This is 1 percentage point lower than the enrollment rate for 2002, and is in keeping with the lower aspiration to enter higher education discussed above.

A disaggregation by race reveals that the ratio of black to coloured to Indian to white learners who, immediately after grade 12, entered higher education institutions in 2006 was, on a scale of percentages, 58 : 8 : 7 : 27. Compare that to the 2006 representation of these four race groups in the general population: on a percentage scale, the ratio was 79 : 9 : 2 : 10 (Statistics South Africa 2006). That same year, the ratio among 15- to 24-year-olds, also on a percentage scale, was 83 : 8 : 2 : 7. This reveals that black students were underrepresented in the first-year intake; coloured students were marginally underrepresented; and Indian and white students were overrepresented. The differentials in the case of three of the race groups— blacks, Indians. and whites—are large, especially in the case of the 15- to

Table 6.2 Percentage Change in Grade 12 Learner Aspiration to Enter Higher Education, 2001 and 2005, by Race

Survey	BA	C	I/A	W	Total
2001 aspiration survey	85.4	69.5	91.7	81.3	84.1
2005 aspiration survey	53.5	43.9	65.0	59.1	53.8
Percentage change between 2001 and 2005	−37.4	−36.8	−29.1	−27.3	−36.0

Note: Figures are percentages.

Source: Author's own table, derived from Cosser with du Toit (2002) and Cosser (2009).

24-year-old age bracket. Racial equity, therefore, was far from having been achieved in the first-year intake into higher education in 2006 of those learners who had been in grade 12 in 2005.

Table 6.3 compares grade 12 learner aspirations to enter higher education in 2005 with actual first-time entering student enrollments in 2006 (among students who had been in grade 12 the previous year).

As table 6.3 shows, there is a fairly strong correlation between the percentages of learners of three of the four race groups who aspired to enter higher education in 2006 and the distribution of 15- to 24-year-olds within these race groups in the general population. The correlation for Indians is weak: the percentage aspiring to enter higher education in 2002 is more than double the Indians' representation among the general population of 15- to 24-year-olds. While in the 2001–2002 transition (see table 6.1) higher percentages of all race groups aspired to enter higher education than were represented in the 15- to 24-year-old population, here we see that slightly lower percentages of black and coloured learners aspired to enter higher education than were represented in the overall 15- to 24-year-old population; meanwhile slightly higher percentages of Indian and white learners aspired to enter higher education than were represented in the 15- to 24-year-old population. A slippage has taken place, therefore, in black and coloured learner aspiration for higher education as compared to black and coloured representation in the overall population of 15- to 24-year-olds. Thirteen years into South Africa's democracy, fewer blacks and coloureds than are represented in the population want to proceed to higher education.

Table 6.3 Aspiration to Enter Higher Education in 2006, Enrollments in 2006 of Students Who Were in Grade 12 in 2005, and Representation in the General Population Aged 15–24 in 2006, by Race

Category	BA	C	I/A	W	Total
Aspiration to enter higher education in 2006	80.6	5.8	5.4	8.2	**100.0**
Enrollment in higher education in 2006	58.4	7.8	7.0	26.8	**100.0**
General population aged 15–24 in 2006	83.0	8.0	2.3	6.7	**100.0**

Note: Figures are percentages.

Source: Derived from Cosser (2009); South African Department of Education (2007a); Statistics South Africa (2006).

As in the case of the 2001–2002 transition, however, the enrollment profile is profoundly out of step with this population correlation for all groups other than coloureds (for whom there is a perfect correlation between representation in the population of 15- to 24-year-olds and enrollment in higher education). Thus, for example, only 58% of enrollments in higher education institutions in 2006 were black, in relation to blacks' 83% representation in the general population of 15- to 24-year-olds. And at the other end of the spectrum, 27% of enrollments in higher education institutions in 2006 were white, in relation to whites' 7% representation in the general population of 15- to 24-year-olds.

ASPIRATION AND ENROLLMENT: A STUDY IN CONTRASTS

What emerges clearly from the above presentation of selected findings of the two surveys, and of the analysis of HEMIS data, is the extent to which higher education enrollment rates are out of step both with learner aspirations for higher education and with the university-aged representation of the four race groups in the general population.

From an aspiration perspective, the 2005 profile reveals that there has been a major decline in aspiration to proceed to higher education not only at the aggregate level (from 84% in 2001 to 54% in 2005) but also at the race-disaggregated level (from 85% for blacks in 2001 to 54% for the same group in 2005, and from 81% for whites in 2001 to 59% for the same group in 2005). What the shift also indicates is that there has been a reversal in aspiration to enter higher education from 2001 to 2005: in 2001, a higher percentage of black than of white learners wanted to enter higher education (85%, as compared to 81%). But in 2005, a higher percentage of white than of black learners wanted to enter higher education (59%, compared to 54%). What factors can have contributed to this reversal?

The difference in response between 2001 and 2005 may be due in part to learners having indicated, in the 2001 survey, that they planned to proceed to higher education when they in fact may have planned to proceed to another type of further learning (e.g., a further education and training, or FET, college). Some of the difference may be attributed to the different ways in which the question regarding aspiration for higher education was asked in the two surveys. In the 2001 survey, learners were asked: "Are you planning to study at a university or technikon within the next three years?" There was no lead-up question probing whether they planned to study further or not; nor was further study disaggregated into various options (higher education, further education, etc.). In the 2005 survey, however, learners were asked: "Are you planning to study further after Grade 12?" and, subsequently, "At which institution type are you planning to study?" The listed options were: "A higher education institution," "A further education and training (FET) college," "A private FET institution," "An agricultural college," and "A nursing college." A total of 60% of learners wanted to study at a higher education institution rather than at one of the other institutional types.

While some of the difference may be ascribed to the question-filtering process in the 2005 questionnaire, however, it is unlikely that so large a difference results from differences in question wording. There are three possible hypotheses for the shift.

First, a greater pragmatism may have set in among black learners regarding the reach of their expectations for further study, with inadequate grade 12 symbols (i.e., grades) for higher education study proving to be a disincentive to admission to higher education institutions. While there have certainly been improvements in the overall Senior Certificate pass rate annually for some years, black learners continue to perform more poorly than their white counterparts, as evinced by the far larger number of formerly black schools than formerly white (Model C) schools with matric pass rates in the bottom two quartiles (South African Department of Education 2000, 2004). There is a positive correlation, at the other end of the spectrum, between intention to enter higher education and the average grade 11 symbols of learners. A regression analysis of the 2001 survey data revealed that learners with an A-average grade 11 symbol were 8.6 times more likely to want to enter higher education than were learners with an F-G symbol. Learners with a B-average grade 11 symbol, in turn, were 4.5 times more likely to want to proceed to higher education than were learners with an F-G symbol, and so forth (Cosser with du Toit 2002).

Second, the reinvented role of FET colleges in addressing the intermediate-level skills needs of the country may have deflected some interest away from higher education study, boosted by state recapitalization of the FET sector and a fairly aggressive marketing campaign that has repositioned the sector in the public eye.

Third, funding for higher education continues to prove a major disincentive to black students entering higher education, despite the annual increases in disbursements by the state-funded loan-cum-bursary scheme (the National Student Financial Aid Scheme, or NSFAS) for academically capable students unable to afford university fees. When the mean values are plotted on a continuum, the 2001 survey reveals that external sources of funding for higher education study (NSFAS, bank loans, bursaries, and scholarships) were more important for blacks than for coloureds, Indians, and whites. The corollary is that internal sources of funding (such as parental finance) are less important influences upon blacks, coloureds, and

Indians than upon whites, in inverse proportion to reliance on external funding sources (for further discussion, see Cosser with du Toit 2002). The 2005 survey confirms that the awareness of the availability of financial assistance for study is highest among black learners on a five-point Likert scale (3.6), but not even significant for Indian and white learners, at 2.9 and 2.4 respectively (Cosser 2009).

The influence of these factors on learner aspiration for higher education needs, however, to be subjected to scrutiny through further research.

Notwithstanding the decline in learner interest in proceeding to higher education, such aspiration remains high. Comparisons between South Africa and the United States may be spurious, given that blacks constitute a minority in the United States and that the race group dynamics in the two countries may differ; however, it is nonetheless interesting to observe that, broadly speaking, the finding that learners of all race groups aspire to a higher education bears out comparative longitudinal research conducted by Schneider and Stevenson (1999). That research reveals that the rise in educational expectations in the United States over the last 40 years is not confined to any particular group of students. The percentages of learners expecting to obtain a first degree rose from 30% of learners in 1955 to 70% in 1992. Similarly, research conducted by Hossler et al. (1989) and by Paulsen (1990) reported that ethnicity has little or no effect on the educational aspirations of learners. However, as the South African profile demonstrates, the proportion of coloureds intending to enter higher education within three years of the survey date is significantly lower than the percentages for each of the other three race groups, while the proportion of Indians wanting to proceed to higher education is notably higher than that for blacks and whites.

From an enrollment perspective, the 2002 and 2006 profiles show a reversal of white and black enrollments in higher education institutions. Relative to the enrollments of the other three groups, black enrollments increased from 53% in 2002 to 58% in 2006, while white enrollments decreased from 31% in 2002 to 27% in 2006. The enrollments of coloured and Indian learners have remained fairly constant (7% for coloureds, with a relatively minor shift from 9% to 7% for Indians), so we can assume that the shift has largely been between black and white enrollments. The 5 percentage point increase in black enrollments, moreover, far outstrips the 1 percentage point growth during this period in the proportion of blacks in the general population aged 15 to 24. Blacks in this age bracket made up 82% of the population in 2002 and 83% in 2006, while the proportion of whites in this age category over the same period dropped marginally, from 7.4% to 6.7%.

While the aspiration profile is disappointing from a black perspective, the enrollment profile from the same perspective is encouraging. The gradual

nature of the change in black enrollments between 2002 and 2006 (on average, about 1 percentage point per year) does underscore, however, the extent
to which discrimination persists in the learning pathway from school to
higher education.

DETERMINANTS OF DIFFERENTIAL RATES OF ENROLLMENT

It might be supposed, given the statutory death of apartheid, that institutional discrimination against blacks would have diminished, if not disappeared, in the wake of the 1994 transition to democracy. The 1994 student
enrollment distribution across the South African higher education system
was 43% black, 5% coloured, 7% Indian, and 45% white (South African
Department of Education 2008). An examination of the racial breakdown of
enrollments in 2006, 13 years into democracy, reveals that 61% were black,
7% each were coloured and Indian, and 25% were white. In other words,
there was a 42 percentage point increase in black enrollments between 1994
and 2006, a 40 percentage point increase in coloured enrollments, no change
in Indian enrollments (which remained static at 7%), and a 44 percentage
point decrease in white enrollments over the period. There is an inverse
relationship, then, in the black-white enrollment pattern over the 13-year
period.

But however dramatic the increase in black enrollment and decline in
white enrollment have been, the distribution still fails to represent the racial
proportions of 15- to 24-year-olds in the general population. In 2006, this
distribution was 83% black, 8% coloured, 2% Indian, and 7% white (Statistics
South Africa 2006). Why this failure?

The answer would seem to be threefold: the implementation of apartheid; the differential growth of cultural capital; and the impact of socioeconomic status (SES). The effect of each of these is explored below.

Apartheid—the policy of separation in every sphere of human activity—
was legislated by the National Party government when it assumed power in
1948. The racial classification upon which apartheid was premised included
four major groups (blacks, coloureds, Indians, and whites), which are still
differentiated to this day. This was the springboard for many apartheid initiatives in racial discrimination and segregation: forced residential segregation (Union of South Africa 1950); the imposition of racial barriers on
marriage and sex (Union of South Africa 1949); racially segregated access to
public facilities (Union of South Africa 1953b); access to urban space (Union
of South Africa 1952); and, most relevant to the present discussion, racially
differentiated schooling (Union of South Africa 1953a). Kallaway (2002)
epitomizes apartheid education as: separate schools for Afrikaans- and

English-speaking children; direct state control of schooling for the black majority, under an education department separate from one catering to white children; a strong rhetorical commitment in the speeches of the notorious Dr. Verwoerd to different kinds of curricula for different racial groups; English (and in some parts of the country, Afrikaans) remaining the language of instruction in high schools;[3] the denial of advanced vocational and technical education to all but whites; and homeland authority governance of education.[4]

The Bantu Education Act of 1953 was abolished and the policies to which Kallaway refers were reversed in the mid-1990s through the promulgation of the South African Schools Act and the Further Education and Training Act (Republic of South Africa 1996, 1998): acts that established a single, unified national Department of Education. As the foregoing analyses have shown, however, practice has not caught up with legislation.

The discrimination practiced under apartheid is the product of historical legacy. But it is due also to the stunting of the growth of cultural capital (Bourdieu and Passeron 1973) among blacks. This took place initially and quite deliberately through the implementation of apartheid, and consequently through blacks needing to play catch-up, in the manner in which latecomer economies in developing countries across the world have had to do. (For a compelling analysis of the catch-up dynamic between "early leaders" and "latecomers," which serves as a useful correlative for failure in the fulfillment of black aspiration, see Abramovitz 1986.) Two of the three subtypes of Bourdieu's cultural capital (Bourdieu 1986: 47)—embodied capital and institutionalized capital—are illuminating.

Embodied capital represents the ways in which time, culture, and traditions bestow elements of the embodied state upon another, usually by the family through socialization. Institutionalized capital represents institutional recognition of the cultural capital held by individuals, usually in the form of academic credentials. Black achievement has been compromised with regard to both. Separate development meant not only the bifurcated charting of black and white developmental pathways along grossly unequal lines but, ironically, the separation, for blacks, of father from family. This occurred through both the migrant labor system (in which men were forced to seek work in white areas far from their family homes) and concomitant disruptions, through family breakdown, to the maintenance and transfer of sociocultural traditions. At the same time, the barring of blacks from entry into most white institutions and their gradual admission to certain institutions from the mid-1980s onward (see Bunting 2002b), on the strength of generally weak academic results, had far-reaching consequences for parity of credentialing. Institutions had to mount academic development programs for black students, bridging courses and alternative learning pathways, so as to meet the requirements for admission to and progression through degree programs. At the other end of the process, the labor market afforded, and continues to afford, differential recognition to black and white graduates (Moleke 2005).

The stunted growth of black cultural capital is equally a function of, and therefore compounded by, depressed SES. An examination of the SES of respondents to the 2001 and 2005 aspiration surveys reveals the low base from which blacks as a group in South Africa must by necessity operate. From a calculation of SES based on the education and income levels of learners' parents or guardians (see Cosser with du Toit 2002; Cosser 2009), we see that 84% of blacks fell into the low SES bracket in 2001, compared with 23% of whites. Four years later, 76% of blacks fell into the low SES bracket, compared with 10% of whites. The percentage changes for blacks and whites in the low SES category differ markedly, with blacks experiencing a 10% reduction and whites a 55% reduction. This suggests that, while there have been improvements in the SES of black people, the lot of poor white people has improved far more than that of their black counterparts over a four-year period.

This finding together with broader findings from SES-race cross-tabulations four years apart (Cosser with du Toit 2002; Cosser 2009) point up the extent of the correlation between low SES and color in South Africa. And they underscore the extent to which SES is likely to be a strong contributory variable in the decline in higher education aspiration over the period in question, as well as in the moderate growth in black enrollments.

I have shown elsewhere (Cosser with Sehlola 2009) that, of a range of sociodemographic variables,[5] academic performance at school is the strongest predictor of higher education enrollment, followed by the level of education of the learner's mother or female guardian. Morgan (1996) shows that students from families with higher SES score much higher on tests than do students from low SES backgrounds. Similarly, children of parents who are college or university graduates perform academically far better than do children of parents without this level of education. Given these findings, the slow rate of growth in black enrollments is hardly surprising.

SES is a component of the class stratification that the Council on Higher Education is keen to have higher education address. In one of its early publications, the council claims that "the extent to which equity and access are actively promoted or frustrated will determine the nature and extent of social and class stratification and have a direct bearing on the nature of South Africa's democracy, labour market and social stability" (Council on Higher Education 2000: 27). This, however, is a two-way path: without a fairly dramatic growth in the proportions of the population in the middle and high

SES brackets, access to higher education for blacks will continue to be restricted and indirect discrimination perpetuated.

GLOBALIZATION AND UNEQUAL EDUCATION

Morgan (2005: 59) asks: "Why is the relationship between educational expectations and subsequent educational attainment weaker for blacks than for whites?" As we have seen from the findings of the surveys and analyses of HEMIS data presented above, the South African experience mirrors the U.S. experience (Morgan 1996) in this regard, notwithstanding the contextual differences between the two countries. I have posited three possible determinants of differential aspiration-enrollment translation in the South African case: the implementation of apartheid, the differential accumulation of cultural capital, and the impact of SES. These go some way toward explaining inequality. But what of the lingering effects of inequality well into the second decade of postapartheid rule?

In 1994, South Africa emerged from the dark age of apartheid rule—white rule on the "dark continent"—into the light of democratic governance. Simultaneously, however, the country emerged into a new world order shaped by the globalizing agenda of developed nations: shifting from a nationalist, racially exclusive, inward-looking economy to one that sought to benefit from external global interaction (Altman and Mayer 2003). This double-edged emergence spawned competing policy options.

Early African National Congress (ANC) policy (the seeds of which were sown in its first election manifesto) championed the Redistribution and Development Programme (RDP), which sought to achieve redress and equity rather than global efficiency and integration. The main objective of the RDP was increased state spending to improve delivery of social services, in the interests of promoting equity (Nicolaou 2001). Subsequent ANC policy, however, was strongly influenced by the notion that social policy could be tempered by fiscal discipline (Marais 1998; King and McGrath 2002). This shift in thinking, fueled by the South African government's acceptance of the General Agreement on Tariffs and Trade (Akoojee and McGrath 2004), led to the devising of the Growth, Employment and Redistribution (GEAR) strategy (South African Department of Finance 1996), which came to replace the RDP as government policy.

This shift in economic policy from the RDP to GEAR had major implications for the development of the country's people, not least of which related to education (Akoojee and McGrath 2004). GEAR was epitomized by fiscal discipline, which in the educational sphere translated into reduced public expenditure, which led in turn to poorer provision in terms of both quantity and quality. The post apartheid Department of Education promoted a policy of reduction in teaching staff, or "rationalization." This resulted in a considerable decline in the number of teachers employed by provincial education departments (an annual growth of 4.9% between 1975 and 1996 was followed by a 1.3% decline between 1996 and 2000) and a concomitant need for an increase in part-time teachers (Nicolaou 2001). Most significant from the perspective of this chapter, teacher rationalization in the provinces was accompanied by a redeployment of teachers, so as to achieve a better mix in the composition of teaching staff. Since, however, many white teachers took voluntary retirement packages, the racial composition of the education system was left largely intact (Akoojee and McGrath 2004). While previously white schools in advantaged areas have witnessed the increasing integration of black and white learners over the past 15 years, schools in disadvantaged areas to this day remain populated by black learners and black teachers, the vast majority of whom were trained under a teacher-training college system notorious for poor quality.

The other face of South Africa's flirtation with globalization is its promotion of a high-skills, high-technology strategy at the expense of the development of skills at the low and intermediate levels (Kraak 2003). This strategy effectively perpetuates the apartheid racial and gender segmentation of the labor market, precluding the vast majority of blacks from accessing the higher-skilled segments of the economy. In the education arena, the closing of the teacher training colleges and the shifting of all teacher education to universities, another result of rationalization, has had the unintended consequence of increasing enrollments of white students with the academic preparedness to achieve the now-required teaching degree (South African Department of Education 2007a), while also producing a decline in the numbers of black students enrolling in teacher education programs. The major implication of this trend is the neglect of teacher development at the foundation and intermediate phases. This might perpetuate inferior teaching in formerly black schools, despite the fact that the Department of Education aimed to address this problem through its closure of the teacher training colleges.

CONCLUSION

We have seen in this chapter that racial discrimination lives on in the differential opportunities, open to black and white learners, to proceed on to higher education the year after graduating from school. The combined effect of globalization (in the forms of teacher rationalization and high skills promotion), together with the legacy of apartheid, the differential accumulation of cultural capital, and the impact of SES, I have argued, account in large measure for the differential rates of entry into higher education.

But has the mere writing of this chapter not contributed to the very perpetuation of discrimination that the writing of this chapter is intended to reverse?

One argument that gained prominence in the early part of this decade was that the perpetuation of racial classification may actually impede rather than promote transformation. Posel (2001: 51) epitomizes this position as follows:

> So it remains the norm for the narratives we hear in public media or in conversation to designate unnamed social actors in terms of their race—as though this reduces their anonymity and renders their actions more intelligible. Nor is this simply an apartheid residue; there are ethical and political arguments— as in the Employment Equity Act, for example—for the renewed salience of racial identification in the project of "transformation." If apartheid's racial categories were previously the locus of racial privilege and discrimination, these very same racial designations are now the site of redress—for, how else can the damage be undone and equitable treatment established? Yet, what are the consequences of these reiterations? Can we continue to construct our social realities in racial terms—in particular, drawing on apartheid's very own catalogue of race—in ways that transcend the ideological burdens of the past? What are the grammars of racial categorisation post-1994? To what extent, and in what ways, might they be at odds with the project of non-racialism?

Given the salience of race in the human consciousness (see, for example, Du Bois 1903; Fanon 1952; West 1994), it may be naïve to suggest that racial categorization can be transcended. Race consciousness aside, while "the project of non-racialism" through the abandonment of racial classification is a noble ideal, it is unlikely to reduce inequality. In this regard, the approach of the Department of Education toward race disaggregation in its reporting of education statistics is illuminating. In its annual publication *Education Statistics in South Africa*, the department (as in, e.g., South African Department of Education 2008) disaggregates statistics by race for the higher education sector, but not for the other education sectors (schooling, Adult Basic Education and Training, Early Childhood Development, FET). Why is this?

One answer may be that, while equity has been achieved in terms of enrollment rates in the sectors for which race disaggregation is not reported, such equity is far from having been achieved in the higher education sector. The counterargument to Posel's view, following from this premise, is that racial classification should be abandoned only once equality as measured by proportional representation of all race groups disadvantaged under the apartheid system has been achieved in every sphere of public life. While this means "drawing on apartheid's very own catalogue of race," it is the only measurable way to demonstrate change. Equality in these terms is by no means consonant with the death of racism; but it is at least consistent with the birth of equal opportunity.

Far from impeding transformation, then, maintaining racial categories in official reporting should assist in foreshortening the lingering effects of apartheid.

Notes

1. The sampling procedure and the methodology deployed are described in detail in the published report on the project (Cosser with du Toit 2002). Of the 14,064 questionnaires taken into the field (48 per each of 293 schools), 12,204 were returned completed, a response rate of 87%.

2. HEMIS is the official Department of Education system for the annual collection of data on enrollments and graduations from all higher education institutions in South Africa.

3. It was the use of Afrikaans as the language of learning that led to the Soweto uprising in 1976.

4. Homelands were a creation of the government ostensibly to promote separate development but actually to keep black people within (arid) rural areas and away from white rural and urban areas.

5. The province in which the learner's family was living in 2006; the province in which the learner was living in 2006; the highest level of education of each of the learner's parents or guardians; the employment situation of the learner's parents or guardians; the monthly income of the learner's parents or guardians; whether the learner had a parent or guardian or a sibling studying at a higher education institution in 2006; whether the learner had a sibling who was a graduate of a higher education institution; the learner's housing type in 2006; the sex and race of the learner; and the province in which the learner went to school.

7

Class, Race, and Social Mobility in Brazil

Carlos Antonio Costa Ribeiro

INTRODUCTION

There has been recurrent public debate over racial and class inequalities in Brazil. Although high levels of inequality are indisputable (Oliveira et al. 1983; Hasenbalg 1979; Hasenbalg and Silva 1988, 1992; Hasenbalg et al. 1999; Henriques 2001), the main issue in such debate remains that of defining whether the inequalities of opportunity are determined either by class or by race prejudice. Some commentators maintain that race prejudice is less important than class origin, while others argue that the former is important and has to be taken into account as a factor that transcends the stigma of lower-class origin.

In analyzing these questions, most studies make use of statistical information on inequalities of individuals' and families' life conditions (income, education, and so on) at a certain time, typically specified by year or month, frequently compared to conditions at a later time. Although this kind of approach allows for observing several forms of race and class inequalities, it cannot be used to decide which is more relevant, race or class, in determining prospects for social ascension. In other words, information on inequality of outcomes is not a substitute for information about inequality of opportunities. This distinction is of paramount importance because the main focus of interest in this debate is the inequality of opportunities between blacks, *pardos*, and whites, and between poor and rich;[1] however, the data used by those studies often relate to inequality of outcomes during a given period of time.

It is essential, however, to study the ways in which class origin and skin color are associated with the prospects for social mobility, since this type of analysis brings us closer to an understanding of the inequality of opportunities between class and racial groups. The relevant questions we need to answer are the following: is it true that people with distinct class origins, belonging to different groups of color or race, have unequal mobility opportunities? How do color of skin and class of origin relate to mobility opportunities?

These are precisely the questions I propose to answer in this chapter, based upon empirical analyses of inequalities of opportunity for social mobility. To carry out these analyses, it is necessary to utilize databases with information on class origin (measured through the father's occupation at the time when the interviewee was 14 years old); class destination (measured by the individual's occupation); color or race; and level of education. The last three variables are present in several research studies that are regularly carried out in Brazil, but the first is not normally included in collected data. The most recent nationally representative database with information on respondents' fathers is the 1996 Pesquisa Nacional por Amostragem Domiciliar (PNAD; Brazil's National Household Sample Survey). I utilize this in all the analyses developed in this chapter.

I conduct three types of analyses. First, I describe the intergenerational mobility between the parents' class or class of origin and the class of destination of whites, *pardos*, and blacks. The intent here is to verify what has a greater influence on the inequality of opportunities for ascensional mobility: the class of origin or skin color. Next, I provide a decomposition of such mobility, taking as an intermediary point the educational level achieved. As is well known, education is one of the most important factors of social ascension: without educational qualifications, one cannot, for instance, occupy professional positions, and thereby obtain relatively more comfortable life conditions. So I analyze the inequality of educational opportunities, seeking to verify the weight of class origin and skin color upon the chances of completing different educational levels. Finally, I analyze the likelihood that mobility opportunities will favor the more privileged classes, according to an individual's educational level, class origin, and skin color. This three-stage analysis enables the disclosure of the main barriers to social mobility, and also an evaluation of the combination of race and class of origin that inhibit such mobility.

Before presenting my empirical analyses, I discuss, in the next section, earlier studies on social mobility of whites, blacks, and *pardos* in Brazil, not only with the purpose of describing previous results, but also to define hypotheses that might be tested and discussed based upon empirical analyses. In the subsequent section, I present the methodology I rely upon in these analyses, while discussing the appropriateness of statistical models to the data. Finally, I discuss the outcome of the analyses and propose answers to this article's initial questions.

EARLIER STUDIES

Although, in the literature on race relations, the topic of social mobility is considered essential for determining whether there is racial prejudice or discrimination, studies using quantitative methodology are relatively rare in Brazil. Until the 1970s, most works were based on qualitative research studies or historical interpretations. Only at the end of that decade did studies using aggregate databases and descriptive statistics start to appear. Most of these studies, however, analyzed the inequalities of conditions, while only a few dealt with the inequality of educational opportunities and social mobility.

In 1979, Carlos Hasenbalg published his book *Discriminação e Desigualdades Raciais no Brasil* (Discrimination and Racial Inequalities in Brazil). This work reviews the literature on race relations in the country and suggests an alternative to the interpretation of Florestan Fernandes (1965) challenging the idea that racial discrimination would be replaced by class distinctions in modern society. According to Hasenbalg, racial discrimination would remain an important factor of social stratification in Brazilian society, even with the expansion of the class society that would result from industrialization. This hypothesis therefore foresees that there would be inequalities in chances of mobility between whites and nonwhites (blacks and *pardos*) regardless of their classes of origin.

Directly or indirectly, Hasenbalg's hypothesis has been the focus of discussion in the studies on race relations carried out since the end of the 1970s—mainly using data collected from 1976 onward, when the IBGE (Brazilian Institute of Geography and Statistics) started conducting sample household surveys on a national basis, collecting information on the interviewees' race or color (especially white, black, and *pardo*). The main empirical works initially have been those developed by Carlos Hasenbalg and Nelson do Valle Silva (1988, 1992; Hasenbalg et al. 1999). Edward Telles (2003) later built upon Silva and Hasenbalg's work, adding new research topics (such as residential segregation) and presenting a valuable review and interpretation of race relations in Brazil. Although most studies focus on inequality of conditions between whites and nonwhites,[2] these authors wrote about inequality of educational opportunities and social mobility as well. Studies on inequality of opportunities generally seek to analyze the relationship between class origin (O), education (E), and class destination (D). Figure 7.1 presents the basic triangle of the analyses of inequality of opportunities.

The studies on inequality of educational opportunities deal with the analysis of the relationship between O and E. They seek, therefore, to determine whether there is a statistical association between class origin and race, on

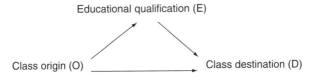

Figure 7.1

the one hand, and educational transitions for different cohorts of age, on the other. This type of analysis uses models of logistic regression, or logits, estimating the logarithm of relative chances of accomplishing or not accomplishing a determined educational transition. Usually, these relative chances are estimated for each of the age cohorts, using one model for each transition[3]—for instance, one model for each cohort's relative chances of completing the fundamental education, another for the relative chances of completing the secondary education after having completed the fundamental education, and so on. Besides the independent variables, class of origin and race, some other variables are used in the analyses. Initially proposed by Mare (1980, 1981), this methodology largely has been used in comparative research studies (Shavit and Blossfeld 1993).

The first study about Brazil using such methodology was an article by Silva and Souza (1986). In that study, the authors were careful to stress that some important variables (especially cognitive capacity and educational aspiration) were not available in the 1976 PNAD database that they utilized. In fact, these extremely important variables still do not exist even in more contemporary databases.[4] The authors still, however, arrive at the important conclusion that, for males aged between 20 and 64 in 1976, the individual's color is as strongly associated with educational transitions as the father's occupation and education. This association, as one would expect, decreases for transitions to the higher levels of the educational system. Subsequently, Hasenbalg and Silva (1992) used the 1982 PNAD data to show that there was racial inequality in the educational transitions for people aged between 6 and 24. Blacks and *pardos* had disadvantages when compared to whites. Silva and Souza (1986) used controls for the individual's ages, but did not analyze the effects of class origins. Afterward, Hasenbalg and Silva (1999a) enlarged the study to include other independent variables besides an individual's color. By including within the model variables concerning family structure, these researchers showed a substantial decrease in the magnitude of the individual's color effect, which nevertheless remained significant, pointing to the existence of a racial bias. They concluded that, effectively, there would likely be racial discrimination involved at the moment of children's registration into the educational system. Finally, also using PNAD data, Silva (2003) analyzes during three different years (1981, 1990, and 1999) the educational transitions of individuals aged between 6 and 19, arriving at the interesting conclusion that the effects of color upon educational transitions "increase as one progresses within the educational system" (p. 132). In addition, the effect of family income (a socioeconomic variable) also increases along these transitions. Another important study about inequality of educational opportunities is a monograph by Fernandes (2005). The author analyzes educational transitions for different age cohorts, using data of the 1988 PNAD. The main conclusion is that the effect of race increases at higher transitions (that is, finishing secondary education).

As for the effects of race and class of origin (socioeconomic characteristics), the studies on inequality of educational opportunities point to the impact of both effects upon educational transitions. White people originating from more privileged classes tend to have better chances of succeeding in educational transitions. Whites get even more advantages from completing secondary school. These conclusions corroborate Hasenbalg's (1979) hypothesis. In other words, inequalities of educational opportunities are marked by racial stratification, which seems to be even more accentuated at the higher levels of the educational system.

Besides studying educational transitions, research on inequality of opportunities has tended to analyze intergenerational mobility in order to verify whether there are class and race advantages or disadvantages when it comes to prospects for social ascension. The study of mobility refers to the association between class of origin (O) and class destination (D). In Brazil, most of the studies on social mobility of different racial groups have been based mainly on the analysis of absolute mobility rates, that is, on the analysis of percentages calculated from table 7.1 (in appendix) by comparing the father's class to the son's class. Later, I will show why this methodology confounds the effects of race and class of origin upon mobility prospects.

The first studies on mobility and race employing quantitative methodology were carried out by Hasenbalg (1979, 1988) and Hasenbalg and Silva (1988). They respectively used data from the 1976 and 1982 PNADs for six states of center-south Brazil. In these studies, the authors show that whites have more upward mobility than nonwhites, interpreting the results as indications that racial discrimination or racial barriers likely affect the process of intergenerational mobility. Hasenbalg's conclusions were later confirmed by Caillaux (1994), who compared data from the 1976 and 1988 PNADs. A new PNAD containing data on social mobility was collected in 1996. Using these data, Hasenbalg and Silva (1999a) and Telles (2003) once more confirmed what they had observed in their previous studies with earlier data:that is, they concluded that racial barriers to intergenerational mobility continued to exist in 1996.

In spite of their importance in the advancement of knowledge about social mobility, the fact that all these studies were based on simple percentage analysis raises doubts as to which were the effects of race and which of class origin upon mobility prospects, since these two variables are correlated. That is, blacks and *pardos* constitute a greater percentage of people raised in lower classes, and a lesser percentage of those raised in higher classes. Thus, in analyzing opportunities for upward mobility, one must be aware of such disproportionate starting points. If one finds more upward mobility of whites, as observed in the above-mentioned studies, this may be due to the fact that the percentage of whites in the more privileged classes is greater than that of the other groups. To solve this problem, one has to use log-linear models capable of controlling the marginal distribution of the mobility tables, that is, capable of controlling the disproportion of whites and nonwhites in the classes of origin.

Aware of this limitation, Silva (2000) and Hasenbalg and Silva (1999b) use log-linear models to analyze the intergenerational social mobility of whites, blacks, and *pardos*. The statistical tests using log-linear models indicate that occupational destination and color are associated, regardless of an individual's class of origin. That is, the models indicate that there is inequality of social mobility opportunities between whites and nonwhites. One of the limitations of the models employed is the fact that they only permit global conclusions, such as those just indicated; however, they do not allow for a more detailed analysis about the interaction between color and class origin. In the analyses developed in this chapter, I use more advanced log-linear models that facilitate the verification of whether there is interaction among class of origin and race upon the prospects for social mobility, and also allow for determining the pattern of such interaction.

Finally, there are some articles seeking to jointly analyze the relationship between class origin (O), educational qualification (E), and class destination (D), as well as their differentials by racial groups. The works of Silva (1988), Carvalho and Neri (2000), and Osório (2003) analyze different aspects of the relationship between origin, education, and class destination.

To understand the process of socioeconomic attainment (status attainment), Silva (1988) proposes linear regression models aimed at explaining the occupational position of and the income obtained by individuals. Such models include as explicative variables the characteristics of socioeconomic origin (the father's occupation and level of education), the residential situation (the region of residence and of birth), and the education achieved (schooling years). Silva (1988: 158) arrives at the following conclusion: "besides the inheritance of a socioeconomic situation by the individuals, there is still a legacy of race, which causes the colored individuals to find themselves in competitive disadvantage in relation to whites in the struggle for positions within the social structure."

Another article dealing with occupational mobility is that of Carvalho and Neri (2000), based on the analysis of data from the Pesquisa Mensal de Emprego (PME; Monthly Employment Research) of 1996. Using logistic regression models, they come to the conclusion that socioeconomic variables are more important than race in regards to intragenerational mobility prospects. Finally, Osório (2003) estimates log-linear models including class origin (O), class destination (D), education (E), sex (S), age (I), and color (C). Even though log-linear models estimated in such a way are subject to complex interpretation, Osório concludes that being white specifically reduces the risk of downward mobility, while for blacks, the prospects are greater. Accordingly, being white enhances one's chances of remaining in the upper classes (Osório 2003: 144).

The results provided by these three articles are important. On the one hand, Silva's (1988) and Osório's (2003) analyses show that there is a difference in the relative chances of mobility between whites and nonwhites. Osório shows that such a difference is more prominent in the higher classes—an outcome that is similar to my findings in this article. On the other hand, Carvalho and Néri (2000) indicate that, in the process of intragenerational mobility, the chances of mobility are better explained by the socioeconomic variables.

Even though they do not discuss directly their theoretical implications, the studies of Osório (2003) and Carvalho and Néri (2000) challenge Hasenbalg's (1979) hypothesis that racial inequality factors are independent from factors of stratification by class. What is suggested by these works is that some form of interaction between class and race likely exists in the development of inequalities. In a certain way, Hasenbalg's theory presupposed this, although the more simplistic of his arguments does not emphasize the interaction between race and class. One of the implications of this chapter's findings is precisely the need to think more coherently about the interactions between race and class in the production of social inequalities.

DATA AND MODELS

In this section, I briefly present the models I use to analyze the inequality of opportunities of social mobility between white, black, and *pardo* males aged from 25 to 64. (More specific explanation about the adjustment and selection of models is included in appendix 1.) The data used here derive from the 1996 PNAD, and they are representative for the entire country. In presenting the characteristics of the models, I describe as well the variables used in each one. Before that, however, I discuss briefly the four strata used for classifying classes of origin (measured from the father's occupation when respondents were 14 years old) and of destination (based on the respondent's occupation in September 1996).

Classes of origin and destination have been classified as follows: (1) professionals, managers, and employers (average income and schooling years for the class of destination: R$2,074.00 and 11 years); (2) nonmanual routine workers, technicians, and owners without employees (average income and schooling years for the class of destination: R$801.00 and 8 years); (3) manual workers and small rural employers (average income and schooling years for the class of destination: R$490.00 and 5 years); and (4) rural workers (average income and schooling years for the class of destination: R$244.00 and 2 years).[5]

All the analyses in this chapter are based on statistical models for categorical data. More specifically, the models used here are log-linear, logit (logistic regression), and conditional multinomial logit. These three types are mathematically equivalent; that is, they are distinct specifications of the same type of model. My analyses proceeds accordingly: initially, I describe the intergenerational mobility and estimate models in order to verify whether the force and pattern of association between class of origin (O) and of destination (D) vary between the three color groups (C). Then, I analyze the association between class origin (O) and educational transitions (E), on the one hand, and the impacts of acquired educational qualifications (E) and of class origin (O) upon the prospects for mobility for the classes of destination (D), on the other. For each of these steps, I use distinct models.

To analyze the intergenerational mobility, I adjusted three log-linear models, crossing four classes of origin (O) by four classes of destination (D) by three groups of color (C) (see appendix 2, table 7.5). The first one is the constant association model, hypothesizing that the association between origin and destination classes is the same for the three racial groups. The second one is the uniform difference model, hypothesizing that the strength of association varies across the three racial groups. The third one is the regression-type model investigating variation in the strength and pattern of origin by destination association across racial groups. A final version of this last model is achieved after including some restrictions (see appendix 1 for details). It is this last model that is presented in the following section.

Besides analyzing intergenerational mobility, I investigate the correlation between class of origin and educational transitions. To analyze these transitions, I use logistic regression models whose equation can be found in several methodology books (e.g., Powers and Xie, 2000: 49). Such models are used to estimate six important educational transitions:

1. Being admitted to school (comparing those who have completed the first grade of primary school with all those who have not)

2. Successfully concluding the fourth grade of primary school (among the group that has completed the first grade of primary school)
3. Successfully concluding the eighth grade of primary school (lower middle school) (among the group of those who have completed the fourth grade)
4. Successfully concluding secondary school (upper middle school) (among the group that has completed lower middle school)
5. Being admitted to college or university (comparing those who completed one year of superior education with all those who have completed the upper middle school)
6. Successfully concluding superior education (comparing those who successfully concluded the course of study at a college or university with those who have completed only one year of the course of study)

Each of these transitions, from the second one onward, is conditional in relation to the former. In other words, to have the chance of making a certain educational transition, one has to have successfully completed the earlier transition. The models estimated for the six transitions are presented in table 7.3 in appendix 1.

Each model analyzes the probabilities of making or not making an educational transition according to color or race, class origin, and age cohort. All the models are adjusted according to the data (the Bayesian information criterion, or BIC, statistics are negative), and will be interpreted farther on.

Finally, I used a conditional model for multinomial logits to explain the association between race, class of origin, and level of education, on the one hand, and the relative chances of entering into one of the four classes of destination, on the other. This type of model is entirely equivalent to a log-linear one, but it allows for the inclusion of three more variables, without rendering the interpretation excessively complex (as occurs with Osório 2003), as first used in sociology by Logan (1983), Breen (1994), and DiPrete (1990). I estimate two models using this specification: the first includes only origin and destination classes, and the second adds race (white and nonwhite) and years of schooling, which significantly improves the fit.[6] My interpretations below are based on this second model; I include parameter estimates and an evaluation of the appropriateness of statistics in table 7.4 in appendix 1.

RACE OR CLASS: THE DETERMINANTS OF SOCIAL MOBILITY

The main methodological problem faced by a study about the prospects for upward social mobility of individuals in different color groups and with distinct class origins is that, in general, these two variables are correlated. That is, blacks and *pardos* constitute a higher percentage of individuals who have grown up in lower classes, and a lower percentage of those reared in the higher classes. Thus, in analyzing the prospects for upward mobility, we need to pay attention to this initial disparity, which we can observe through the 1996 data (see appendix 2, table 7.7). While 61% of *pardos* and 56% of blacks were sons of rural workers, only 49% of whites had this family origin. Historically, rural workers' families are the poorest in Brazil. So we can easily conclude that blacks and *pardos* have grown up in poor families in a larger proportion than whites. The opposite occurs with richer families. Among all whites, 9% are sons of professionals and small entrepreneurs, whereas only 4% of *pardos* and 2% of blacks have a similar origin. Thus, whites come from well-to-do families in a larger proportion than do blacks and *pardos*.

This larger proportion of blacks and *pardos* with origin in low classes, and whites with high-class origins, is reflected in the class destination, the occupations in which the individuals find themselves. In 1996, 56% of blacks, 48% of *pardos*, and 43% of whites were urban manual workers (a class that is also very poor). At the top of the destination scale, there are more whites and fewer blacks and *pardos*. In 1996, 18% of whites were professionals and small entrepreneurs, while only 7% of *pardos* and 5% of blacks held these positions.

Hence, the difference in class position in 1996 is partly determined by the difference in the class position of origin. We cannot simply say, for instance, that the disproportionately low percentages of blacks and *pardos* in the class of professionals and small entrepreneurs in 1996 results from racial prejudice because, as we have seen, blacks and *pardos*, more than whites, are concentrated in low classes of origin, which reduces their chances of upward social mobility.

To define the role of race and class of origin as relates to upward social mobility, we need to use models that are capable of statistically controlling disparities in the classes of origin. After implementing the different statistical analyses presented in the previous section, I arrived at a model (M4 model in appendix 1, table 7.1) that, although mathematically complex, clearly expresses the interaction between race and class of origin upon the prospects for upward mobility. The chief manner in which this model expresses outcomes is to start from a numerical value known as odds ratio, which defines the relative chances of people with similar class origins, in distinct color groups, to attain the same classes of destination. These odds ratios or, rather, their logarithm, permit the design of figure 7.2, which shows the differential in relative chances of upward social mobility between whites, *pardos*, and blacks, controlled by disproportions in their classes of origin. If the straight line connecting blacks, *pardos*, and whites is completely horizontal to the color scores axis in each graph of figure 7.2, then the odds ratios, or relative prospects for mobility, are identical for blacks, whites, and *pardos*. Otherwise, there is inequality between the color groups in their relative prospects for upward mobility.

Although figure 7.2 is rather complex, what it reveals is quite simple and quite significant. The first two graphs in lines 2 and 3, indicate that there is no difference in relative prospects for upward mobility between blacks, *pardos*, and whites whose parents were in the lowest classes. Those graphs compare the relative chances that sons of rural workers and manual urban workers will achieve upward mobility into the classes of professionals and nonmanual urban workers. In none of these comparisons is there any difference between the relative chances of mobility for black, *pardo*, and white males. For example, regardless of their color or race, sons of urban manual workers have 1.3 times more chances of reaching the professional class than do the sons of rural workers. In short, the chances of upward mobility among people with origins in the lowest classes are entirely determined by their class origin, and the color of their skin is not relevant. There is no racial inequality in chances of upward mobility for people who originate in the lowest classes.

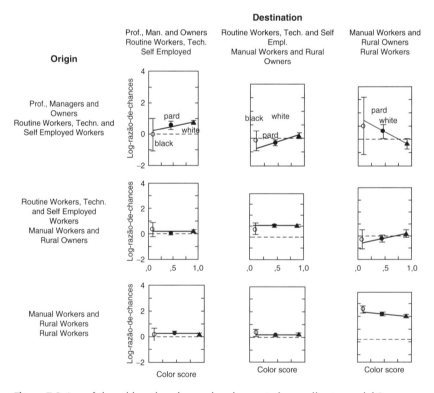

Figure 7.2 Log of the odds ratios observed and expected according to model 3, by color score, origin, and destination

If we observe, however, the relative chances of professionals' and non-manual routine workers' sons (represented on the first three graphs of the first line of figure 7.2), we find out that the relative prospects for immobility at the top, and for downward mobility, are different for blacks, *pardos*, and whites. For instance, white sons of professionals have a two times greater chance of remaining in this class than they do to descend to the class of routine nonmanual workers. Meanwhile, black sons of professionals have only 1.2 times more chance. In short, the chances of downward mobility and of immobility of persons originating from higher classes are significantly influenced by the color of their skin. There is racial inequality in chances of downward mobility and immobility for people with origins in the higher classes.

What is suggested by these analyses is that, in Brazil, racial prejudice becomes more relevant as we go upward in the class hierarchy. People with origin in lower classes find difficulties as relates to upward mobility because they belong to lower classes, and not because of their color or race. There are, however, important indications suggesting that black persons originating from higher classes have fewer opportunities than do whites who originate in those same classes, of remaining at the top; similarly, they have more likelihood of downward mobility. The analyses reveal that the inequality of opportunity of social mobility is racial only in the high classes, and not in the low ones. This is a very important conclusion, for it indicates that racial prejudice is likely to be more strongly present at the top and not throughout the class hierarchy.

INEQUALITY OF EDUCATIONAL OPPORTUNITIES

In contemporary society, one of the most important paths to social mobility is formal education. To occupy certain prestigious positions, an educational qualification is essential; to be a son of someone qualified is not enough. To become a doctor or a judge, one needs to have higher education. Being the son of a doctor or a judge does not qualify anybody as a doctor or judge: the essential qualification is successful study at a school of medicine or law. It is, however, widely recognized that sons of qualified professionals have greater chances of attaining higher educational levels than do sons of non-qualified workers. Meanwhile, much is said in Brazil about unequal educational opportunities between whites and nonwhites. Such presuppositions must be empirically investigated.

Modern sociological methodology for the study of educational stratification points to the need for studying several significant educational transitions. Thus, we must determine which are the main characteristics that influence the chances of children and youngsters of making successful educational transitions. In this chapter, I analyze six educational transitions: (1) admission to school; (2) conclusion of the fourth grade of elementary education; (3) conclusion of the eighth grade of elementary education (lower middle school); (4) conclusion of secondary education (higher middle school); (5) admission to college or university; and (6) conclusion of university education.

One of the expected consequences throughout these educational transitions is that inherited characteristics (class of origin, race, or gender) tend to have more weight during the earlier rather than the later transitions, since each transition produces a selection in terms of educational qualifications. For instance, people with different class origins, when admitted to university, share an important similarity: they all have concluded their secondary education.

Although different characteristics influence the chances of success in each of the educational transitions (please note: I have included class of origin, age, and color in the models of logistic regression I used), I present in figure 7.3 only the weight of people's class origin and color at each transition. The purpose, in this case, is that of verifying, for each transition, the magnitude of the inequality of educational opportunities in terms of race and class origin.

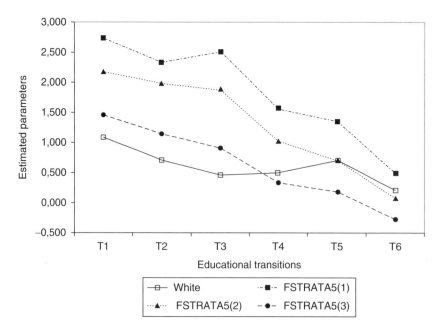

Figure 7.3 Origin, class, and race effects for log of educational transition chances for men in four birth cohorts: Brazil.

Figure 7.3 effectively reveals that the influence of people's class origin and color decreases progressively along the continuum of educational transitions. Moreover, class origin seems to have greater effect than color upon people's chances of accomplishing transitions. That is, people whose parents were in the higher classes (professionals, for example) have more chances of success in educational transitions than those whose parents were in lower classes. Whites also have more chances of success than nonwhites; however, the weight of class origin is bigger than that of race. In other words, we can say that there is more inequality of educational opportunities in terms of class than in terms of race. In the later transitions, however, the effect of race becomes similar to the effect of class; that is, chances of entering and completing university are unequal in racial and class terms. Consider this example: the sons of professionals are 15 times more likely to enter primary school than are the sons of rural workers, and whites are 3 times likelier to enter primary school than nonwhites. Inequality of educational opportunities exists in terms of class origin as well as in terms of race, although the first factor is stronger than the second. When it comes to entering university, sons of professionals are 4 times more likely than sons of rural workers to do so; and whites are 2 times likelier than nonwhites to do so. In short, at the early stages of an educational career, class inequality is much stronger than race inequality, while at the higher educational levels both types of inequality decrease in relation to what occurs in the first transitions, becoming more similar. That is, at educational transitions of higher levels, inequalities of race and class have similar magnitudes.

These findings about educational transitions reinforce the conclusions on upward mobility presented in the previous section. In terms of opportunities, class inequality is much stronger than race inequality at the early transitions. In contrast, compared to class inequality, racial inequality starts to become more relevant in the higher transitions of the educational system. As we go upward in society's socioeconomic hierarchy, racial inequality seems to become more important than, or at least as important as, class inequality.

CLASS DESTINATION: THE EFFECTS OF RACE, CLASS ORIGIN, AND EDUCATIONAL QUALIFICATIONS

Having analyzed, in the two previous sections, intergenerational social mobility and educational stratification, we turn now to the task of integrating these two analyses. What remains to be known, in other words, is the effects of class origin, color, and level attained in education upon the chances of social mobility for the classes of destination in 1996.

It is also useful here to rely upon statistical models that can control for different proportions of whites, *pardos,* and blacks with origins in high and low classes. Additionally, I have introduced the variable "completed schooling years" as one of the main factors determining social mobility. The model I employed is known as the conditional multinomial logit model (see appendix 1).

The outcomes of the model (according to table 7.4 in appendix 1) reinforce my earlier conclusions. Racial inequality seems to effectively have a stronger effect upon the entering of higher rather than lower classes. That is, there are unequal entrance opportunities into the lower classes because of class origin rather than of race; meanwhile, when it comes to entering the higher classes, there is inequality of opportunities between whites and nonwhites (i.e., *pardos* and blacks), which indicates that racial discrimination becomes stronger as one moves upward in the class hierarchy.

Figure 7.4 presents the relative likelihood of white and nonwhite males entering the class of urban manual workers instead of entering that of rural workers, given the schooling years they have completed. The calculation of these chances also takes into account the class of origin. In statistical language, we say that we are controlling by the class of origin; that is, we are observing the conditional chances (in terms of education and class of origin) of whites and nonwhites entering the manual workers' class.

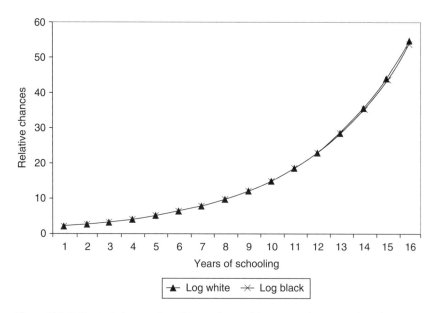

Figure 7.4 Estimated chances for white and nonwhite men to be manual workers instead of rural workers by years of schooling (model 2 and table 7.4): Brazil, 1996.

What the graph shows is that there is no difference between whites and nonwhites, and only an effect of education on the chances of entering the class of urban workers (which is hierarchically higher than that of rural workers).

An entirely different outcome is found when we analyze the chances of entering the professional class instead of that of the rural workers. (These are the two extremes of the class hierarchy.) Figure 7.5 details this comparison according to the same model used for designing figure 7.4.

Figure 7.5 reveals that there is a significant difference in whites' and nonwhites' chances of entering the professional class. With the same schooling years as whites, the nonwhites have relatively smaller chances of becoming professionals (these data control by class origin). For instance, between those males who have completed 15 schooling years (having completed university education), whites are three times likelier than nonwhites to become professionals. It is interesting to observe that, in spite of the absence of racial inequality when it comes to the prospects for completing university education, there is strong evidence that nonwhite graduates experience more difficulty in entering professional positions than whites with the same educational level.

These analyses, once more, confirm my earlier observations. In the process of upward mobility, racial inequality is present mainly on the higher

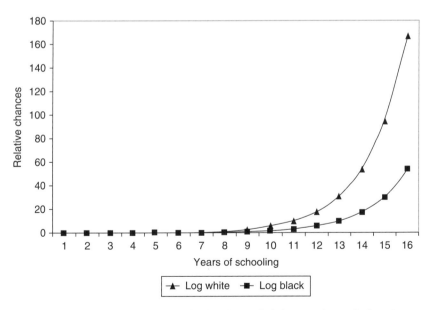

Figure 7.5 Relative chances to be professionals or administrators instead of rural workers for white and nonwhite men by years of schooling (model 2, table 7.4): Brazil, 1996

levels of the class hierarchy, while the social mobility chances of those originating in lower classes are determined by class position, and not by race or
color of skin.

CONCLUSION

This article's main conclusion is that racial inequality in social mobility
prospects is only present for individuals with origin in the higher classes.
White, *pardo*, and black males with origin in lower classes have similar
chances of social mobility. I have arrived at this outcome from a detailed
analysis of three aspects of social mobility: (1) inequalities of intergenerational mobility opportunities between classes of origin and destination; (2)
inequalities in chances of accomplishing educational transitions; and (3)
effects of attained education and of the class origin upon the prospects for
social mobility. In all these analyses, I have emphasized comparisons
between the effects of skin color and class of origin.

The main problem in the analysis of intergenerational mobility of whites,
pardos, and blacks is that the first group tends to be represented in greater
proportion in the higher classes of origin, and the last two in the lower
classes of origin. This produces greater mobility opportunities for whites
than for blacks and *pardos*. Hence, in analyzing the chances of mobility
using only the gross rates (percentages), it is difficult to separate the effect
of class origin from that of skin color. For this reason, I used statistical models that control this disproportion in class of origin and allow for analyzing
the variation, between the color groups, of the pattern and force of association between classes of origin and of destination. These models make it
possible to verify not only which are the effects of class origin and skin color
upon the prospects for mobility, but also to determine whether, and if so
how, these effects combine (i.e., interact) or not.

The findings of this analysis lead to the conclusion that, for males with
origin in lower classes (rural workers, urban manual workers, and small
rural employers), there is no racial inequality in prospects for upward mobility; that is, in the lower strata, whites, *pardos*, and blacks face similar difficulties concerning upward mobility. In contrast, white, *pardo*, and black males
with origin in higher classes (professionals, managers and small employers,
routine workers, technicians, and independent workers) have different
prospects for immobility and downward mobility. Whites have more chances
of immobility on the top of the class hierarchy than do *pardos* and blacks,
while the latter face greater likelihood of downward mobility. That is, there
is racial inequality in the opportunities of intergenerational mobility for
males with origins in the higher classes. These outcomes reveal that the

inequality of opportunities is present at the top of the class hierarchy, but not at its bottom. This conclusion leads us to suggest that racial discrimination occurs mainly when valued social positions are at stake.[7]

Another fundamental aspect of the social mobility process is the acquisition of formal education. Schooling is one of the main factors that affect social mobility. The analysis of inequalities of educational opportunities is, therefore, fundamental for understanding the mobility process. In this sense, I have analyzed the effects of race and class of origin upon the chances of accomplishing six educational transitions: (1) completing the first grade of primary school; (2) completing the fourth grade of primary school, having accomplished transition 1; (3) completing fundamental education, having accomplished transitions 1 and 2; (4) completing secondary education, having accomplished the previous transitions; (5) completing one year of university studies, having accomplished the previous transitions; and (6) completing university studies, having accomplished all previous transitions. According to current interpretation (Shavit and Blossfeld 1993), the effect of the variables concerning class origin tends to decrease along with educational transitions. This theoretical tendency is confirmed by my analyses. My major objective, however, has been to verify the impact of skin color and class of origin upon the chances of accomplishing educational transitions.

The analyses show the inequality of these chances for accomplishing transitions, in terms of both color and class origin; however, they also reveal that the second type of inequality is stronger than the first. Additionally, while class inequality decreases along with transitions, racial inequality increases at the fifth transition (completing or not completing the first year of university studies). Until the fourth transition (completing secondary education), the class-of-origin effects are at least six times greater than the effect of race. In other words, until the fourth transition, inequality of class is greater than inequality of race. At the fifth and sixth transitions (completing the first year of university studies, and finishing university graduation), racial inequality becomes more similar to class inequality, with the impact of the class of origin only 2.5 times more than the impact of skin color on prospects for accomplishing these transitions. Being the son of someone in higher classes increases the chances of success in accomplishing educational transitions, whether one is white or nonwhite (black or *pardo*). In short, at those educational transitions leading up through admission to secondary school, class inequality is much greater than race inequality, while when it comes to completing one year of university studies and finishing university graduation, racial inequality is almost as great as class inequality.

Finally, I analyzed the effects of attained level of formal education, of race, and of class of origin upon the prospects for upward mobility. In these analyses, which combine the previous two as well, it is clear that the effect of race upon prospects for mobility (taking into account level of formal education and class of origin) is apparent only in people with more than 10 or 12 schooling years who are entering the class of professionals, managers, and employers. With more than 12 schooling years, whites have on average a three times greater likelihood than do nonwhites of experiencing upward mobility toward the more privileged classes. Although education is important for any type of upward mobility, racial inequality is present only when it comes to the chances of mobility toward the top of the class hierarchy. Once more, the outcomes confirm that there is racial inequality only when it comes to prospects for upward mobility toward the hierarchically higher classes.

The outcomes of this research are extremely relevant for the debate on racial inequality in Brazil. Today the dominant theory—which is best represented by the works of Carlos Hasenbalg, Nelson do Valle Silva, and Edward Telles—states that the effect of race on social mobility prospects is independent of the effect of social class. In other words, the effects of race and class would be additive in explaining inequality of opportunity. My analyses advance this current view, indicating it is the interaction between race and class that has an effect on social mobility chances. Moreover, this interactive effect is based on a dominance of class inequality for those coming from lower class positions, on the one hand, and on a combination of race and class inequality for those competing for higher class and educational positions, on the other hand. Although I am not directly measuring racial discrimination—if this is ever possible—my analyses suggest that it is only when higher class positions are in contest that such discrimination occurs. In any case, it is clear that the competition for hierarchically higher social positions is marked by racial inequalities, while the prospect for ascension by those with lower class origins is entirely determined by their class position. This outcome indicates that racial inequality is present at the top of the class hierarchy, but not at its bottom.

The outcomes of the analyses presented in this chapter point to the need for new theoretical syntheses on the relation between class, race, and social mobility. The answer cannot simply be that there is, or there is not, racial discrimination and racial inequality in chances of mobility. This sort of Manichean vision, which seems to be present in most of the current debate, does not help the development of new theories and analyses about race relations in Brazil. In fact, new studies on race relations in Brazil should follow some of the chapters presented in this book. There are important studies showing that racial inequality in socioeconomic conditions are present and widespread in Brazil (see the literature review above). In this book, similar types of inequality also are studied: for South Africa in terms of race, and for

Japan in terms of gender. The studies following some type of audit methodology (such as those used to study India in this book) are highly recommended to evaluate the effects of racial discrimination in Brazil; to my knowledge, there is only one study of this type that was ever carried out in Brazil, and it was inconclusive. My findings in this chapter take, so to speak, a middle course between these two approaches. Instead of only reporting the levels of racial inequality in living conditions, I study racial inequality in social mobility opportunities. This approach is arguably better when it comes to understanding discrimination, but it is far from ideal. My hope is that future studies of race relations in Brazil will not only advance the analyses of inequality of opportunity in terms of race, but also be inspired by this book's good example to combine these types of analyses with direct studies of racial discrimination, using both audit and qualitative methodologies.

APPENDIX 1

Three types of model were used in this chapter: (a) log-linear models to analyze overall intergenerational mobility from father's to son's occupation; (b) logit models to analyze educational transitions; and (c) conditional multinomial logit models to analyze intergenerational mobility, taking into account educational attainment. In this appendix, I present these models and their fit to the data.

a. Log-linear Models Used to Analyze Intergenerational Mobility

The three models adjusted to table 7.5 are the following. The first is the model of constant association:

$$\log F_{ijk} = \mu + \lambda_i^O + \lambda_j^D + \lambda_k^C + \lambda_{ik}^{OC} + \lambda_{jk}^{DC} + \lambda_{ij}^{OD} \qquad \text{(M1)}$$

Where $\log F_{ijk}$ is the logarithm of the odds ratio that measures the association between origin i and destination j conditional in color k; the term μ is the general average; the terms λ_i^O, λ_j^D, and λ_k^C control the marginal distributions of origin, destination, and color; the term λ_{ik}^{OC} controls the association between origin and color; and the term λ_{jk}^{DC} controls the association between destination and color. As this model includes a term for the association between origin and destination (λ_{ij}^{OD}), and does not include a term for the interaction between origin, destination, and color (λ_{ijk}^{ODC}), if it is adjusted to the data, one should conclude that the association between origin and destination is the same for the three color groups.

The second model that I adjust to the data is the log-multiplicative proposed by Xie (1992), whose general formula is:

$$\log F_{ijk} = \mu + \lambda_i^{O} + \lambda_j^{D} + \lambda_k^{C} + \lambda_{ik}^{OC} + \lambda_{jk}^{DC} + \exp(\Psi_{ij}\phi_k) \qquad (M2)$$

The only difference of this model (M2) relative to the former (M1) is that the term λij^{OD} of M1 is replaced by $\exp(\psi ij_\Phi k)$. ψij describes a single pattern of association between origin and destination, and is multiplied by ϕk, which defines the variation, by color group, of the force of association between O and D. If this model provides a better adjustment to the data than that of M1, we can conclude that the force of the association is different for each color group, according to the numerical value of ϕk.

Finally, I make use of a third model that permits not only that the force of the association between origin and destination vary according to the color groups, but also that the pattern of this association be different. This model, proposed by Goodman and Hout (1998), is the following:

$$\log F_{ijk} = \mu + \lambda_i^{O} + \lambda_j^{D} + \lambda_k^{C} + \lambda_{ik}^{OC} + \lambda_{jk}^{DC} + \exp(\Psi_{ij}\phi_k) \qquad (M3)$$

This formula (M3) simply adds the term λij^{OD} to the previous model (M2). This inclusion allows for analyzing the difference in the pattern of association between the three racial groups, besides analyzing the difference in the force ($\exp[\psi ij\phi k]$). This third model may be rewritten to render its formula similar to that of a linear regression, including an intersection (that measures the pattern of association—μij) and a slope (measuring the force of the association—$\mu' ij$). This alternative manner of conceiving the same model permits a clearer interpretation, helps to improve the adjustment of the model, starting from restrictions to its estimators, and is responsible for the model's denomination: regression-type layer effect model (Goodman and Hout 1998). The alternative formula is:

$$1n\theta_{ij/k} = \mu_{ij} + \mu'_{ij}\phi k \qquad (M3')$$

This third model (formulas M3 and M3') is rather complex, and its accurate interpretation depends on the inclusion of restrictions to the terms of intersection (μij) and/or of slope ($\mu' ij$). Table 7.1 shows the adjustment of the three models (M1, M2, and M3) to table 7.5, crossing four classes of origin by four classes of destination and three color groups. In addition, I present the adjustment of the perfect mobility model (MO), according to which there is no association between origin and destination, and the M4 model that imposes restrictions to the M3 model.

In order to evaluate the adjustment of the models, one uses the chi-square test (χ^2) and the BIC test, giving preference to the first. The perfect mobility model (MO) does not adjust itself to the data; the model of constant association (M1) adjusts itself according to the BIC (the more negative the BIC, the better the adjustment of the model); the log-multiplicative model (M2) is adjusted as well, but does not represent a significant improvement in

Table 7.1 Adjustment Statistics of the Models of Association Applied to Table 7.5: Tables of Intergenerational Mobility for White, *Pardo*, and Black Males Aged 25–64 Years, Brazil 1996 (N = 40.635)

#	Model	L²	X²	df	Bic	L_m^2/L_o^2	p
M0	Perfect Mobility	9.726,05	9.453,23	27	9.440	100,0%	<0,001
M1	Constant Social Fluidity (CSF)	80,19	77,94	18	−111	0,8%	<0,001
M2	Layers Multiplicative Effect	68,01	66,67	16	−102	0,7%	<0,001
M3	Regression Type Layers Effect	11,23	10,38	7	−63	0,1%	<0,129
M4	Regression Type Layers Effect + mu6	15,75	14,93	11	−101	0,1%	<0,497

Source: PNAD/IBGE (1996)

relation to M1. Finally, the regression-type model (M3) is adjusted according to the BIC and the chi-square. This model should be chosen as the better adjustment, but it is still rather complex, for it uses nine degrees of freedom more than the M2 (df = 16-7 = 9), which is the reason why the BIC statistics, which penalize models that are rather complex, is less negative than in the former models. Because of this type of complexity, Goodman and Hout (1998) suggest specific restrictions to the estimated parameters of the intersection and/or the inclination. These parameters for the M3 model are presented in table 7.2.

Table 7.2 Intersection, Slope Parameters, and Color Score for Model 3, Estimated by Maximum Likelihood: Mobility Table for White, *Pardo*, and Black Males

			j	
Parameters	i	1	2	3
Intersection (:*ij*)	1	0.264	−0.67	1,569
	2	0,055	0,887	−0,555
	3	0,342	0,185	2,378
Slope (:*ij'*)	1	0,523	0,992	−2054
	2	0,156	0,213	0,803
	3	−0,099	0,071	−0,460
Score (N_j)	–	0,900	0,460	0,100
		brancos	pardos	pretos

Source: Author's elaboration based on analysis of data from PNAD (1996).

Considering that the slopes between -0.3 and $+0.3$ are practically equal to zero, we can define the slopes in the coordinates i and j (2,1), (2,2), (3,1), and (3,2) as being equal to zero. Once this restriction is applied, we have the M4 model of table 7.2. This model (M4) uses fewer degrees of freedom than the M3 (it is less complex), is better adjusted to the data than the other formerly proposed models (for M4, the χ^2 = 14.93 with the value of p = .497), and, therefore, is the selected one for interpreting the variation between the three racial groups in the association between class origin and destination.

b. Logit Models for Analyzing Educational Transitions

Table 7.3 presents parameter estimates and appropriateness-of-fit statistics for the six models used to analyze the six educational transitions referred to in the section on data and models. All models present a significant adjustment to the data.

c. Conditional Multinomial Logit Models Used to Analyze Mobility Taking into Account Educational Attainment

The formula for the version of the model I use in this chapter is as follows:

$$L_{ij} = \gamma_i - (\alpha_1 r_{i.1} + \alpha_j r_{ij}) + \delta u a_{ij} + \beta_{j1} C_i + \beta_{j2} e_i$$

Where L_{ij} is the logit for the individual i in class of destination j; γj (j = 2, 3, and 4) indicates class of destination; ($\alpha_1 r_{i.1}$ + $\alpha j r_{ij}$) are the parameters of class heritage (probabilities of immobility); δ is the effect of origin upon destination, according with the pattern of uniform association (linear association with identical scale of origin and destination) for the individual i in class of destination j; βj_1 is the effect of being white in class j for individual i; and βj_2 is the effect of each schooling year attained by individual i. I have adjusted two versions of the former model: (a) one of them excluding the independent variables for race and education ($\beta j_1 c i_+ \beta j_2 e i$), which is equivalent to the log-linear model of uniform association with restrictions for the diagonal; and (b) another including all the independent variables. This second version greatly improves the model's adjustment, as becomes clear by the value of the pseudo R^2 in table 7.4. The effects of immobility and of uniform association decrease when we include race and schooling years. The whites' advantage is more accentuated for entering class 1 than for classes 2 and 3; and each schooling year has a positive effect, enhancing the chances of upward mobility.

Table 7.3 Goodness of Fit, Estimated Parameters, and Standard Deviation for Educational Transitions Logit Model: Men Aged 25–64 Years, Brazil, 1996

	Transitions 1		Transitions 2		Transitions 3		Transitions 4		Transitions 5		Transitions 6	
L^2	5777		3942		4146		1115		827		165	
d.f..	7		7		7		7		7		7	
p-valu	0,000		0,000		0,000		0,000		0,000		0,000	
Cox & Snell R Square	0,14		0,12		0,15		0,08		0,09		0,04	
Nagelkerke R Square	0,23		0,18		0,20		0,11		0,12		0,06	
BIC	−5.703		−3.869		−4.075		−1.049		−763		−108	
N	38.106		31.556		24.931		13.024		8.104		3.652	
	B	**S.E.**	**B**	**S.E.**	**B**	**S.E.**	**B**	**S.E.**	**B.**	**S.E.**	**B**	**S.E.**
Non-whites (ref.)												
Whites	1,087	0,030	0,709	0,030	0,457	0,029	0,479	0,040	0,706	0,056	0,209	0,100
Origin Class 4 (ref.)												
Origin Class 1	2,739	0,157	2,332	0,106	2,506	0,064	1,579	0,069	1,347	0,075	0,483	0,128
Origin Class 2	2,172	0,089	1,988	0,070	1,887	0,044	1,027	0,055	0,699	0,070	0,079	0,125
Origin Class 3	1,457	0,042	1,148	0,035	0,903	0,031	0,340	0,046	0,177	0,068	−0,278	0,122
Cohort 55–64 (ref.)												
Cohort 25–34	1,182	0,046	0,931	0,049	0,570	0,056	−0,336	0,048	−0,707	0,103	−1,308	0,195
Cohort 35–44	1,037	0,044	0,829	0,048	0,598	0,055	−0,335	0,084	−0,266	0,101	−0,773	0,192
Cohort 55–54	0,503	0,044	0,399	0,050	0,360	0,059	0,185	0,090	0,029	0,106	−0,367	0,202
Constant	−0,231	0,038	−0,323	0,045	−1491	0,057	−0,278	0,088	−0,929	0,113	1,653	0,219

Table 7.4 Multinomial Logit Models in Conditional Form for Probabilities of Entering into Four Occupational Strata in Brazil, 1996: Males Aged 25–64

Model Adjustments	Conditional Multinominal logit Models							
	Quasi-Uniform Association Model				Quasi-Uniform Association Model with Independent Variables (Race and Schooling Years)			
Log likelihood	−43921,27				−38570,38			
Number of cases (4 times expanded)	152736,00				152424,00			
LR chi2(8)	18025,99				28511,51			
g.l.	8				14			
Prob> chi2=	0,00				0,00			
Pseudo R2=	0,17				0,27			
Estimated Parameters								
Intersections	**Coef.**	**Standard Error**	**z**	**P>|z|**	**Coef.**	**Standard Error**	**z**	**P>|z|**
Intersections for Manual vs. Rural Work (3 vs 4)	1,033	0,050	20,630	0,000	0,418	0,062	6,75	0,000
Intersections for Non-Manual vs. Rural Work (2 vs 4)	−0,585	0,060	−9750	0,000	−2039	0,076	−26,94	0,000
Intersections for Prof. vs. Rural (1 vs 4)	−1849	0,078	−23860	0,000	−4690	0,101	−46,38	0,000
Immobility Effects								
Stratum 4 - Rural Workers	1,297	0,047	27,790	0,000	1,175	0,050	23,45	0,000
Stratum 3 - Manual Workers	0,285	0,026	10,770	0,000	0,384	0,029	13,25	0,000
Stratum 2 - Non-Manual Workers	0,353	0,037	9,610	0,000	0,294	0,038	7,67	0,000
Stratum 1 Professionals and Managers	−0,045	0,056	−0,810	0,420	0,113	0,362	1,84	0,066
Class Origin Effects (UA)	0,449	0,010	42,880	0,000	0,134	0,012	10,95	0,000

Independent Variables Effect

Schooling Years by Stratum 3 vs. 4	0,214	0,006	37,46	0,000
Schooling Years by Stratum 2 vs. 4	0,405	0,007	62,05	0,000
Schooling Years by Stratum 1 vs. 4	0,569	0,008	75,2	0,000
Race (White) by Stratum 3 vs. 4	0,007	0,030	0,24	0,807
Race (White) by Stratum 2 vs. 4	0,110	0,038	2,88	0,004
Race (White) by Stratum 1 vs. 4	0,568	0,049	11,68	0,000

Table 7.5 Crossing Class Origin (O) by Class Destination (D) by Color (C) for Males Aged 25–64 Years, Brazil, 1996

	Class Origin (Father)	Class Destination (Son)				
		1	2	3	4	Total
Whites						
1	Professionals, Managers, and Owners with Employees	1056	571	354	39	2020
2	Non-Maual Routine Workers, Techinicians, and Owners without Employees	935	1045	822	67	2869
3	Manual Workers and Small Rural Employers	1157	1590	3632	357	6736
4	Rural Workers	946	1655	4905	3514	11020
	Total	4094	4861	9713	3977	22645
Pardos						
1	Professionals, Managers, and Owners with EmployeesNon-Manual Routine Workers, Technicians, and Owners without	129	167	241	19	556
2	Employees	226	513	556	81	1376
3	Manual Workers and Small Rural Employers	351	848	2591	305	4095
4	Rural Workers	331	1127	4103	3977	9538
Blacks						
1	Professionals, Managers, and Owners with Employees Non-Manual Rouine Workers, Technicians, and Owners without	7	14	31	1	52
2	Employees	24	46	87	8	165
3	Manual Workers and Small Rural Employers	57	155	595	40	847
4	Rural Workers	37	118	648	558	1361
	Total	125	333	1361	606	2425

Source: PNAD (1996). Author's Tabulation.

Table 7.6 Classes and Strata Hierarchies by Averages of Schooling Years and Monthly Income, and Association Coefficients, Brazil, 1996

4 Strata	16 Classes	Average of Schooling Years (Standard Deviation)		Average of Monthly Income (Standard Deviation)	
		16 Classes	4 Strata	16 Classes	4 Strata
1	I — Professionals and Managers, Higher level	14,4 (2)	11 (2.1)	2661.8 (261.64)	2074.44 (407.9)
	II — Professionals and Managers, Lower level	11.7 (2.9)		1392.9 (379.72)	
	IVa — Small Owners, Employers	10.2 (2.6)		2133.6 (224.79)	
2	IIIa — Non-Manual Routine Workers, Higher level	11.1 (2.7)	8 (2.2)	969.42 (333.14)	800.95 (79.3)
	V — Technicians and Labor Work Supervisors	9.5 (3.1)		897.29 (192.83)	
	IIIa1 — Non-Manual Routine Workers, Higher level (Office Workers)	8.5 (3.1)		575.34 (175.05)	
	IVb — Small Owners without Employees	701 (2.5)		766.08 (134.08)	
3	VIa — Qualified Manual Workers, Modern Industry	7,4 (2)	4 (2.1)	608.81 (122.72)	490.48 (49.1)
	VIc — Qualified Manual Workers, Services	6.7 (2.5)		599.99 (140.26)	
	VIIa2 — Non-Qualified Manual Workers, Modern Industry	6.6 (1.9)		507.92 (138.82)	
	IVc1 — Small Rural Owners, with Employees	6.4 (2.6)		1173.25 (388.14)	
	VIIa1 — Non-Qualified Manual Workers, Street Vendors	5.7 (2.1)		440.52 (159.31)	
	VIb — Qualified Manual Workers, Traditional Industry	5 (2.1)		408.88 (166.63)	
	VIIa3 — Non-Qualified Manual Workers, Home Services	5 (2.2)		287.44 (114.45)	
	VIIa1 — Non-Qualified Manual Workers, Traditional Industry	4.9 (2.2)		345.84 (120.81)	
4	VIIb — Rural Manual Workers	2.2 (1.6)	2.2 (1.6)	240.9 (72.42)	244.34 (61.4)
Total		6,7	5,7	710,9	715,0
Association Coefficient (Eta ao quadrado)		0,45	0,38	0,25	0,20

Table 7.7 Classes of Origin and Destination Distribution, and Indexes of Absolute Mobility for White, Pardo, and Black Males Aged 20–64 Years, Brazil, 1996

Strata	White Origin (%)	White Destination (%)	Pardos Origin (%)	Pardos Destination (%)	Blacks Origin (%)	Blacks Destination (%)
1 Professionals, Managers, and Owners with Employees	8,9	18,1	3,6	6,7	2,1	5,2
2 Non-Manual Routine Workers, Technicians and Owners without Employees	12,7	21,5	8,8	17,1	6,8	13,7
3 Manual Workers, and Small Rural Employers	29,7	42,9	26,3	48,1	34,9	56,1
4 Rural Workers	48,7	17,6	61,3	28,2	56,1	25,0
Indexes of Absolute Mobility	**Whites**		**Pardos**		**Black**	
Total Mobility	59		54		50	
Upward Mobility	49		45		43	
Downward Mobility	10		9		7	
Upward/Dwnward Mobility Ratio	5 to 1		5 to 1		6 to 1	
Dissimilarity between Origin and Destination	31		33		31	

Source: PNAD (1996)

Notes

Several colleagues and students, with different views about the theme of racial quotas and affirmative action in Brazil, have read this essay before its publication. As thanking them individually would take too long to enumerate, let me here simply express my gratitude to them all. All those readings and comments have helped me in improving the essay's argument. As usual, I am entirely responsible for the final outcome.

1. *Pardos* are individuals whose ancestry is a mixture of white and black, generally with a light brown skin color.

2. I use the category nonwhite to emphasize that the sum of blacks and *pardos* is rather a methodological necessity than a political choice or a choice based in some theoretical grounds.

3. There are cases of joint analyses of all the transitions in a single model, but this has not yet been done for the Brazilian data.

4. On this subject, see the criticisms of Cameron and Heckman (1998) of Mare's (1980, 1981) methodology.

5. This scheme of four groups of classes is an aggregation of the 16 groups described by Ribeiro (2007, chapter 2). These 16 classes are obtained in base of the occupational variables (which include the position in the occupation as well) present in the PNAD, with the purpose of constructing a Brazilian version of the international scheme described in chapter 2 of Erickson and Goldthorpe (1993) and obtained in base of the methodology proposed by Ganzeboom and Treiman (1996). In the case of the Brazilian data, the classes of qualified (VI) and nonqualified (VIIa) manual workers can be divided into seven categories according to the type of industry in which the work is concentrated. To analyze the intergenerational mobility of the groups of color (whites, blacks, and *pardos*), I have been obliged to diminish the number of class categories because the group of blacks is very small, which leads to the methodological impossibility of analyzing the mobility table for this group. In face of this limitation, I have aggregated the class groups, from 16 to 4 categories, taking into account the work characteristics of each group and the socioeconomic conditions expressed in the respective averages of education and of income provided by the main work activity. The averages of income and schooling years for the schemes with 16 and with 4 categories are presented in appendix 2, table 7.6.

6. The difference between blacks and *pardos* was not statistically significant.

7. Conclusions about discrimination based on statistical studies as I present in this chapter are not unequivocal. It is possible that a series of other factors could lead to the pattern of racial inequality exposed here. An interesting alternative for directly studying discrimination would be quasi-experimental studies. For a methodological discussion based on the American case, see Pager (2003).

8

Sex-Based Discrimination Trends in Japan, 1965–2005

The Gender Wage Gap and the Marriage Bar

Kunihiro Kimura

1. SEX DISCRIMINATION IN JAPAN DURING THE ERA OF GLOBALIZATION

During the era of globalization, Japan might seem a peculiar society. On the one hand, it is the most successful society in East Asia with respect to industrialization and modernization, especially during the period after World War II. Yet it is well known that gender inequality and sex discrimination remain serious problems within Japanese society.

As the United Nations Development Programme (2008) reports, Japan's economic performance is relatively strong; however, some unfavorable conditions persist for women. The nation's GDP in 2005 was US$4,534.0 billion, which ranked second after the United States among 177 countries worldwide. Japan's per-capita GDP in 2005 ranked 14th, at US$35,484. Meanwhile, though, the value of Japan's Gender Empowerment Measure (GEM) is 0.557, ranking 54th among nations. This lackluster performance is surprising since the first sentence of Article 14 of the Constitution of Japan, which was promulgated in 1946 and enforced the following year, declares equality between the sexes: "All of the people are equal under the law and there shall be no discrimination in political, economic or social relations because of race, creed, sex, social status or family origin."

This chapter aims to describe sex-based discrimination trends in Japan and to propose hypotheses that might explain these trends. We must recognize, however, that there are at least two types of sex discrimination in this country. One is the gender gap in wages (or income). The other is the "marriage bar," that is, the sex discrimination that typically takes the form of excluding married women from full-time employment. These two types of sex-based discrimination are considered to have some important societal consequences, among them the declines in marriage and fertility rates. Within this chapter, I describe trends relating to these two types of sex discrimination in Japan, during the period between 1965 and 2005, using aggregated data from official statistics. I also propose my hypotheses, which may help to explain these trends. Let me note that although some scholars might assume that the Japanese still share patriarchal Confucian ideals or values, emphasizing the superiority of men over women, I believe that such a cultural and particularistic hypothesis cannot avoid tautology or ad hoc explanations. Moreover, if we manage to formulate this kind of hypothesis in a falsifiable manner, we can easily find evidence to refute it. Therefore, I offer more general hypotheses instead, building upon preexisting social scientific studies, especially those relating to rational choice and institutional settings.

My focus in this chapter is upon regular or full-time employment in Japan's nonagricultural sectors, although I acknowledge that there are other important and related issues: for example, occupational sex segregation; gendered labor markets (the most pronounced examples of which include labor market segmentation within the full-time or regular employment sector, in which the majority of workers are male, and the part-time or irregular employment sector, in which the majority of workers are female); and the gendered division of labor within households. Despite the significance of these related issues, I have chosen this focus here because the nature of women's prospects for obtaining full-time or regular employment is of deep-seated concern, not only for social scientists but also for policymakers and the Japanese population as a whole. Another factor influencing my choice is that in contemporary Japan, as in most other industrial societies, the proportion of workers in the agricultural sector is very small.

In section 2, I briefly describe the official statistics that provide the source of the data I will analyze throughout this chapter. In section 3, I describe trends in Japan's gender wage gap from 1965 to 2005, demonstrating that the gender wage gap has dramatically decreased although not disappeared. To explain this development, I propose a hypothesis that highlights the effect of educational attainment on wages. This hypothesis is derived from educational economic theories such as human capital theory (Becker 1993; Mincer 1974) and the signaling model (Spence 1974). In section 4, I compare the proportions of full-time or regular employees[1] who are unmarried women and married women, analyzing the difference between these two proportions during this time period. The results of my analysis suggest that the marriage bar remains a source of sex-based discrimination. To explain this trend, my hypothesis assumes the persisting process of statistical discrimination (e.g., Aigner and Cain 1977; Coate and Loury 1993; Phelps 1972; Schwab 1986) by employers and the reproduction of gender role stereotypes (cf. Brinton 1993), in what may be an example of a self-fulfilling prophecy (Merton 1968, chapter 13). I also discuss why Japan's Equal Employment Opportunity Law, enforced in 1986, seems to have been ineffective in reducing or eliminating the marriage bar. In section 5, I discuss the research that is necessary to improve our understanding of sex discrimination in Japan.

2. DATA: OFFICIAL STATISTICS OF JAPAN, 1965–2005

The data are taken from two surveys conducted by the Japanese government. The Basic Survey on Wage Structure (Policy Planning and Research Department, Ministry of Labour, Japan, 1966–2001; Statistics and Information Department, Ministry of Health, Labour and Welfare, Japan, 2002–2006) provides data on wage distribution for full-time or regular employees in total, by gender, and by age group, as well as other detailed information on wage distribution. The Labour Force Survey (Statistical Bureau, Management and Coordination Agency, Japan 1966–2001; Statistical Bureau, Ministry of Public Management, Home Affairs, Posts and Telecommunications, Japan 2002–2004; Statistical Bureau, Ministry of Internal Affairs and Communications, Japan 2005–2006) provides data on frequency distribution of various types of workers, such as full-time or regular employees, part-time or irregular employees, and self-employed workers. This survey also tracks the unemployment rate.

Social scientists studying the Japanese economy or society in general typically employ the aggregated data from these surveys in order to simply report the gender wage gap in total, the female labor force participation rate[2] (in total, by age group, or by educational attainment), or the nation's unemployment rate. (An exceptional study is Kawashima and Tachibanaki 1986.) I utilize survey data differently, however, in order to describe first, the trend in the gender wage gap by age group, and second, the trend as relates to the the marriage bar, demonstrated by the difference in the proportions of full-time or regular employees who are unmarried women and married women, by age group.

I concentrate on data relating to women aged 25 to 39. This is because most Japanese women have experienced their first marriage and first childbirth within this age range.

3. TRENDS IN THE GENDER WAGE GAP

Figure 8.1 shows trends in the gender wage gap in Japan from 1965 to 2005. The degree of the gender gap is measured in terms of the ratio of the median

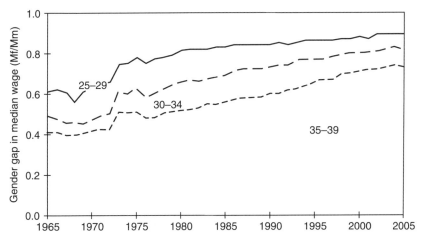

Figure 8.1 Gender wage gap (*Mf/Mm*) for three age groups in Japan, 1965–2005. *Note*: *Mf* stands for the median wage of female full-time or regular employees and *Mm* for the median wage of male full-time or regular employees. The ratio of *Mf* to *Mm* represents the degree of the gender gap in wages. *Source:* Basic Survey on Wage Structure, Japanese Ministry of Health, Labour and Welfare. http://www.mhlw.go.jp/english/database/db-l/index.html

wage (per month) of female full-time or regular employees (*Mf*) to that of their male counterparts (*Mm*). (As the ratio approaches 1, the gender wage gap becomes smaller, while as the ratio approaches 0, the gender gap becomes greater.) We can observe that the gender wage gap has dramatically decreased although not disappeared. In 1965 the ratio of the median wage for female full-time or regular employees aged 25–29 to that of their male counterparts was equal to 0.61, while in 2005 it was 0.89. In 1965, the ratio of the median wage for female full-time or regular employees aged 30–34 to that of their male counterparts was equal to 0.49, while in 2005, it was equal to 0.82. In 1965, the ratio of the median wage for female full-time or regular employees aged 35–39 to that of their male counterparts was equal to 0.41, while in 2005 it was equal to 0.73.[3]

3.1 Hypothesis: Effect of Higher Education

Why has Japan's gender wage gap dramatically decreased? Increasing rates of advancement by Japanese women to higher education partly may explain this trend. We note that this rate has been increasing since 1961 (Hara and Seiyama 2005: 123). Yet in 1965, the rate of advancement to higher education for men was 22.4% compared to an advancement rate for women of

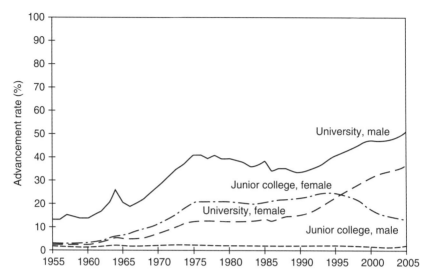

Figure 8.2 Trends in advancement rates to higher education in Japan, 1955–2005.
Source: Basic School Survey (Japanese Ministry of Education, Science and Culture, 1956–2001; Japanese Ministry of Education, Culture, Sports, Science and Technology, 2002–2006)

only 12.3%. By 2005, however, when men advanced to higher education at a rate of 53.1%, the female advancement rate was nearly as high, at 49.8%. Significantly, during 2005, women's advancement rate to universities (36.8%) was nearly three times greater than their advancement rate to junior colleges (13.0%) (figure 8.2).[4] Educational economic theory, either human capital theory or the signaling model, leads us to expect that higher education promotes an individual's level of wage or income. Thus, increasing advancement rates of women to higher education may lead the gender wage gap to decline.

4. TRENDS RELATING TO THE MARRIAGE BAR IN JAPAN, 1965–2005

Contrary to the trend in Japan's gender wage gap, the degree to which the marriage bar serves as a form of sex-based discrimination does not seem to have changed. Although the proportions of full-time or regular employees among both unmarried women and married women gradually have increased, the difference between the former and the latter has decreased only slightly.

Figure 8.3 Trends in the marriage bar in Japan, 1965–2005. (1) Percentages of full-time or regular employees among unmarried women and married women (aged 25–29). *Notes:* Data for 1967 are missing. The figures for 1965 and 1966 represent the percentages of employees among unmarried women and married women (aged 25–29). *Source:* Labour Force Survey, Japanese Ministry of Internal Affairs and Communications, Statistics Bureau. http://www.stat.go.jp/english/data/roudou/index.htm

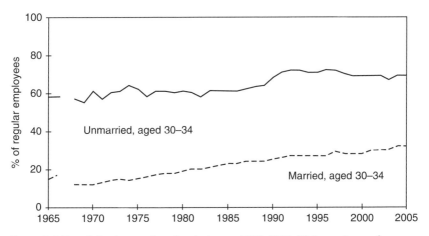

Figure 8.4 Trends in the marriage bar in Japan, 1965–2005. (2) Percentages of full-time or regular employees among unmarried women and married women (aged 30–34). *Notes:* Data for 1967 are missing. The figures for 1965 and 1966 represent the percentages of employees among unmarried women and married women (aged 30–39). *Source:* Labour Force Survey

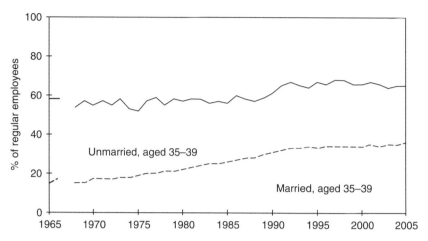

Figure 8.5 Trends in the marriage bar in Japan, 1965–2005. (3) Percentages of full-time or regular employees among unmarried women and married women (aged 35–39). *Notes:* Data for 1967 are missing. The figures for 1965 and 1966 represent the percentages of employees among unmarried women and married women (aged 30–39). *Source:* Labour Force Survey

Figure 8.3 shows the proportions of full-time or regular employees among unmarried women aged 25–29 and married women aged 25–29. In 1968, the difference between these two proportions was equal to 0.52, while in 2005 the difference was equal to 0.38. Figure 8.4 shows the proportions of full-time or regular employees among unmarried women aged 30–34 and married women aged 30–34. In 1968, the difference between these two proportions was equal to 0.45, while in 2005 the difference was equal to 0.37. Figure 8.5 shows the proportions of full-time or regular employees among unmarried women aged 35–39 and married women aged 35–39. In 1968, the difference between these two proportions was equal to 0.39, while in 2005 the difference was equal to 0.29.

We can look from another perspective as well at the difference between the percentages of full-time or regular employees among unmarried and married women. Let us introduce the concept of birth cohorts and trace two trajectories of the percentages of full-time or regular employees among unmarried women and married women by birth cohort. In so doing, we find that the former is decreasing while the latter is increasing by a small amount for every cohort.[5] This implies that the difference between the percentages of full-time or regular employees among unmarried and married women decreases for every cohort as women get older within the age range of 25–39. However, the difference remains significant, at about 30 percentage points even at the maximum of each age cohort (figure 8.6).

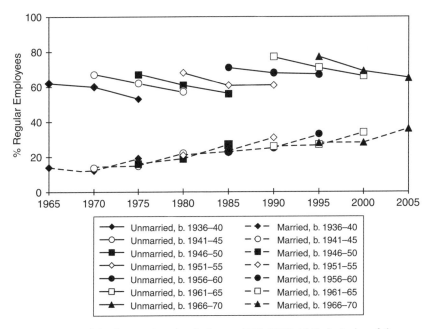

Figure 8.6 Trends in the marriage bar in Japan, 1965–2005. (4) Trajectories of the percentages of full-time or regular employees among unmarried women and married women by birth cohort. *Source:* Labour Force Survey

In summary, figures 8.3–8.6 reveal that the marriage bar remains in full force in contemporary Japan, although, on average, the proportions of full-time or regular employees among unmarried women and women gradually have increased regardless of the age group. The difference in the proportions of full-time or regular employees between unmarried and married women has been about 0.4 (40 percentage points) on average. This applies to all three age groups, that is, women aged 25–29, women aged 30–34, and women aged 35–39, with one exception: women aged 35–39 in the period since 1980.

4.1 Hypothesis: Statistical Discrimination and Reproduction of Gender Stereotypes

Why has the marriage bar remained in effect in Japanese society? One plausible hypothesis is that there has been a persisting process of statistical discrimination (e.g., Aigner and Cain 1977; Coate and Loury 1993; Phelps 1972; Schwab 1986) by employers and a reproduction of gender role stereotypes (cf. Brinton 1993).

This process starts with the belief on the part of most Japanese employers that, based on their experiences, observations, and statistical inferences, women tend to quit their jobs at marriage or childbirth. Given this belief or gender role stereotype, it is rational for employers to prefer men over women when it comes to decisions relating to job assignments, promotions, and other kinds of opportunities that enhance an employee's career prospects. (This is because employers believe that, if they awarded these opportunities to women they could not expect the same level of economic return from their investments as they would be likely to receive from men.) Facing such discriminatory decisions, many female employees come to expect that women have fewer career options than men do. As a consequence, many female employees do in fact decide to quit their jobs at marriage or childbirth. This pattern confirms employers' initial belief or gender role stereotypes. We can observe a self-fulfilling prophecy (Merton 1968, chapter 13) here (figure 8.7).

Brinton (1993: 96–108) already has pointed out that such a process of gender role stereotype reproduction leads to Japanese women's lower rates of labor force participation, especially among Japanese female university graduates. We note that Brinton also assumes that internalization of values or socialization of daughters by parents is necessary for this process to take effect; she also maintains that parents are likely to regard a university education as job preparation for sons and general education for daughters. However, I do not think that internalization of values or socialization of daughters by parents is necessary for this process to happen. It is my assertion that it is employers' beliefs that really matter.

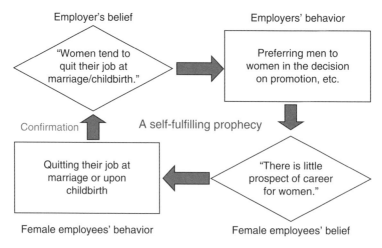

Figure 8.7 A hypothetical process for the persisting marriage bar: statistical discrimination and reproduction of gender-role stereotypes.

In fact, we can observe evidence against Brinton's argument. Hara and Seiyama (2005: 130–32) report that the percentage of those who agree with the idea that "men should work outside and women should look after the home" substantially dropped from 1985 to 1995 among women from most academic backgrounds and cohorts. If women internalized gendered values, such drops in the percentage of those who agree with the idea quoted above might rarely occur. Moreover, Kimura (2007) detects other significant facts by analyzing the survey data relating to high school students and their parents. First, it is worth pointing out that there are very low associations between gender role attitudes of female high school students and those of their mothers (table 8.1).[6] Second, the proportion of female students who aspire to enter a university is greater among those who disapprove of the gendered division of labor than among those who accept it (table 8.2). Third, the proportion of female students who would like to work after marriage or childbirth is greater among those who disapprove of the gendered division of labor than among those who accept it (table 8.3). In other words, it seems that female students regard higher education as a springboard for occupational attainment and lifelong work or careers, rather than as an institution that could provide them with general education that might be useful when they become homemakers or mothers. We can observe similar results in the analyses of the data sets of female high school students from the 1980s and 1990s. These findings provide additional evidence against Brinton's argument about the importance of socialization of daughters by parents and the greater significance of universities in providing general education (rather than job preparation) for Japanese women.

Table 8.1 Association between Gender Role Attitudes in Female High School Students and Their Mothers

Female Student	Mother %	
	Positive	Negative
Positive	19.3	17.9
Negative	80.7	82.1
(N)	(119)	(263)
		$r = 0.017$

Source: The Fifth Survey on Social Consciousness of High-School Students and Their Parents, conducted by the Work Group on Education and Culture, Tohoku University, in 2003.

Table 8.2 Educational Aspirations and Gender Role Attitude among Female
High School Students

Educational Aspirations	Gender Role Attitude %	
	Positive	Negative
University	28.2	47.6
Junior college	5.9	5.9
Vocational school	12.9	19.0
Postsecondary employment	40.0	20.2
Depending on achievement/ Undetermined	12.9	7.3
(*N*)	(85)	(357)

Note: A vocational school (*senmon-gakko*) is a postsecondary school that provides
students with specialized and practical courses for vocational education.

Source: The Fifth Survey on Social Consciousness of High-School Students and Their
Parents, conducted by the Work Group on Education and Culture, Tohoku University,
in 2003.

Table 8.3 Work/Career Aspirations and Gender Role Attitude among
Female High School Students

Work/Career Aspirations	Gender Role Attitude %	
	Positive	Negative
Desire to continue to work	11.9	41.9
Desire to quit job once but return to work	38.6	26.8
Desire to quit job at marriage or childbirth	27.7	10.9
Undetermined	21.8	20.5
(*N*)	(101)	(396)

Source: The Fifth Survey on Social Consciousness of High-School Students and
Their Parents, conducted by the Work Group on Education and Culture, Tohoku
University, in 2003.

4.2 Ineffectiveness of Japan's Equal Employment Opportunity Law

It is worth noting here that Japan's Equal Employment Opportunity Law
seems to have had no effect on the marriage bar, although this law prohibits
it. We can observe little decrease in the difference between the proportions
of full-time or regular employees among unmarried women and married
women, even after the mid-1980s, as shown in figures 8.3–8.6.

In European countries and the United States, discrimination based upon marital status has been illegal since the 1960s (Cohen 1985: 97–115; Goldin 1990: 161–79; Hakim 1996: 123–25). The marriage bar was prohibited in Japan about 20 years later. The Equal Employment Opportunity Law of Japan, which was established in 1985, enforced in 1986, and revised in 1997 and 2006, has consistently prohibited the marriage bar. But the law did not dictate an explicit punishment for employers who failed to observe it until the 2006 revision. It is my assumption that the absence, until recently, of explicit punishment explains the curious fact that the law seems to have had no effect on the marriage bar.

5. SUMMARY AND CONCLUDING REMARKS

5.1 Summary

We can observe different trends in Japan's two types of sex-based discrimination, that is, the gender wage gap and the marriage bar, during the period from 1965 through 2005.[7] The gender wage gap in Japan has dramatically decreased although not disappeared. The rate of increasing advancement by Japanese women to higher education may partly explain this trend. During this period, however, the degree to which the marriage bar has served as a form of sex discrimination does not seem to have changed. I think that this is due to the persisting process of statistical discrimination by employers and the reproduction of gender role stereotypes, although I disagree with the hypothesis posed elsewhere that internalization of values or socialization of daughters by parents is necessary for this process to occur.

5.2 Concluding Remarks: A Call for Future Research

I would like to point out some problems of the analyses and theoretical examinations in this chapter in order to envision the type of research that would be valuable in the future.

First, let me mention that the above analyses utilize only aggregated data. Such analyses cannot avoid the ecological fallacy (Robinson 1950) in principle. To confirm whether my hypotheses are valid or not, we need analyses of microlevel data, that is, analyses of data from social surveys that not only define individuals as the respondents but also make their data sets available. Unfortunately, the Japanese government does not make the data sets of either the Basic Survey on Wage Structure or the Labour Force Survey available. Thus, we have to use other relevant data sets. I intend, however, to examine whether my hypotheses are valid using the data from the Fourth and Fifth Survey of Social Stratification and Social Mobility in Japan, which were conducted nationwide in 1985 and 1995, respectively.

Second, while my analyses of the aggregated data concern only Japanese women's wage and employment status, my hypotheses involve assumptions about the attitudes and behaviors of both Japanese women and Japanese employers. Thus, we need historical analysis of employers' attitudes to explain trends relating to the marriage bar in Japan. It is worth pointing out that most social scientists have been more concerned with Japanese women's attitudes and behaviors, and, as a consequence, there have been few empirical studies that depict Japanese employers' attitudes and behaviors.[8]

Third, we need a more detailed comparative analysis of the effects of institutional settings on individuals' behaviors: most especially of the characteristics of laws that may influence gender inequality. This will be useful because the reason for the ineffectiveness of the Equal Employment Opportunity Law of Japan in eliminating the marriage bar may not be explained as simply as I argued in section 4.2.

In fact, Foote (1996) proposes an alternative hypothesis that takes into account not only the role of the courts but also the supplementary effect of another act. First, he emphasizes that the Equal Employment Opportunity Law of Japan only codified standards that the Japanese courts already had developed, especially those relating to retirement ages and dismissal policies. As a result, the law required employers only to "endeavor" to treat women the same way that men were treated in recruitment, hiring, assignments, and promotions. Additionally, Foote elucidates the significance of the Worker Dispatching Act, which was enacted just one month after the Equal Employment Opportunity Law. The Worker Dispatching Act, along with the Cabinet Order that designated which types of jobs were covered by the act, enabled private temporary employment agencies to hire women as dispatched workers for clerical or "pink collar" jobs (such as file clerk, purse bearer, secretary, receptionist, translator, programmer, demonstrator, and cleaner) with little job security. In other words, thanks to the Worker Dispatching Act, Japanese companies could continue to assign young women to jobs like these, on the assumption that they would leave the workforce upon marriage or childbirth.[9]

Can the lack of explicit punishment simply explain the ineffectiveness of the Equal Employment Opportunity Law in eliminating the marriage bar? Or do we need to take into account the standards developed by the courts as well as the effect of the Worker Dispatching Act to sufficiently explain the ineffectiveness of the Equal Employment Opportunity Law? To answer these questions, we should conduct a comparative analysis of various societies and investigate the effects of the characteristics of labor laws on the behaviors of employers as well as workers.

Let me conclude this chapter by pointing out a somewhat ironic trend in the unemployment rates for younger men and women in Japan (that is, those aged 25–29), as shown in figure 8.8. Although unemployment rates seem relatively low in Japan, they have been increasing since the early 1990s. This may reflect a change in the hiring policies of most large companies in Japan. As the recent wave of globalization penetrated Japanese society, following the collapse of the "bubble economy" in the early 1990s, most large companies began limiting the employment of young people to cut personnel expenses and thereby strengthen their own international competitiveness. It is worth noting here that the difference between the unemployment rates for these men and women has been decreasing, especially since 2000, with little difference between the two rates in 2005. This implies that young Japanese men have lost the privilege of having a higher chance to get and retain a job than their female counterparts. In other words, young Japanese men and women are currently more equal than their seniors had been in the past, because the employment situation for young men is worse than previously was the case. Ironically enough, the prospects for young men in this regard have now declined to approximate those of young women.

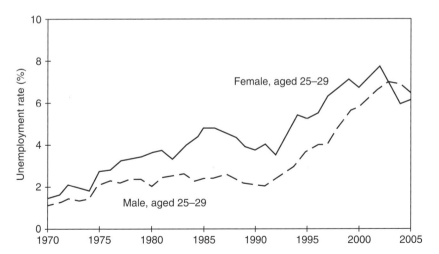

Figure 8.8 Trends in the unemployment rate for men and women aged 25–29 in Japan, 1970–2005. *Source:* Labour Force Survey

Notes

This study was supported by the Japan Economic Research Foundation and by the Center for the Study of Social Stratification and Inequality (the 21st Century/Global Center of Excellence Programs, Director Yoshimichi Sato) of Tohoku University.

1. Strictly speaking, full-time employment is not exactly the same as regular employment and vice versa. However, many social scientists point out that the overlap or intersection of full-time employment and regular employment is broad within Japanese society, although, in some cases, part-time or irregular employees work as if they were full-time or regular employees with respect to working hours or job descriptions (cf. Stockman et al. 1995: 95–96).

2. For Japan, using the female labor force participation rate as an indicator of gender empowerment is sometimes misleading. This is because the labor force includes part-time or irregular workers as well as unemployed persons. Moreover, the definition of the unemployed in the Japanese Labour Force Survey is different not only from that of the International Labour Organization but also from those definitions relied upon by some other countries, including the United States.

3. Chapter 9 in this volume by Koyo Miyoshi analyzes Japan's gender wage gap more intensively and inclusively than this chapter does by applying elaborate methods to the data of the first wave of a panel survey.

4. A junior college (*tanki-daigaku*) is a two-year school for higher education in Japan.

5. It is a puzzling fact that the percentage of full-time or regular employees among married women increases a little for every cohort. I offer three conjectures to explain this fact. The first is that women in some professional or semiprofessional occupations, such as school teachers, pharmacists, and nurses, can enjoy maternal leave designated by the regulations of their workplaces or are easily able to return to work owing to their qualifications, even if they quit their jobs for childbearing or child rearing. The second is that some part-time or irregular employees may become full-time or regular employees if they manage to continue to work in the same workplaces for many years. The third is the possibility of response/nonresponse biases.

6. Gender role attitude is measured by the respondent's answer when asked whether she agrees ("Positive") or disagrees ("Negative") with the statement: "Men should work outside the home, and married women should stay home."

7. It is worth noting that Japanese women, facing these two different trends of sex discrimination, may experience satisfaction as a result of cognitive dissonance reduction (e.g., Festinger 1957; Harmon-Jones and Mills 1999; Thibodeau and Aronson 1992), rather than frustration caused by (egoistical) relative deprivation (e.g., Crosby 1982; Merton [1949] 1968, chapters 10–11; Runciman 1966; Stouffer et al. 1949; Walker and Smith 2002). Kimura (2000: 186–87) reports that most Japanese married women aged 30–59 feel that there exists unfairness in terms of gender in Japanese society, regardless of their educational attainment and employment status. This may be an expression of "fraternal relative deprivation" (Runciman 1966) among Japanese (married) women. However, some other studies reveal that most Japanese women are satisfied with their daily lives (e.g., Umino and Saito 1990: 108–9; Yonemura 1998: 183). This satisfaction may be a result of cognitive dissonance reduction. Notice that the simultaneous expression of feeling or recognition

of societal unfairness and life satisfaction is similar to what Crosby (1982) described as the typical attitude of women in a suburb of a city in the United States in the late 1970s.

8. Devah Pager's methodological argument on the measurement of discrimination in chapter 3 in this volume will be very suggestive when we study Japanese employers' discriminative attitudes and behaviors.

9. The nature of those jobs to which the Worker Dispatching Act is applied has been extended and defeminized by several revisions since 1986.

9

Male-Female Wage Differentials in Japan
The Importance of the Choice of Work Status

Koyo Miyoshi

1. INTRODUCTION

Several studies have pointed out that the gap between the average pay of males and females in Japan has been the largest among developed countries (see Mincer 1985; Jacobsen 1998; Blau and Kahn 2003). For example, the Japanese Equal Employment, Children and Families Bureau (2004) reports the ratio of the average hourly earnings of women to men in Japan is 0.67, while it is 0.81 for the United Kingdom, and 0.79 for the United States. Even in recent research like Johnes and Tanaka (2008) or Miyoshi (2008), the wage gap still exists. Johnes and Tanaka (2008) demonstrate that, although the Japanese gender wage gap narrowed between 1993 and 2000 during a period in which it widened in Russia and the United States, the wage gap unexplained by observable characteristics in Japan persists, remaining markedly larger than in those two other countries.

Houseman and Abraham (1993) point out that, because strong job security applies only to full-time regular workers, peripheral nonregular workers, who are predominantly females, are more vulnerable to contract termination. This difference in job security between regular and nonregular workers may affect the gender wage gap because nonregular workers are mostly females. However, the data used in past studies of male-female wage differentials in Japan, for example, Higuchi (1991), Kawashima and Tachibanaki (1986), and Johnes and Tanaka (2008), contain insufficient information on nonregular workers. Because the data they use contain only information on regular workers who are continuously hired by companies, the data do not cover all part-time workers. As a result, past studies have ignored the possible differences in the wage structures of full-time regular workers and nonregular workers. A comprehensive household survey conducted yearly since 2004 by Keio University contains a wealth of information, not only on regular workers but also on a sample of Japanese households, including their detailed work histories. The aim of this chapter is to examine empirically what produces Japan's large male-female wage differential, taking account of the possible differences in the labor market structures for regular and nonregular workers.

To eliminate bias resulting from endogeneity and selectivity, this chapter estimates both the work status function and wage function simultaneously, in line with the approach of Ermisch and Wright (1993), Nagase (2003), and Matsuura and Shigeno (2005). To demonstrate what causes the gender wage gap, this chapter follows Neuman and Oaxaca (2004), a more sophisticated version of the traditional decomposition approach developed by Oaxaca (1973), which compares the results of wage equations estimated for a male sample with those estimated for a female sample.

Compared to previous research relating to Japan's gender wage gap (Higuchi 1991; Kawashima and Tachibanaki 1986; Nagase 2003; Johnes and Tanaka 2008), this chapter offers the following features. First, since this chapter uses a data set that contains a wealth of information on individuals' work histories, it can take account of the differences in human capital accumulation caused by differences in work histories. As relates to this, the chapter takes account of the possibility of a difference in human capital accumulation between regular and nonregular work experience, significant since nonregular work experience is typically longer for females than males. Additionally, this chapter takes account of the possibility of the existence of firm-specific human capital accumulation that increases with job seniority, typically shorter for females than males. The chapter takes account as well of the possibility of human capital depreciation during periods of no work, which are typically longer for females than males.

Second, since this chapter takes account of the choice of work status (that is, regular worker, nonregular worker, or not in employment or education) to eliminate selectivity bias in the wage equation, it clarifies the impact of individual household characteristics, such as the number of infants, on an individual's wage.

The estimation results can be summarized as follows. First, there are significant differences between males and females in the reasons why they choose to be regular workers. For example, having a child under age six significantly decreases the probability of being a regular worker for females, while this is not the case for males. Second, even among regular workers, the wage gap unexplained by observable characteristics in Japan still remains after the effects of selectivity bias have been removed. There are four important reasons why, for regular workers, the wage gap is so large between the average pay of males and females in Japan. First, regular work experience and seniority, both of which tend to be shorter for females than males, significantly affect wages. Second, there are significant differences in the evaluation of regular work experience between males and females. Third, there are significant differences in the evaluation of university degrees between males and females. Fourth, there are many more males than females who have university degrees, which significantly affects wages.

The remainder of this chapter is as follows. Section 2 explains the empirical model. Section 3 describes the data and the characteristics of work experience in our sample. Section 4 presents the empirical results, and section 5 contains a conclusion.

2. EMPIRICAL STRATEGY

This section briefly describes the empirical strategy. This chapter follows the traditional approach introduced by Oaxaca (1973). It first assumes a standard Mincerian wage function, but takes account of possible sample selection bias caused by estimating a wage equation only for workers. In line with Nagase (2003) and Matsuura and Shigeno (2005), this chapter estimates the following reduced-form work status choice function:

$$P_{sjg} = Z_{jg}\delta_g + X_{jg}\gamma_g + \varepsilon_{jg},\tag{1}$$

where P_{sig} stands for the choice of work status (i.e., regular worker, nonregular worker, or not in employment or education), g stands for gender (i.e., male or female), Z_{jg} stands for the individual's household characteristics, such as the number of infants (typically, children aged zero–three) and net financial assets, which are assumed to affect the utility obtained by those who choose the status of not in education or employment. X_{jg} stands for the degree of human capital accumulation (such as work experience and education level), which is assumed to affect wages. This chapter uses the following variables to take account of the utility obtained when an individual chooses not to work: the number of children whose age is three or younger, the number of children aged between four and six (considered separately since the cost of nursery services for infants aged zero–three can be assumed to be higher than the cost for children aged four–six), the average income of the individual's spouse over a three-year period (=0 if the individual is not married), and the net financial assets of the household. Given that there are three work choices, the work status choice models are estimated using the multinomial logit model.

Using the results obtained from estimating the work status choice function (1), this chapter then estimates the following wage functions:

$$\ln W_{kjg} = X'_{jg}\beta_{kg} + IMR_{kjg}\lambda_{kg} + v_{kjg} \quad k = r, nr \quad g = m, f, \tag{2}$$

where W_{kjg} denotes the offered wage rate for worker j in work status k (regular or nonregular workers) with gender g (male or female); X_{jg} is a vector of characteristics; IMR_{kjg} denotes the inverse Mill's ratio computed using the estimates from the work status choice model; and v_{kjg} is a disturbance term. IMR_{kjg} is used to remove the impact of sample selectivity bias caused by the unobservability of wages. Because the estimates of IMR are computed from the estimated results of (1), equation (2) will suffer from a generated regressor problem. This needs to be taken into account when estimating the variance-covariance matrix of the parameter estimates of equation (2). To calculate the variance-covariance matrix of the estimated coefficients, this chapter uses the bootstrapping method.

In line with Mincer (1985), this chapter uses the individual's education level and work experience as explanatory variables in the wage function. To account for different education levels, schooling dummy variables for junior high school, universities, and other schools like specialized school or two-year colleges are included. As a result, senior high school is the base education level.

To specify work experience variables, this chapter focuses on three possibilities raised in previous research. First, the chapter focuses on the possibility that wages rise with job seniority, as Topel (1991) pointed out, and distinguishes between work experience as a whole and work experience in the current workplace. Work experience in the current workplace is typically shorter for females than males in Japan. Second, this chapter focuses on possible differences between the impact of regular work experience and nonregular experience on wages, as in Mincer and Higuchi (1988), and distinguishes between regular work experience and nonregular work experience. Nonregular work experience is typically shorter for males than females in Japan. Third, this chapter focuses on the possibility that years not in employment or education (NEE) depreciate human capital, utilizing NEE, which is typically longer for females than males, as a proxy variable for human capital depreciation, as Mincer and Ofek (1982) suggested. As a result the following variables relate to work experience: the years of regular work experience, the years of nonregular work experience, NEE, the number of years of tenure as a regular worker, and the number of years of tenure as a nonregular worker. Work experience is defined as the number of years of experience prior to the year in which the individual chooses his or her work status. The squares of the work experience variables also are included to allow for the possibility of nonlinear responses to changes in work experience. To take account of the possibility that labor markets are geographically segmented, regional dummy variables also are used in both the work status function and the wage functions.

If the values of β_{km} and β_{kf} in equation (2) differ, then male and female workers will not receive the same wages even if they have the same characteristics, which implies the existence of a male-female wage differential. Hence, our main null hypothesis is $H_0 : \beta_{km} = \beta_{km}$, and the alternative hypothesis is $H_1 : \beta_{km} \neq \beta_{km}$ for $k = r, nr$.

To analyze which are the main factors affecting the male-female wage differential, this chapter uses the decomposition method introduced by Oaxaca (1973) and extended to the sample selection case by Neuman and Oaxaca (2004). The decomposition method is described in the appendix.

3. DATA

This chapter utilizes data from the Keio Household Panel Survey (KHPS) conducted by Keio University in 2004, 2005, 2006, and 2007. The first wave of KHPS, KHPS2004, sampled about 4,000 households with respondents aged 20 through 69, including both married and unmarried males and females. Kimura (2005) contains details of the sampling methods used to obtain KHPS and the sample characteristics of KHPS2004. KHPS2004 asked each respondent to detail his or her work status from age 18 until the time of the survey. Table 9.1 contains an English translation of part of the question relating to work status. Respondents are asked to describe their work status at each age, according to the following categories: worked as a regular worker, worked as a nonregular worker, in education, stopped work, worked as a self-employed worker, did piecework at home, worked with a family business, or looked for a job. Respondents are asked also to report when they changed jobs. This data enables the computation of the number of years of actual work experience when we estimate wage and labor participation functions. In line with OECD (2006), this chapter defines nonregular workers as part-time workers, dispatched workers (employed by temporary worker agencies), and temporary and short-term contract employees. It should be noted that there are a few individuals who worked as nonregular workers while also having a regular worker job, and there are a few individuals who worked as nonregular workers while also attending an educational institution (i.e., he or she was in education). In neither instance were individuals dropped from the sample. To compute the number of years of regular or nonregular work experience for these individuals, this chapter assumes the following. First, individuals can accumulate regular worker and nonregular worker specific human capital simultaneously. Second, individuals can accumulate nonregular worker specific human capital even while they are in education. There are therefore a few individuals whose years in actual work experience are shorter than the sum of their years of regular work experience and nonregular work experience.

Table 9.1 Question Relating to Work Status

Age	In Education	Searching for a Job	Non–Regular Worker	Regular Worker	Self-employed	Doing Piecework at Home	Family Worker	Changed Jobs	Age
18									18
19									19
20									20
21									21
22									22
23									23
24									24
25									25
64									64
65									65
66									66
67									67
68									68

Note: Respondents are asked to indicate for each age which of these choices applied to them.

In this chapter, the sample is restricted to individuals aged 18 through 59 who are not self-employed (*jieigyo*). The reason for imposing this upper age limit is that most Japanese workers face retirement at age 60; postretirement wages tend to be set quite differently from preretirement wages (see Ohashi 2005). Hourly wage rates are calculated by dividing an individual's reported income by his or her working hours. Work experience and seniority, up to the year prior to that in which the individual chooses his or her work status, is calculated using the information collected from responses to the question in table 9.1.

For people who were in their 50s or 60s at the time of the KHPS survey, some of the information requested relates to events that might have occurred as much as 40 years earlier. There is a question about how reliable the data are given the possibility of recall bias (see Horvath 1982; Oyer 2004). To minimize some of the effects of recall bias that may occur in response to the question in table 9.1, the following process was implemented: KHPS2004 asks those currently working, "How many years have you been working in the current place?" and "When did you start working in the current place?" If the information obtained from the answers to these questions and the information from table 9.1 are contradictory, the individual is dropped from the sample. In addition, individuals were also excluded if they reported that their last school attended was junior high school while also answering that they were still in education after reaching the age of 18. As a result of these two checks, about 100 individuals were excluded.

Table 9.2 Descriptive Statistics

	Whole Sample				Nonregular Workers Only				Regular Workers Only			
	Male		Female		Male		Female		Male		Female	
	Mean	S.E.	Mean	S.E.	Mean	S.E.	Mean	S.E.	Mean	S.E.	Mean	S.E.
Junior high	4.30%	—	2.90%	—	7.90%	—	3.10%	—	3.70%	—	1.60%	—
High dchool	45.90%	—	50.80%	—	42.80%	—	54.10%	—	47.00%	—	44.10%	—
University	40.60%	—	14.80%	—	38.60%	—	13.00%	—	40.40%	—	20.50%	—
Two- year college	9.10%	—	31.40%	—	10.70%	—	29.80%	—	9.00%	—	33.80%	—
Age	41.5	10.6	40.5	10.3	38.1	13.0	40.9	9.9	41.9	10.1	38.2	10.3
Actual experience	20.1	10.9	12.7	8.4	16.2	12.3	13.9	7.4	20.9	10.4	16.3	9.6
Regular worker experience	19.2	11.2	8.7	7.6	12.1	12.0	6.8	5.3	20.2	10.6	14.5	9.4
Tenure as regular worker	—	—	—	—	3.9	7.9	1.1	3.1	14.5	11.2	10.0	9.5
Nonregular worker experience	1.0	2.9	4.0	5.2	4.1	4.4	7.1	5.6	0.6	2.4	1.8	3.5
Tenure as nonregular worker	—	—	—	—	2.3	3.5	4.0	4.9	0.4	1.7	0.9	2.4
Years in NEE	1.0	3.3	8.5	8.7	2.3	5.1	8.2	7.1	0.7	2.6	2.1	4.3
Number of kids (age 4–6)	0.1	0.3	0.1	0.3	0.0	0.2	0.1	0.3	0.1	0.3	0.0	0.2
Number of kids (age 0–3)	0.2	0.5	0.2	0.5	0.1	0.3	0.1	0.3	0.2	0.5	0.1	0.3
Income of spouse	82.1	157.6	412.6	372.1	38.9	94.9	394.9	346.1	88.3	162.5	252.9	324.6
Net financial assets	−65.2	1,794.5	76.3	2,006.2	−58.3	972.6	−120.6	2,188.9	−92.4	1,867.1	244.8	1,369.4
Hourly wage rate	—	—	—	—	1,441.9	1,471.3	1,169.2	1,143.9	2,712.7	2,127.7	1,918.8	1,507.4
Obs	2,421		2,685		215		1,004		2,119		698	

Source: Keio University Japan Household Panel Survey 2004, 2005, 2006, and 2007.

According to the OECD (2002), Japanese females have a stronger tendency to leave the labor market when they marry than do females in any other developed country. Japanese males, however, tend to work at the same workplace. Table 9.2 demonstrates some of the differences between the work experiences of males and females in Japan. Actual work experience is defined as the numbers of years each respondent says he or she worked as either a regular worker or a nonregular worker. As can be seen from table 9.2, for females, actual work experience is on average about seven years shorter than for males. For females, a quarter of their work experience is in nonregular worker jobs, while for males almost all of their work experience is in regular worker jobs. The number of years when an individual is neither in employment nor in education (NEE) is nearly nine years for females; however, it is very short for males. Even for a sample limited to nonregular workers, NEE is approximately eight years for females.

4. ESTIMATION RESULTS

Table 9.3 shows the results of estimating a reduced-form work status choice function. Rather than reporting the estimated coefficients of the multinomial logit model, which are extremely difficult to interpret, this table only reports marginal effects of each variable and their standard errors. The marginal effects indicate how the probability of a particular work status choice will change when the associated explanatory variable is changed by one unit.

The results are generally consistent with theoretical predictions. For the sample as a whole and for females, acquiring a university degree increases the probability of choosing to become a regular worker. The factors that affect the work status choice differ between males and females. For example, the income of a spouse and the number of children significantly impact the choice of NEE for females, but not for males.[1] As the income of the spouse increases, more males choose to work as regular workers, while more females choose to work as nonregular workers. Net financial assets significantly affect the work status choice of females, but not of males.

The effects of experience and seniority differ by gender and by the type of worker. For example, while an increase in tenure as a regular worker increases the probability of working as a regular worker for both males and females, it decreases the probability of working as a nonregular worker for males, while it decreases the probability of working for females. On the other hand, tenure as a nonregular worker has the opposite effect: an increase in tenure as a nonregular worker increases the probability of working as a nonregular worker and, for males, decreases the probability of

Table 9.3 Occupational Choice Function: Reduced Form

	Whole Sample			Male			Female		
	NEE	Nonregular	Regular	NEE	Nonregular	Regular	NEE	Nonregular	Regular
Female	0.007***	0.181***	-0.188	—	—	—	—	—	—
	[0.003]	[0.024]	[0.025]						
Junior high	0.0001	0.065	-0.065	0.0003	0.041*	-0.042	-0.043	-0.16	0.204
	[0.002]	[0.067]	[0.068]	[0.0004]	[0.024]	[0.024]	[0.018]	[0.120]	[0.124]
University	0.002	-0.048	0.046*	0.0001	0.006	-0.006	0.001	-0.112	0.111**
	[0.002]	[0.026]	[0.027]	[0.0001]	[0.007]	[0.007]	[0.017]	[0.046]	[0.046]
Two-year college	-0.0003	-0.017	0.018	0.0001	0.014	-0.014	-0.001	-0.047	0.049
	[0.001]	[0.027]	[0.027]	[0.0001]	[0.013]	[0.013]	[0.011]	[0.031]	[0.031]
Regular worker experience	-0.009	-0.156	0.164***	-0.0001	-0.018	0.018*	-0.114	-0.057	0.171***
	[0.003]	[0.041]	[0.041]	[0.0001]	[0.010]	[0.010]	[0.030]	[0.065]	[0.057]
Regular worker experience^2	0.002***	0.030**	-0.032	0.00002	0.005*	-0.005	0.052***	-0.026	-0.025
	[0.001]	[0.012]	[0.012]	[0.00003]	[0.003]	[0.003]	[0.013]	[0.027]	[0.022]
Nonregular worker experience	-0.003	0.526***	-0.523	-0.00005	0.113***	-0.113	-0.147	0.481***	-0.334
	[0.001]	[0.071]	[0.072]	[0.0001]	[0.025]	[0.025]	[0.039]	[0.081]	[0.079]
Nonregular worker experience^2	0.001	-0.239	0.238***	-0.00001	-0.046	0.046***	0.073***	-0.217	0.144***
	[0.003]	[0.036]	[0.036]	[0.00004]	[0.013]	[0.013]	[0.022]	[0.044]	[0.042]
Tenure as regular worker	-0.066	-0.609	0.676***	-0.001	-0.088	0.089***	-0.647	-0.039	0.686***
	[0.017]	[0.048]	[0.049]	[0.0009]	[0.012]	[0.012]	[0.080]	[0.105]	[0.075]

	(1)	(2)	(3)	(4)	(5)	(6)	(7)	(8)	(9)
Tenure as regular worker²	0.016***	0.143***	-0.159	0.0002	0.020***	-0.02	0.145***	0.019	-0.164
	[0.004]	[0.016]	[0.095]	[0.0002]	[0.004]	[0.004]	[0.023]	[0.037]	[0.027]
Tenure as nonregular worker	-0.061	0.540***	-0.479	0.00001	0.115***	-0.115	-0.911	1.152***	-0.241
	[0.021]	[0.092]	[0.053]	[0.0002]	[0.030]	[0.030]	[0.153]	[0.150]	[0.109]
Tenure as nonregular worker²	0.021***	-0.144	0.124**	-0.000001	-0.051	0.051**	0.300***	-0.335	0.036
	[0.001]	[0.052]	[0.053]	[0.0002]	[0.008]	[0.008]	[0.008]	[0.031]	[0.109]
Years in NEE	0.017***	0.347***	-0.365	0.0005	0.061***	-0.061	0.125***	0.175**	-0.3
	[0.006]	[0.052]	[0.053]	[0.0005]	[0.018]	[0.018]	[0.031]	[0.071]	[0.069]
Years in NEE2	-0.003	-0.084	0.087***	-0.0002	-0.022	0.022***	-0.011	-0.027	0.038
	[0.001]	[0.022]	[0.022]	[0.0002]	[0.018]	[0.008]	[0.008]	[0.071]	[0.069]
Number of kids (age 4–6)	0.001	-0.05	0.048	—	—	—	0.032**	0.002	-0.034
	[0.001]	[0.038]	[0.039]	—	—	—	[0.014]	[0.045]	[0.044]
Number of kids (age 0–3)	0.006***	-0.052	0.046	—	—	—	0.102***	-0.076	-0.026
	[0.002]	[0.028]	[0.029]	—	—	—	[0.022]	[0.040]	[0.034]
Income of spouse	0.119***	1.727***	-1.845	-0.0012	-0.5101	0.511*	1.152***	0.891*	-2.042
	[0.044]	[0.485]	[0.495]	[0.0018]	[0.2735]	[0.274]	[0.281]	[0.508]	[0.470]
Net financial assets	0.008**	-0.066	0.058	0.0003	-0.0036	0.003	0.079**	-0.178	0.098
	[0.004]	[0.059]	[0.060]	[0.0003]	[0.0165]	[0.017]	[0.032]	[0.084]	[0.082]

Note: This table reports marginal effects. Figures in brackets are standard errors. *, **, and *** indicate a coefficient is significant at the 10%, 5%, and 1% level, respectively. Details of the regional dummies and year dummies are not reported.

working as a regular worker. But for females, it decreases the probability of stopping work. Similar effects also can be seen from the estimated marginal effects of the experience variables. These results imply that there is a market segregation between regular and nonregular workers.

Table 9.4 presents the results of estimating wage functions for regular and nonregular workers, adjusted for sample selectivity. Standard errors are computed using the bootstrapping method with 500 replications. The estimated coefficients are consistent with theoretical expectations, and generally are significant except for nonregular work experience in the wage function for male workers.

It should be noted that the results in table 9.4 suggest that not all experience increases wages. While work experience as a regular worker seems to increase the wages of both regular and nonregular workers, work experience as a nonregular worker does not affect wages. Job seniority (tenure) as a regular worker increases the wages of regular workers, while job seniority as a nonregular worker does not significantly increase wages. It appears that neither the experience nor the seniority of nonregular workers are evaluated when wages are set; in contrast, both experience and seniority are evaluated if individuals are regular workers. This implies that there is a dualism in the Japanese labor market. That is, although regular workers accumulate human capital, nonregular workers hardly accumulate human capital, as OECD (2006) points out.

According to results from the whole sample, the female dummy is significantly negative. There appears to be direct gender discrimination after taking account of regular and nonregular worker wage differentials.

To examine the gender wage gap in more detail, the results of the Neuman-Oaxaca decomposition are presented in table 9.5. Although Johnes and Tanaka (2008) demonstrate that unjustifiable male-female wage differentials narrowed from 1994 onward, wage differentials that cannot be explained by observable characteristics still exist. All the decomposition results in table 9.5 show that there are significant wage differences between males and females that cannot be explained by differences in the observable characteristics of the two groups. That is, female workers will not receive the same wages as males even if they have the same characteristics as males and even if they are regular workers. There appears to be a significant difference in the effect of a university education on the wages of male and female regular workers. This also appears to be the case as relates to the effect of regular work experience on males and females. This implies that there exist male-female wage differentials due to the evaluation of human characteristics immediately after leaving school; these differentials widen as individuals accumulate regular work experience. This result also suggests there are differences in the promotion of males and females. It should be noted that as Neumark (1988) points out, this decomposition may be somewhat

Table 9.4 Wage Functions

	Whole				Male				Female			
	Regular Worker		Nonregular Worker		Regular Worker		Nonregular Worker		Regular Worker		Nonregular Worker	
	Coef	SE	Coef	SE	Coef	SE	Coef	SE	Coef	SE	Coef	SE
Junior high	-0.266***	0.066	-0.056	0.067	-0.339***	0.074	-0.002	0.186	0.153	0.102	-0.133	0.186
University	0.277***	0.023	0.223***	0.043	0.284***	0.025	0.148	0.096	0.173***	0.053	0.277***	0.096
Two-year college	0.136***	0.029	0.077**	0.031	0.081**	0.040	-0.068	0.133	0.139***	0.049	0.089	0.133
Regular worker experience	0.304***	0.046	0.099*	0.051	0.353***	0.058	0.371***	0.142	0.348***	0.104	0.086	0.142
Regular worker experience	-0.058***	0.012	-0.026	0.017	-0.067***	0.014	-0.098**	0.041	-0.099***	0.034	-0.039	0.041
Nonregular worker experience	-0.022	0.134	-0.083	0.108	-0.332*	0.199	-0.979	0.939	0.244	0.203	-0.073	0.939
Nonregular worker experience	0.080	0.063	0.050	0.047	0.186*	0.104	0.451	0.631	-0.105	0.101	0.049	0.631
Tenure as regular worker	0.225***	0.049	0.033	0.109	0.254***	0.052	0.350	0.360	0.269**	0.129	0.104	0.360
Tenure as regular worker	-0.006	0.014	-0.004	0.050	-0.012	0.014	-0.063	0.093	-0.003	0.040	-0.086	0.093
Tenure as nonregular worker	0.019	0.159	0.028	0.111	-0.014	0.247	0.152	0.666	0.292	0.275	-0.036	0.666
Tenure as nonregular worker	-0.011	0.108	0.026	0.056	0.059	0.152	-0.096	0.564	-0.267	0.213	0.052	0.564
Years in NEE	-0.184*	0.100	-0.213***	0.055	-0.186	0.149	-0.189	0.386	-0.214	0.134	-0.245	0.386
Years in NEE	0.085*	0.051	0.064***	0.023	0.119	0.082	0.080	0.168	0.003	0.071	0.074	0.168
Female	-0.163***	0.026	-0.104**	0.050	—		—		—		—	
IMR	-0.035	0.062	0.016	0.055	-0.246**	0.113	0.434	0.326	-0.014	0.089	0.005	0.326
Constant	6.991***	0.047	7.105***	0.099	6.900***	0.062	7.569***	0.575	6.859***	0.104	7.060***	0.575

Note: Standard errors are computed using bootstrapping with 500 replications. *, **, *** indicate a coefficient is significant at the 10%, 5%, and 1% level, respectively. Details of the regional dummies, and year dummies are not reported. IMR denotes the inverse Mill's ratio.

Table 9.5 Results of Neuman-Oaxaca Decomposition

	Nonregular Workers		Regular Workers	
	Unexplained	Explained	Unexplained	Explained
Junior high	5.50%	−3.40%	−5.5%***	1.00%
University	−26.30%	37.3%*	13.7%*	10.4%*
Two-year college	−8.90%	−9.00%	−1.60%	−10.5%*
Regular worker experience	90.7%*	−20.10%	53.9%**	−6.1%**
Nonregular worker experience	−120.10%	−0.40%	−5.40%	−5.70%
Tenure as regular worker	59.30%	−14.40%	−16.10%	35.8%***
Tenure as nonregular worker	9.30%	−3.00%	−0.60%	−2.20%
Years in NEE	7.70%	41.80%	3.0%**	9.30%
Total	77.6%**	22.4%**	66.0%**	34.0%**

Note: *, **, *** indicate significance at the 10%, 5%, and 1% levels, respectively. Details of the regional dummies, year dummies, and constant term are not reported. Decomposition results for wage differences that are due to differences in the sample selection term (third term in equation (6) are not reported.

ambiguous because the results may change when the decomposition basis changes from males to females. To avoid this ambiguity, this chapter tried another decomposition and compared the two results. While there are some differences in the significance levels of some variables and the signs for the explained differences of certain variables, the sign of the impact for regular worker experience is changed but still significant. This may be because Oaxaca's (1973) decomposition is not intended to analyze wage equations that include squared terms. However, the effect of tenure as a regular worker is unambiguous even when the decomposition base is changed. This implies that differences in tenure as a regular worker between males and females contribute to the gender wage gap for regular workers.

5. CONCLUSION

This chapter analyzes the gender wage gap, taking account of differences in the wage structures between regular workers and nonregular workers in Japan, using the new KHPS data set, which contains a wealth of information on the work history of individuals. The main empirical findings can be summarized as follows. Even for regular workers, the wage gap unexplained by observable characteristics in Japan still remains. There are four important reasons why the regular wage gap between the average pay of males and females in Japan is so large. First, regular work experience and seniority, which tend to be shorter for females than males, significantly affect wages. Second, there are significant differences in the evaluation of regular work experience in the wages of males and females. Third, there are significant differences in assessment of the value of a university degree, when it comes to the wages of males and females. Fourth, there are more males than females with university degrees, which significantly affects wages. In addition, there are significant differences between males and females as to the reasons why individuals choose to be regular workers. For example, having a child under age six significantly decreases the probability of a female being a regular worker, while this is not the case for males. This is one possible reason for the existence of the unexplained Japanese gender wage gap analyzed by Johnes and Tanaka (2008) and Miyoshi (2008), because this implies that females tend to leave the labor market more often or earlier than males do, and as a result accumulate less human capital.

These results are consistent with Johnes and Tanaka (2008), Miyoshi (2008), and Kimura (chapter 8, this volume). Although Johnes and Tanaka (2008) and Kimura (chapter 8) demonstrate that the gender wage gap has been shrinking recently, there still exists a gender wage gap in Japan. Kimura demonstrates that increases in working females with university degrees contribute to a shrinking gender wage gap, yet there are still significant gender differences in the evaluation of the value of a university degree.

These empirical results are also consistent with the marriage bar that Kimura describes. Having a preschool child significantly decreases the probability of a female being a regular worker who would receive higher pay.

Although the pattern that females of child-rearing age may exit the labor market is also evident in other countries, it is unique to Japan that educational attainments of females do not affect their employment decisions. According to the OECD (2002), the employment rate of Japanese females who have completed higher education (including the tertiary level) is 62.7%, the second lowest among listed OECD countries, and far less than the 82.1 % OECD average. The OECD (2002) notes that the employment rate of females with higher education is similar to that of lower-educated females in both Japan and Korea. The reason why the employment rate of females with higher education in Japan is lower than elsewhere is a topic of interest for researchers and deserves further study.

APPENDIX

This appendix briefly describes the decomposition method introduced by Neuman and Oaxaca (2004). Let X_m, X_f be the average values of the explanatory variables for males and females, respectively. Then, from equation (2) we obtain:

$$\overline{\ln W_{km}} = \overline{X_m}\beta_{km} + \overline{IMR_{km}}\lambda_{km}, \tag{3}$$

$$\overline{\ln W_{kf}} = \overline{X_f}\beta_{kf} + \overline{IMR_{kf}}\lambda_{kf}, \tag{4}$$

where the mean of the log of male (female) wages for group k is denoted by W_{km} (In W_{km}), and μ_{km} and μ_{kf} are the mean of the sample selection correction terms for males and females, respectively. Taking the difference of (3) and (4) and some simple manipulation means the mean of log of the wage gap can be written as:

$$\overline{\ln W_{km}} - \overline{\ln W_{kf}} = \overline{X_f}(\beta_{km} - \beta_{kf}) + \overline{IMR_{kf}}(\lambda_{km} - \lambda_{kf}) + (\overline{X_m} - \overline{X_f})\beta_{km} + (\overline{IMR_{km}} - \overline{IMR_{kf}})\lambda_{km} \tag{5}$$

Then the average logarithm of the wage gap can be decomposed as follows:

$$100\% = \frac{\overline{X_f}(\beta_{km} - \beta_{kf})}{(\overline{\ln W_{km}} - \overline{\ln W_{kf}})} + \frac{\overline{IMR_{kf}}(\lambda_{km} - \lambda_{kf})}{(\overline{\ln W_{km}} - \overline{\ln W_{kf}})} +$$
$$\frac{(\overline{X_m} - \overline{X_f})\beta_{km}}{(\overline{\ln W_{km}} - \overline{\ln W_{kf}})} + \frac{(\overline{IMR_{km}} - \overline{IMR_{kf}})\lambda_{km}}{(\overline{\ln W_{km}} - \overline{\ln W_{kf}})}. \tag{6}$$

The first two terms at the right-hand side of equation (6) are called the "unexplained difference," a difference in wages that may result from discrimination. The last two terms stand for wage differences that are due to differences in the observable characteristics of male and female workers, which are called the "explained difference."

Notes

The author is grateful to Colin McKenzie, Hideo Akabayashi, Miki Seko, Ryuhei Wakasugi, Souichi Ohta, and Yoshio Higuchi for their extremely helpful and constructive comments on an earlier draft, and also wishes to thank the participants at the Public Economics Seminar at Keio University, the annual meetings of the Japanese Economic Association in 2005 at Chuo University and the Conference on Global Studies Discrimination in Princeton in 2007. Research support, especially in relation to the supply of the data used in this chapter, provided by the Japanese Ministry of Education, Culture, Sports and Technology's 21st Century Center of Excellence Program, Development of a Theory of Market Quality and an Empirical Analysis Using Panel Data, awarded to the Graduate Schools of Economics, and Business and Commerce at Keio University, is gratefully acknowledged.
   Respondents are asked to indicate for each age which of these choices applied to them.
   1. All men who have children also participate in the labor market, so the coefficients relating to the number of children cannot be estimated for males.

10

Roadblocks at the High End

The Role of Caste in Postuniversity Employment

Katherine S. Newman and Ashwini Deshpande

Charges of reverse discrimination are commonplace in all countries with affirmative action. Underlying the issue of reverse discrimination is a popular view that, for instance in the United States, minorities are reaping enormous benefits from affirmative action, while qualified whites are languishing on the unemployment lines. To explore the legitimacy of the critique, sociologist Deirdre Royster (2003) developed a longitudinal study that inspired the present essay. Royster's project ferrets out these underlying attitudes and, more important, investigates the role that race plays in creating divergent and highly unequal patterns of employment and mobility among equally qualified blacks and whites.

In this chapter, we mimic Royster's methods to investigate the ways in which caste in India shapes the experience of students in elite universities, both while they are in the midst of their education and as they venture out into the labor market. In this context, public controversy over quota systems that provide for places in universities and public employment for the historically disenfranchised Dalits function similarly to debates in the United States over affirmative action. As Newman and Jodhka (chapter 11, this volume) point out, this "reservation" system has been in place in India since the constitution was ratified in 1949 and hence constitutes the oldest system of remedies for discrimination in the world.

Dalit students who qualify for reservations and their non-Dalit counterparts, who also face extraordinary competition for access to higher education, come together in the proving ground for future employment: the nation's top universities. It cannot be overstated how narrow this bottleneck is. Access to higher education is severely constrained relative to the demand; every place is coveted by hundreds, if not thousands, of applicants in India.

With so much at stake, claims about special privilege associated with quotas take on a particularly strident tone. Beneficiaries of reservations are often made to feel that they have stolen a place that rightfully belongs to someone more qualified, and their peers believe they lack the talent and drive to measure up. The less celebrated aspects of inequality—from differential school quality to the investments well-heeled families can afford in test preparation and tutoring, from the availability of legacy privileges to the upper hand that family resources provide in making donations to secure admissions—are rarely identified as unfair or responsible for special privileges that should be reexamined.

The claim of reverse discrimination often proceeds from the assumption that the playing field that leads to university entrance is level enough or that determining admission on any basis other than pure merit is inimical to modern practice, which should be based on competitive success alone. We have seen these attitudes in play among employers in the previous chapter.

THE ROYSTER STUDY AS A MODEL

Deirdre Royster (2003) followed 50 graduates (25 black and 25 white) from Baltimore's Glendale Vocational High School to examine the school-to-work transition for working-class black and white men.[1] She finds that in her carefully matched sample, race continued to be a powerful predictor of wages and employment. The median black man earned only 73% of the earnings of the median white man. Black men were 10% less likely than their white counterparts to be employed at the time of interviews. White men enjoyed an enormous advantage over black men with respect to job quality: 19 out of 25 white men had already held at least one desirable blue-collar job in the first two to three years after graduating, while only 8 out of 25 black men had done so.

These findings are particularly sobering in light of the fact that a substantially larger number of black men increased their skill sets and employability by paying for additional training themselves. Black and white men's trajectories began to diverge only two or three years after high school graduation. Despite equal or greater effort to develop marketable skills and work experience, black men were unable to either successfully pursue the trades they had studied in high school or to recover successfully after switching trade preferences, as their white peers seemed to do easily.

Why was this the case? Racial bias in hiring? Unmeasured differences in human capital? Royster (2003) argues that the most powerful explanations for the differentials lie in the constitution of social networks that can be mobilized in pursuit of employment. "Other things being equal—and in this study they are," she points out, "the stronger one's network, the better one's chances of making stable labor market transitions." (176)

In the United States, there was a time when families took primary responsibility for assisting non–college bound students with work entry difficulties, but now that families no longer have access to jobs in the manufacturing sector, schools are increasingly called upon to find ways to assist students in finding and getting work. This should help to level the racial playing field, particularly for students who are graduating from the same trade schools, as the blacks and whites in Royster's study have done.

Royster finds the contrast between how schools assist college-bound and work-bound students very stark. Students headed for higher education get abundant information on application procedures, selection criteria, placement rates, prestige ratings, and so forth from their high schools. Students aiming for the labor market are comparatively underserved: there is very little information on training or career options. For this reason, most work-bound students tend to rely on friends and family, rather than schools, for help in finding training and jobs. However, for minority youth, who are more likely than white youth to lack ties to employers, job trainers, and other employed people in general, schools may provide the only available information about and connections to employers or other post–high school options. Thus, school-based connections could be a potentially equalizing resource between white and black students but, in fact, seem not to be operating in this fashion because they do relatively little for students in either race group.

This leaves the private information system as virtually the only resource for the "forgotten half" of non–college bound workers.[2] Here, though, at every turn, white men are at an advantage compared to black men. Black men mainly know workers, while white men know bosses as well as workers. White contacts can recommend young men for jobs for which they have little or no training, whereas black men recommend young men only when there is evidence of training or expertise in the field. White men with contacts would be hired for desirable blue-collar jobs without interviews; black men would face screening interviews for all but the most menial jobs, and sometimes even for those.

Young white workers are neither permanently ejected from nor unduly stigmatized within networks if they act out or get into trouble. Young black men have to be extra careful not to confirm widely held stereotypes regarding their alleged irresponsibility and unfitness as workers. Young white men get many of their first experiences working in the small businesses of family members or neighbors, where mistakes can be quickly and quietly corrected. Young black men's first jobs may be in white-owned firms where early mistakes confirm racially biased suspicions.

While these major racial differences in early employment outcomes are clear, Royster considers two questions that could be raised about these results: (a) that these findings could indicate progress over an even worse situation— "things are bad but getting better"; and (b) these unequal outcomes may not reflect discrimination but hidden differences in school performance, motivation, and character. Based on detailed and pointed questions to measure the latter, she finds that in this sample, black and white men demonstrated similar academic, character, and motivation and preparedness levels.

Tragically, these are the young men who have done everything society could have asked of them and still they face rampant inequality in life chances, as Royster (2003: 102) explains:

> These findings are even more troubling when we recall that these are the young people who have done what society suggests they should: they have stayed in school, taken the "dirty" jobs, gone to school regularly, performed at a satisfactory level, stayed out of police trouble, and impressed school personnel. They have followed the rules, and yet they have been unable to get returns on their educational and behavioral investments comparable to those of their white peers.

She terms this result "ghetto results without ghetto residence," that is, "the three black disadvantages—lack of networks, lack of transportation, and the presence of discrimination—operate irrespective of class and residential advantages associated with being a member of the stable working or lower middle class."

Was the pattern of black disadvantage and white success recognized by the men she followed into the labor market? Interestingly, not only was the answer no, but a folk theory of white disadvantage developed instead. White men, who were extremely successful compared to their black peers, thought that racial quotas had limited their occupational options, giving their black peers an unfair advantage over them. None of the white students saw themselves as uniquely privileged compared to their black peers, not even those who admitted to having seen black workers put up with harassment on the job.

White men described the job process as meritocratic if they got the job but as biased in favor of blacks if they did not or suspected that they would not get the job. These convictions created disincentives for whites to incorporate blacks into their more effective networks. Why let the "advantaged" into that tent? The answer is that they did not.

RESEARCH DESIGN

In this chapter, we examine the experience of similarly qualified Indian students in some of the nation's most selective institutions of higher education as they move toward the labor market and ask to what extent they expect and then experience a level playing field or one tilted by caste advantage. Accordingly, we identified two groups of comparable university students from different caste backgrounds (in particular, reserved category or Dalit students, and the general category[3]) on the eve of their entry into the labor market and compare them in terms of job expectations, job search methods, actual placements, and the differential role that social networks (friends and family) play in determining their options in the world of work. The students in question have similar educational credentials, although they come from divergent personal backgrounds.

The students in this study were first interviewed during what they expected would be their last year of university.[4] One set of follow-up interviews has been completed so far with the students who graduated from the Delhi School master of arts program in economics, but because very few reservation students were in that sample, much of what we know at this point about the Dalit experience comes from informants who are still in graduate school.

The present chapter follows all of our respondents—Dalit and non-Dalit alike—for a period of about two years. For those who were in university for the duration, we have learned about their anticipatory experience as they prepare for work. But many respondents, particularly the Dalit students who are from poorer backgrounds, took jobs during their student years and hence already had significant employment experience. Finally, many had already landed full-time positions before graduating and hence had considerable knowledge of the matching process even if they had not been on the job yet.

The baseline questionnaire was administered to an initial sample of 108 students from Delhi University (DU, all in economics), Jawaharlal Nehru University (JNU), and Jamia Milia Islamia (JMI, in mixed disciplines) in April 2005. Given that Dalit students were a small proportion of the DU sample (owing to a low number of reservation students who met the rigorous minimum entrance standards and the high dropout rates from the economics program[5]), we added a second cohort of students in April 2006 from DU (again in economics) and from a mix of disciplines at JNU and JMI, with matching Dalit and non-Dalit students in each disciplinary cell.

The first follow-up was conducted in November and December 2006, which is roughly a year and a half after the baseline survey for the first part of the sample, and roughly six months after the baseline survey for the second part of the sample. Common to longitudinal studies everywhere, retaining our respondents has been a challenge.[6] Moreover, contrary to our initial (and their professed) expectation, not everyone from the initial sample entered the job market. Some failed to graduate, and among those who dropped out without the diploma, we were unable to contact any of the reservation students.[7] Some decided to repeat the final year of the master's program to improve their grades and for this reason did not enter the job market. However, this latter group is contactable and we have been in touch with them.

Our sample is primarily drawn from the three national universities: Delhi University (masters' students in economics), JNU (different disciplines), and JMI (different disciplines).[8] DU, JNU, and JMI would be considered among the best universities in India by any measure. It would be a reasonable guess that these universities enjoy a 10% acceptance rate. Even more grueling would be the Indian Institutes of Technology, which are on a par with MIT or Cal Tech in the United States. But the institutions out of which we have recruited our sample are next in line in the hierarchy of Indian higher education (table 10.1).

All the students in our sample completed their undergraduate programs and we have information about their final exam performance, that is, whether they qualified with a first (60% and above), second (50–59%), or a third (40–49%) division. We consider these data first since they help us to determine just how closely matched the two groups (reservation and non-reservation students) actually are.

We do find differences in undergraduate academic background, but they are not as stark as might be expected. Fewer Dalit students had first-class honors in their undergraduate degrees than nonreservation students (40% versus 46.3%) but this gap is modest, owing no doubt to the selection pressure induced by minimum scores on the postsecondary entrance exams. For both groups, most had entered their postgraduate training with second-class undergraduate degrees (57.14% of Dalits, and 53.7% of nonreservation students).

Over half of nonreservation students reported previous job experience, compared to about one-third of Dalit students. Nonreservation students were also more likely to report various computer skills. Most students had computer word-processing skills, but nearly 13% of Dalit students (and only 7% of non-Dalits) lacked that skill. Most students knew how to use the Excel spreadsheet program, but 27% of Dalits and 13% of nonreservation students lacked those skills. Nonreservation students were also much more

Table 10.1 Sample Composition

	Nonreserved	Reserved	Total
JNU	31	33	64
Jamia Milia Islamia	9	5	14
Delhi University	83	9	92
IGNOU	1	1	2

likely to have skills in constructing computer presentations with PowerPoint (79% compared to 55% of Dalit students).

Since Royster's (2003) respondents were in several ways atypical, she believes that her sample may have reflected "creaming" because the "sample may reflect those who were most likely to rise to the top or be seen as the cream of the crop, rather than those of average or mixed potential" (58). This is an advantage in her study since she deliberately sought to compare black and white men with as much potential for success as possible. Our Indian sample is part of the "creamy layer": it too captures students with a very high potential of success given their educational background. However, the selection is operating at different levels of human capital. The Indian study is looking at the very top of the educational hierarchy, where students are all aiming for the professional labor market.

PRELIMINARY RESULTS

These analyses include 173 students who were completing postgraduate degrees from four universities in the Delhi area. Over half (53%) were graduating from the MA program in economics from Delhi University. Most of the remaining students (38%) were completing degrees at JNU. About 35% were women and 65% were men.

Nearly 28% were reserved category students. Reserved category students were disproportionately men: 83% of the reserved category students, compared to 58% of nonreservation students, were men. In terms of religious or communal background, for the sample as a whole, 71% were Hindus and 12.7% were Muslims. The remaining students were Sikhs, Buddhists, Christians, and Jains.

Reservation students were found in all the religions other than Jainism. All of the Buddhist students, 60% of the Sikhs, 27% of Muslims, 25% of Hindus, and 14% of Christians were reservation students. These percentages are based on respondents' self-reporting about their eligibility for reservations. These percentages diverge from what we would obtain based on official reservation policy. Reservation applies mainly to Hindu and Sikh "Scheduled Castes" and not to Muslims and Christians, even if they are marked by caste internally within their faith.[9]

Diverging Expectations

Long before our sample confronted the labor market, their expectations of what they would find diverged by reservation or nonreservation status. These students were in the final months of their postgraduate studies, so that they had given considerable thought to their job prospects. In bivariate comparisons, graduating reservation students had significantly lower occupational expectations than their nonreservation counterparts. The average expected monthly salary for reservation students was Rs. 19,510, while nonreservation students expected to earn about Rs. 24,470. The median salary for the nonreservation students was Rs. 22,500 and that for the reserved category students was Rs. 15,000. While the average salary for the reserved group was lower, the variability (spread) of expected salary was higher.

We asked each student to describe their ideal job but also to tell us what job they realistically expected to find. The contrasts were sharp. The majority of Dalits listed jobs in the public sector: 45% mentioned administrative services/Indian Police Service, and another 28% would ideally seek jobs as teachers or academics or researchers. This reflects the operation of the affirmative action policy, which is applicable only to public sector enterprises and leaves the private sector completely untouched.

Nonreservation students were much more likely to report an ideal job as a business analyst or corporate planner (19% of nonreservation students, compared to 9% of Dalits) or in the social or development sector (15% compared to 2% for Dalits). Relatively few nonreservation students viewed administrative services as an ideal job (12% compared to 45% of Dalits).

The largest area of overlap in terms of an ideal job was in teaching, academic, and researcher jobs: many nonreservation students thought that ideal (30%), as did 28% of Dalits. Also confirming the lower expectations of Dalit students, a small minority of Dalit students (2%) thought of clerical-type office jobs as ideal, whereas none among the non-Dalits did.

There was a big disparity, for both categories, between their ideal job and the job they realistically expected to get. This is hardly surprising in view of the enormous glut of well-educated but unemployed or underemployed men and women in India. A large number of nonreservation students expected to find work as business analysts and planners (19%), while only 9.2% of Dalits had this expectation. Many nonreservation students also expected to find work as teachers, academics, or researchers (29.5%), but the proportion of reservation students expecting to find work in those occupations was slightly higher (30.5%).

Surprisingly, even though few Dalit students had listed planning or development as their ideal job, only about 2.4% listed this as the most realistic kind of job they thought they would actually find. The expectation among Dalit postgraduates that they would find jobs in the public sector is further confirmed by the proportion who had taken the requisite civil service exams. At the time of the baseline survey, far more reservation students (nearly 67%) had taken the civil service exam than nonreservation students (34%).

Family Businesses, Family Connections, Parental Education

The differential ability of reservation and nonreservation students to benefit from family resources—ranging from businesses where they might find employment to social networks that could be activated in the search for employment, to the cultural capital (or know-how) that will help inform a student of advantageous options—is very pronounced. For example, nearly 18% of nonreservation students said that someone in their family owned a business where the student might be employed, compared to only 8.5% of reservation students.

Students were asked whether they expected to rely on family connections in finding a job. About 20% of nonreservation students said they were likely to use family connections for this purpose, compared to about 10% of Dalit students. These two findings parallel Royster's observations about the advantages white men can call on in turning to friends and family members for employment in the small business sector.

Differences in family background (measured by parents' occupations) for the two groups of students are quite stark. The occupational distribution of fathers of the nonreservation students shows that the single largest category (16.5%) is either self-employed or in big business. Thereafter, we find fathers who are managers or in the banking sector (11.5%), are in voluntary retirement (11.5%), are doctors, engineers, software engineers, or in the information technology sector (10%), or are farmers (10%). Smaller proportions (around 5% each) are lawyers or chartered accountants and academics or researchers.

In contrast, the fathers of almost 33% of reservation students are farmers. This is followed by 15% of the fathers who are academics or researchers and lawyers, chartered accountants, and VRS (9% each). Another 8.6% are government servants or members of the civil service. Other than farming, all the other professions either have reservation quotas for public sector jobs, or the courses that lead to these occupations (medicine, engineering, law) can be pursued in government institutions via quotas. There is a small proportion, roughly 4% each, in the development sector and management or banking.

We asked the students if their mother was working outside the home. Some 58% of the nonreservation students had nonworking mothers, compared to 81% of Dalit students. Thus, an overwhelming majority of Dalit students in our sample came from single-income families. The distribution of occupations for mothers who were working was much wider for the nonreservation students compared to the Dalit students.

Reading this together with the disparities in the parental education level, we can get a sense of how different the family background for the two sets of students is. As the qualitative section shows, family background plays a huge role in the selection process during job interviews.

Job Search

Both reservation and nonreservation students searched for jobs in similar ways, using university-sponsored on-campus interviews (placement cells), answering newspaper advertisements, submitting résumés by mail and over the Web, turning to family connections, and off-campus "head hunters" or placement firms. However, reservation students were significantly less likely to use campus job fairs or placement cells and were significantly more likely to depend on newspaper ads than their nonreservation counterparts. Again, this illustrates the preference for public sector, government, and university jobs on the part of Dalit students, as a lot of private sector jobs are not advertised and government and public sector organizations cannot recruit without advertising.

Time to Find a Job

About 47% of the nonreserved students expected to find a job in two months; 75% expected to find a job in eight months; and 92% expected to find a job within a year. The maximum time quoted was two years. The average expected time was 5.25 months.

The expected time was, on the whole, longer for reservation students than general category students: 45% of the reserved students expected to find their ideal jobs in eight months; 82% of this category expected to find a job within a year; and 91% of the sample expected to find a job within 18 months (as compared to 12 months for the general category). The average time expected was 9.6 months.

MOVING INTO THE LABOR MARKET

These group differences are clearly reflected in the follow-up interviews. We begin with the perceptions and experiences of the Dalit students and then contrast their perspectives on educational opportunity, labor market entry, and the political conflicts surrounding the extension of reservation policy to the private sector, with those of their nonreservation counterparts.

Reservations Are Critical

Almost without exception, the Dalits in our sample endorsed the purpose of reservation policy and were convinced that without it, they would have had no chance to obtain a higher degree. "I am here because of reservations," noted Mukesh, a political science student at JNU. "Because of my background, even though I had the talent, I could not study because of financial problems. We never got a chance to buy books, to get tuition. But we got through because of reservations. I am ahead by a few steps because of reservations. There is nothing wrong with that."

Indeed, for Mukesh, quotas in higher education not only enabled his ascent in the university world, it literally enabled him and his fellow reservation students to "open their mouths," meaning to speak their minds and "go to the center of society," where they could "meet other people…and get a platform." The silence imposed by marginality, caste prejudice (enforced by atrocities, especially in rural areas), and poverty was broken by introducing these Dalit students to another world and a different future. They were well aware that without this social policy intervention, they could have remained stuck in a life that would never provide the kind of options they see before them now.

For those aware of the history of the political struggle that resulted in the creation of this quota system, reservation is seen as a noble commitment to equality, struck by the hero of the Dalit social movement, B. R. Ambedkar, the architect of the Indian constitution. This lineage is sacred to Dalit students, for it represents the first victory in a long and unfinished struggle for human rights and full equality. As Bir Singh, another politics student at JNU explained, that campaign remains as vital as ever as a source of inspiration for the poor and excluded:

> Ambedkar…used his education to free the SC/ST and OBC [Other Backward Castes] and to…solve their problems…on the basis of equality, liberty, and fraternity. He wanted to make them live with self-respect, and why he was able to do that? Because of education, because of the participation in this society in the form of reservation in every sphere of life.
>
> Education has created an ideal image in the minds of those people who are illiterate, an example where a person (girl or boy) who comes from a rural area [can] enjoy taking reservation in education institutions. He is learning, reading, and becoming a very high-status profile person. That gives an example which…gives courage and pride to the rest of the illiterate, poor people, who are not getting [an] education, who are suppressed socially and educationally.

These opportunities are critical not only because they promote social mobility, but because reservations literally rescue Dalits from a lifetime of exploitation at the hands of landlords, abusive employers, and neighbors who can turn on them without provocation and remind them forcefully of their subordinate status. Legal guarantees in the form of anti-atrocity regulations mean nothing in the context of weak enforcement.

Karunanidhi, a student of history at JNU, comes from a rural area near Madurai in Tamil Nadu, and is all too familiar with life under the heel.

"I am from a very remote background," he explained. Without reservations, he would have been stuck in a community where his safety was at risk.

> In my [native] place . . . [it] is very brutal, very uncivilized. They can kill anybody for a simple reason. . . . Because of reservations in higher education, I am here. I could not even imagine being here at JNU without reservations. . . .
>
> After my graduation [from undergraduate school], I worked continuously from six to eight hours [in a factory near my home]. If there is work, we have to work. We cannot delay. "Sir, I am tired. I worked so long!" You can't say that. If they call you, you have to go and work there whether you are sick or not, whether your father is sick or not. . . . This kind of exploitation is there. . . . I was working in Tiruppur [and the] rules and regulations of the company were on the wall . . . in English and Tamil.[10] But whatever goes on in the company is just the opposite. . . . There is no clean toilet . . . no hygienic environment [in the factory] for the workers.
>
> The girls are really exploited by the [hiring] agents and higher-positioned people in the factory. If these people asked girls to go to bed with them, they cannot [be] denied. They force the girls, though these people are educated. I think educated people do this kind of exploitation more than others.

Reservations rescued Karunanidhi from a future of this kind.

The policy has always been important to those at the bottom of a social pecking order that was resistant to change, grounded as it was in abiding caste hierarchies and the traditional, pernicious practice of pollution taboos that surrounded the lives of untouchables, especially in the more remote rural regions of India. Today, however, the importance of reservations—and the fear that their impact may diminish—is heightened by the recognition that the public sector is shrinking. The one sphere where these students could hope to find respectable employment is shedding jobs as liberalization puts pressure on government budgets. Globalization is creating enormous opportunities for the Indian economy, all of which fall into the private sector. High growth rates in corporate India have opened opportunities of the kind rarely seen before and it is common knowledge that the big money is to be made there. Increasingly, the public sector is seen as a backwater of inefficiency, and students who can manage it are flocking to the high technology sector.

Our interview subjects were well aware of this trend and worried by it since reservations do not presently apply to the private sector. Even if they are willing to trade lucrative opportunities (that may or may not be available to them on the grounds of bias or skill) for the accessibility and security of the public sector, this alternative is disappearing. The solution, they argue, is to see reservations extended to the private sector, to continue Ambedkar's mission of social justice to the domain where all the action is for the foreseeable future.

Amit, a political science student at JNU, argued that "both sectors should have reservation.... Now in India, it is the private sector that is getting bigger. Even in Delhi, just see the size of the public sector. It is very small. So SC/ST, OBC, and minorities should all get reservations. If they don't... where will these people adjust?"

This view was universally shared by the Dalit students for whom reservations policy is nothing more than a form of social engineering designed to address centuries of oppression and discrimination, extreme inequities in the distribution of educational opportunity, and the formation of a huge class of Indian citizens who are not equipped to compete without this assistance. These are not matters of history. Students cite countless examples from their own experience where they have been interrogated about their caste identities, castigated by prospective employers for their support of reservations, subjected to harassment or disrespect, and denied jobs (as far as they know) solely on account of their caste background.

As long as this injustice persists, they argue, reservations will be needed. The policy levels the playing field at the vital choke points of social mobility. They are not special privileges that unfairly advantage; they are compensation for historic and contemporary injustice that creates some measure of equality in outcomes. As Bhim, a reservation student studying Korean at JNU, points out, social engineering is necessary to modernize the country, to move it past a traditionalist, antiquated social system ridden with superstitious beliefs that are themselves antimeritocratic. "Because of reservations," he notes, "people of backward classes are developing."

> I think there should be reservation in both private and public sectors. Upper-caste people are holding important positions in both sectors. In [the] public sector all the positions at the top level are held by upper-caste people and they are also filling these positions with their relatives. If we are getting any jobs, we are getting only low-level jobs.
>
> Reservation is being misused by some people like one of my classmates, who was from the general category [but] made fake certificates [for himself] of SC/ST and captured one seat that [was supposed to be] for SC candidates. So there is need of proper implementation of policy. [Still,] because of this policy, people are coming from remote areas, they are getting admission, doing their courses and progressing well in their lives.

Of course, these students are aware that their sense of legitimacy is not shared by the dominant classes and castes in India. Reservations policy is condemned for punishing innocent nonreservation students for the damage done in the past, reinforcing caste lines rather than striving for a caste-free society, and exempting Dalits from the rigors of market competition. Critics argue that reservations replace one form of discrimination (again Dalits) with another, equally pernicious form (against nonreserved students or workers).

These arguments are unconvincing from the viewpoint of our reservation interviewees, though, who argue that the most powerful special privileges actually accrue to high-caste Hindus who can tap into exclusive social networks, bank on the cultural capital their families bequeath to them, or pay the bribes that are demanded by employers for access to jobs. As Rajesh, a student of Korean language and culture at JNU, notes, these forms of advantage are never criticized as unfair:

> Some people get admission in medical [school] after giving Rs. 25–30 lakh [in bribes]....They don't get admission on the basis of capability. The entry of these people is not ever opposed, but people are against the SC/ST/OBCs who get in on quota. They say that these SC/ST/OBC doctors are [incompetent], leaving their scissors and thread inside the patients' bodies during surgery. But people who [gain] admission through capitation fees, paying huge donations, why are these things [not] said about them?

Entry into the Labor Market

At this point in our study, 73% of the reserved students are still enrolled in advanced degree programs at the three universities from which we pulled our sample. However, given the needs they face to support themselves and their families, they are often seasoned in the ways of the labor market even at this point. In this section, we examine their experiences to date, for they lay the groundwork—both in terms of expectation formation and actual employment—for the more intense exposure to the competitive matching process to come when they seek positions commensurate with their educational credentials.

Our first observation is that despite their position as students from elite universities seeking employment, they are reminded at every turn that caste matters in the eyes of hiring managers. For many civil service positions, the lists of candidates to be interviewed are organized by caste and the information is not received in a neutral or respectful fashion. Om Prakash, a sociology student at JNU, applied for a teaching position—one of the 1,500 positions advertised that year. "They had written in the list...in a bracket [next to my name] 'SC.' Some [interviewers] were asking something of the SC candidates, but some other person was talking like this: 'Yeah, one knows how much talent they are having and what they can do' [sarcastically, derisively]."

Many complained that they would present themselves for job interviews only to discover that they were never given serious consideration, that the selection process had been unfair. Some said that the interview had clearly been a formality as the selection committee members had already made up their minds, and hence the questions they were asked concerned irrelevant matters having no bearing on the job at issue.

Several of the Dalit respondents explained that because they lacked "push" (influence), it was clear that they had no chance. An influential network of supporters is required to emerge from the crowd for desirable jobs both in the public and private sectors. At times money is the issue. Bribery is reportedly quite widespread. One respondent reports giving Rs. 10,000 for a job he did not get and explained that he was unable to get the money back. For most of these students, jobs known to require bribes are simply off limits: they don't have the money and cannot apply.

Chandrabhan, a politics student at JNU, applied for a civil service position in a Panchayat (council) in the district headquarters of home village. He was required to submit the application at the home of the council's headman rather than the official office. But when he tried to get information on the requirements of the post through his father, the headman excoriated his father for thinking that his highly qualified son would be seriously considered: "He told my papa, 'Why is [that boy] going for that job?' Actually, some influential people were going for that job, he told us. You cannot give money; you need to give a lot of money. That was really a shock for me. Someone like me goes for a job, then you get such a response."

Even perfectly legal hiring practices impose barriers on Dalit students from poor backgrounds. For example, traveling to an interview may be prohibitively expensive. Rakesh sat three examinations for jobs with the national railway company and when called for interviews far away, could not afford the expense of staying overnight or paying for his food. "One interview was in Calcutta," he explained; "another was in Guwahati. I had to go there and stay there and have meals there. For this, I need money that I was not having, so I could not attend that interview."

The signals of persistent caste barriers can be subtle as well as direct. Employers recognize surnames that are caste identified and then engage in questions that non-Dalits are never asked. Private-sector employers often raise pointed questions about the legitimacy of reservation policy, which does not presently apply to these firms, in order to place students on the defensive.

Kabir, a reservation student in political science at JNU, went for a job interview in a Delhi hotel in which this topic dominated the conversation:

> They asked me...what is the caste system in India? I answered that Indian society is divided by caste and religion. So they asked me...should there be reservations for SC/ST? I answered because SC people are facing problems, they are being discriminated against; their position is not good, they are backward. Why should there be this difference?...They said they have got reservation for 50 years. Why should [this] continue? I said because they want to be equal with others, so that is why reservation should be there for some more years.

They said it is not fair because some SC/ST people are getting privileges. They don't have knowledge. They don't have talent. Taking admissions in good universities/colleges and then coming out [as if they were equivalent to] general category students. I said, madam, they are working hard because they are not in good position economically and socially. But it will take time to be equal to the others.

As Newman and Jodhka (chapter 11, this volume) make clear, employers are given to asking questions of all applicants about their family background. For students from nonreservation backgrounds, the questions appear innocuous, and indeed they are regarded by everyone as normal human resources practice. For reservation students, however, honest answers will often lead them into the territory of the stigmatized. Employers want to test the suitability of applicants by learning whether or not their family members ratify their own claims to a particular status. They rarely do. Dalit fathers do not have the kinds of occupations that confirm the student applicant's suitability for professional jobs; their families are too large (a mark of poverty); and most of all, students are burdened by demands for support from their families (a quality that might be regarded as positive in the United States, for it denotes a responsible child, but seems to signal distraction or lack of flexibility in the Indian context).

Nathu Prasad, a politics student at JNU, applied for a job at a national research center. He expected to be asked "about my NET exam or my MA, but there was no need to ask about my background, income source and all these things."[11]

They asked me about my parents, what they do. So I said they own a small bit of land, they are farmers, but they also do small business. I got the feeling that I was being singled out for these kinds of questions. I later asked some other boys who were there and they said that they had not been asked. The psychological effect of those questions is very negative. Suppose you get selected. Then even after that, you will remain conscious since the person knows about your family background and that person may try to ... exploit you.

I don't think that these questions were neutral.... I knew the topic that I had to speak on. They knew my qualifications, so if they had asked about that I wouldn't have had any problem. Problem is that by asking other questions, they can find out about our "low label."

Nathu Prasad landed the job, but felt awkward that his family background factored into the equation; instead of being taken solely on his own merits, personal information that did not pertain to his qualifications was known by "company strangers."

Bidyut faced a harsh barrage over his family's circumstances following an equally discomfiting litany of remarks about reservations policy from the director of a firm. Everything from his regional origins to his parents' occupation was at issue:

> Explain where you belong to [I was told]. I said I am from Orissa.[12] "So how did you come here to Delhi?"...He asked me so many questions about my caste, my family, about my questions. First he asked me, "If you are from Orissa, why don't you settle down there?"...I said that in Orissa, the opportunities are very less, there is no chance [to make it]. I have been in Delhi already for one decade, so I want to join a job here because there are more opportunities. I am very interested in joining a good institute like yours. Then he asked, "Tell me about your background. What does your father do?" I told him I come from a very poor background. My father was a farmer. He died recently. Now my mother is there. My elder brother is there. I am very much responsible for my family, so I want to earn some money.

The director went on to imply that someone from his background should be applying elsewhere, forcing Bidyut on the defensive to make the case for why he should be considered at all. It was made clear that people who come from his family background were not welcome: "You people are struggling for life, so you are not that competent, [he told me]. I answer that is not true....They don't like SC/ST candidates in the private sector."

Dalit students are aware that these barriers are out there in the labor market well before their graduation from higher-degree courses. For some, concern runs so high that they decide to conceal the truth in hopes of landing the jobs they want. Arshad, a computer science student at JMI, knew that he would face discrimination on this basis and hence reconfigured his biography to look less stereotypically lower caste:

> Family background was asked, but I did not tell them reality, that we are six brothers and sisters. I told them that I have one brother and one sister. They asked me, "What is your father?" I told them he is a teacher. I thought it could have some positive impact because my family background will look like a small family and [my] father is a teacher.

It is a sad irony that in order for reservations policy to work in education and public employment, caste identity must be affixed to qualify. SC status is made clear in official records from high school graduation certificate to university files. If this knowledge was merely part of a bureaucratic record, the story would stop at that. But it becomes part of a moral narrative in which the student's right to the education he has received, his genuine talents, and his fitness for a job are questioned by those who hold negative assumptions on all three counts. In a society where educational opportunity is extremely scarce relative to the demand, in which good jobs are highly coveted since there are too few for all of the qualified people seeking them, the job interview becomes more than a means of matching applicants to positions. It becomes an occasion for political debate that throws Dalit students on the defensive.

THE OTHER SIDE OF THE FENCE

Royster's (2003) book chronicles the embittered views of white working-class students in the United States who also face a competitive labor market in which opportunities have been shrinking, even for skilled blue-collar labor. Lacking much of a grasp of the structural dimensions of this shift, her white interviewees relapse into a politics of blame, focusing on affirmative action and unfair racial preferences for minorities to explain declining opportunities. They certainly saw no particular advantages to being white, either in terms of the social networks they could rely on or in terms of employers' preferences.

Indian students—reserved and nonreserved alike—also face extraordinary competition for spaces in higher education and public and private employment. At the same time, India's unparalleled growth has opened up opportunities for university graduates, and the sense throughout our interviews was that students with advanced degrees can look forward to a much better future than might have been true in the past. These truths coincide and help to explain the fractured nature of nonreserved students' opinions on their own opportunity structure, the legitimacy of set-asides in higher education and employment, and their views on the best use of available resources for creating equal opportunity. The fractures are best understood as a consequence of deep and pervasive inequality in primary and secondary education (acknowledged by virtually all nonreserved students) and the inherent competition for scarce mobility resources, coupled with pronounced advantages in India (and the United States) for those at the top of the educational hierarchy.

Those inequalities are powerfully reflected in the overall experience of nonreserved (henceforth general) students in the labor market. These respondents reported far more favorable interviews and selection procedures when job hunting than reserved students, as well as a more positive "interpretive disposition." By this we mean that matching procedures that reserved and general students both experience are interpreted by the former as indicative of questionable intent, while experienced as neutral or even positive by general students.

Few general students were asked about their caste or religious background.[13] When asked about their family background, general students saw the questions as neutral in intent or an opportunity for them to shine because their families are more middle class in size and occupational background.

They were able to bring to bear on the job interview fluency in English, confidence in their academic skills, and advanced knowledge of what they would be expected to demonstrate in the way of fitness for the firm than Dalit students, whose cultural capital was weaker.

General students did not see themselves as privileged because of these qualities, even if they recognized that the distribution of these skills was differential. These are merely the talents that firms are looking for, including ease in social situations like interviews. This parallels one of Royster's findings that white men did not see themselves as advantaged, but rather as the neutral case.

Job Interviews

Bharat, a sociology student at JNU, typified the reaction of general students to their job interview experience. It is an occasion overlaid with tension, because an evaluation is in progress. But on the whole, interviews are a learning experience, not a test of cultural fitness: "The interview . . . teaches you a lot to handle the tension. . . . Just adjusting to the ambience, the environment of the interview, helps a lot. So many questions are asked and one question is followed by another. You need to keep your mind cool enough in special circumstances."

The only negative experience Bharat could remember from his many rounds of interviews was one where he was "asked to come at 10 A.M. and the interview began at 1:30 P.M." This was a "bitter experience," he noted.

General students experienced a problem that many reserved students interpreted as caste discrimination: the wired interview. For general students, the idea that a job has already been handed over to an inside candidate or someone with social connections superior to their own is a recognized fact. It happens all the time. Preeti, a Delhi School economics student, described the experience in detail:

> I went to another college [for an interview]. There was an internal candidate, so she was given the job and my interview lasted only two or three minutes. It was virtually decided that she had to be taken in. [The interview] was a formality for me. I did ask my professor [who was on the interview board], "You won't ask anything else?" He said, "Yes, I won't ask anything." They were not treating me seriously. I know because just 15 days [before] I faced [an interview at another college] and the interview lasted a complete half hour and asked lots of questions.

Preeti did not understand this experience as a commentary on her fitness; indeed, she regarded herself as perfectly well qualified, but outmaneuvered. The wired interview does not lead general students to believe that they will be shut out of upward mobility. If anything, it indicates to them that they too must cultivate their networks. For the Dalit student, a wired interview is one more piece of evidence that they are going to face a very long uphill struggle for mobility because they don't have easy access to the inside track.

The value of cultural capital, of understanding the social skills that need to be on display in an interview, cannot be overstated. With so many applicants qualified on the grounds of skills and knowledge, Indian firms are looking for people who fit, a matching process noted by American researchers of the labor market as well (Kirshenmann and Neckerman 1991). For general students, a university education is often a continuation of a lifelong process of cultivation not unlike what elite students in American Ivy League universities experience. They move into the task of job hunting with a degree of confidence that they have the social skills to function appropriately, to avoid being overly nervous, to project an air of cosmopolitanism that may be the final element that distinguishes them from other students with similar technical credentials.

Abhijit, a Delhi School general economics student, described his experience with job interviews in tones strikingly different from even the most positive encounters among the Dalit students:

> Most of my interviews are very relaxed. No one was assessing my knowledge or anything, but…seeing how well and efficiently I contribute to the company. So, positive feedback purely in fact that I had high success rate in terms of clearing interviews, that is making me feel good. I was competitive enough to get a job later if I wanted to.…
>
> None of my interviews were stressful at all. They were all very friendly for me. For example, when I had my interview with [information firm], he asked me why I want to work in Bombay. That is one of the cities that never sleeps and lots of stuff to do there. So the interview was more in terms of what I like, what I dislike, and general chitchat about what I was looking to do in the future rather than quizzing me about, let's say what particular topics I had done in a particular [academic] subject or something like that.

None of the Dalit students we interviewed expressed this kind of confidence. Even those who managed to land jobs were apprehensive and stressed by the interviews. They never had the feeling that their interest in the nightlife of the city where a firm was located was a centerpiece of conversation. Instead, they were often interrogated about their command of the academic subjects they had studied, and put on the defensive about the impact of the quota system.

Lacking cultural capital when they arrive in elite universities, Dalit students—most especially those from rural backgrounds—are not in a position to improve their cultural exposure beyond what they acquire inside the university itself. Those on-campus opportunities are important, of course. Coming to a place like JNU from a remote tribal region does indeed create occasions for exchange and personal growth in a cosmopolitan direction. But if one must work at the same time, it will be hard to take this any farther. Not so for non-reservation students who may have many opportunities to widen their horizons outside of the university during their years as students. Shreekant, a Delhi School economics student, commented on the ways in which he had been able to move outside of the university context to broaden himself:

> What I expected, I got from my study at Delhi School.... Other avenues ... like travel, I got enough chances to travel around India or other places through the university. After some time, university education helped me to form a general (overall) understanding and also a social circle. Also helped me to gain general skills....
>
> There are so many ingredients [to being successful]. The most important thing is the peer group. There is a circle of friends/acquaintances in which one gains confidence, learns skills. A person like this will get access easily and he can be identified as a suitable candidate. Now here the background is equally important. So things other than intelligence matter a lot. Most of these ingredients are acquired with money. So [a person's] economic background gives a lot of privileges and it becomes a requirement to access several things. But someone who is less qualified at entry can be trained and learn the requirements of the job.

The Family Background Test

Virtually all of our study subjects reported being asked about their family background during employment interviews. Questions about where they come from, what their parents do for a living, the types of jobs their siblings do, and the like were very common. However, nonreservation students can offer biographies that are much closer to the middle-class, professional ideal. Hence the questions are rarely interpreted as offensive or prying. And the answers are almost always in line with positive images of family life, as Aditya, a Delhi School economics student, recounted:

> [A] couple of people asked me about my family background, about what my father does, whether I have any siblings or what my mother does. No one asked me about my religion or caste. I told them that my dad is a government servant, he is working in the Indian railways and my mom is also in the bank of [my region]. My sister is a doctor. So that was more courtesy, interested kind of questions that the interviewer broached up. They made me more comfortable rather than judging me on what my parents do or not do. I am sure I did not make any negative kind of influence at all in my case. It might have had positive impact to see in terms of my parents are well educated and my sister is also well educated and everyone is doing well.

While Dalit students often perceive a hidden agenda in family background questions, for nonreservation students the same questions appear to be innocuous or sensible inquiries from a human resources perspective. They are not gotcha questions designed to discredit an applicant who is presenting herself as an educated, highly trained protoprofessional.[14] When asked, in our interviews, what these questions were there for, these students invariably had answers that made the whole subject seem completely uncomplicated. For example, Ashok, a Delhi School general economics student, noted, "Yes, I was asked about family background. 'Where do you come from? What is your family business?' I tell them I come from UP and my family is in agriculture." We then asked Ashok, "What do you think they were trying to get at?"

> Maybe they were trying to understand if I will stay on in the organization or leave soon. Because the one major problem that companies face is attrition. So, they do need a bit of an idea.... They try and gauge if I will stay or not looking at a variety of factors. The way I told them, it should have been positive information for them. Or at least I felt that way. They must have thought that I will work there.

It is impossible to judge who has the "right story" on family background from these interviews, and it is not clear that they are contradictory either. It is entirely possible that family background questions are used to identify caste or other background information that would be disqualifying in the eyes of employers who are not willing to employ Dalit applicants, or applicants with particularly needy families. It is also quite possible that human resource practice inclines firms to ask questions that help them ascertain the risks of attrition. The questions themselves do not provide a window on what they are used for when the winnowing process begins.

Yet if we couple these findings with the observations from studies of employer interviews (see chapter 10, this volume), there is some reason for concern that family background is used to ratify the claims presented on the surface by a job candidate to be a suitable person for a position, with siblings whose trajectories confirm his or her own "impression management" (to use Erving Goffman's well-known term). To the extent that this is the case, being able to give a socially acceptable answer about parental occupation or family size will be helpful. The converse could knock an otherwise qualified candidate out.

Equal Opportunity

Two distinct positions were evident among nonreservation students with respect to quotas aimed at increasing the representation of Dalits, Scheduled

Tribes, and OBCs in higher education and employment. The first simply rejects the notion that this is appropriate at all, since reservation policy is deemed a violation of fairness principles and therefore an unfair tipping of the scales in what is meant to be a competition on the basis of merit. A variant of this view sees quotas as perfectly appropriate, but not if drawn along caste lines. Instead, economic deprivation or social backwardness should be the appropriate test. Here we see lines of convergence with many Dalit students from rural areasm who also resent the application of reservation to the "creamy layer" within their own caste.

The second recognizes the legitimacy and purpose of reservations and seems to be enhanced by the interactive relations between Dalit and high-caste students. The more conservative posture falls in line with Royster's findings among white working-class students. The more liberal position emerges from contact and social relations that may be the positive by-product of desegregation. Indeed, when advocates in the United States argue for diversity in higher education, they make the point that mixing students up and ensuring that classrooms represent a rainbow of experience will enrich learning and create tolerance. Both outcomes are clear in our sample.

Akhilesh, a sociology general student from JNU, exemplifies the conservative reaction to quotas:

> I am not very happy with the Indian government actually bringing in such reservation. I feel that the people who actually need it the most do not get it. There should be a proper identification of who needs it. Since it is absolutely impossible for the Indian government to develop the skill to look for such people, they are giving it to the wrong people. Implementing it means they are actually dividing society. When we are looking for harmony, we are looking towards unity being in the same country.
>
> I think such barriers should not be allowed because when we are competing, we should compete on the basis of merit. Today one person is getting into IIT [Indian Institute of Technology[15]] with no brains whatsoever, just by virtue of reservations. Whereas certain excellent students are not getting into IIT because general quota is full....
>
> In jobs, also the same thing. Somebody who is an SC...gets the job and somebody like me who is not getting a job because I don't have any caste certificate....It should be equal because we are all living in the same country. If you can really identify the poorest people who have very low annual income...I think then there is some reason to support reservation.

As this quote suggests, Akhilesh objects to reservations on a number of grounds. First and foremost, they are benefiting a generation whose parents have already moved up in the social structure and have been able to give them benefits denied to other, much poorer and more remote young people. Second, unqualified students are displacing highly qualified students in the race to the top of the educational heap. Many—including the employers discussed at length in chapter 10 (this volume)—who share this view argue strenuously that the application of reservations will destroy the competitiveness of the Indian economy and drive away foreign investors because of the privileges ensured by reservation. Hence they fuse personal exclusion with a national downfall in the making.

Other critics of reservations argue that the policy may indeed be positive—in the sense that it redresses tremendous inequities—but ends up being a colossal waste because the high dropout rates that SC and ST students suffer from negates their impact. These places could have been taken by nonreservation students who would complete their demanding courses, but instead are taken by people who had almost no chance, by virtue of poor preparation. Kavita, an economics student at Delhi University, was sympathetic in many ways to the cause of reducing inequality, but discouraged by the outcomes on both sides:

> When I was a student, there were about 80 of us in college. Out of these, about 20 were from the quota. But by the time we reached the third year, virtually all of the reserved students dropped out, because they could not clear [pass] the courses.... Reservation should be given to them only in things that help them gain employment. If the cutoff [on entrance exams] is 90% and you are admitting a person with 35 or 40% in a course like econ, medical, or engineering, you very well know that he/she cannot be. He is not fit to clear the course.

This student went on to explain that forms of social segregation inside the universities did not help matters:

> They are not treated well when they go to colleges. [SC/ST students] have separate tables [for] lunch in college [dorms]. They get separate treatment. I don't know whether these people actually gain out of these quotas because lots of stress. OK, there have been people who completed their degree, but see in our college, there were hardly any.... General category students who were eligible could not get admission and had to go to other colleges or get into worse courses.... So this reservation policy is not achieving its objectives at all.

What is the value, she asks, of a policy that produces dropouts and deprives the capable of a place because they lack a quota on their side? This is a view many nonreservation students embrace.

But they do not speak with a monolithic voice. On the other side of the equation are nonreserved students for whom equality is a high principle, and the barriers to achieving it for historically oppressed peoples clear enough. They embrace the purpose of reservation and see in it the possibilities of upward mobility. Among these supporters, there are differences of opinion nonetheless about the effectiveness of reservations for some of the same reasons that critics voice: high dropout rates. The lesson to be learned for these more progressive students, though, is not to abandon reservations but to redouble efforts to address educational inequality at much younger ages. Without a massive commitment to improving primary school education, they argue, we cannot really expect reservations to succeed. If not for reasons of equity, then for reasons of efficiency, differential investment is required.

CONCLUSION

Following the lead of Deirdre Royster, this study traces the differential pathways that Dalit and non-Dalit students, from comparable, elite educational backgrounds, traverse in their journey from college to work. As was true in Royster's study, students from these two groups bring very different levels of resources—in the form of family connections, financial security during their university years, obligations to support parental households, and the like—to the starting gate. Hence while the training they receive in the university world and the credentials they can claim when they finish are quite comparable, Dalit students lack many advantages that turn out to be crucial and are subject to skepticism on the part of employers who doubt the legitimacy of reservations (and by extension, the legitimacy of the credentials they present during the job search).

Perhaps as a result, Dalit students from comparable degree programs as their high-caste counterparts have lower expectations and see themselves as disadvantaged because of their caste and family backgrounds. Because they arrive in college with weaker skills on average, they are playing catch-up and often do not succeed in pulling even with more advantaged students, and hence enter the job markets with weaker English language and computing skills.

Direct questions about caste affiliation are rare for both Dalit and non-Dalit students, but the catch-all question on family background is extensively used by employers to gauge the social and economic status of the applicant. One sees a clear class divide among Dalits, with those from rural backgrounds with relatively less educated parents at a clear disadvantage compared to their urban, second- or third-generation affirmative action beneficiary counterparts (the so-called creamy layer). Financial constraints are a serious stumbling block for rural Dalits and the good fortune of admission to the university is followed by significant burdens both for self-support and for contributions to their natal families' survival.

The competitive pressures experienced by general students from these elite universities are not insignificant, but they are encountered against a background of overwhelming advantage created by cultural and social capital, not to mention financial resources that smooth their way through a university education without the burden of providing for a poor family back home. They are confident that their educational advantages will pay off in the labor market and that the growth and modernization of India will place people like themselves in coveted positions. None of the signals they receive—from the admissions process, from instructors, or from employers—lead them to feel they must defend their right to compete. Their social experience is entirely different and leads to differential expectations, even at the starting gate of postuniversity employment.

These are the lasting legacies of caste inequality in India and in this chapter we see how they are internalized in the expectations and actual experiences of these two groups of students and job seekers.

Notes

1. She uses the case study method (in contrast to the existing studies that rely on survey and archival data) to answer what she calls the how and why questions: causal factors in processes or events that develop over time. As she points out, the case study approach, which differs from aggregate-level surveys and intimate ethnographic methodologies, nevertheless combines aspects of both. This is because it relies on semistructured interviewing techniques that use some of the same questions with all subjects but allow for considerable unstructured discussion between the interviewer and the respondents.

2. The William T. Grant Foundation issued an influential book in 1988 titled *The Forgotten Half: Pathways to Success for America's Youth and Young Families*, in which they drew attention to the wholly inadequate educational and training options for non–college bound youth in America.

3. We have used the term nonreserved for symmetry.

4. Our research design consists of administering a baseline questionnaire that respondents completed while they were still students but were very close to graduating. The plan is to track these students with a follow-up questionnaire at periodic intervals that has more focused questions about their job search efforts, interview experiences, and, if they have found a job, details about their job, their job satisfaction, and their overall views about the affirmative action policy.

5. Because the dropout rate of Dalit students is very high, by the time they reach the final semester, it is impossible to match the non-Dalit numbers with Dalit numbers.

6. While at the time of the baseline survey all respondents willingly gave their contact information, by the time we pursued them for the first follow-up survey, we found that either their contact information had changed or they were simply unreachable.

7. Given the difficulties of reaching those who dropped out, it is reasonable to surmise that the data presented in this chapter represent a best-case scenario for the Dalit respondents, since they are—on average—likely to be doing better than those we could not contact, who left the university without completing their degrees.

8. We also have two students from the Indira Gandhi National Open University (IGNOU), a distance learning university.

9. In several surveys, Christians and Muslims report themselves as Other Backward Castes (OBCs) and/or deserving of reservations. It needs to be noted that this reflects their self-perception about their relative disadvantage and/or discrimination toward their communities rather than the actual reservation policy. In the case of Muslims, it is more complicated because the government OBC list does include some Muslim jatis.

10. Tiruppur is a rapidly growing, important garment production and assembly center in Tamil Nadu.

11. Passing the NET (National Eligibility Test), an all-India examination conducted by the University Grants Commission, is a necessary condition to apply for a lecturer's (assistant professor) job. For higher-level teaching jobs (reader, professor), one is exempt from this examination.

12. One of the poorest states in India.

13. Although caste affiliation can often be identified by the use of occupationally connected surnames, religious background is much more apparent from last names.

14. Goffman (1959) uses the term "discrediting" information when describing the fault lines in an interactive setting that occur when someone makes a gaffe and inadvertently reveals that their claims to a particular identity are false.

15. Indian Institutes of Technology (IITs) are extremely prestigious engineering schools. They were established explicitly with the purpose of providing cutting-edge training in engineering and other science programs. Admission into IITs is highly competitive: the acceptance rate for undergraduate courses is about 1 in 55, with about 300,000 annual entrance test takers for 5,500 seats across the seven IITs. For SC/ST students, the cutoff for the entrance exam is lowered by 5%. IITs are not bound to fill the quota: in 2004, 112 out of 279 seats for ST and 11 out of 556 seats for SC were left vacant.

11

The Language of Globalization
Meritocracy, Productivity, and the Persistence of Caste-Based Stereotypes among Indian Employers

Katherine S. Newman and Surinder S. Jodhka

More than a decade ago, Joleen Kirshenman and Kathryn Neckerman interviewed Chicago area employers to try to understand the role they played in the production of unequal employment outcomes by race and gender. Recognizing that young black men, in particular, were plagued with high levels of unemployment, these sociologists sought to understand how hiring managers viewed the landscape of job applicants, how the stereotypes they employed affected their judgments about the qualifications of those who sought work. In their oft-cited chapter, "We'd Love to Hire Them, But..." Kirshenman and Neckerman (1991) discovered that employers believed black men were unreliable, unruly, poorly educated, and low skilled.

Audit experiments like those conducted by the Urban Institute and Princeton sociologist Devah Pager (2003, 2007) make it clear that racial discrimination is an ongoing problem in the United States and a key contributor to the employment gap between majority and minority members of the labor force. Employer interviews contribute to our understanding of the pathway by which this might occur. Hiring agents, who are choosing among people whom they don't know personally, are filtering the information presented to them—in applications and interviews—through a set of lenses that create higher hurdles for stigmatized groups.

The example of Kirshenman and Neckerman has seldom been followed, even in the United States, much less elsewhere in the world.[1] But the same goals that led them to study the social attitudes of employers and hiring managers in Chicago animated the present study of Indian employers in the formal sector.

BACKGROUND

India is a country with a huge unemployment problem, one so vast that it is hard to estimate with confidence its real contours. Like many third world countries, the growth of the informal sector—particularly pronounced among the low-skilled, rural migrants to large cities—has been enormous. Even so, the increasing importance of the formal sector in India's megacities has thrust the question of labor market discrimination in this domain to the fore.

Attewell and Thorat (chapter 12, this volume) have demonstrated in their audit experiment that lower-caste and Muslim job seekers are less successful than equally (or even less) qualified applicants from high-caste Hindu backgrounds. Their findings help to explain the enormous discrepancy in unemployment rates between higher- and lower-caste Indians and between Hindus and members of minority faiths.[2] But as is true in the U.S. case, the mechanism by which this differential develops requires further elucidation. To fill in some of the elements of that black box, we turn to the present study of employer attitudes in the formal sector in India.

We must note at the outset that one cannot extrapolate from the data contained here that the patterns of unemployment and underemployment of stigmatized groups in India can be laid fully at the feet of discriminatory actors, acting either consciously or unconsciously on stereotypical expectations to overlook or eliminate qualified workers. Our interview data cannot speak to the question of whether managers act on their preconceptions. They do not tell us whether clear statements, to the effect that "merit is the only thing that matters," are the real watchword of employment decisions either.

For evidence of discriminatory outcomes, we have to turn to the field experiment presented in chapter 12.[3] But because their analysis turns up fairly persistent evidence of discrimination under controlled conditions, the question of employer attitudes is important to pursue as one ingredient that contributes to the pattern of unemployment that plagues religious or caste-based minorities in India.

Accordingly, this chapter presents the results from a qualitative pilot study based on a convenience sample of 25 human resources (HR) managers in large firms based in New Delhi, but with satellite offices, manufacturing plants, and retail outlets all over the country. While this is a small sample, worthy of replication on a much larger scale, the firms involved are generally large, established, and responsible for a significant number of hiring decisions in any given year. We have employment totals for 22 of the 25 firms, and together they employ over 190,000 core workers (meaning they are on direct payroll), and data on contract or temporary employees for only eight firms, usually hired via outsourcing, for another 63,000 workers (table 11.1).[4]

Table 11.1 Sample Characteristics: Firm Types and Number of Employees

Firm Type	Core Workforce	Contract Employees
Construction	8,000	
Hotel	550	(100)
TV and magazine	700	
Auto manufacturer	4,500	(3,500)
Shoe manufacturer	10,000	(2,000)
Daily newspaper	3,000	(800)
Chemical company	1,100	
Tobacco manufacture/hotels	20,000	
Health care	4,000	(1,800)
Steel manufacturer	11,000	(10,000)
Food processor	150	
National airline	6,000	(2,400)
Security firm	100,000	
Alternative medicine	3,000	
Air conditioning manufacture	300	(700)
Courier/cargo	No data	
Public toilet placement/cleaning	3,500	
Retail home furnishings/clothing	No data	
Hotel	1,000	(100)
Automobile manufacturing	7,000	(42,000)
Watch manufacturing	2,800	
Hotel/restaurant/food processing	2,000	
Ice cream manufacturer	No data	
Communications/video	800	
E-commerce	135	

Lengthy on-site interviews were conducted in 2005–2006 with the heads of human relations or managers holding equivalent responsibilities for hiring and employment policy in each firm.[5] They were told that the purpose of the study was to explore employer perceptions of the Indian labor force and challenges involved in hiring policy. Our informants were first asked to describe the firm's history, size of the workforce, categories of employees, and labor search practices. They were then asked if they had any views on why members of the Scheduled Caste population display high levels of unemployment. Finally, we asked for their opinions of reservations policy, the longest-standing quota system in the world. In particular, we wanted to know their views on whether this policy instrument, which is legally required in public higher education, public employment, and the legislative branch of government, should be extended to the private sector. This is a matter of considerable controversy in India today, with business groups rallying to make their positions known. This is one of the first pilot studies to assess, in a formal fashion, the views of industry human relations leaders on this issue.

The smallest of the firms has only 135 core employees, while the largest has approximately 100,000. They range from manufacturing—still heavily represented in the city of Delhi—to service firms, especially hotels and restaurants. Many of the firms were founded as family enterprises and some still are. A number of them began as British-owned production companies in the colonial era, transferred to Indian management after Independence, and have now been absorbed into multinational firms. Most were family-run firms that have now transitioned to what interviewees refer to as professional management, by which they mean that network-based hiring has declined in favor of more formal sources of recruitment, including Web sites, newspaper advertisements, on-campus interviews, and "headhunters." These avenues do not entirely preclude the exercise of personal ties, as we shall see below, but it has become a matter of pride to move away from total reliance on in-group recruitment as the former is regarded as too traditional, while more formal and open routes have been deemed more modern.

MODERNISM AND MERIT

The most striking finding in the interviews was the view, expressed in virtually every interview, that workers should be recruited strictly according to merit. That this has not previously been the case in Indian industry was clearly understood and readily acknowledged. India is a country with a very long commercial history and for most of it, jobs were doled out in a nepotistic fashion, according to personal ties first, village ties second, and caste affinity third. These traditional practices served India well for centuries, and the notion that a precious resource, a job opportunity, should willingly be deeded over to a complete stranger—no matter how well qualified—was a perspective born of an entirely different culture.

Instead, the most natural practice of all was to trade jobs along the lines of personal networks, much as other resources would be exchanged. With labor in plentiful supply, competition for scarce employment prospects was severe enough on the inside of these networks to guarantee at least some level of competence.

Of course, India is not alone in this history. As the sociologist Max Weber (1968) pointed out in his classic work on the evolution of bureaucracy, the same practices obtained in Western countries, and whatever inequalities emerged as a result were simply accepted as the norm. It was not regarded as unfair or unfortunate; it was simply the way things worked. The rise of the professions in the West, with their elaborate systems of credentialing, interjected a different conceptual framework and corresponding practices. Qualification was now important and competition built up at the gateway to the institutions that certified the most desirable would-be businessmen, lawyers, doctors, teachers, accountants, and so forth. To be sure, nepotism and other forms of preferential selection played a role in the admission to credentialing institutions, but the concept of merit took hold as a public declaration in opposition to the old tradition of inherited privilege or I-scratch-your-back cronyism.

This attitude received a powerful shot in the arm with the invention of the civil service, a reform intended to break the back of corruption and distribute jobs more fairly than the traditional practice of rewarding friends, family, and coethnics. Civil service employment was a coveted good in Western counties and, throughout the colonial period, in India as well. Stable jobs, relatively well paid, respected (to a degree) by authorities, these jobs and the pathways that led to them were the essence of modernism in the marketplace.

The concept of merit as the sole legitimate basis for employment was built into the foundation of what Western employers see as modern. Belief in the paramount importance of merit as the key to productivity and economic efficiency remains high to this day, even though studies of the job matching process continue to show a powerful role for personal connections.[6]

Indian employers speak about the past—which was dominated by localism and favoritism—as a period best left behind. The more India takes its place as an economic powerhouse in the modern world, they explain, the more it must operate strictly in accord with meritocracy and utilize hiring practices that will achieve this goal. To do otherwise—either in the service of a potentially laudatory goal, like the advancement of Scheduled Castes or Scheduled Tribes, or goals that no one would admit to in public, the exclusion of these groups from employment—is to stick the country (and the firm in question) in the historical mud. Hence the language of meritocracy is firmly linked to modernism, efficiency, and productivity—all virtues to be nurtured in contemporary India—and anything that departs from this model must naturally be rejected (including all forms of social policy that are motivated by the intent to eradicate discrimination, as we discuss at length in the last section of this chapter).

A good example of the meritocratic perspective is found in our interview with a hiring manager at Global Productions—a major media company with its publishing headquarters in Delhi (interview 6) and bureaus in 16 Indian states.[7] The firm is about 80 years old and has a workforce of 3,000 core employees and another 800 who are hired through outsourced contracts. They recruit new employees on a national level for their main news staff and locally for their auxiliary bureaus. It is a publicly listed company, though the majority of the shares belong to the Indian family that purchased the firm after Independence.

When asked about whether particular groups compose the workforce, the manager responded, "Our workforce is quite diversified. No concentration on caste, creed, and colour...talent and merit does not go with one particular caste or creed." Pressed about whether popular stereotypes of castes or religious groups influence hiring, he was adamant that prejudice plays no role:

> No, things have changed. This was the perspective of the 1980s [before liberalization]. Today when you are casting your own future in an unknown market, the internal flexibility is very important. We don't put any kind of template on any individual.... We focus completely on merit. As our main goal is standardization...we also have defined what merit is.... We need people who are more exposed [to the world]. We believe power of imagination comes with exposure. Exposure makes you observe certain things and this stimulates the power of the imagination. If you have to be part of global culture, your leadership should be...defined by your capability of redefining...the company. And this can be...made possible only through the power of imagination.

For Global Productions, which relies on projecting a cosmopolitan image as part of its market appeal, there is a bottom-line value to recruiting people who are worldly, sophisticated, and well educated. In principle, individuals with this kind of cultural capital could come from any background. In practice, the institutions and experiences that produce cosmopolitanism are rarely accessible to members of the Scheduled Castes. Nowhere in the discourse of Global Productions' hiring practices do we see antagonism or exclusion toward the least favored members of Indian society. Indeed, quite the opposite. Throughout the interview, we see consistent pronouncements about talent and merit, without respect to "caste, creed, and color." But the production of merit is itself a highly unequal business and, hence, the linkage of modernism with merit, and merit with cultural capital, effectively eliminates Dalits, for example, from the competition.

Perhaps this is to be expected in a media company where image is so critical to the bottom line. Let us turn, then, to a manufacturing firm where this pressure is less evident. Food Futures, a 20-year-old company that sells processed agricultural products, is a small family-owned firm. They have a total workforce of 150 people, some of whom work in the Delhi headquarters, while others work in an industrial town in Punjab. As a fairly new firm, they embrace management practices that they believe are consistent with modern techniques. As the HR director explained, he sees no relationship between the quality of one's work and background characteristics such as caste:

> I haven't seen any kind of correlation between the religion of a person and his work. It is basically his caliber, attitude, and commitment that are seen. I have seen people from various castes. Some hailed from the so-called BIMARU states,[8] but they are very active and committed towards their work.... So, I never thought about caste and creed.

He acknowledges that not everyone shares his enlightened perspective and some actively practice an affirmative form of caste discrimination:

> Some owners of Indian companies come from a particular caste and the people who belong to this community may have some kind of positive discrimination. For example, a person who is a thriving businessman is always helped by people from his own caste or community, or the kind of friends he has also belong to the same caste.

Yet, from his perspective, this is not a modern attitude and it is fading quickly. It is more likely to be found outside major cities or in rural areas. "Such things are not very strong today," he explained. "About the impact of these stereotypes in recruitment, I don't think it works. No one recruits anyone on the basis of his caste or the region he comes from if he is not going to be useful."

Even so, he notes that "caste is a politically sensitive issue and there are people who are very particular about caste." They would tend to be people in smaller organizations who are more likely to "belong to the caste of the person who set up the company." But these practices are going the way of the past because globalization creates competitive pressures that wipe the conservative or backward practices of the past out of the way:

> I do see among my colleagues a kind of bias against these communities, stated or unstated. But now because of the competition being intensified, the corporations have started to overcome these issues. These things may be carried in small organizations ... as [they] are run by one single individual. Also, in family-owned organizations, there are these people who recruit people from their families, relatives, and villages. In professional organizations, these things have gone.

Hence, it is not that "casteism" or its cousin, in-group preference, has disappeared completely. As this manager sees the matter, an evolutionary trend is in progress. The firms most exposed to international competition and modern management have abandoned these vestiges of discriminatory tradition, while the smaller firms, that cater to local markets or rural employers who are far from the influences of large markets, are slower to accommodate. It is there, and only there, that these retrograde practices will persist.

The language of merit, the morally virtuous credo of competitive capitalism, subtracts from the conversation the many forms of institutional discrimination and disinvestment that prevent all members of a society from competing on a level playing field. It assumes that we begin from the same starting point (regardless of evidence of deprivation), enter equally efficacious credentialing institutions (despite the clear inequalities in schooling that take a heavy toll on the poor and low castes), and come out ranked objectively in terms of sheer quality.

FAMILY MATTERS

The American language of meritocracy similarly relies on the subtraction of institutional inequality, as well as the ability to overlook the persistent impact of historical discrimination that has left deep tracks in test score gaps and differential educational attainment by race and class. Whatever the consequences of these handicaps, the American variant nonetheless clings to the principle that the only thing that matters is individual capacity.

For Indian employers, there is no contradiction between an emphasis on individual merit and the notion of valuing family background, which, virtually every hiring manager emphasized, was critical in evaluating a potential employee. At least officially, Americans would view this notion as a contradiction in terms. The whole concept of the American dream rests on the notion that rising above one's station at birth, one's family of origin is essential to the very notion of merit. On this theory, it is no more legitimate to "dock" a job candidate for characteristics of his family than it is to reject him on the grounds of race, age, or gender.

This does not mean that background plays no role in the production of qualifications, for it surely does, but as explicit criteria for hiring, family characteristics are formally beyond the pale. In practice, of course, hiring at all levels of the American labor market is powerfully affected by kinship connections and friendship networks. But even when employers would admit that these linkages matter in introducing them to applicants, they would maintain that merit matters as the ultimate criterion of selection.

What kind of information is an Indian hiring manager seeking when she asks about a candidate's family background? For some, the concept is amorphous and would stretch to include virtually anything that was not directly related to educational credentials or work experience. For others, the idea was quite specific.

The HR manager of the India Shoe Company, a firm employing 10,000 core workers and 2,000 casual workers, focused on a variety of qualities entirely beyond the control of applicants, including:

1. Good background
2. Educated parents
3. Brother and sister working
4. Urban residence

The ABC firm employs more than 20,000 people over 60 locations throughout India. It has been an important corporation for over 100 years, selling agricultural items, clothing, and paper goods, among other diversified products. The 45-year-old Brahmin manager of ABC's HR department was clear that family background and the kind of setting in which a candidate was raised makes the difference between success and failure in a job applicant. "We ask them about family background," he noted, "depending upon the position applied [for] and the kind of task allotted with the position." The need to prove one's worthiness through family characteristics is most important for managerial workers, he explained. For lower-level workers, the assumption is that they would not pass muster on these grounds. Instead, they want to know whether a potential janitor (for one of the firm's hotels) has the same standards as those that the company wants to promote:

> Say, for example, in housekeeping, we generally avoid keeping people from slum areas because his appreciation for cleanliness will be different from us. For him, a dusty room would also be a clean room. If he is trainable, then there is no problem of taking him in the company. But in front office, we go for trained and professional people and they all belong to higher castes.

Whether or not someone appears to be "trainable" is going to be judged according to the interviewer's estimation of how far away from an assumed list of traits, born inexorably out of the neighborhood characteristics of his upbringing, the applicant can be coaxed to come. There is a barrier to be overcome, rather than a blank slate on which to build.

Why does family background matter so much? It seemed unnecessary to explain for nearly all of our informants; it is so important a part of the hiring system that the question seemed surprising. But when asked for more detail, respondents answered with a theory of socialization: merit is formed within the crucible of the family. The HR manager of Food Futures provided the most coherent expression of this theory:

> Personal traits are developed through the kind of interaction you have with society. Where you have been brought up, the kind of environment you have in your family, home, colony, and village—these things shape up your personal attributes. These determine a person's behavior and working in a group

with different kind of people. We have some projects abroad, and if a person doesn't behave properly with the people abroad, there is a loss for the company. Here, family comes in between whether the person behaves well and expresses himself in a professional way for a longer term and not for a short term. This is beneficial.

What one sees on the surface—credentials, expressed attitudes—is shaped in the bosom of the family. For the hiring manager, who cannot delve more deeply into the character of the applicant than surface characteristics, the successes of the rest of the job applicant's family stand in for proof that the individual before him is reliable, motivated, and worthy. If the answers do not come back in a desirable form, the surface impressions may be misleading. Doubt is cast on the qualities of the individual.

Mr. Soames, the hiring manager of a major manufacturing firm that employs over 2,800 people to produce some of the finest jewelry in India, echoed this sentiment in explaining what he learns from answers to questions about family background:

> We also ask a lot of questions related to family background: questions like how many family members are there, how many are educated, etc. The basic assumption behind these questions is that a good person comes from a good and educated family. If parents have good education, the children also have good education. Some questions about their schooling, such as what type of schooling and where did they [grow up].

The HR manager of the Cool Air Corporation, a family-run manufacturing firm that produces air conditioning units, echoes the same idea: "A good culture comes from a good family, good parenting. The person is also then stable. Not like people who come from worker's background."

As these managers see it, background characteristics of this kind are the source of "soft skills" that are an asset for the firm. The person who can manage adroitly in the organizational context of a firm hierarchy in India and abroad is going to contribute to the bottom line; the person who has trouble in these interactions will detract. But the surface evidence of soft skills is difficult to judge in an interview and, by the time it matters, managers seem to believe, it would be too late if the judgment of the hiring manager at the outset had been faulty. Hence, they search for corroborating information to shore up their estimation of an applicant's personal qualities and find it in the "data" on family background.

In Erving Goffman's (1959) terms, the employment or educational status of family members is a source of discrediting or corroborating information that either undermines or reinforces a job applicant's impression management. One could create a smooth persona, projecting the ability to work well in a corporate environment, but if the rest of the family does not line up with this projected self, the manager is alert to the cracks in the façade.

This is as close as we can come to pinpointing the underlying rationale behind questions on family background. A more compelling explanation for the practice, however, probably lies in the history of recruitment over the long run in which a scarce commodity like a job would rarely be given over to a stranger, but would become a gift in a reciprocal exchange system. One's status as a member of a family was (and still is, in many places) an integral part of personal identity and, in many respects, was only fully understood within the social coordinates of local society as a representative of the family, the village, or the caste. A firm is, therefore, not hiring an individual but, in some sense, is employing a representative of a larger social body: the family, the village, the tribe, the caste.

Regardless of the origins or the contemporary purpose of screening applicants on family background, the practice, almost by definition, will eliminate Dalits, Other Backward Castes (OBCs), and others for whom historic (and contemporary) patterns of discrimination have made it difficult to assemble the necessary credentials in employment or education. While there are Dalit families that have managed, through the reservation system, to overcome caste bias and find jobs that are respectable enough to help launch the careers of the next generation, the odds are against them. Of the 160 million Dalits in India, the majority are rural, landless laborers. Unemployment among them is high, and the occupations they hold will not lend credence to the efforts of an educated job applicant looking for work in the formal sector in India today. Urban Dalits are largely relegated to the informal sector and, if employed, are more likely than not to be in low-prestige positions. While pollution taboos have faded in the large urban centers, social exclusion remains pronounced and limits the mobility of Dalit families. The fortunate few who manage to get an education are far less likely to be able to produce the kind of evidence of sterling family background that an employer seeks.

We would be on safe ground in surmising that invoking family background in hiring decisions will act as a barrier to low-caste Indians in their search for employment. Ironically though, HR personnel point out that it will effectively put the brakes on the prospects of the well-to-do as well. If Dalits are too lowly, the scions of rich families are considered bad material for employment. As the HR managers see it, they are pampered and lazy and accustomed to getting jobs on the basis of connections alone. In the competitive world of global capitalism, this won't do either.

Security Services Inc. (SSI) is an enormous firm of over 100,000 employees. Begun in 1989, SSI provides security guards, training, and protection of everything from private firms to ATM machines. They operate in all of

India's major cities and can brag of over 500 client firms. Typically, they hire guards from rural areas, recruited for their physical strength and imposing stature. Their employees are "mostly from interior places where the state doesn't provide them jobs," the HR manager, Mr. Smith, explained. "[There is] no availability of jobs and poverty is more....They generally come out [of the hinterlands] and join us."

When the firm first began, Mr. Smith explained, they recruited workers informally and made heavy use of nepotism, tribalism, and local connections to address their almost chronic labor shortage. "Many people came up through references, children of earlier employees, people from the neighborhood." As time progressed, this was deemed "not professional," and now they recruit from regional colleges and "B-grade institutes" as well as the armed forces as sources of labor. Family background, however, continues to play a role. What the manager is trying to weed out, though, are people from families that are too elevated: "Somebody from a high-profile family—for him, the job is not very exciting. For example, a chartered accountant, he has to do a lot of work in the company. That kind of professionalism is not there [in a high-profile person]. So, that kind of person we may not like."

A car-manufacturing firm, now half foreign owned, employs 3,800 workers in one plant alone. It is in the process of building another and, hence, has been recruiting new workers of late. What do they look for in a new employee? "First is the qualification and relevant background," the HR manager explains. "If the person frequently changes jobs, he is not preferred." But this is not sufficient. One must be willing to work hard and that is a quality which this manager believes is absent from those at the top of the social structure: "We judge and prefer a person who is humble, not aggressive, and open to all....We see the family background. People who come from high-profile families are not preferred as they have an inner pride within them, which makes them arrogant. People from middle class are preferred."

Of course, the cost of exclusion for someone from the upper registers is not nearly so punishing as it is for those at the bottom. Nonetheless, it is important to recognize that the meritocratic model, which places family background in a central position, favors those industrious members of the middle classes or castes and makes life harder for those at the very top and the very bottom.

REGIONAL STEREOTYPES

Americans are familiar with the stereotypical reputations assigned to our regional cultures and the workers who come from them. America's southern states are often deemed languid and slow. Northeastern residents—particularly New Yorkers—are described as brusque, fast paced, and almost genetically rude. Californians are characterized as laid back and informal, superficially friendly, and obsessed with physique. Midwesterners are sober and plain, befitting the Scandinavian and German heritage of so many. Relatively little research has been done on the impact of these regional stereotypes on hiring patterns, at least compared with what we know about racial bias in employment decisions. Nonetheless, region is certainly in play as a background characteristic that, like height or weight, may play a role in determining an individual's life chances.

While India is known for its hierarchical caste system, our interviews suggest that equally pronounced regional stereotypes inhabit the minds of HR managers, particularly those whose firms hire a large part of the workforce from outside of large urban centers. Not only do they have firm ideas about the qualities that different regions inculcate in their residents, but they also worry about the social consequences of either throwing workers together in unbalanced combinations of antagonistic local groups or about the opposite, endangering solidarity within the workforce, based on caste, tribe, or village membership, in the service of opposition to management. India's states diverge sharply in their levels of economic development, though even the most prosperous cities (Mumbai, Delhi, etc.) are surrounded by vast slums. Still, Orissa and Bihar, to name only two examples, are among the poorest regions of the country, and are popularly regarded as backward economically and, concomitantly, economically.

The Kilim Chemical Company is a family owned business, founded 45 years ago to supply caustic soda to the aluminum manufacturing industry. They run manufacturing firms in remote regions of India where the raw materials are extracted and refined. One family owns 65% of the shares, but the firm is professionally managed, meaning it employs managerial staff that are not beholden to the family. Kilim has over 1,000 core workers on the payroll and, in addition, employs thousands of seasonal workers who are involved in salt manufacture, an essential element of caustic soda production. The HR manager, an economist employed by the firm for two years, tells that the firm is very stable. "We have extremely good industrial relations," he explained. "We have never had workers going on strike."

The firm is "widely recognized for [its] generosity.... There are people who have been working here for 20 years, 25 years, and 50 years." As is typical of many family firms, a paternalistic relationship obtains between the owners and the community surrounding the manufacturing plants. "[The owner] has a bungalow in [the township where the plant is located]. He goes there every two, three months and visits and then goes around the place. So everybody knows who he is. He is a *mai-baap* [mother-father], but in terms of welfare."

Though described as a shy man, the owner nonetheless makes a habit of turning up at village weddings to make contributions to the bride's father. In this respect, the firm is a kind of family, with obligations that stretch beyond the work world to the private sphere of kinship and households. Given this kind of integration, it is perhaps not surprising that the professional management can rattle off images of local ethnic groups that are strikingly categorical. "Are there any kind of stereotypes about labor?" we inquired. "I understand what you're talking about," the HR manager replied.

> Now it is a little impolite thing to say it on a tape recorder. There is a great deal [of stereotyping] about Uttar Pradesh people. There is a constant mimicking of Bihari laborers. Lazy guys, come in, drop in without work, you know, but we have no choice, we have to work with those kind of people, rather than people from Gujarat and Maharashrata....
>
> I can manage with these people, but in casual [conversation] we say he is so laid back. We have to adjust. The work I expect to be done in three minutes would probably take an hour and a half, but it will get done.

National Airlines, a fairly new transportation company, serves 45 cities in India and a variety of international destinations. It employs 8,400 workers, including those on regular and contract hiring agreements. Its core work-force tends toward management and high-level jobs, including pilots, air hostesses, and the like. Low-level jobs like loaders, cleaners, data entry operators, and sweepers are almost entirely contracted out, a common practice in Indian firms. A self-consciously modern firm, National Airlines maintains a Web site for employment applications, its preferred recruitment method.

When asked about the kinds of workers they employ with respect to background, region, or religion, the HR manager was completely open about the fact that they select on appearance, fluency in English, and cultural sophistication. "This is a service-providing industry," Mr. Gupta explained.

> We need good people, people who have some style and looks. A stylish guy, who also communicates well, speaks good English, who is very much educated, well grown, and who comes from a particular class, is preferred. So, we do not recruit anyone and everyone. We have identified some regions and communities from where we get our people. Say in north India, Punjabi culture is very much open; their faces have glow. But that is not the same case with Haryana culture, Uttar Pradesh, or Bihari culture. They are not good for us. Their cultures, their way of speaking and dealing with others, would not work in our company or in this industry. They don't have that openness.

A majority of air hostesses come from Punjabi families, as they are open. They can speak or communicate well. Some of them are from the northeast.

Mr. Gupta went on to explain that National Airlines likes to recruit *sardar* (Sikh) girls who are also well spoken. But they are not interested in just any *sardar*. Instead, they specifically seek out "those who come from good families.... Sardar girls won't speak well if they come from Himachal Pradesh. They may not be cultured."

Physical appearance is integral to Gupta's image of the right kind of employee for National Airlines. He has very definite ideas about whether one finds people with the right features, the requisite "glow on their faces." "Frankly speaking, people from urban areas are preferred more than those coming from a rural area in this company, because rural mentality does not suit us and the company."

He is of the view that girls whose fathers are in the military are a particularly good bet for jobs in the airline industry. "People who come from this particular culture," he notes, "have a tendency to come together and work for the company."

Security Services, discussed earlier in the context of family background, combines views about the appropriateness of particular regions as a source of employment with straightforward caste bias. Recruiting in rural areas, where laborers move in and out of agricultural labor and seasonal employment with firms like this one, they have come to know the Scheduled Tribes in the region. They know that when the harvest season arrives, their workforce will disappear for a month or two. But this varies by region, and the HR manager has developed very strong views of who will work out and who will flake out:

> If we go down to the south, say Chennai, Bangalore... that part of the country has a different attitude and they work much better. Basically, it is the culture of the area. The feedback from the customer is that the service in those regions is much better.
>
> If I go to Noida area [in Uttar Pradesh], the social system is not balanced. If I go to Gurgaon, it is the most horrifying because of the concentration of Jats there. They are very arrogant. In India, this is the community which is the most unsophisticated. The roughest community is the Haryanvi community. They don't understand logic; their blood starts boiling fast. In terms of discipline, commitment, and confinement to rule, I find it is least in these people.

Hiring managers who are themselves from urban areas are particularly uneasy about rural and tribal peoples and are prone to regard them in terms of group characteristics. They see tribals moving en masse into employment niches where they multiply through personal networks and then become a source of trouble. Urban dwellers are generally regarded as less trouble-some, even if they descend from rural populations that fall under suspicion. The tempering influence of a heterogeneous urban environment reduces tribal affiliations, or so the managers seem to see it. Hence, as long as these communities mix with others and appear less as a block, they are more acceptable targets for recruitment. Nonetheless, underlying stereotypes prevail, as Security Services sees the matter:

> In Delhi, they have a mixed background. There are Biharis, Oriyas, Gadwalis, Pahadis (Nepalese). So, these people behave well with high-profile people. If a group of Gadwalis [from the hills of north India] come together, then their behavior changes. Same is the case with Biharis. If they are one, one each, then there is no problem. If they come in masses, there is a problem.

India Motors, an automobile manufacturer based in Punjab, is now a multinational firm, jointly owned now by one of the major Japanese firms. Two production firms—one in Gurgaon and one in Dharuhera—have been in operation for more than 20 years. The India Motors payroll lists 4,500 workers, but the actual workforce is nearly double that number, since contract employees are brought on as temps. The senior HR manager, Mr. Vincor, who had been with the firm for 15 years, explained that the workforce that mans the plants is drawn from nearby areas and, hence, is dominated by the indigenous peoples of the area:

> The social profile of labor varies significantly in the two plants. The first plant in Dharuhera is dominated by the labor from nearby villages, which means they are mostly from Haryana. Since they were recruited from available labor locally, they are not very educated. In fact, most of them were trained by us.

Caste plays an important role in organizing the rural labor force. As Mr. Vincor explained, even the unions are structured by caste:

> Nearly 450 workers [in the first plant] belong to the local dominant caste of Jats and another 250 to 300 come from another dominant caste of Ahirs. Around 100 to 150 would be from different backward castes. Our workers are also organized on caste lines. Trade union elections are mostly on caste lines....
>
> Jat group is arrogant. It does not listen to anyone. Ahirs are tamed. Brahmans are more learned and they speak well, and SCs are not vocal.

These are not neutral observations. The social organization of caste provides a platform for collective grievances, and the firm has been on the receiving end of labor actions that can be more easily organized, given the caste lines in the workforces. "At times they are very aggressive," Vincor complained. "We have seen a lot of bad phase, strikes and lockouts."

The firm tries to temper the power of ethnic or caste-based organizing in two ways. First, the firm's owner maintains a paternalistic relationship that they hope will cut through these solidarities and engender loyalty to the firm. As part of its civic relations, India Motors builds hospitals, schools, water wells, and health camps. In this, they resemble the company towns of the American past. Between the personal gestures to family members and the infrastructure the firm provides, the link between worker and firm tightens into a dependency.

> The plant is everything for them, their *mai-baap*. They are loyal to the [owner's family]. Middle-level officers directly communicate with the chairman. The chairman also patronizes them. There are some occasions when workers can meet the chairman directly. The chairman also attends the employees' weddings or their children's weddings.

Second, they try, where possible, to "divide and rule" by limiting the number of like-caste individuals in any given part of the production process: "If we recruit 50 people, not more than 10 to 12 Jats are recruited and the rest should be from diverse background. We need loyal and obedient workforce: people who will listen to us and work religiously."

India Motors relies on hiring practices that promote a mix of castes rather than permitting the dominance of a single group. And they avoid those groups that management regards as oppositional in character, likely to refuse management dictates and threaten labor actions instead.

The company's second plant is described in very different terms. Here labor relations are more professional and less personalistic. Mr. Vincor regards the second plant as more modern, closer to the rest of the world economy in part because of its more impersonal labor practices. The language of globalization, which equates patrimonial bureaucracy and ethnic or caste-based hiring with the past, and formal mechanisms for hiring rather than personal networks, meritocratic principles (albeit in the context of family background), and national rather than local recruitment, represents a self-conscious effort to align India with international business culture, rather than traditional, customary, and ancient local practice.

The flip side of caste prejudice is a preference for specific groups, regional ethnicities, and religions, based on the view that they are particularly suited to a given occupation. Fitness Health Corporation, a relatively new firm owned by an upper-caste Sikh family, employs about 4,000 people in northern India, while another 1,800 workers—ranging from "ward boys to nurses, cleaners and receptionists"—are contract workers. Fitness is a new industry of private health providers that caters to relatively wealthy families. They are particular about the people they hire because they are serving an elite clientele.

The majority of our employees are local, most north Indians. We have peoples who have migrated from Noida and Gaziabad. However, most of our nurses are females coming from South India, especially from Kerala (Malu Christian girls).... They are better in knowledge than other girls and this is because they are doing the job from generation to generation and the knowledge is passed from one...to another.

Higher-caste people are reluctant to send their daughters in this nursing profession. They think that this is not a good profession, looking after the patients, cleaning them, and other things. The nurses [we hire] are mostly Christians, must be converted (from low-caste [Hindus]) or born Christians. They generally don't belong to Scheduled Castes. People coming from north India are mostly Punjabis, an average Punjabi girl.

As the HR manager—an upper-caste Hindu woman—makes clear, there are channels of recruitment in operation that have been, if not restricting, then at least providing insider advantage to regionally based religious groups. These preferences are based in part on traditional views of who will be willing to come into physical contact with patients and who patients will accept in that role. One could argue that this manager is merely describing a labor migration flow, rather than unveiling a preference that affects who the firm will hire among those who present themselves as applicants. There hardly seems to be a difference in practice. Fitness Health searches among the groups it sees as fit for the job and neither looks for nor entertains others easily.

Such a preferential policy often exists side by side with a bright line that excludes those who do not fit these stereotypical expectations. For Fitness Health, this clearly includes Dalits, who need not apply. "Among SCs," the manager explains, "there is a lack of technical skills. And their attitude is unmatchable for the company." Is this an unfair, an example of bigotry? No, she insists. "We have no prejudices about SCs and Muslims. This is a mind-set issue."

A "mind-set issue" echoes a global language of "psychological fit," often determined through the use of psychometric tests that have become popular among modern managers in multinational firms. These multiple choice personality assessments are considered scientific instruments that will assist employers in matching the needs of the firm with the intrinsic qualities of applicants. Only a few of the firms we studied employ them, but the ones that do tend to be in the most globalized industries, particularly communications.

RESERVATIONS

The constitution that marks India's founding as an independent nation was passed in 1949 in the midst of fierce political battles over the religious and ethnic composition of the country. Dalits, or untouchables as they were then termed, seeking to gain some leverage during Independence, agreed to remain inside the Hindu fold if they were guaranteed quotas in the public sector, especially higher education, employment, and in Parliament itself. Today 22.5% of public university seats, including those in the most elite institutions, are set aside for Scheduled Castes and Scheduled Tribes who are primarily rural landless laborers whose standard of living is abysmally poor.[9] In the 60 years since the creation of this reservation policy, a small (though impossible to measure with any certainty) proportion of these traditionally shunned groups have been able to claim places in public education, the civil service, and, finally, in the government itself.

These opportunities are vital to the upward mobility of the Dalit population. Even though only a small proportion ever gets this far, it is a right that is fiercely protected. Indeed, other groups (including the so-called OBCs) have lobbied to extend the policy to themselves, arguing that an additional 27% of seats in higher education be set aside for them.[10] The proposal sparked riots across India in 2006, as medical students and doctors took to the streets and fought pitched battles with the police, insisting that merit should be the only criterion for entry into these coveted programs and medical professions.

As eye-opening as these protests were, they are but the tip of a larger iceberg. The Indian economy has been gradually opening itself up to international competition, trade, and foreign investment. Pursuing a liberalization strategy, the state has been contracting in size while the growth of the private sector has been significant. Over the past three years, the country has averaged growth rates of about 7%, and today it represents the third largest economy in the world, behind only the United States and China (Walker 2007). It is a matter of some controversy as to whether or to what extent the nation's poor have benefited from these trends. In any case, the ground is slipping out from under public sector workers as the government continues to pursue the liberalization strategy and the future increasingly seems to lie with private employment.

This trend, in turn, has turned the attention of legislators and advocates concerned about continuing discrimination against lower castes to suggest that reservations policy be extended to the private sector. They argue that only if the private sector commits to affirmative action through quotas will the rights guaranteed in the constitution be protected.

Reservation in the private sector was uniformly opposed by the HR managers interviewed for this study. Not one in the entire portfolio of research subjects had anything positive to say about quota-based hiring. Ultimately, their objections trace back to the first topic raised in this chapter: the relationship between modernity and meritocracy. The future of the Indian economy, they argue, lies in increasing productivity and this, in turn, requires that each firm permit the "creamy layer" to rise, while the incompetent fail and disappear. There should be little need to justify this perspective, as the employers and managers see the matter: it is the natural way of Adam Smith's hidden hand, the only means to achieve the greater good.

From the perspective of HR managers, reservations policy inserts ascriptive criteria into the hiring process and short-circuits the competitive processes essential to the market. This way lies the ruination of India's economy and, hence, the policy must be stopped dead in its tracks. Interference in the name of social engineering will ultimately defeat the purpose of national growth, and the loss of international investment that would accompany quota regulations would strip the whole country of the capital it needs.

Beyond this general attack on reservation, there were a variety of subthemes worth exploring for the images they throw off of the underlying nature of low-caste workers. The first is the view that discrimination is not a problem at this stage in the development of India's labor market. It might have been an issue in the past, but India has turned a corner and as a modern nation, no longer thinks in terms of caste at all.

The most surprising example of this view came from the founder of an organization dedicated to reforming the occupation most often populated by Dalits, the urban scavengers. This firm runs public waste facilities in urban areas and provides employment, ostensibly to members of any caste, but in practice heavily subscribed by Dalits. The firm's birth was inspired by Gandhi's 1917 campaign to destigmatize the ex-untouchables by insisting that every caste Hindu should clean his own toilets, a principle adopted by the Congress Party and promoted by the government in the late 1950s. Waste Management Corporation was founded as a response to a public health initiative started in the late 1970s that was ideologically compatible with the destigmatization campaign and has spread all over India as an industry intended both to improve sanitation and to provide employment for those without more appealing options. Given this background, one might imagine the leadership of the firm would be acutely aware of employment discrimination. Not so.

"I haven't come across anywhere where a Scheduled Caste has been denied a job because he is a Scheduled Caste," the director explained. "Nobody can do it, even in the private sector. Private sector is more concerned about its profit and production. If someone is an asset, he or she is accepted....If a Schedule Caste person comes to me and he is brilliant, I will employ him."

Confidence in the basic fairness of the employment system was echoed in our interview with Mr. Palin, the manager of a large retail firm started 15 years ago to supply the growing Indian market with household products.

Today, the firm has 3,500 workers all over India and competes for workers who are not from the top universities and institutes, since the wages in retail are modest, but rather the graduates of less prestigious training programs. When asked whether reservations were a good idea or a necessary practice, he answered, "If a person is capable enough, he or she doesn't need reservation. There are enough jobs in the market; one can easily achieve what he wants."

What matters—according to those who believe that opportunity is ample and, therefore, reservations are unnecessary—is talent. Those that have it will find work, regardless of their caste background, and those who do not have it lack the necessary qualities and deserve to fail. As Mr. Sunasi, the HR manager of a large transportation firm, emphasized, cream rises:

> We don't hire people based on their caste and creed. The company sees only one thing and that is merit and that is the only one criteria.... I don't think there should be reservation on the basis of caste. Talent should be talent and should not be manipulated....
> There should be no reservation in the private sector. No company will allow it. They need educated people and recruit only on the basis of merit.

Virtually every interview we collected includes a statement to the same effect. Yet managers are aware that inequality is persistent, that low-caste individuals have less opportunity than others in the labor market. Few would argue that this state of affairs comes about just because talent is differentially distributed. Instead, they suggest that a human capital problem, created by an educational system that disadvantages Dalits and OBCs, is producing a talent deficit in this population. The hiring manager for Global Productions insisted that unequal education is the root of the problem. When asked why it was that Dalits are virtually never employed in top private sector jobs, she responded:

> I haven't thought [about] it that way. I don't think that it is true [that discrimination is at work]. I think it could be a lot to do [with] the way our society is developed. There could be possibility that because Dalits are economically weaker, so they haven't gone to best schools and colleges. That could be a reason. But if you have a level and a degree, no one can stop you.

Hence, the explanation for poverty and disadvantage in the lower castes has shifted away from the pollution taboos and enforced exclusion toward the institutions that certify talent. Almost to a person, the view among employers is that education—not affirmative action—is the key to uplifting the low-caste population.

And here, some would admit, India lags behind. It has not invested as heavily in education as it needs to do and should feel some obligation to remedy the problem. Dalit students attend inferior schools and this, business leaders agree, needs to be addressed. Pradeep Wig, the owner of Kwality Ice-Creams, is the author of an important report from the business community submitted to the prime minister in July 2006.[11] Wig is concerned that the government would even contemplate the idea of extending reservation to the private sector and likens the idea to the confiscation of private property.

What, then, is the appropriate diagnosis and remedy? "Frankly, corporations have no solution to the problem," he explained.

> We cannot progress in this regard [equal hiring] unless there is integrated schooling in India. In countries like USA, where you have integrated schooling, the young people grow up together. For 15 to 20 years of their life, they have been together in the school despite the difference of colors.... Industries have little role to play. One should not have more expectation from industry.

Hence, investment in education and encouraging integration to break down barriers that divide Indians by caste will pay off in leveling the playing field. Then, and only then, can business be expected to show equal hiring rates, because it will be choosing from among equally qualified applicants.

Business elites express confidence in the notion that once a greater investment has been made, the playing field will be level and the natural, market-driven sorting devices will be able to operate as they should. Yet it was striking in our interviews how often HR managers argued that the business community should forge ahead in hiring as if equality of educational opportunity was already a reality. Hence, Mr. Sunasi suggests, "Instead of reservation, provide them free schooling and, then, let them face the competition. If talent is there in them, it will come out. I am personally against reservation even in colleges and jobs."

His counterpart at Global Productions agrees. "Reservation," she told us, "this is a bad move."

> The caste or a particular social background does not qualify a person for any specific job. Why is a person getting into academics? A person gets in to perform, to achieve. So, you are killing the very purpose by letting people enter through reservation. You are killing your own institution.

She believes that investment in education for the poor will pay off as long as it is earned through hard work. Scholarships for the economically disadvantaged represent a sound response to the problem of underrepresentation of SCs in the formal sector:

> See [a lower-caste person's] economic situation, if you have to help him. Let him study well, let him get his marks and then wave off his fees. Do a favor! Yes, do a favor, wave off his fees and do that for any other, not for a particular caste, but that can be for anybody who provides the proof of income.

The fact that primary education is so weak in India, according to the manager of Security Services, puts the Scheduled Caste and poor children at a disadvantage from the very beginning:

> In my perspective, elementary education has to be strengthened. Any parent who doesn't send their children to school—the roadside beggars, the street children—they should be provided with primary schooling and it should be strengthened. They should be rigorous at the primary level; there should be standardization of education. Instead of giving them reservation in jobs and compromising merit, provide them elementary education.... Give them extra slots in schools for their personal grooming, overall personality development, and personal education. But [if we go] beyond this point, the country will go to hell.

His counterpart at the India Shoe Company echoes the same notion:

> We do not support reservation. Productivity will suffer and the company will suffer. The Scheduled Castes should be given opportunities in education and after that, they should compete on their own.... There should be no reservation for any category of population in education either.

What are the pitfalls of insisting on reservation for the moment? Here, a litany of problems emerges. First, employers argue, acquiring a job through a reservation policy destroys the incentive to be productive. The HR manager of Kilim Chemical Company is certain that anyone who gets a job as a consequence of government-induced social engineering will behave as if there is no relationship between performance and his ability to hold onto the job. He will take the position for granted and underperform. "In a corporate environment," he explained, "[reservation policy] is disastrous because people use it as a trick.... People take advantage and do not do any work.... This guy, like he says, because I am a Scheduled Caste, I will get away with anything that is not acceptable and it happens. That's number one."

This manager worries that grievances will follow if a scheduled caste person is passed over or not hired, not unlike the problems he encounters with trade unions, which, he thinks, make trouble when they don't get what they feel is their due. The trouble brings production to a halt and costs the company on the bottom line. "See, *main chamar hun is liye muj ko nahin select karte* [because I am a Chamar (SC), that's why I am not selected]. That kind of thing is bad. In the private sector, if you reserve, they will bring productivity down."

Americans familiar with the debate over welfare reform will recognize the language here, though it is oddly transposed into a work context. Charles Murray (1994), Lawrence Mead (2001), and other critics of the U.S. system of public assistance argued that it was fundamentally flawed because it removed all incentives to work and recommended dismantling non-work-related benefits in order to drive recipients into the labor force where they would have to sink or swim. Murray's and Mead's complaints had to do with what they saw as incentives to avoid the labor market altogether. Indian employers complain that reservation will incline low-caste workers not to work as hard as they would if they had to earn their job and worry about whether they could retain it. Multiply that times the millions of workers who would come into their organizations by virtue of quotas and, they argue, the productivity of their firms would collapse.

The assumption at work here is that the purpose of reservation is not to level the playing field or permit a deserving Dalit to gain a job he would otherwise be denied for reasons of prejudice. Instead, reservation represents a political victory that enables the unqualified to game the system, forcing firms to permit indolent time servers into a labor force that is scrambling to meet production targets. The hiring manager for Security Services says that he sees this problem at work when he recruits new employees from universities that practice quotas for Dalits in higher education. Their qualifications are simply not equal:

> In terms of caliber, competence, and delivery, these people are far lower than their batch mates [nonreservation classmates]. I had an engineer from [SC] background. We had to take this person because the salary structure was not so good and, hence, the lower rungs of IIT [Indian Institute of Technology] graduates will come in the company.
>
> He terribly disappointed me. No discipline, no competence, and no confidence. The person did not understand the basic rules and fundamentals. . . . He was looking for small personal benefits, cutting corners, low comprehensiveness, losing the character of the company because of low job delivery.
>
> I have experience of five to six people coming from such background. These people were from SC background, only carrying the tag of IIT, but no way compared to their batch mates.

The outcome of the experience, he explained, was that the firm raised wages to avoid being left with the dregs of the technical institutions.

For further proof of the damage reservation would do to firms' competitiveness, employers point to government organizations in their own fields. India has had public hospitals for many decades. The employment manager of Fitness Health, a private health care firm that operates hospitals for paying customers, looks upon his competition with contempt and believes that if his firm were forced to comply with reservation policy, they would end up in similar condition:

> If there [is] reservation in this company, nurses and ward boys won't work and pay less attention to patients. See what is happening in government departments. Incapable people are pushed in and, ultimately, we all lose.

These people do not work hard. They enter with low [grades]. Our job is very technical and incompetent people cannot be relied upon to [do] such work. There is no place for poor education and technical skills in our institution. Our company will resist any kind of caste-based reservation.

According to these employers, not only does reservation policy let the scheduled caste beneficiaries off the hook, but it also has the potential to spread a watered-down work ethic to others, or so the manager of Global Productions explains. We inquired, "What has the reservation system done to India's education system?" He responded, "Somewhere, it affects the people who work hard. It demotivates them."

Dalits fail under reservation, we were told, in part because they have internalized the negative expectations that underlie the policy. Here employers reflected an acquaintance with the position taken by some American black conservatives that affirmative action casts doubt on the capabilities of its beneficiaries, as well as race mates who compete and succeed without any assistance from social policies. This view posits that white students or employees in American schools and firms will come to see any black person as substandard and able to gain entry to an elite institution only with the special help of a selection system that gives him or her preference for ascriptive reasons. Conservatives like Ward Connerly go on to argue that these preferential admissions policies undermine the self-confidence of minority students who come to believe that they are not really good enough to be in elite institutions.[12] If the policy is dismantled, the only people who will be admitted are those who meet universal standards.

Pradeep Wig, the author of the report from the business community to the Prime Minister on the subject of inclusive employment, is inclined to extend this diagnosis to the Indian case as well. "The lower-caste people are scared," he insists. "They have already accepted that they are smaller [less capable] than the high-caste people.... They have a low confidence level. I had one person from SC background; he is a scared fellow. He doesn't even speak with me. They are so much oppressed that he doesn't even question me."

Reservation exacerbates the problem, he claims, because it reinforces the view that absent a special boost, the SC employee would never hold the job he has. What is more, Wig worries, reservation will increase rather than decrease "casteism" in Indian firms. It will "increase the divide in companies" as positions are doled out via background characteristics rather than personal qualities. Groups will form to protect their positions within the private sector, and the result will be division everywhere.

Trouble will follow as groups align themselves in opposition to the privileges extended to some. Employers can see that something of this kind has already happened in higher education, as upper-caste students rally outside the medical schools to protest the claims of OBCs to a reservation quota for themselves. They fear similar forms of disruption in their own organizations if reservations are imposed on the private sector.

Finally, we see in some interviews arguments for fairness that see in reservation the creation of unfair advantage and inherited rights. On this account, reservation is itself unequally distributed. The Jodor Steel Company is 30 years old and has production facilities all over India. The firm produces pipes that supply gasoline and oil, and employs 12,000 core employees and an equal number of temporary workers. Owned by a Baniya family, traditional traders from northern India, the Jodor Company is a powerful manufacturing firm that employs tribal peoples in the hinterlands all over India. The manager, who participated in this project, had experience of working in both the private and public sector. He was of the firm opinion that reservation policy is a disaster because it has become the preserve of one class of Dalits:

> It is high time we should get out of [the quota system]. We must stop this. No one should avail of such a facility. It has become a privilege for them. Father was taking it; then his son and now his great-grandson. It then becomes institutionalized. Government should stop it. Only the urban Dalits take the benefit of it and [the] rural class is kept deprived.

Readers familiar with William Julius Wilson's (1996) argument in *The Truly Disadvantaged* will recognize a common theme here. Wilson argued that race-based affirmative action, while beneficial in many ways, ultimately would do little for the poor. Middle-class African Americans would be best able to compete under these conditions, while the poor would be unable to benefit. This is why Wilson argued for economic disadvantage as the basis for affirmative action. Both for reasons of political appeal to color-blind policy and because the poor are the most likely to need recognition of special barriers, Wilson argued in favor of more universal policies with targeted benefits.

In the end, though, it would appear that reservation policy is a complete no-go from the corporate perspective. In the 25 interviews we had, there was not a single supporter of the idea. At most, hiring managers were willing to support policies of educational investment, scholarships to reward deserving students, as a means of encouraging meritorious behavior and the future benefits that are presumed to go with high achievement.

As the HR manager of Security Systems summed up the situation, nothing in the Indian experience of reservation policy since Independence inspires confidence that it is a viable or desirable route for the private sector. Instead, it should be dismantled everywhere else:

> Why should we need reservation after 60 years of [it]? We have not done our jobs, as corporate ventures, as politicians. It is just a waste of the country. Sixty years and every 10 to 15 years, their generations have changed and there is no material change at all. Sixty years and that's enough. No more reservations are required.

India's success in the international marketplace provides ample justification, as this manager sees it, for the wisdom of promoting competition, meritocracy, and investment in the best. The least well off will receive the trickle-down benefits of high growth if the country avoids fettering itself with anticompetitive policies.

> All our Indian universities have tied up with foreign universities, and now what for we need reservation? Today it has reversed; foreign companies are coming and tying with us. Indian firms are opening up campuses outside [of India] because they have intellect to cater to others. Why can't people from SCs come up?
>
> We have spoiled the country and played with the people for 50 years.... It is people like us who are paying for these people.

IN THE NAME OF GLOBALIZATION

The language of meritocracy has spread around the globe along with the competitive capitalism that gave birth to it. Largely gone is the notion that patrimonial ties, reciprocal obligations, and birthright should guarantee access to critical resources like jobs. That those ascriptive characteristics continue to matter—now dressed up as family background rather than caste—hardly causes the managers we interviewed to skip a beat. They are convinced that modernism is the future of their firms and the future of the country. It calls for the adoption of labor market practices that the advanced capitalist world embraces and a blind eye to the uneven playing field that produces merit in the first place.

What are the consequences of this cultural shift, of the spread of a common language that resonates with moral precepts of fairness and level playing fields? Can one argue against meritocracy in the modern world? Two responses come to mind. First, as we have suggested in this chapter, the belief in merit is only sometimes accompanied by a truly caste-blind orientation. Instead, we see the commitment to merit voiced alongside convictions that merit is distributed by caste or region and, hence, the qualities of individuals fade from view, replaced by stereotypes that—at best—will make it harder for a highly qualified low-caste job applicant to gain recognition for his or her skills and accomplishments. At worst, they will be excluded simply by virtue of birthright. Under these circumstances, one must take the profession of deep belief in meritocracy with a heavy grain of salt. Antidiscrimination law is required to insist on the actual implementation of caste-blind policies of meritocratic hiring and, we submit, to question common and accepted practices of assessing family background as a hiring qualification, for it may amount to another way of discovering caste.

Second, the findings in this chapter return us to the question of how merit is produced in the first place. The distribution of credentials, particularly in the form of education, is hardly a function of individual talent alone. It reflects differential investment in public schools, health care, nutrition, and the like. Institutional discrimination of this kind sets up millions of low-caste Indians for a lifetime of poverty and disadvantage. As long as the playing field is this tilted, there can be no real meaning to meritocracy conceived of as a fair tournament.

This is not to suggest that a commitment to competition is, in and of itself, a bad idea or a value to be dismissed. It is a vast improvement over unshakeable beliefs in racial, religious, or caste inferiority, for it admits of the possibility that talent is everywhere. Until the day that institutional investments are fairly distributed, policy alternatives will be needed to ensure that stereotypes do not unfairly block the opportunities of low-caste Indians and rural job applicants.

Notes

1. An exception would include Philip Moss and Chris Tilly (2001), *Stories Employers Tell: Race, Skill and Hiring in America.* For a perspective of employer attitudes based on survey research, see Harry Holzer (1999), *What Employers Want: Job Prospects for Less-Educated Workers.*

2. The official unemployment rate among the Scheduled Castes in urban India is 10.5% as against 8.2% for the other backward castes and 6.8% among upper-caste Hindus. It was 8.1% among Muslims and 10.9% among other minorities. Unemployment for the entire urban population was 8.3%. These figures are based on the 61st round of the National Sample Survey carried out in 2004–2005. Government of India (2006).

3. It is more likely the case that employers and hiring managers understate the degree to which bias influences hiring than that they overstate it. As Pager and Quillian (2005) show in a comparison of results from an audit study and a telephone survey of the same employers, those who indicate an equal willingness to hire black and white ex-offenders actually display large differences by race in audit experiments where they are given an opportunity to consider matched pairs differentiated only by race.

4. Hiring managers often do not know exactly how many contract or temporary workers their own firms employ, particularly if they are spread out all over the country. Hence, it could easily be the case that the total workforce of these firms is closer to 300,000 than the 210,000 we can total up. But the data on the demographics of

contract labor are less reliable by far than what we have on the core labor force and, in any case, the hiring managers who participated in this study are not responsible for actual hiring decisions where contract labor is concerned. This is an important limitation, though, because for many low-skilled Dalits, the opportunities provided by contract positions are undoubtedly more important than the positions that are at issue for the core labor force.

5. All interviews were conducted by Surinder Jodhka in English or Hindi, depending on the linguistic comfort of the interviewee.

6. Ott et al. (2008) provide survey data to show that 74% of job seekers rely on friends and family when looking for employment.

7. All company names have been changed and identifying details modified slightly to protect the privacy of the firm and that of our interview subjects.

8. BIMARU is an acronym coined by demographer Ashish Bose to refer to India's less developed states of Binhar, Madhya Pradesh, Rajasthan, and Uttar Pradesh. The word *bimaru* in Hindi means someone who is perennially ill.

9. Having long suffered from pollution taboos that forbid the higher castes to associate with them, Dalits were confined to jobs (often no more than forced labor) as "scavengers," responsible for cleaning latrines, dealing with dead bodies or animals, and working with leather, which must be cured in urine. All of these traditional occupations are regarded with disgust by other castes. Gandhi famously insisted that his fellow Brahmins clean their own toilets and for this, he was regarded as a turncoat by millions of high-caste Hindus.

10. Sengupta and Kumar (2006). OBCs pushed for an additional 27% of positions in higher education to be reserved for them.

11. ASSOCHAM report, *Concrete Steps by Indian Industry on Inclusiveness for the Scheduled Castes and Scheduled Tribes*, submitted to the Prime Minister of India, July 27, 2006. Pradeep Wig is the only participant in our project whose real name is being used here because he is speaking as a public figure, the author of a major government report, rather than as a business owner whose hiring practices are at issue.

12. Ward Connerly is the former regent of the University of California who has sponsored successful ballot initiatives to make affirmative action by race or ethnicity illegal, on the grounds that it diminishes the confidence of minority students, causing them to question the legitimacy of their own achievements, as well as the illegitimacy of policies that are not "color blind."

12

Caste Is Not Past

The Persistence of Discrimination in India's Formal Labor Market

Paul Attewell and Sukhadeo Thorat

INTRODUCTION

Current patterns of socioeconomic inequality within nations are often inter-twined with much older systems of stratification and social exclusion. In most nations, however, groups at the bottom of the stratification order have either won or have been granted rights of equal citizenship. Nowadays, modern constitutions and legal codes outlaw the more violent or oppressive forms of social exclusion that were common in the past. In some countries, lawmakers have gone further to offer group-specific rights and privileges intended to redress past wrongs (Darity and Deshpande 2003).

Ironically, the existence of these rights and protections leads many persons in the social mainstream—those not from a stigmatized or economically disadvantaged group—to conclude that discrimination is a thing of the past (Pager 2007). The fact that certain social groups remain disproportionately poor, despite these legal safeguards, is often attributed to the group's low levels of education, or to their concentration in economically backward sectors. When continuing discrimination is acknowledged, it is frequently viewed as a fading survival from the past, an aberration that is antithetical to a modern capitalist economy. Consequently, advocates for stigmatized groups face an uphill battle in persuading their fellow citizens that discrimination remains a powerful ongoing force that explains the persistence of inequality even in modern sectors of society (Thorat et al. 2005).

Field experiments provide a useful tool for determining the extent of present-day discrimination (Fix et al. 1993; Massey and Lundy 2001; Bertrand and Mullainathan 2004; Pager 2003; Blank et al. 2004; Quillian 2006). In this chapter, we apply one of these methods—a correspondence study of job applicants—to college-educated members from the lowest caste within India (ex-untouchables or Dalits) and upon similarly college-educated individuals from the Muslim religious minority in India.

We study what happens when highly educated Indians from different caste and religious backgrounds apply for jobs in the modern urban private sector, encompassing multinational corporations as well as prominent Indian companies. This is the part of the Indian economy where supposedly caste and communal discrimination are things of the past. Yet our findings document a pattern of decision making by private sector employers that repeatedly advantages job applicants from higher-caste backgrounds and that disadvantages low-caste and Muslim job applicants with equal qualifications.

PREVIOUS RESEARCH AND THEORY

Caste and Communal Exclusion in India

There is a huge scholarly literature about caste (*jati*) in India that spans disciplines from history to sociology, from anthropology to economics. There are many thousands of *jati* within India; they have names and are usually associated with a certain regional or geographic base.[1] Sometimes, members of a caste share a distinctive surname. Castes are endogamous descent groups: most people marry within their own caste, and there are strong social norms against cross-caste marriage. Castes also have a hierarchical dimension. Each *jati* claims to be or is viewed by others as being located within a hierarchy of *varnas* described in the Hindu scriptures: Brahmin or scholars, Kshatriya or warriors, Vaisyas or traders, and Shudras or cultivators. Below these four is a very large group of people whom those scriptures describe as spiritually impure and defiling. Once known as pariahs and untouchables, members of this lowest stratum, which contains many *jati*, are today called Dalits, a nonpejorative term connoting oppressed or ground down.

Historically, because Dalits were viewed by higher-caste people as physically and spiritually polluting, they were not allowed to live close to persons of higher caste, or to use the same water supply, or to enter temples. They could not own land or be educated and were excluded from many occupations. Even their presence was polluting; in public places they had to keep physical distance from higher-caste persons.

Many Dalits worked in stigmatized occupations that handled "impure" materials: human waste, dead animals, hides. Tanning, scavenger, sweeper, and cleaning jobs remain distinctively Dalit occupations in modern India.

However, the majority of today's 167 million Dalits work as landless or near-landless laborers in agricultural production or in the lowest-paid kinds of manual labor (Thorat and Umakant 2004). They constituted 16.2% of the Indian population in the 2001 census.[2]

In the modern period, Dalits have won important legal rights, including a reservation system that provides a quota of positions in government and the universities, though not in private sector businesses, that are reserved for Dalits and for "other backward classes." This has led to the emergence of a stratum of university-educated and professional Dalits, known as the "creamy layer," but census data document that the great majority of Dalits remain in or close to poverty, with rates of illiteracy and malnutrition that are substantially higher than the rest of the Indian population.

Within India there is intense contention over the reservation system, with some commentators claiming that it is unfair to higher-caste persons or that it allows less competent individuals to rise to higher occupational positions. Within this context, a debate has been underway over whether reservation should be extended to private sector companies. Dalit advocates claim that employer discrimination continues to prevent low-caste applicants from accessing any but the lowest-level jobs in the modern private sector, while business spokespersons claim that discrimination is a thing of the past and that reservation would be inimical to efficiency in the modern private sector, since they currently hire the best-qualified applicants for jobs, irrespective of caste and communal background (Thorat et al. 2005).

This chapter examines the relationship between caste (and being a member of a minority religion) and labor market discrimination in today's urban India. Akerlof (1984) and others have developed theories to explain why an economically irrational phenomenon such as caste discrimination might persist in a modern economy (cf. Scoville 1991, 1996; Deshpande 2005).[3] Jodhka (2002) and colleagues have shown that multiple identities (caste, religion, migrant status, gender) together affect patterns of employment and exclusion in Indian cities. Darity and Deshpande (2003) have drawn parallels between Dalits and disadvantaged groups in other countries. Thorat (2004) provides a compilation of data from Indian government surveys, contrasting Dalits with higher-caste Hindus on indicators such as earnings, unemployment, education, and health. Thorat and Umakant (2004) compile articles that debate caste and discrimination against Dalits, in the context of the United Nation's world conference against racism in Durban.

Prior research relies on four kinds of data: (a) descriptive statistics from surveys of the standing of Dalits relative to other groups in India on social indicators; (b) government accounting of "atrocities" against Dalits (the term encompasses a variety of discriminatory behaviors penalized by Indian law, ranging from harassment to violence); (c) qualitative fieldwork and community studies; and (d) media descriptions of incidents against Dalits. There is similar material regarding discriminatory treatment of Indian Muslims (Perry 2003).

However, previous research has certain limitations. The qualitative studies often highlight caste oppression in rural contexts, strengthening the impression that caste inequality is a survival in traditional parts of India. Much of the quantitative evidence is not multivariate; thus there are few studies that separate human capital differences from job and wage discrimination. Important exceptions are Banerjee and Knight (1985), Lackshmanasamy and Mahdeswaran (1995), and Madheswaran (2004), which rely on data from 1981 or earlier. Attewell and Madheswaran (chapter 13, this volume) update the econometric approach and apply it to more recent data.

Even the econometric studies are not ideally suited to separating current discrimination from the legacy of past discrimination. By contrast, the correspondence methodology employed in this chapter is designed to assess the extent of present-day discrimination in the modern urban economy.

Hiring, Favoritism, and Social Exclusion

The Weberian perspective on social stratification emphasizes the enduring importance of status groups within capitalist societies: communities that enjoy different amounts of social honor. Status groups may encompass racial, ethnic, or religious groups but can also involve strata such as "gentlemen," "the educated classes," the working class, and castes. Communities that constitute status groups share a certain style of life and maintain their solidarity through rituals, shared tastes, and social activities on the one hand, and through social closure on the other, reducing their intercourse with social inferiors (Weber 1968).

One important element in this Weberian conception is that status groups seek to monopolize valued economic opportunities. Collins (1979) has detailed how, in the U.S. context, educational credentialism allows status groups to claim that lucrative occupations require certain degrees, thus limiting competition for privileged positions. Certain jobs come to resemble sinecures and social monopolies; their high earnings reflect the kinds of people who occupy them, rather than objective skills, according to Collins. Residential segregation of status groups by education and income, along with differences in childrearing practices and in familial cultural capital, produces differential access to superior schooling opportunities and to elite universities, reproducing status group inequalities across the generations (Domina 2006; Lareau 2003; Massey and Denton 1993).

People who hold privileged positions within large organizations develop a sense that a certain kind of person is especially effective in their role, leading many managers to favor potential recruits who are socially similar to themselves, a process that Kanter (1977) has termed "homosocial reproduction." Conversely, employers hold stereotypes about certain out-groups as being unsuitable for employment (Holzer 1999; Kirschenmann and Neckerman 1991). One corollary is that a person's social networks prove important for finding jobs in the United States, both at the professional end (Granovetter 1974) and at the blue-collar end (Royster 2003) of the labor market, because social networks often run along status group lines, sponsoring people who are "like us" (Elliott 2001; Smith 2003).

This macrosociological view of stratification and employment opportunity is paralleled by an extensive social psychological literature about the cognitive processes of prejudice and stereotyping that underlie both in-group preferences and social exclusion (see Fiske 1998; Massey 2007 for overviews). An additional body of research charts the consequences of social exclusion for those groups at the bottom of the status order (Hills et al. 2002).

Taken as a whole, this literature implies that social favoritism in hiring is not a matter of aberrant or unfair individuals, but rather a consequence of widespread in-group and out-group dynamics. Favoritism only recedes when bureaucratic practices limit the discretion of those who hire. A reliance on exams or tests, reporting to superiors about applicant pools and hiring outcomes, and formalized collective decision making enhance universalistic hiring (Moss and Tilly 2001). In the absence of these mechanisms to ensure fairness, favoritism and discrimination are likely to proliferate.

METHODS AND DATA

Beginning in October 2005 and continuing for 66 weeks, we collected advertisements announcing job openings from several national and regional English-language newspapers, including the *Times of India* (New Delhi and Mumbai editions), the *Hindustan Times*, the *Hindu* (Mumbai, Delhi, and Chennai editions), the *Deccan Herald* (Bangalore), and the *Deccan Chronicle* (Hyderabad).

From these we chose only advertisements for openings in private-sector firms. There are important government-owned enterprises in India—including some banks, steel companies, and railways—but we deliberately excluded public enterprises from this study. We also avoided advertisements for positions that were highly specialized or that required many years of on-the-job experience. Our aim was to select jobs that a university graduate might be eligible for within the first few years after graduation: entry-level or near entry-level positions.

These job advertisements specified the educational credentials and the on-the-job experience (if any) desired from applicants. The ads sometimes indicated the degree subject as well as the level of degree, for example, an MBA, a bachelor's degree in pharmacy or science, or a bachelor's in engineering. There was a bifurcation: some ads asked for applicants with a master's or higher degree, while others required a bachelor's degree. In the Indian labor market, higher degrees are frequently required for better-paid administrative and sales jobs in large corporations, even for entry-level positions that in the United States would be filled by employees with BA degrees. In the private sector in India, bachelor's degrees tend to be required for lower-paid white-collar positions.

However, job titles often overlapped at both credential levels. Many advertisements sought management trainees, branch managers, and marketing managers. Accountants, account managers, account executives, and sales officers were another large group found at both credential levels. Ads seeking engineers, assistant engineers, and engineer/sales were also common but tended to require only the bachelor's degree. Service, sales, and administrative jobs predominated.

The companies whose advertisements we responded to included securities and investment companies; pharmaceuticals and medical sales; computer sales, support, and IT services; manufacturing of many kinds; accounting firms; automobile sales and financing; marketing and mass media; veterinary and agricultural sales; construction; and banking.

The correspondence methodology we adopted involved submitting by mail several artificial applications to each job advertisement. (All our applicants were young men; the issue of gender discrimination in Indian labor markets was beyond the scope of our study.)

The research staff prepared sets of three matched application letters and résumés (in English) for each type of job. These experimental applications were carefully constructed to have identical educational qualifications and experience. For example, we prepared a set of three résumés, each of which indicated a BA degree and major from a university of similar prestige, with the same class of degree, and that listed equal amounts of sales experience, in order to respond to advertisements for a sales officer.[4] Another set of résumés and cover letters was prepared for managerial trainee openings, and so on. All the experimental résumés and cover letters were prepared so that they presented strong applicants for the job opening: they claimed suitable degrees from reputable universities and (where indicated in the advert) appropriate job experience and skills. This was done to maximize the likelihood that an applicant would be contacted by the employer to proceed to the next stage of hiring, typically the interview stage.

For each advertised job, we constructed a set of matched applications that differed only in terms of the name of each male applicant. No explicit mention of caste or religious background was made in the application. However, in each matched set, one application was for a person who had a stereotypically high-caste Hindu family name. A second was for a job applicant with an identifiably Muslim name. A third applicant had a distinctively Dalit (low-caste) name. In India, Muslim names are very distinguishable from Hindu names; one can immediately tell who is a Muslim from their name. Some Hindu family names also clearly signal the family's caste, although many other Hindu names are ambiguous in this respect. We therefore chose both Dalit and high-caste names that were very distinctive in terms of their caste origins.

To ensure that there were no effects from very minor differences in format between applications, the résumés and application letters were rotated after each job application. So the résumé and letter that were used for a Dalit for the first job advertisement were used for a Muslim in a subsequent job application, and for a high-caste applicant in the next application, and so on.

A record was kept for each job advertisement applied to. Over the course of the study, we sent at most two sets of applications to any particular employer: one set in response to an ad from that employer for a higher-credential job, and one set for an ad from the same employer for a lower-credential job. Thereafter we ignored any additional job advertisements we encountered from that employer.

Each experimental application listed a home address and a cell phone number where the employer could contact the applicant. Employers usually made contact by phone. Research staff answered these cell phones or read mail responses and recorded employers' replies to the job applications. The most common answer to an application was no response whatsoever. Rejection letters were rare: only 17 applications (one-third of 1%) resulted in rejection letters. In other cases, those we classified as positive outcomes, employers either phoned or wrote to certain applicants asking to interview the person (or in some cases requesting that the applicant appear for a written test). There were 450 positive outcomes of this type (9.4% of all experimental applications).

We reiterate that a successful outcome as defined in this study involves simply being admitted to the second stage of the job selection process: being contacted for an interview or for testing. The type of discrimination being assessed is whether some kinds of college-educated applicants are disproportionately successful, and others disproportionately unsuccessful, at this earliest stage in seeking employment.

On those occasions when employers did contact an experimental applicant to schedule an interview, the applicant always declined the interview,
saying that he had already found another job. Thus we sought no data on the
ultimate decision of who was offered the job.

The core of the correspondence method involved three identically qualified applications for the same job: one a Dalit, one a high-caste Hindu, and
one a Muslim. However, we added one "discordant" application to these
three. For jobs that requested a higher degree, we sent in one additional
application from a person with a high-caste name who only had a bachelor's
degree. In other words, this discordant applicant was an academically underqualified person but from a socially high-ranking group. For jobs that
demanded BA degrees, we added a different kind of discordant application,
from a person with a Dalit name who had a master's degree. In other words,
this second type of discordant applicant was overqualified in academic terms
but had a socially lower status. The purpose of these two kinds of discordant
applicants was to act as yardsticks, to determine whether, in the application
process, the effect of caste might outweigh or overcome that of academic
qualifications or vice versa.

Throughout the study we submitted job applications to employers in sets
of four: three identically qualified plus one discordant applicant. When the
research began, we sent one group of four applications to each job advertisement. However, after we discovered that positive responses were relatively
rare, we shifted to submitting three sets of four applications to each job
advertisement: 12 applicants per opening.

FINDINGS

Table 12.1 provides simple descriptive statistics for the job applications.
A total of 4,808 applications were made to 548 job advertisements over 66
weeks.

Table 12.1 Descriptive Statistics

Variable Name	N	Mean	SD	Minimum	Maximum
Muslim	4,808	0.25	0.43	0.00	1.00
Dalit	4,808	0.25	0.43	0.00	1.00
High caste	4,808	0.25	0.43	0.00	1.00
Overqualified	4,808	0.13	0.33	0.00	1.00
Underqualified	4,808	0.13	0.33	0.00	1.00
Outcome	4,808	0.09	0.29	0.00	1.00

Our analytical goal was to determine whether the likelihood of receiving a positive response from an employer differed according to whether the application was made with a high-caste, a Muslim, or a Dalit name. Since applications were clustered within jobs, multilevel or hierarchical models are appropriate. Since outcomes were dichotomous (either a positive response or not) we employed a random effects logistic regression model. In this kind of model, there is a random effect of the particular job on the likelihood of receiving a positive outcome. The effects of caste and religion are represented in the model by two dummy variables, Muslim and Dalit, with high-caste Hindu as the reference category. Two additional dummy variable predictors are included in the model: one indicates whether the applicant was underqualified (the anomalous high-caste person with a BA applying for an MA position), and the last dummy variable indicates whether the applicant was overqualified (a Dalit with an MA applying for a lower-level job).

This model may be written:

$$\text{Log}[p_{it}/(1-p_{it})]=\alpha_i+\beta D_{it}+\gamma M_{it}+\delta O_{it}+\lambda U_{it}$$

Where D_{it} is a dummy variable for an appropriately qualified Dalit applicant; M_{it} is a dummy variable for an appropriately qualified Muslim applicant; O_{it} is a dummy variable for an overqualified Dalit applicant; and U_{it} is a dummy variable for an underqualified high-caste applicant. The subscript i refers to the job applied for ($i = 1,\ldots548$), such that α_i is a random effect for each job. The job effect α_i implies a correlation among applications to the same job and reduces the standard errors.

The results are reported in table 12.2. The logistical regression model (on the left) was estimated using STATA's xtlogit procedure with a random effect for job. This procedure fits the data and calculates estimates using an adaptive Gauss-Hermite quadrature algorithm (STATA Corporation 2005: 161–69). The effects are reported as odds ratios. Table 12.2 provides two different significance levels for each predictor in this model. The first is the default method in STATA and assumes clustering. The second used a jack-knife method involving 250 replications, and calculated the standard error from this distribution.

As table 12.2 indicates, there are statistically significant effects of both caste and religion on job outcome. Appropriately qualified applicants with a Dalit name had odds of a positive outcome that were 0.67 of the odds of an equivalently qualified applicant with a high-caste Hindu name. Similarly qualified applicants with a Muslim name had odds of 0.33 of an otherwise equivalent applicant with a high-caste name.

A second model (on the right in table 12.2) was estimated using the program HLM6 (Raudenbusch et al. 2004). It reports a two-level hierarchical

Table 12.2 Modeling Differences in Job Outcomes

	Random Effects Logistic Regression				Bernoulli HLM Unit-Specific Model	
	Odds Ratio	SE	p Value	Jackknife p Value	Odds Ratio	Robust p Value
Predictors: (Compared to high caste)						
Dalit	.6724	.1202	0.026	0.014	.6835	0.013
Muslim	.3318	.0649	0.000	0.000	.3475	0.000
Underqualified high caste versus:						
Qualified high caste	.5711	.1409	0.023	0.033	.6028	0.037
Qualified Dalit	.8493	.2134	0.516	0.538	.8819	0.609
Overqualified Dalit versus:						
Qualified high caste	.7818	.1689	0.255	0.193	.7718	0.146
Qualified Dalit	1.162	.2571	0.495	0.435	1.129	0.503

nonlinear Bernoulli model, with applications nested within jobs, fitted using a penalized quasi-likelihood estimator. The coefficients are reported for the level 1 effects in a unit-specific model with robust Huber-White standard errors that correct for heteroskedasticity. The estimated effects are quite close to those from the random effects logistic regression in the previous model. For a positive job outcome, Dalits had an odds ratio outcome of 0.68 that of an otherwise equivalent high-caste applicant. Muslims had an odds ratio of 0.35 compared to a high-caste applicant. Both coefficients were statistically significant.

In sum, both models yielded consistent findings that job applicants with a Dalit or Muslim name were on average significantly less likely to have a positive application outcome than equivalently qualified persons with a high-caste Hindu name.

The two discordant application types provide additional insights into the likelihood of gaining a positive job outcome. The odds of a positive outcome for an underqualified high-caste applicant applying for a higher-level job were statistically significantly lower than the odds for a high-caste applicant with an appropriate qualification (an odds ratio of .57). The odds of success for an underqualified high-caste applicant were not significantly different from the odds of success for an appropriately qualified Dalit. Having a high-caste name considerably improves a job applicant's chances of a positive outcome, but if a high-caste applicant lacks the requested credential, his chances of success are considerably reduced.

The odds of a positive outcome for an overqualified Dalit applicant (a Dalit with an MA applying for jobs that required only a BA) were larger than the odds for a qualified Dalit but were smaller than the odds ratio for a BA-qualified high-caste applicant. Although the effects were substantial in size, neither of these differences in odds was statistically significant, probably due to insufficient statistical power. This leaves us unable to draw any firm conclusions about the relative importance of qualifications versus caste in this specific context.

DISCUSSION

This field experiment study of job applications observed a statistically significant pattern by which, on average, college-educated lower-caste and Muslim job applicants fare less well than equivalently qualified applicants with high-caste names, when applying by mail for employment in the modern private-enterprise sector. The only aspect of family background that was communicated in these applications was the applicant's name, yet this was enough to generate a different pattern of responses to applications from

Muslims and Dalits, compared to high-caste Hindu names. These were all highly educated and appropriately qualified applicants attempting to enter the modern private sector, yet even in this sector, caste and religion proved influential in determining a person's job chances.

These discriminatory outcomes occurred at the very first stage of the process that Indian university graduates go through to apply for a job. We did not collect data on who was ultimately hired for these particular jobs. Nor is it possible to determine the employment composition of private sector enterprises in India, because corporations are not obliged to report the caste and religious composition of their workforces to the government. (By contrast, U.S. law requires companies of a certain size to report the gender and racial composition of their workforces to the federal government, and these data are monitored by the Federal Equal Employment Opportunity Commission.)

Other chapters in this volume study the job search process in India at later stages. Newman and Deshpande (chapter 10) describe the frustrations that Dalit graduates from prestigious Indian universities experience when they apply for jobs at the end of their university training. They are looked on with great suspicion by interviewers, and many Dalit applicants abandon their expectations of getting a private sector job and instead hope for government jobs where the reservation system assists Dalit applicants. Chapter 11, by Newman and Jodhka, takes us to the other side of the hiring process, and reports that managers who hire have strong beliefs about kinds of workers. They prefer applicants from "good families," which usually means families with many university-educated members who work in professional jobs. Such preferences make it very difficult for upwardly mobile Dalits to be hired. Young Dalits are often the first in their families to gain a university degree.

It is clear from these studies that social exclusion is not just a residue of the past clinging to the margins of the Indian economy, nor is it limited to people of little education. On the contrary, it appears that caste favoritism and the social exclusion of Dalits and Muslims are widespread in private enterprises even in the most dynamic modern sector of the Indian economy.

If Muslims and Dalits are discriminated against simply because of their names, what is to be done? Other nations have responded vigorously to entrenched systems of communal privilege and discrimination in employment. In the United Kingdom, intercommunal conflict between Catholics and Protestants in Northern Ireland historically generated severe job discrimination. In its efforts to overcome that legacy, the British government instituted systems of monitoring employment and laws that monitored and regulated hiring. In the United States, one outcome of the civil rights struggles of African Americans was legislation on equal employment opportunity. Few scholars believe that employment discrimination has disappeared in the United States as a result of these laws, but most would acknowledge that large corporations have committed themselves to fairness in employment, and that companies expend considerable effort to monitor their own hiring and promotion behavior. Over a period of decades, corporate cultures have shifted and discrimination is less widespread. Women and minorities are employed in increasing numbers in higher-level corporate jobs.

These kinds of institutional, legal, and policy changes need to be embraced in India and other nations where employment discrimination prevents individuals from historically stigmatized groups from fully participating in the modern economy.

Notes

1. The most current list or schedule of Dalit *jati* (Scheduled Castes), is available on the Indian Census Web site: http://www.censusindia.net/scstmain/SC%20Lists.pdf.

2. The Indian government refers to Dalits as Scheduled Castes, a bureaucratic term dating from the colonial period when an official list or schedule identified certain *jati* as untouchables. In many current government reports, Scheduled Castes are combined with Scheduled Tribes (SC/ST) who are indigenous tribal groups, most of whom are very poor. The figure of 166,635,700 was the count of Scheduled Caste persons in the 2001 India Census, constituting 16.2% of the nation's population. The Scheduled Tribe population is about 84 million or an additional 8.2% of the Indian population (see http://www.censusindia.net/t_00_005.html). In recent legislation, an additional category, Other Backward Classes (OBCs) has been granted certain rights under the reservation system. OBCs are not untouchables, but they are the poorest of the historically agricultural *jati*. The number of persons in the category OBC, which does not include the SC/ST, is a matter of great contention, with one estimate being 32% of the Indian population.

3. These scholars draw upon economic theories that argue that discriminatory hiring may be economically rational in situations where employers have few ways for evaluating the quality of job applicants. Employers therefore undertake statistical discrimination, using past experiences with employees from certain groups as a basis for selecting individuals (cf. Arrow 1972, 1998). This approach differs from sociological theories, reviewed below, that emphasize discrimination as an outcome of competition for jobs among status groups.

4. Based upon performance on final examinations, an Indian university student receives a certain class of degree that is noted on the diploma: first class, second class, and so on. Our experimental applicants had degrees of the same class.

13

The Price of Globalization
Wage Penalties and Caste Inequality in Urban India

Paul Attewell and S. Madheswaran

1. INTRODUCTION

Though the occupational placement of caste groups varies across India, a common feature is the sharp contrast in status and income between Scheduled Castes (SC) and Scheduled Tribes (ST) on the one hand, and so-called forward castes (FC) on the other. Since Independence, the Indian government has sought to alleviate these inequalities by instituting affirmative action in political representation, in higher education, and in government and public sector employment. These policies reserve seats in local and national legislatures for SC and ST applicants and mandate a certain quota of jobs in the government and public sector for them.

Despite these efforts, the educational level of the scheduled castes continues to lag behind that of the general population, and the overwhelming majority of the SC/ST population is still found in less-skilled and lower-paying jobs. This chapter examines inequalities in employment, occupation, and earnings, between SC/ST and FC Indians, as measured by government survey data, and then statistically decomposes those gaps into separate components, one explainable through differences in factors such as education, and the other representing discrimination in employment and wages.

Many commentators acknowledge the prevalence of caste inequality in rural India, but believe that caste discrimination is much less important in urban India. Others believe that caste discrimination occurs primarily in the informal labor market and in manual jobs, but not in regular salaried white-collar positions. This chapter focuses upon inequality in the formal sector in urban India—the part of the economy that is more integrated into the global economic system—and pays special attention to caste-related income and employment gaps among highly educated employees.

2. SOURCES OF DATA

Data for this study come from Round 38 (1983), Round 50 (1993–1994), and Round 55 (1999–2000) of the all-India household survey conducted by the National Sample Survey Organization (NSSO) of the government of India (NSSO 2001c). Our study confines itself to urban regular- or salaried-sector workers aged between 15 and 65 years old. The wage distribution was trimmed by 0.1% at the top and bottom tails. Nominal wages were converted to 1993 prices using an inflation index for wages of urban industrial workers (CPIIW).

3. THE DECOMPOSITION METHODOLOGY

Three different empirical approaches for studying caste discrimination can be found in prior research. The first of these includes caste as a predictor while predicting earnings from the characteristics of all workers (a single-equation technique). Unfortunately, this approach yields a biased result because it assumes that the wage structure is the same for both NSC (Nonscheduled Castes) and SC/ST (Scheduled Castes). It thus constrains the values of coefficients of explanatory variables, such as education and experience, to be the same for SC/ST and for NSC (Gunderson 1989; Madheswaran 1996).[1]

A second approach employs a decomposition technique to partition the observed wage gap into an endowment component and a coefficient component. The latter is derived as an unexplained residual and is termed the discrimination coefficient. This method was first developed by Blinder (1973) and Oaxaca (1973) and later extended to incorporate selectivity bias (Reimer 1983, 1985) and to overcome the index number problem (Cotton 1988; Neumark 1988; Oaxaca and Ransom 1994).

A third expanded approach incorporates the occupational distribution into the earnings estimation and was first proposed by Brown et al. (1980). One advantage of using this expanded method is that both job discrimination (differential access to certain occupational positions) and wage discrimination (differential earnings within the same job) can be estimated simultaneously.

We have employed all three of the methods mentioned above to estimate the extent of discrimination against lower-caste workers in urban India. We have also contributed a new refinement to the expanded decomposition approach by combining Oaxaca and Ransom (1994) and Brown et al. (1980) to produce a more detailed decomposition analysis of occupational and wage discrimination. In the appendixes to this chapter, we lay out the mathematical logic of this decomposition.

4. ECONOMETRIC RESULTS

4.1. Mincerian Earnings Function Results

To estimate the earnings differences attributed to discrimination, we estimated an augmented Mincerian earnings function separately for NSC, SC,
and Other Backward Castes (OBC) in the regular or salaried labor market.
The logarithm of the daily wage rate was used as the dependent variable, and
age, level of education, gender, marital status, sector, job tenure, union status,
occupation, and region were predictors. Generally the results are consistent
with human capital theory and a priori expectations. The earnings function
results for the year 1999–2000 are given in table 13.1. Due to space constraints,
we have not reported the earnings function for the years 1983 and 1993–1994.
A longer version of the report that provides the estimates from earlier surveys
used for comparing trends over time is available from the authors.

First, we examined the returns on education for NSC and SC workers
and the changes in these returns following the economic liberalization of
the 1990s. In common with other studies, the marginal wage effects of education are found to be significantly positive and monotonically increasing
with education level. Duraisamy (2002) and Dutta (2004) are the only other
national studies that compare returns on education in India over time.
However, those studies calculated rates of return on education by gender
and by sector. To the best of our knowledge, no previous study in India has
determined rates of return on education by caste using a nationally representative sample. The average rate of return on each education level, rj, can
be estimated as follows:

$$\gamma_k = \frac{(\beta_k - \beta_{k-1})}{(S_j - S_{j-1})}$$

where j = primary, middle, secondary, higher secondary, and graduate
school; β_j is the coefficient in the wage regression models and Sj the years of
schooling at education level j.

The rate of return to primary education is estimated as follows:

$$\gamma_{Primary} = \frac{\beta_{Prim}}{S_{Prim}}$$

The omitted category for the education dummy variables is that of those
workers who are illiterate or have less than two years of any type of formal
education. The estimated rates of return on additional years of schooling are
reported in table 13.2.

Table 13.2 suggests that there is an incentive to acquire more education
if the individual is in regular wage employment—the returns on acquiring
education are all positive. An interesting observation is that the labor market
return is the highest for a secondary level of education in 1983, whereas the

Table 13.1 Earnings Function: OLS Results, Regular Workers, Urban India

Variables	1999–2000					
	Other Caste		SC		OBC	
	Coeff.	t Value	Coeff.	t Value	Coeff.	t Value
Age	0.04186	14.28	0.063607	10.86	0.050079	12.78
Agesq	−0.00034	−9.24	−0.00062	−8.32	−0.00045	−9.23
Bprim	0.118523	4.46	0.125573	3.53	0.110725	3.74
Primary	0.155207	6.48	0.095845	3.09	0.177313	6.79
Middle	0.231942	11.06	0.225104	7.87	0.292325	12.14
Secondary	0.457122	22.85	0.388247	13.15	0.456787	19.28
High school	0.586235	27.78	0.564215	16.33	0.574385	21.6
Graduate	1.217369	46.13	1.030238	11.64	1.154985	26.52
Grad/other	0.874313	44.76	0.723349	22.42	0.820725	32.55
Male	0.226024	19.79	0.266195	11.22	0.375886	22.44
Married	0.108977	8.64	0.03983	1.56	0.097785	5.54
Public	0.275494	27.34	0.309054	14.54	0.335282	21.25
Unionmem	0.216788	21.53	0.268418	12.19	0.335363	21.64
Permanent	0.278837	25.18	0.268317	11.55	0.178827	12.05
South	0.072278	6.1	0.171682	7.27	0.091458	6.18
West	0.066188	6.59	0.065884	3.11	0.090175	4.82
East	−0.04017	−2.93	0.006045	0.2	0.119431	4.17
_cons	2.667867	49.88	2.264271	22.18	2.31265	33.37
R square	0.514		0.5287		0.5515	
Adj.R²	0.5136		0.5267		0.5507	
F	1267.12		287.65		699.94	
N	20,706		4,380		9,695	

Table 13.2 Average Private Rate of Return on Education by Caste (as a Percentage)

Educational Level	1983		1993–1994		1999–2000		
	NSC	SC	NSC	SC	NSC	SC	OBC
Primary	4.21	4.48	3.26	1.39	3.10	1.92	3.55
Middle	5.05	6.43	3.54	3.19	2.56	4.31	3.83
Secondary	16.95	16.28	9.86	4.77	11.26	8.16	8.22
HSC	NA	NA	5.21	12.92	6.46	8.80	5.88
Graduate professional	9.61	7.47	9.67	7.23	12.62	9.32	11.61
Graduate general	8.08	5.98	7.87	4.65	9.60	5.30	8.21
Prof. deg compared to Gen. deg	12.66	10.44	12.37	11.10	17.15	15.34	16.71

return to a professional graduate degree is greatest in 1993 and 1999–2000 for both NSC and SC.

When rates of return on education are compared across castes, we see that the rate of return on education is considerably lower for SC workers and for OBCs than for other (higher-caste) workers. If we look at the 1999–2000 results, the rate of return is usually higher for OBCs than for SC workers. These differential rates of return on education between castes suggest a substantial amount of labor market discrimination.

The premium on skill appears to be increasing over time due to economic liberalization, and this has led to increasing levels of wage inequality in urban India (Kijima 2006). Several other studies have found evidence of increasing educational returns for the more educated during periods of rapid economic change. For instance, Foster and Rosenzweig (1996) found that during the Green Revolution in India, increasing educational returns were concentrated among the more educated. Kingdon (1998) finds in her review of the returns on education in India (mainly computed from specialized surveys in urban areas of a particular state or city) that the rate of return on education, as in table 13.2, tends to rise with education level. Newell and Reilly (1999) also found in their study on transitional economies during the 1990s that the private rates of return on education rose after a period of labor market reforms. However, we find that there is a markedly lower rate of return for Scheduled Castes and OBCs compared to other caste workers.

4.2. Decomposition Results

As mentioned in our methodology section, we initially adopted a single equation method. We found that, compared to FC employees, SC workers earned 5.0% less in 1983, 8.4% less in 1993–1994, and 8.9% less in

1999–2000. OBCs earned 10.9% less than FC employees in 1999–2000. These coefficients are all statistically significant. A single-equation approach assumes that the slope coefficients are the same for all social groups. To overcome this limitation, we next estimated an earnings function separately for each social group over the period of time and subjected the earnings

Table 13.3 Blinder-Oaxaca Decomposition Results

Components of Decomposition	1983	1993–1994	1999–2000	1999–2000 FC vs. OBC
Amount attributable:	30.9	15.2	−9.7	−0.5
Due to endowments (E):	25.1	18.8	24.4	23.8
Due to coefficients (C):	5.8	−3.6	−34.1	−24.4
Shift coefficient (U):	−1.9	11.8	40.4	35.5
Raw differential (R): {E + C + U}:	29	26.9	30.6	35
Adjusted differential (D): {C + U}:	3.9	8.2	6.2	11.2
Endowments as % total (E/R):	86.55	69.6	79.0	68.1
Discrimination as % total (D/R):	13.45	30.4	21.4	31.9

Note: A positive number indicates advantage to forward caste; negative numbers indicate advantage to Scheduled Caste. The results from decomposition are presented using Blinder' (1973) original formulation of E, C, U, and D. The endowments (E) component of the decomposition is the sum of (the coefficient vector of the regressors of the high-wage group) times (the difference in group means between the high-wage and low-wage groups for the vector of regressors). The coefficients (C) component of the decomposition is the sum of the (group means of the low-wage group for the vector of regressors) times (the difference between the regression coefficients of the high-wage group and the low-wage group). The unexplained portion of the differential (U) is the difference in constants between the high-wage group and the low-wage group. The portion of the differential due to discrimination is C + U. The raw (or total) differential is E + C + U. The unexplained component is the difference in the shift coefficients (or constants) between the two wage equations. Being inexplicable, this component can be attributed to discrimination. However, Blinder also argued that the explained component of the wage gap also contains a portion that is due to discrimination. To examine this, Blinder decomposed the explained component into: (1) the differences in endowments between the two groups, "as evaluated by the high-wage group' wage equation"; and (2) "the difference between how the high-wage equation would value the characteristics of the low-wage group, and how the low-wage equation actually values them." Blinder called the first part of the amount "attributable to the endowments" and the second part of the amount "attributable to the coefficients," and he argued that the second part should also be viewed as reflecting discrimination: "[this] only exists because the market evaluates differently the identical bundle of traits if possessed by members of different demographic groups, [and] is a reflection of discrimination as much as the shift coefficient is." Conventionally, the high-wage group' wage structure is regarded as the "nondiscriminatory norm," that is, the reference group. The average endowment differences are now weighted by the high-wage workers' estimated coefficients, and the coefficient differences are weighted by the mean characteristics of the low-wage workers. One can also do the reverse.

equation to decomposition, following the Blinder-Oaxaca approach. The results are reported in table 13.3.

Table 13.3 indicates that the endowment component is larger than the discrimination component. Nevertheless, discrimination explains 13.45% (in 1983), 30.4% (in 1993–1994), and 21.4% (in 1999–2000) of the lower wages of SC workers as compared to FCs in the regular urban labor market. Similarly, discrimination causes 31.9% of the lower wages for OBCs as compared to FCs.

Two points are especially noteworthy. First, the large endowment difference in developing countries like India implies that premarket discriminatory practices with respect to education, health, and nutrition are more crucial in explaining wage differentials than labor market discrimination. The endowment difference has decreased over the period from 1983 to 1999–2000. This is consistent with evidence available about the impact of the reservation system in Indian education. Student enrollment, including that of students under the reservation system, has been increasing (Thorat 2005; Weisskopf 2004b). However, reservation quotas in employment and educational institutions still fall short of their targets for some levels of education and for some categories of jobs.

Second, in the decomposition, wage discrimination appears to have increased soon after the economic liberalization of 1993–1994, but it had come down by the year 1999–2000. Nevertheless, raw wage differentials have increased over this period.

We also assessed the relative contribution of each independent variable to the observed wage gap. Table 13.4 shows which part of the wage gap can be attributed to differences in endowments and which part is due to differences in rewards (discrimination) in the earnings function.

If we look at the total difference column, the proxy for experience—the age variable–was favorable to FCs in 1993–1994, but the result was quite the reverse in 1999–2000. Note that the large contribution of age during 1999–2000 in favor of SC is more than offset by the constant term, which is in favor of FCs.

The next important variable is level of education. Secondary/higher secondary and higher education both favor FCs. The public sector and union membership variables are rather prominent in their effects on the earnings difference. There is a favorable treatment of SCs in the public sector— SCs gained an earnings advantage of 27.1% in 1993–1994 and 9.8% in 1999–2000. The permanent job variable favors FCs. The regional effect on earnings difference is meager but it favors FCs. Finally, there is a large effect of the constant or intercept term that works in favor of FCs; its contribution increases over time.

When we include occupational variables in our model, the discrimination coefficient is reduced to 24% from 30% in 1993–1994, and to 15% from

Table 13.4 Relative Contribution of Specific Variables to the Decomposition

Variables	1993–1994			1999–2000		
	Explained Diff	Unexplained Diff	Total Diff	Explained Diff	Unexplained Diff	Total Diff
Age	0.0	10.8	10.8	3.6	–126.5	–122.9
Less than secondary	–7.4	14.5	7.1	–8.8	2.6	–6.2
Secon/HSC	20.1	11.5	31.6	14.7	4.2	19.0
Higher education	63.6	5.9	69.5	70.3	6.5	76.8
Male	1.1	–46.5	–45.4	1.6	–10.8	–9.2
Married	–1.5	4.8	3.3	0.3	17.3	17.6
Public	–5.9	–21.2	–27.1	–4.9	–4.9	–9.8
Union	–4.5	–0.4	–4.8	–2.9	–8.2	–11.1
Permanent	1.9	10.4	12.3	4.9	2.3	7.2
Region	3.0	–3.3	–0.4	1.3	5.2	6.5
Constant	—	43.9	43.9	—	132.0	132.0
Subtotal	69.6	30.4	100.0	79.6	20.4	100.0

Note: A positive number indicates advantage to forward castes. A negative number indicates advantage to Scheduled Castes.

20% in 1999–2000. This implies that discrimination partially operates through occupational segregation, an issue that we study in greater detail in an ensuing section.

4.3. Discrimination in the Public and Private Sectors: Decomposition Results

The reservation system that sets aside a certain proportion of jobs for SC/ST applicants operates only within the public sector of the Indian economy; the private sector is exempt. One important issue, therefore, is to look at caste-based wage inequalities separately for the public and private sectors of the urban economy. We estimated separate earnings functions for the public and private sector for each social group, and then decomposed the earnings differentials between FC and SC/ST for each sector. The results are reported in table 13.5.

The decomposition in table 13.5 reveals that SC/ST workers are discriminated against both in the public sector and the private sector, but that the discrimination effect is much smaller in the public sector. The government policy of protective legislation therefore seems to be partly effective. Over time the discrimination coefficient has decreased slightly in the public sector, whereas the discrimination coefficient has not changed significantly in the private sector. Discrimination still arises in the public sector in part because the reservation quota for lower-caste applicants is close to full in the less-skilled class C and D government jobs but is far from filled in the higher-category A and B jobs, where higher castes predominate.

These findings have important implications for the public-private divide and for affirmative action in India. The evidence provided by these decompositions contradicts the argument that there is no discrimination in the private sector. Claims that discrimination does not occur in the Indian urban private sector are based neither on the economic theory of discrimination nor on empirical facts.

Table 13.5 Decomposition Results for the Public and Private Sectors

Components	1993–1994		1999–2000	
	Public	Private	Public	Private
Endowment difference	82.0	69.0	86.0	70.1
Discrimination	18.0	31.0	14.0	29.9

4.4. Cotton, Neumark, and Oaxaca/Ransom Decomposition Results

We calculated decomposition results using the Cotton (1988), Neumark (1988), and Oaxaca and Ransom (1994) approaches. These reveal that the wage difference due to skill is 81.8% using Cotton's method and 85% for a pooled method (Oaxaca/Ransom). This skill or productivity advantage is estimated as it would have been in the absence of discrimination. The NSC treatment advantage is 5.2% in Cotton's method and 4.1% in the pooled method. This is the difference in wages between what the FCs currently receive and what they would receive in the absence of discrimination. The treatment disadvantage component for SC is about 13% in the Cotton method, and the corresponding figure is 11.2% for the pooled method. This is the difference in the current SC wage and the wage they would receive if there were no discrimination. If we look at table 13.6 at the last two columns of the estimates using the Oaxaca method, as expected, the fourth column evaluated at SC means somewhat underestimates the true value of the skill difference, whereas the fifth column evaluated at FC means does the reverse.

This form of decomposition procedure yields more accurate estimates of the wage differential but it also models the true state of differential treatment by estimating the cost to the group discriminated against as well as the benefits accruing to the favored group.

We estimated standard errors for each of the three estimates to determine which of the three was least objectionable. The pooled method has the smallest standard error and should probably be preferred. When this method

Table 13.6 Cotton-Neumark-Oaxaca/Ransom Approach, Urban India, 1999–2000 (Percentages)

Components	Cotton/ Neumark	Oaxaca/ Ransom (Pooled Method)	Oaxaca-Blinder Using SC Means as Weight	Oaxaca-Blinder Using FC Means as Weight
	81.8	85.0	79.0	88.1
Skill diff (end diff)	(0.010214)	(0.01010)	(0.01246)	(0.01038)
Unexplained diff	18.2	15.0	21.4	11.9
(discrimination)	(0.010249)	(0.008235)	(0.01242)	(0.010611)
Overpayment to FC	5.2	4.1	—	—
Underpayment to SC	13.0	11.2	—	—

Note: Unexplained component = overpayment and underpayment component. Figures in parentheses indicate standard errors.

Table 13.7 Expanded Decomposition Results: Urban India, 1999–2000

Occupation	Job Explained	Job Discrimination	Wage Explained	Wage Discrimination	Wage Overpayment to FC	Wage Underpayment to SC
Professional	−0.06206	0.706537	0.014075	0.00456	0.00512	0.016564
Administration	−0.00232	0.249214	0.015555	0.00321	0.00123	0.012567
Clerical	0.049441	0.169439	0.014127	0.01343	0.00033	0.00123
Sales	−0.07005	0.213229	0.002345	0.01527	0.00434	0.017725
Service	−0.11033	−0.66201	0.018874	0.01649	0.00225	0.001123
Production	0.25565	−0.56178	0.015537	0.01474	0.00177	0.003143
Total	0.060324	0.114629	0.080514	0.06771	0.01504	0.052352
(%) to overall raw wage differentials	18.66	35.46	24.91	20.95	4.78	16.17
Overall wage differentials between FC and SC				0.323177		

is used, the discrimination coefficient is somewhat smaller in magnitude (15%), but there is still clear and substantial evidence of discrimination in the labor market against SCs and STs.

4.5. Combining Wage and Job Discrimination: Expanded Decomposition Results

We analyzed occupational attainment within the framework of a multinomial logit model. Using the occupation attainment results, a predicted distribution for SC ($\hat{P}^{SC}$), and for NSCs ($\hat{P}^{Nsc}$) was obtained. The earnings functions by occupation are needed to complete the decomposition based on the full model. Table 13.7 reports a decomposition of the actual earnings difference into its skill difference, an overpayment to FC, and an underpayment to SC.

Of the gross wage difference, 24.9% can be explained by education and experience, 18.6% by occupational differences, 20.9% by wage discrimination, and 35.4% by occupational discrimination. Thus, discrimination accounts for a large part of the gross earnings difference, with job discrimination (inequality in access to certain occupations) being considerably more important than wage discrimination (unequal pay within a given occupation, given one's educational and skill level) in the regular salaried urban labor market. This result is contrary to an earlier study in India by Banerjee and Knight (1985). However, their study focused on migrant workers in Delhi, a small sample compared to our nationwide survey.

5. CONCLUDING OBSERVATIONS

Almost everyone acknowledges that wage inequality in India is very high, and most commentators acknowledge that, on average, income is associated with caste background. However, many commentators explain away this inequality as a manifestation of economic backwardness. Rural India is poorer than urban India. Less educated people suffer poverty at higher rates than more educated people. Those who work in the informal economy earn less than those in the regular salaried sector. Since lower-caste Indians are overrepresented in rural areas and in informal jobs, and are less educated on average than higher-caste Indians, they are likely to be poorer.

There is clearly some truth in this picture. Policies are urgently needed to bring more education to the rural poor and to lower-caste communities in general. India also needs to develop more job opportunities for individuals to move from the informal into the formal sector. However, the point of this chapter is to argue that discrimination in modern India is not simply a matter of discrimination against less educated lower-caste Indians working in the most backward areas of the economy. On the contrary, our analyses of government data show clearly that discrimination operates powerfully in the modern educated urban sector and in the parts of India that are part of the global economy.

Caste discrimination occurs among educated salaried workers in both the state sector and the private sector. The magnitude of caste discrimination is greater in the private sector than in the public sector, which suggests that the reservation system has helped to lessen caste inequality in the public sector. However, the reservation system does not currently extend to the private sector, and industrialists and their supporters argue strongly against extending reservations into that sector.

However, discrimination is clearly operating among urban salaried workers in the modern Indian private sector. Both wage discrimination—unequal pay for people in the same job—and job discrimination are present, but the latter is more pronounced. Lower-caste employees do not have equal access to better jobs; high-caste individuals consistently win out in the competition for these higher-paying jobs. Not only is discrimination worse in the private than in the public sector, but the immediate aftermath of liberalization—the shrinkage of public employment relative to private enterprise employment—led to higher levels of discrimination over time in the private sector.

Other chapters in this volume reveal how job discrimination comes about in the urban economy. India has a glut of college-educated labor, and good jobs are hard to find, even among the most advantaged parts of the population. Many educated and skilled Indians emigrate to North America and Europe because better job opportunities are often to be found overseas. For those who remain in India, obtaining a well-paid job is an extraordinary challenge.

Chapter 10, by Newman and Deshpande, shows that lower-caste (Dalit) students who graduate from some of the best Indian universities nevertheless confront great skepticism (and sometimes hostility) from interviewers who are selecting a handful of persons to hire out of hundreds of applicants. Many lower-caste (Dalit) college graduates lower their hopes and focus on public sector jobs because they are repeatedly rebuffed in their attempts to obtain professional employment in private sector companies. Chapter 11 shows that employers utilize stereotypes about who is a good worker, and who comes from a good family, when they hire. Those stereotypes tend to work against college-educated lower-caste applicants, because employers assume that the most productive professional and white-collar employees come from families where parents, brothers, and sisters are all in professional jobs. This emphasis on hiring persons from "good families" sustains caste and class discrimination. Chapter 12, by Attewell and Thorat, shows that college graduates who reply to job advertisements and have recognizably low-caste or Moslem names are significantly less likely to be called in for an interview than otherwise equally qualified applicants with higher-caste names. Taken together with our analyses of government income data, these studies demonstrate that job discrimination based on caste and religious background are commonplace in the most modern economic sectors in India: among multinationals and large Indian-owned firms.

Evidently, economic globalization is quite compatible with caste- and communal-based employment discrimination. Becker (1962) and other Western economists argued that discrimination is inimical to capitalism, and that economic competition will drive out enterprises that discriminate. In retrospect, that belief seems naive. In places like India, modern enterprises do not suffer shortages of skilled labor if they discriminate. On the contrary, educated job applicants are lining up at their doors. Moreover, Indian employers are primed to believe that many job applicants are below par; they distrust the educational qualifications and work ethic of many applicants. Because there are so many applicants for each opening, firms often delegate the early stages of the hiring process to outside firms, who run the job ads, do initial interviews, and forward short lists of candidates. In this kind of atmosphere where applicants are plentiful and job openings are precious, it is very easy for nepotism, caste, class, communal bias, sexism, regional preferences, and other forms of discrimination to flourish.

Globalization in the sense of global enterprise has not prevented job discrimination from flourishing in modern India. But perhaps globalization in a different sense can provide a solution. There have been long-standing struggles against social exclusion in employment in many economically developed countries, and some of these struggles have resulted in various legal, policy, and bureaucratic instruments aimed at preventing discrimination. In the United States, for example, federal statutes outlaw discrimination based on gender, race, and ethnicity. There is a body of equal opportunity legislation, and there are agencies like the federal Equal Employment Opportunity Commission that are empowered to collect data from private sector employers about the numbers of applicants and employees, broken down by gender, race, ethnicity, and so forth. Similar statutes and administrative entities exist across Europe.

These laws and agencies limit, even if they do not eradicate, grosser forms of employment discrimination. They shine a light on the employment practices of firms and create incentives for private sector companies to operate in a nondiscriminatory fashion. They create a transparency in the hiring process and encourage the development of company policies and formal procedures to guarantee fairness and nondiscriminatory hiring and promotion. Regulatory agencies also monitor private firms and provide avenues for adjudicating complaints regarding discrimination.

These institutions have become a relatively uncontroversial feature in several Western nations. Private sector companies thrive despite this regulatory and legal oversight. We conclude that an equal employment enforcement system, along the lines of those in the United States or Northern Ireland, would be very desirable in India, as a first step toward lessening the grip of caste discrimination on the modern private sector in India. Until policymakers and executives can see data about the unequal caste composition of their own workforces, and unless transparency and accountability are brought to the hiring process, caste discrimination is likely to continue.

APPENDIX 1: THE DECOMPOSITION LOGIC

The Blinder-Oaxaca Decomposition Method

Decomposition enables the separation of the wage differential into one part that can be explained by differences in individual characteristics and another part that cannot be explained by differences in individual characteristics. The gross wage differential can be defined as:

$$G = \frac{Y_{nsc} - Y_{sc}}{Y_{sc}} = \frac{Y_{nsc}}{Y_{sc}} - 1 \tag{1}$$

where Y_{nsc} and Y_{sc} represent the wages of higher or NSC individuals and wages of individuals belonging to the lower-caste SC categories, respectively. In the absence of labor market discrimination, the NSC and SC wage differential would reflect pure productivity differences:

$$Q = \frac{Y_{nsc}^0}{Y_{sc}^0} - 1 \tag{2}$$

where the superscript 0 denotes the absence of market discrimination. The market discrimination coefficient (D) is then defined as the proportionate difference between $G + 1$ and $Q + 1$:

$$D = \frac{(Y_{nsc} / Y_{sc}) - (Y_{nsc}^0 / Y_{sc}^0)}{(Y_{nsc}^0 / Y_{sc}^0)} \tag{3}$$

Equations (1)–(3) imply the following logarithmic decomposition of the gross earnings differential:

$$\ln(G + 1) = \ln(D + 1) + \ln(Q + 1) \tag{4}$$

This decomposition can be further applied within the framework of semilogarithmic earnings equations (Mincer 1974) and estimated via OLS (ordinary least squares) such that:

$$\ln \overline{Y}_{nsc} = \sum \hat{\beta}_{nsc} \overline{X}_{nsc} + \varepsilon_{nsc} \ (\text{NSC wage equation}) \tag{5}$$

$$\ln \overline{Y}_{sc} = \sum \hat{\beta}_{sc} \overline{X}_{sc} + \varepsilon_{sc} \ (\text{SC wage equation}) \tag{6}$$

where $\ln \overline{Y}$ denotes the geometric mean of earnings, $\overline{X}$ the vector of mean values of the regressors, $\hat{\beta}$ the vector of coefficients, and ε the error term with zero mean and constant variance. Within this framework, the gross differential in the logarithmic term is given by:

$$\ln(G + 1) = \ln(\overline{Y}_{nsc} / \overline{Y}_{sc}) = \ln \overline{Y}_{nsc} - \ln \overline{Y}_{sc} = \sum \hat{\beta}_{nsc} \overline{X}_{sc} - \sum \hat{\beta}_{sc} \overline{X}_{sc} \tag{7}$$

The Oaxaca decomposition simply shows that equation (7) can be expanded. In other words, the difference in the coefficients of the two earnings functions is taken as a priori evidence of discrimination. If, for a given endowment, SC individuals are paid according to the NSC wage structure in the absence of discrimination, then the hypothetical SC earnings function can be given as:

$$\ln \overline{Y}_{sc} = \sum \hat{\beta}_{nsc} \overline{X}_{sc} \tag{8}$$

Subtracting equation (8) from equation (7), we get

$$\ln \overline{Y}_{nsc} - \ln \overline{Y}_{sc} = \sum \hat{\beta}_{nsc} (\overline{X}_{nsc} - \overline{X}_{sc}) + \sum \overline{X}_{sc} (\hat{\beta}_{nsc} - \hat{\beta}_{sc}) \tag{9}$$

Alternatively, the decomposition can also be done as

$$\ln \overline{Y}_{nsc} - \ln \overline{Y}_{sc} = \sum \hat{\beta}_{sc} (\overline{X}_{nsc} - \overline{X}_{sc}) + \sum \overline{X}_{nsc} (\hat{\beta}_{nsc} - \hat{\beta}_{sc}) \tag{10}$$

In equations (9) and (10), the first term on the right-hand side can be interpreted as education and other endowment differences. The second term in these equations has been regarded in the literature as the discrimination component. Studies use either of these alternative decomposition forms (equation 9 or 10) based on their assumptions about the wage structure that would prevail in the absence of discrimination. Some authors prefer to take the average of the estimates of the two equations (Greenhalgh 1980). This particular issue is known as the index number problem.

The Cotton, Neumark, and Oaxaca/Ransom Decomposition Method

To resolve the index number problem, Cotton (1988) and Neumark (1988) and Oaxaca and Ransom (1994) have proposed an alternative decomposition that extends the wage discrimination component further. They calculate nondiscriminatory or competitive wage structures that can be used to estimate overpayment and underpayment. The true nondiscriminatory wage would lie somewhere between the NSC and SC wage structure. The Cotton logarithmic wage differential is written as:

$$\ln \overline{Y}_{nsc} - \ln \overline{Y}_{sc} = \sum \beta^*(\overline{X}_{nsc} - \overline{X}_{sc}) + \sum \overline{X}_{nsc}(\hat{\beta}_{nsc} - \beta^*) + \sum \overline{X}_{sc}(\beta^* - \hat{\beta}_{sc}) \quad (11)$$

where β^* is the reward structure that would have occurred in the absence of discrimination. The first term on the right-hand side of equation (11) is skill differences between SC/ST and NSC, while the second term represents the overpayment relative to NSCs due to favoritism, and the third term the underpayment to SC due to discrimination. The decomposition specified in equation (11) cannot be made operational without some assumptions about the salary structures for SC and NSC in the absence of discrimination. The theory of discrimination provides some guidance in the choice of nondiscriminatory wage structure. The assumption is operationalized by weighting the NSC and SC wage structures by respective proportions of NSC and SC in the labor force. Thus, the estimator β^* used above is defined as:

$$\beta^* = P_{nsc}\hat{\beta}_{sc} + P_{sc}\hat{\beta}_{sc} \quad (12)$$

where P_{nsc} and P_{sc} are the sample proportions of NSC and SC/ST populations, and $\hat{\beta}_{nsc}$ and $\hat{\beta}_{sc}$ the NSC and SC pay structures respectively.

Another versatile representation of a nondiscriminatory or pooled wage structure is proposed by Neumark (1988) and Oaxaca and Ransom (1994). It can be written as:

$$\beta^* = \Omega\hat{\beta}_{NSC} + (I - \Omega)\hat{\beta}_{SC} \quad (13)$$

where Ω is a weighting matrix. I is the identity matrix. The weighting matrix is specified by:

$$\Omega = (X'X)^{-1}(X'_{NSC}X_{NSC}) \quad (14)$$

where X is the observation matrix for the pooled sample. X_{NSC} is the observation matrix for the NSC sample. The interpretation of Ω as weighting matrix is readily seen by noting that:

$$X'X = X'_{NSC}X_{NSC} + X'_{SC}X_{SC} \quad (15)$$

where X_{sc} is the observation matrix of the SC sample, Given $\hat{\beta}_{NSC}, \hat{\beta}_{SC}$ and equation (13), any assumption about β^* reduces to an assumption about Ω.

An Expanded Decomposition to Estimate Both Wage and Job Discrimination

Both the Oaxaca (1973) and Cotton (1988) and Neumark (1988) methods can be criticized on the grounds that they do not distinguish between wage discrimination and job discrimination.

Brown et al. (1980) incorporated a separate model of occupational attainment into their analysis of wage differentials. Banerjee and Knight (1985) used this decomposition by introducing a multinomial logit model that could estimate both wage and occupational discrimination for migrant laborers in India, where the latter are defined as "unequal pay for workers with same economic characteristics, which results from their being employed in different jobs." In the following section, we combine elements from Oaxaca and Ransom (1994) and Brown et al. (1980) to form a more detailed decomposition analysis of occupational and wage discrimination. We believe that this represents a theoretical advance in terms of examining discrimination as the combined consequence of unequal access to certain jobs and unequal pay within jobs.

We have seen that equation (7) was used (following Oaxaca 1973) to estimate the gross logarithmic wage differential between caste groups. Our concern is with estimating occupational discrimination as well as wage discrimination. The proportion of NSC (P_{iNSC}) and the proportion of SCs (P_{iSC}) in each occupation i are included in the decomposition. Equation 7 is thus expanded to:

$$\ln(G+1) = \sum [P_{iSC} \ln \overline{Y}_{iNSC} - P_{iSC} \ln \overline{Y}_{iSC}] \tag{16}$$

Using the method in Brown et al. (1980), Moll (1992, 1995), and Banerjee and Knight (1985), this can be further decomposed as:

$$\ln(G+1) = \sum \ln \overline{Y}_{iNSC}(P_{iNSC} - P_{iSC}) + \sum P_{iSC}(\ln \overline{Y}_{iNSC} - \overline{Y}_{iSC}) \tag{17}$$

The first term on the right-hand side of the equation represents the wage difference attributable to differences in the occupational distribution, and the second term is attributable to the difference between wages within occupations. Each of these terms contains an explained and unexplained component. If we define $\hat{P}_{iSC}$ as the proportion of SC workers that would be in occupation i if they had the same occupational attainment function as NSC, then decomposing equation (17) further yields:

$$\ln(G+1) = \sum_i \ln \overline{Y}_{iNSC}(P_{iNSC} - \hat{P}_{iSC}) + \sum_i \ln \overline{Y}_{iNSC}$$

$$(\hat{P}_{iSC} - P_{iSC}) + \sum_i P_{iSC}(\ln \overline{Y}_{iNSC} - \ln \overline{Y}_{iSC}) \tag{18}$$

where the first term represents the part of the gross wage differential attributable to the difference between the observed NSC occupational distribution and the occupational distribution that SC workers would occupy if they had the NSC's occupational function; the second term is the component of the gross wage differential attributable to occupational differences not explained on the basis of personal characteristics, and may be termed job discrimination; and the third term represents the within-occupation wage differential. The proportions P_{iNSC} and $\hat{P}_{iSC}$ are estimated using a multinomial logit model. First we estimate an occupational attainment function for NSC and then we use these estimates to predict the proportion of SC workers that would be in occupation i if they had the same occupational attainment function as NSC. This predicted probability of SC occupation is used in the further decomposition.

The third term in equation 18 represents the within-occupation wage differential and is normally decomposed into a wage discrimination and a caste productivity term. However, instead of doing this, the term can be decomposed into an NSC overpayment term, an SC underpayment term, and a within-occupation wage differential explained by productivity characteristics of the two groups. To calculate these three terms, the "pooled" methodology of Oaxaca and Ransom (1994) is used. Equation 19 presents the within-occupation gross caste wage differential defined as:

$$\sum_i P_{iSC} \ln(G+1) = \sum_i P_{iSC}[\ln \overline{Y}_{iNSC} - \ln \overline{Y}_{iSC}] \tag{19}$$

The actual proportion of SC workers in each occupational group is dropped for simplicity until the final equation is derived. It will be noted that equation 19 is identical to equation 7 but for the occupation subscript. Following the methodology of Oaxaca and Ransom (1994), the within-occupation gross wage differential is decomposed into a productivity differential and an unexplained effect that may be attributed to within-occupation wage discrimination. The within-occupation logarithmic productivity differential is defined as $\Sigma_i \ln(Q+1)$, where Q is the gross unadjusted productivity differential. To calculate the logarithmic term, a nondiscriminatory or competitive wage structure is required so that:

$$\sum_i \ln(Q+1) = \ln \overline{Y}^*_{iNSC} - \ln \overline{Y}^*_{iSC} \tag{20}$$

where $\ln \overline{Y}^*_{ir}$ is the average nondiscriminatory wage structure for caste r in occupation i. To calculate the pooled wage structure, the NSC and SC logarithmic wage structures are estimated using an earnings function, with the assumption that:

$$\ln \overline{Y}_{ir} = \tilde{\beta}_{ir}(\overline{X}_{ir}) \tag{21}$$

where $\tilde{\beta}_r$ and $\overline{X}_r$ are the vector of coefficients and average productivity characteristics of the different caste workers, estimated by OLS. The calculation of the nondiscriminatory wage structure depends on the weighting given to the NSC and SC wage structures. We have discussed the pooled wage structure in equations (13) and (14) (see Oaxaca and Ransom 1994). Given the pooled wage structure in equation (13), within-occupation logarithmic wage discrimination is calculated by subtracting equation (20) from equation (19) to give us:

$$\sum_i \ln(D+1) = (\ln \overline{Y}_{iNSC} - \ln \overline{Y}_{iNSC}^*) + (\ln \overline{Y}_{iNSC}^* - \ln \overline{Y}_{iSC}) \qquad (22)$$

The gross wage differential is thus decomposed into a productivity and a discriminatory term, meaning that the final within-occupation gross logarithmic wage differential is equivalent to:

$$\sum_i P_{iSC}[\ln(G+1)] = \sum_i P_{iSC}[\ln \overline{Y}_{iNSC}^* - \ln \overline{Y}_{iSC}^*] + \sum_i P_{iSC}$$

$$[\ln \overline{Y}_{iNSC} - \ln \overline{Y}_{iNSC}^*] + \sum_i P_{iSC}[\ln \overline{Y}_{iSC}^* - \ln \overline{Y}_{iSC}]$$

$$(23)$$

Substituting equation (23) for the third component in equation (18) yields the final decomposition of the gross-logarithmic wage differential:

$$\ln(G+1) = \sum_i \ln \overline{Y}_{iNSC}(P_{iNSC} - \hat{P}_{iSC}) + \sum_i \ln \overline{Y}_{iNSC}(\hat{P}_{iSC} - P_{iSC}) + \sum_i P_{iSC}$$

$$[\ln \overline{Y}_{iNSC}^* - \ln \overline{Y}_{NSC}^*] \sum_i P_{iSC}[\ln \overline{Y}_{iNSC} - \ln \overline{Y}_{iNSC}^*] + \sum_i P_{iSC}[\ln \overline{Y}_{iSC}^* - \ln \overline{Y}_{iSC}] \quad (24)$$

Hence a multinomial logit nondiscriminatory model can be calculated that can distinguish between within-occupation SC underpayment, within-occupation NSC overpayment, and occupational discrimination. Finally, to estimate this model, equations (21) and (13) are substituted into equation (24) to give final extended decomposition as:

$$\ln(G+1) = \sum_i \tilde{\beta}_{iNSC}(\overline{X}_{iNSC})(P_{iNSC} - \hat{P}_{iSC}) \textbf{ (Job Explained)}$$

$$+ \sum_i \tilde{\beta}_{iNSC}(\overline{X}_{iNSC})(\hat{P}_{iSC} - P_{iSC}) \textbf{ (Job Discrimination)}$$

$$+ \sum_i P_{iSC}[\hat{\beta}_i^*(\overline{X}_{iNSC} - \overline{X}_{iSC})] \textbf{ (Wage Explained)}$$

$$+ \sum_i P_{iSC}[\overline{X}_{iNSC}(\tilde{\beta}_{iNSC} - \tilde{\beta}_i^*)] \textbf{ (Wage overpayment to NSC)}$$

$$+ \sum_i P_{iSC}[\overline{X}_{iSC}(\tilde{\beta}_i^* - \tilde{\beta}_{iSC})] \textbf{ (Wage underpayment to SC)}$$

$$(25)$$

The wage overpayment and underpayment together constitute wage discrimination.

APPENDIX 2

See table 13.8 on pages 276–277.

Table 13.8 Descriptive Statistics of Main Variables in the Earnings Function

Variables	Description of the Variables	1999–2000					
		FC		OBC		SC	
		Mean	SD	Mean	SD	Mean	SD
Lwage	logarithm of daily wage (in rupees)	4.952815	0.846096	4.603097	0.866684	4.64658	0.826999
Age	Age in years	37.16764	11.00094	35.99369	11.41067	36.53055	11.18109
Agesq	Age square (in years)	1502.448	846.3519	1425.737	861.2629	1459.47	845.4274
Bprim	If the worker has completed below primary education = 1; 0 otherwise	0.042584	0.201922	0.06867	0.252905	0.084835	0.278667
Prim	If the worker has completed primary school = 1; 0 otherwise	0.065295	0.247052	0.118916	0.323706	0.134506	0.341232
Middle	If the worker has completed middle school = 1; 0 otherwise	0.13343	0.340046	0.18798	0.390716	0.187033	0.389981
Secon	If the worker has completed secondary school = 1; 0 otherwise	0.206962	0.405138	0.219212	0.413733	0.161758	0.368269
Hsc	If the worker has completed higher secondary school = 1; 0 otherwise	0.136175	0.342983	0.115172	0.319246	0.094066	0.291953
Grad_prof	If the worker has completed professional degree = 1; 0 otherwise	0.045842	0.209147	0.023744	0.152258	0.00989	0.098967
Grad_other	If the worker has completed general degree = 1; 0 otherwise	0.312887	0.46368	0.162168	0.368623	0.114945	0.318991
Male	If the individual's sex is male = 1; 0 otherwise	0.835435	0.370796	0.837833	0.368623	0.810989	0.39156
Married	If the individual is married =1; 0 otherwise	0.767255	0.422591	0.72197	0.44805	0.756264	0.429383

Variable	Description						
Public	If the worker is working in public sector = 1; 0 otherwise	0.384558	0.486502	0.309754	0.462415	0.436703	0.496032
Unionmem	If the worker is a union member = 1; 0 otherwise	0.429097	0.494959	0.381084	0.485677	0.464835	0.498817
Permanent	If the worker has permanent job = 1; 0 otherwise	0.72267	0.447691	0.678325	0.467142	0.658901	0.474131
South	If the individual works in south = 1; 0 otherwise	0.188207	0.390886	0.529458	0.499156	0.22	0.414292
West	If the individual works in west = 1; 0 otherwise	0.341416	0.474196	0.166108	0.372196	0.285495	0.451699
East	If the individual works in east = 1; 0 otherwise	0.127798	0.333873	0.051724	0.22148	0.101978	0.302653
Professional	If the individual's occupation is professional = 1; 0 otherwise	0.222832	0.416156	0.140394	0.347413	0.104615	0.306091
Admn	If the individual's occupation is administration = 1; 0 otherwise	0.058175	0.234079	0.025025	0.156208	0.016703	0.128171
Clerical	If the individual's occupation is clerical = 1; 0 otherwise	0.233444	0.423032	0.186995	0.389927	0.178681	0.383127
Service	If the individual's occupation is service = 1; 0 otherwise	0.093359	0.290941	0.120985	0.326126	0.26022	0.438803
Farmer	If the individual's occupation is farmer, fisherman, etc. = 1; 0 otherwise	0.007633	0.087032	0.02069	0.14235	0.024396	0.154291
Prodn	If the individual's occupation is production = 1; 0 otherwise	0.278308	0.448176	0.394483	0.488763	0.343956	0.475079

Note: The occupation is based on one-digit national Classification of Occupation. Professional = professional, technical, and related workers; administration = administrative, executive, and managerial workers; clerical = clerical and related workers; service = service workers; farmer = farmers, fishermen, hunters, loggers, and related workers; production = production-related workers, transport equipment operators, and laborers.

Notes

1. This approach allows only the intercept to vary by caste, but not the slope. To overcome this problem, we present earnings functions separately by caste.

2. See Mincer (1974) for a discussion of labor market earnings functions.

References

Abramovitz, Moses. 1986. "Catching Up, Forging Ahead, and Falling Behind." *Journal of Economic History* 46 no. 2 (June): 385–406.

Aguero, Jorge M. 2005. "Negative Stereotypes and Willingness to Change Them: Testing Theories of Discrimination." Working paper. Riverside: Department of Economics, University of California, 2005.

Aigner, Dennis J. and Glenn G. Cain. 1977. "Statistical Theories of Discrimination in Labor Markets." *Industrial and Labor Relations Review* 30 no. 2 (January): 175–187.

Akerlof, George. 1970. "The Market for Lemons; Quality Uncertainty and the Market Mechanism." *Quarterly Journal of Economics* 8 no. 43 (August): 488–500.

———. 1984. *An Economic Theorist's Book of Tales.* Cambridge: Cambridge University Press.

———. 1997. "Social Distance and Social Decisions." *Econometrica* 65 no. 5 (September): 1005–28.

Akoojee, Salim, and Simon McGrath. 2004. "Assessing the Impact of Globalization on South African Education and Training: A Review of the Evidence so Far." *Globalisation, Societies and Education* 2 no. 1 (March): 25–45.

Alesina, Alberto, and Eliana LaFerrara. 2000. "The Determinants of Trust." Discussion paper. National Bureau of Economic Research. In NBER database, http://www.nber.org/papers/w7621 (accessed July 1, 2009).

Altman, Miriam, and Marina Mayer. 2003. "Overview of Industrial Policy." In *Human Resources Development Review 2003: Education, Employment and Skills in South Africa*, edited by Human Sciences Research Council, 64–83. Cape Town: HSRC Press.

Aranoff, D., and J. Tedeschi. 1968. "Original Stakes and Behavior in the Prisoner's Dilemma Game." *Psychonomic Science* 12 no. 2: 79–80.

Arrow, Kenneth. 1972. "Models of Job Discrimination." In *Racial Discrimination in Economic Life*, edited by A. H. Pascall. Lexington, MA: D.C. Heath.

———. 1973. "The Theory of Discrimination." In *Discrimination in Labour Markets*, edited by Orley Ashenfelter and Albert Reeds, 3–33. Princeton, NJ: Princeton University Press.

———. 1998. "What Has Economics to Say about Racial Discrimination?" *Journal of Economic Perspectives* 12 no. 2 (Spring): 91–100.

Ashraf, Nava, Iris Bohnet, and Nikita Piankov. 2004. "Is Trust a Bad Investment?" Working paper RWP03–047, Kennedy School of Government, Harvard University. In KSG Working Paper Series database, http://www.hks.harvard.edu/wappp/research/working/ABP_Final.pdf (accessed July 1, 2009).

Ayres, Ian, and Peter Siegelman. 1995. "Race and Gender Discrimination in Bargaining for a New Car." *American Economic Review* 85 no. 3 (June): 304–21.

Azevedo, Thales de. 1996. *As Elites de Cor numa Cidade Brasileira: Um Estudo de Ascensão Social, Classes Sociais e Grupos de Prestígio.* Salvador: Edufba.

Banaji, Mahzarin R., Curtis Hardin, and Alexander J. Rothman. 1993. "Implicit Stereotyping in Person Judgment." *Journal of Personality and Social Psychology* 65 no. 2: 272–81.

Banerjee, Abhijit, Sebastian Galiani, Jim Levinsohn, Zoë McLaren, and Ingrid Woolard. 2006. "Why Has Unemployment Risen in the New South Africa?" Working Paper no. 134, Centre for International Development, Harvard University.

Banerjee, B., and J. B. Knight. 1985. "Caste Discrimination in the Indian Urban Labour Market." *Journal of Development Economics* 17 no. 3: 277–307.

Bardhan, Pranab. 2006. "Globalization and the Limits to Poverty Alleviation." In *Globalization and Egalitarian Redistribution*, edited by Pranab Bardhan, Samuel Bowles, and Michael Wallerstein, ch. 1. Oxford: Oxford University Press.

Becker, Gary. 1962. *The Economics of Discrimination.* Chicago: University of Chicago Press.

———. 1993. *Human Capital: A Theoretical Analysis with Special Reference to Education*, 3rd ed. Chicago: University of Chicago Press.

Bendick, Marc Jr., Lauren Brown, and Kennington Wall. 1999. "No Foot in the Door: An Experimental Study of Employment Discrimination against Older Workers." *Journal of Aging and Social Policy* 10 no. 4: 5–23.

Bendick, Marc Jr., Charles Jackson, and Victor Reinoso. 1994. "Measuring Employment Discrimination Through Controlled Experiments." *Review of Black Political Economy* 23: 25–48.

Berg, Joyce, John Dickhaut, and Kevin McCabe. 1995. "Trust, Reciprocity, and Social History." *Games and Economic Behaviour* 10 no. 1 (July): 122–42.

Bertrand, Marianne, and Sendhil Mullainathan. 2004. "Are Emily and Greg More Employable Than Lakisha and Jamal? A Field Experiment on Labor Market Discrimination." *American Economic Review* 94 no. 4: 991–1013.

Bickford-Smith, Vivian, Elizabeth van Heyningen, and Nigel Worden. 1999. *Cape Town in the Twentieth Century.* Cape Town: David Philip.

Blank, Rebecca M., Marilyn Dabady, and Constance F. Citro. 2004. *Measuring Racial Discrimination.* Washington, DC: National Academies Press.

Blau, Francine D., and Lawrence M. Kahn. 2003. "Understanding International Differences in the Gender Pay Gap." *Journal of Labor Economics* 21 no. 1 (January): 106–44.

Blauner, Robert. 1972. *Racial Oppression in America.* New York: Harper & Row.

Blinder, A. S. 1973. "Wage Discrimination: Reduced Form and Structural Estimates." *Journal of Human Resources* 8: 436–55.

Bobo, Lawrence, James Kluegel, and Ryan Smith. 1997. "Laissez-Faire Racism: The Crystallization of a 'Kinder, Gentler' Anti-Black Ideology." In *Racial Attitudes in the 1990s: Continuity and Change*, eds. Steven A. Tuch and Jack K. Martin. Westport, CT: Praeger.

Bodenhausen, Galen. 1988. "Stereotypic Biases in Social Decision Making and Memory: Testing Process Models of Stereotype Use." *Journal of Personality and Social Psychology* 55: 726–37.

Bogardus, Emory. 1947. "Changes in Racial Distances." *International Journal of Opinion and Attitude Research* 1: 55–62.

Bohnet, Iris, and Bruno Frey. "Social Distance and Other-Regarding Behaviour in Dictator Games: Comment." *American Economic Review* 89 no. 1 (March): 335–39.

Bolton, Gary E., and Elena Katok. "An Experimental Test for Gender Differences in Beneficent Behaviour." *Economic Letters* 48 no. 3–4 (June): 287–92.

Bouckaert, Jan, and Geert Dhaene. 2004. "Inter-Ethnic Trust and Reciprocity: Results from an Experiment with Small Businessmen." *European Journal of Political Economy* 20 no. 4 (November): 869–86.

Bourdieu, P. 1985. "The Forms of Capital." In *Handbook of Theory and Research for the Sociology of Education*, edited by John Richardson, 241–58. New York: Greenwood.

Bourdieu, P., and J.-C. Passeron. 1973. "Cultural Reproduction and Social Reproduction." In *Knowledge, Education and Cultural Change*, edited by Richard K. Brown, 71–112. London: Tavistock.

Bowles, Samuel. 2006. "Egalitarian Redistribution in Globally Integrated Economies." In *Globalization and Egalitarian Redistribution*, edited by Pranab Bardhan, Samuel Bowles, and Michael Wallerstein, ch. 5. Oxford: Oxford University Press.

Bowles, Samuel, and Ugo Pagano. 2006. "Economic Integration, Cultural Standardization, and the Politics of Social Insurance." In *Globalization and Egalitarian Redistribution*, edited by Pranab Bardhan, Samuel Bowles, and Michael Wallerstein, ch. 11. Oxford: Oxford University Press.

Breen, Richard. 1994. "Individual Level Models for Mobility Tables and Other Cross-Classifications." *Sociological Methods and Research* 23 no. 2: 147–73.

———. 1996. *Regression Models: Censored, Sample Selected, or Truncated Data*. Sage University Paper no. 111. Thousand Oaks, CA: Sage.

Brewer, M. B., and R. M. Kramer. 1986. "Choice Behaviour in Social Dilemmas: Effects of Social Identity, Group Size, and Decision Framing." *Journal of Personality and Social Psychology* 50: 593–604.

Brinton, Mary C. 1993. *Women and Economic Miracle: Gender and Work in Postwar Japan*. Berkeley: University of California Press.

Brown, Colin, and Pat Gay. 1985. *Racial Discrimination 17 Years after the Act*. London: Policy Studies Institute.

Brown, R. S., M. Moon, and B. S. Zoloth. 1980. "Incorporating Occupational Attainment in Studies of Male/Female Earnings Differentials." *Journal of Human Resources* 15: 3–28.

Bunting, I. 2002a. "The Higher Education Landscape under Apartheid." In *Transformation in Higher Education: Global Pressures and Local Realities in South Africa*, edited by N. Cloete, R. Fehnel, P. Maassen, T. Moja, H. Perold, and T. Gibbon, 58–86. Landsdowne, Cape: Juta.

———. 2002b. "Students." In *Transformation in Higher Education: Global Pressures and Local Realities in South Africa*, edited by N. Cloete, R. Fehnel, P. Maassen, T. Moja, H. Perold, and T. Gibbon, 147–70. Landsdowne, Cape: Juta.

Burns, Justine. 2006. "Racial Stereotypes, Stigma and Trust in Post-apartheid South Africa." *Economic Modelling* 23 no. 5 (September): 805–21.

———. 2008. "Inequality Aversion and Group Identity in a Segmented Society." Mimeo. University of Cape Town.

Buss, David M. 1999. *Evolutionary Psychology: The New Science of the Mind*. Boston: Allyn and Bacon.

Caillaux, E. L. 1994. "Cor e Mobilidade Social no Brasil." *Estudos Afro-Asiáticos* no. 26: 53–66.

Camerer, Colin. 1997. "Individual Decision Making." In *The Handbook of Experimental Economics*, edited by John Kagel and Alvin Roth, 587–704. Princeton: Princeton University Press.

———. 2002. *Behavioural Game Theory.* Princeton: Princeton University Press.

Cameron, Steven, and James Heckman. "Life Cycle Schooling and Dynamic Selection Bias: Models and Evidence for Five Cohorts of American Males." *Journal of Political Economy* 106 no. 2 (April): 262–333.

Cancio, A. Silvia, T. David Evans, and David J. Maume, Jr. 1996. "The Declining Significance of Race Reconsidered." *American Sociological Review* 61: 541–56.

Cardoso, Fernando H., and O. Ianni. 1960. *Cor e Mobilidade Social em Florianópolis: Aspectos das Relações entre Negros e Brancos numa Comunidade do Brasil Meridional.* São Paulo: Companhia Editora Nacional (Coleção *Brasiliana*, vol. 307).

Carmichael, Stokely, and Charles Hamilton. 1967. *Black Power: The Politics of Liberation in America.* Cambridge, MA: Blackwell.

Carpenter, J. 2002. "Measuring Social Capital: Adding Field Experimental Methods to the Analytical Toolbox." In *Social Capital and Economic Development: Well Being in Developing Countries*, edited by Jonathan Isham, Thomas Kelly, and Sunder Ramaswamy. Cheltenham, UK: Biddles.

Carr, Deborah, and Michael A. Friedman. 2005. "Is Obesity Stigmatizing? Body Weight, Perceived Discrimination, and Psychological Well-Being in the United States." *Journal of Health and Social Behavior* 46: 244–59.

Carter, M. R., and M. Castillo. 2003. "An Experimental Approach to Social Capital in South Africa." Staff Paper Series 448, University of Wisconsin, Agricultural and Applied Economics.

Carter, Stephen. 2005. *Reflections of an Affirmative Action Baby.* New York: Basic Books.

Carvalho, A. P., and M. C. Neri. 2000. "Mobilidade Ocupacional e Raça: Origens, Destinos e Riscos dos Afro-Brasileiros." *Ensaios Econômicos*, no. 392, EPGE/ Fundação Getulio Vargas Editora.

Chandra, Kanchan. 2003. *Why Ethnic Parties Succeed: Patronage and Ethnic Headcounts in India.* Cambridge: Cambridge University Press.

Chaudhuri, A., and L. Gangadharan. 2002. "Gender Differences in Trust and Reciprocity. Paper presented at the AEA meetings, Atlanta, GA, January.

Choi, Minsik. 2006. "Threat Effects of Capital Mobility on Wage Bargaining." In *Globalization and Egalitarian Redistribution*, edited by Pranab Bardhan, Samuel Bowles, and Michael Wallerstein, ch. 3. Oxford: Oxford University Press.

Christopher, A. J. 2005. "Further Progress in the Desegregation of South African Towns and Cities, 1996–2001." *Development Southern Africa* 22 no. 2 (June): 267–76.

Coate, Steven, and Glenn Loury. 1993. "Will Affirmative Action Policies Eliminate Negative Stereotypes?" *American Economic Review* 83 no. 5 (December): 1220–40.

Cohen, Daniel. 2005. *Globalization and Its Enemies.* Boston: MIT Press.

Cohen, Samuel. 1985. *The Process of Occupational Sex-Typing: The Feminization of Clerical Labor in Great Britain.* Philadelphia: Temple University Press.

Collins, Randall. 1979. *Credential Society: A Historical Sociology of Education and Stratification.* New York: Academic Press.

Conley, Dalton. 1999. *Being Black: Living in the Red: Race, Wealth and Social Policy in America.* Berkeley: University of California Press.

Cornell, Bradford, and Ivo Welch. 1996. "Culture, Information, and Screening Discrimination." *Journal of Political Economy* 104 no. 3 (June): 542–71.

Corrigan, Patrick, Vetta Thompson, David Lambert, et al. 2003. "Perceptions of Discrimination among Persons with Serious Mental Illness." *Psychiatric Services* 54 no. 8: 1105–10.

Cosser, M. 2009. *Studying Ambitions: Pathways from Grade 12 and the Factors That Shape Them.* Cape Town: HSRC Press.

Cosser, M., with du Toit, J. 2002. *From School to Higher Education? Factors Affecting the Choices of Grade 12 Learners.* Cape Town: HSRC Press.

Cosser, M., with Sehlola. 2009. *Thwarted Ambitions: Grade 12 Learner Destinations One Year On.* Cape Town: HSRC Press.

Costa Pinto, L. 1952. *O Negro no Rio de Janeiro: Relações de Raça numa Sociedade em Mudança.* São Paulo: Companhia Editora Nacional.

Costa Ribeiro, Carlos Antonio. 2010. *Estrutura de Classe e Mobilidade Social no Brasil.* Bauru: Edusc.

Cotton, C. J. 1988. "On the Decomposition of Wage Differentials." *Review of Economics and Statistics* 70: 236–43.

Cox, J. 2002. "Trust, Reciprocity, and Other Regarding Preferences: Groups vs. Individuals and Males vs. Females." In *Advances in Experimental Business Research*, edited by Rami Zwick and A. Rapoport, 331–50. Boston: Kluwer.

Cragg, J.C. 1971. "Some Statistical Models for Limited Dependent Variables." *Econometrica* 39: 829–44.

Crosby, Faye J. 1982. *Relative Deprivation and Working Women.* New York: Oxford University Press.

———. 1984. "The Denial of Personal Discrimination." *American Behavioral Scientist* 27 no. 3: 371–86.

Croson, Rachel, and Nancy Buchan. 1999. "Gender and Culture: International Experimental Evidence from Trust Games." *American Economic Review Papers and Proceedings* 89 no. 2: 386–91.

Cross, Harry, Genevieve Kenney, Jane Mell, and Wendy Zimmerman. 1990. *Employer Hiring Practices: Differential Treatment of Hispanic and Anglo Job Seekers.* Washington, DC: Urban Institute Press, 1990.

Daniel, William Wentworth. 1968. *Racial Discrimination in England.* Middlesex: Penguin Books.

Darity, William, and Ashwini Deshpande. 2003. *Boundaries of Clan and Color.* New York: Routledge.

Darity, William, and Patrick Mason. 1998. "Evidence on Discrimination in Employment: Codes of Color, Codes of Gender." *Journal of Economic Perspectives* 12 no. 2 (Spring): 63–90.

DeParle, Jason. 2007. "A Good Provider Is Someone Who Leaves." *New York Times Magazine*, April 22.

Deshpande, Ashwini. 2005. "Do Markets Discriminate? Some Insights from Economic Theories." In *Reservation and the Private Sector*, edited by Sukhadeo Thorat, Aryma, and Prasant Negi. New Delhi: Ramat Publishers.

DiPrete, Thomas, and David Grusky. 1990. "Structure and Trend in the Process of Stratification for American Men and Women." *American Journal of Sociology* 96: 107–43.

Domina, Thurston. 2006. "Brain Drain and Brain Gain: Rising Educational Segregation in the United States 1940–2000." *City and Community* 5 no. 4: 387–407.

Du Bois, W. E. B. 1903. *The Souls of Black Folk*. Chicago: A.C. McClurg.

Dudley-Jenkins, Laura. 2003. *Identity and Identification in India: Defining the Disadvantaged*. New York: Routledge.

Dufwenberg, Martin, and Astri Muren. 2002. "Discrimination by Gender and Social Distance." Discussion paper, Department of Economics, Stockholm University.

Duraisamy, P. 2002. "Changes in the Returns to Education in India, 1983–94: By Gender, Age-Cohort and Location." *Economics of Education Review* 21 no. 6: 609–22.

Dutta, P. V. 2004. "Structure of Wages in India, 1983–1999." Working paper no. 25, Poverty Research Unit, University of Sussex. In PRUS database, http://www .sussex.ac.uk/Units/PRU/wps/wp25.pdf (accessed July 1, 2009).

Eckel, Catherine, and Philip Grossman. 1996. "Altruism in Anonymous Dictator Games." *Games and Economic Behaviour* 16 no. 2 (October): 181–91.

———. 1998. "Are Women Less Selfish Than Men? Evidence from Dictator Experiments." *Economic Journal* 108 no. 448 (May): 726–35.

Eckel, Catherine, and R. Wilson. 2003. "Conditional Trust: Sex, Race and Facial Expressions in a Trust Game." Discussion paper, Virginia Tech and Rice University.

Elliot, James. 2001. "Referral Hiring and Ethnically Homogeneous Jobs." *Social Science Research* 30: 401–25.

Erickson, Robert, and John Goldthorpe. 1993. *The Constant Flux: A Study of Class Mobility in Industrial Nations*. Oxford: Clarendon Press.

Ermisch, John F., and Robert E. Wright. "Wage Offers and Full-Time and Part-Time Employment by British Women." *Journal of Human Resources* 28 no. 1: 111–33.

Fanon, Frantz. 1952. *Peau Noire, Masques Blancs*. Paris: Éditions du Seuil.

Farkas, George. 2003. "Cognitive Skills and Noncognitive Traits and Behaviors in Stratification Processes." *Annual Review of Sociology* 29: 541–62.

Fazio, Russell H., and Michael A. Olson. 2003. "Implicit Measures in Social Cognition: Their Meaning and Use." *Annual Review of Psychology* 54: 297.

Feagin, Joe R., and Melvin P. Sikes. 1994. *Living with Racism: The Black Middle-Class Experience*. Boston: Beacon Press.

Fehr, Ernst, and Georg Kirchsteiger. 1997. "Reciprocity as a Contract Enforcement Device: Experimental Evidence." *Econometrica* 65: 833–60.

Fehr, Ernst, Georg Kirchsteiger, and Arno Riedel. 1993. "Does Fairness Prevent Market Clearing? An Experimental Investigation." *Quarterly Journal of Economics* 108: 437–60.

Fernandes, D. 2005. "Estratificação Educacional, Origem Socioeconômica e Raça no Brasil: As Barreiras de Cor." Prêmio IPEA 40 Anos-IPEA-CAIXA 2004 (Monografias Premiadas), Brasília, IPEA.

Fernandes, Florestan. 1965. *A Integração do Negro na Sociedade de Classes*. São Paulo: Companhia Editora Nacional.

Fernandez, Roberto, and Celina Su. 2004. "Space in the Study of Labor Markets." *Annual Review of Sociology* 30: 545–69.

Fershtman, Chaim, and Uri Gneezy. 2001. "Discrimination in a Segmented Society: An Experimental Approach." *Quarterly Journal of Economics* 116: 351–77.

Fershtman, Chaim, Uri Gneezy, and F. Verboven. 2002. "Discrimination and Nepotism: The Efficiency of the Anonymity Rule." Discussion paper, Eitan Berglas School of Economics, Tel Aviv University.

Festinger, Leon. 1957. *A Theory of Cognitive Dissonance*. Stanford, CA: Stanford University Press.

Fiske, Susan. 1998. "Stereotyping, Prejudice, and Discrimination." In *The Handbook of Social Psychology*, edited by Daniel Gilbert, Susan Fiske, and Gardner Lindzay. New York: Oxford University Press.

Fix, Michael, George Galster, and Raymond Struyk, eds. 1993. *Clear and Convincing Evidence: Measurement of Discrimination in America*. Washington, DC: Urban Institute Press.

Foote, Daniel H. 1996. "Judicial Creation of Norms in Japanese Labor Law: Activism in the Service of—Stability?" *UCLA Law Review* 43 no. 3: 635–709.

Forsythe, Robert, Joel Horowitz, N. Savin, and Martin Seftin. 1994. "Fairness in Simple Bargaining Experiments." *Games and Economic Behaviour* 6: 347–69.

Foster, Andrew D., and Mark R. Rosenzweig. 1996. "Technical Change and Human-Capital Returns and Investments: Evidence from the Green Revolution." *American Economic Review* 86 no. 4 (September): 931–53.

Frohlich, Norman, and Joe Oppenheimer. 1984. "Beyond Economic Man." *Journal of Conflict Resolution* 28 no.1: 3–24.

Fryer, Ronald G. Jr., and Steven D. Levitt. 2004. "The Causes and Consequences of Distinctively Black Names." *Quarterly Journal of Economics* 119 no. 3 (August): 767–805.

Fryer, Roland G. Jr., and Glenn C. Loury. 2005. "Affirmative Action and Its Mythology." *Journal of Economic Perspectives* 19 no. 3: 147–62.

Ganzeboom, Harry, and Donald Treiman. 1996. "Internationally Comparable Measures of Occupational Status for the 1988 International Standard Classification of Occupations." *Social Science Research* 25 no. 3: 201–39.

Gibson, James L. 2004. *Overcoming Apartheid: Can Truth Reconcile a Divided Nation?* Pretoria: Human Sciences Research Council Press.

Gibson, James L., and Amanda Gouws. 2003. *Overcoming Intolerance in South Africa: Experiments in Democratic Persuasion*. Cambridge: Cambridge University Press.

Gilens, Martin. 1999. *Why Americans Hate Welfare: Race, Media, and the Politics of Antipoverty Policy*. Chicago: University of Chicago Press.

Gillborn, D. 1999. "Race, Nation and Education: New Labour and the New Racism." In *Education Policy and Contemporary Politic*, edited by Jack Demaine, 82–102. Basingstoke: Macmillan.

Glaeser, Edward, David Laibson, José Scheinkman, and Christine L. Soutter. 2000. "Measuring Trust." *Quarterly Journal of Economics* 115 no. 3: 811–46.

Goff, Philip Atiba. 2005. "The Space between Us: Stereotype Threat for Whites in Interracial Domains." Doctoral dissertation submitted to the Department of Psychology, Stanford University.

Goffman, Erving. 1959. *The Presentation of Self in Everyday Life*. New York: Doubleday.

Goldin, Claudia. 1990. *Understanding the Gender Gap: An Economic History of American Women*. New York: Oxford University Press.

Goodman, Leo, and M. Hout. 1998. "Statistical Methods and Graphical Displays for Analyzing How the Association between Two Qualitative Variables Differs among Countries, among Groups or Over Time: A Modified Regression-Type Approach." *Sociological Methodology* 28: 175–230.

Government of India, Prime Minister's Office. 2006. *Social, Economic, and Educational Status of the Muslim Community of India*. New Dehli.

Granovetter, Mark. 1974. *Getting a Job: A Study of Contacts and Careers*. Cambridge, MA: Harvard University Press.

Greenhalgh, C. 1980. "Male-Female Differentials in Great Britain: Is Marriage an Equal Opportunity?" *Economic Journal* 90: 751–75.

Gunderson, Morley. 1989. "Male-Female Wage Differentials and Policy Responses." *Journal of Economic Literature* 27 no. 1 (March): 46–117.

Hakim, Catherine. 1996. *Key Issues in Women's Work: Female Heterogeneity and the Polarisation of Women's Employment.* London: Athlone.

Hakken, Jon. 1979. *Discrimination against Chicanos in the Dallas Rental Housing Market: An Experimental Extension of the Housing Market Practices Survey.* Washington, DC: U.S. Department of Housing and Urban Development.

Harbough, William T., Kate Krause, and Lise Vesterlund. 2002. "Risk Attitudes of Children and Adults." *Experimental Economics* 5: 53–84.

Hasenbalg, Carlos. 1979. *Discriminação e Desigualdades Raciais no Brasil.* Rio de Janeiro: Graal.

———. 1988. "Raça e Mobilidade Social." In *Estrutura Social, Mobilidade e Raça,* edited by C. Hasenbalg and Nelson do Valle Silva. Rio de Janeiro: Iuperj/Vértice.

Hasenbalg, Carlos, and Nelson do Valle Silva, eds. 1988. *Estrutura Social, Mobilidade e Raça.* Rio de Janeiro: Iuperj/Vértice.

———. 1992. *Relações Raciais no Brasil Contemporâneo.* Rio de Janeiro: Rio Fundo Editora.

———. 1999a. "Educação e Diferenças Raciais na Mobilidade Ocupacional no Brasil." In *Cor e Estratificação Social,* edited by Carlos Hasenbalg, N. V. Silva, and M. Lima. Rio de Janeiro: Contracapa.

———. 1999b. "Race, Schooling and Social Mobility in Brazil." *Ciência e Cultura* 51 (1999): 457–63.

Hasenbalg, Carlos, Márcia Lima, and Nelson do Valle Silva. 1999. *Cor e Estratificação Social.* Rio de Janeiro: Contracapa.

Hara, Junsuke, and Kazuo Seiyama. 1999. *Inequality amid Affluence: Social Stratification in Japan.* Reprint, Melbourne: Trans Pacific Press, 2005.

Harbaugh, William, Kate Krause, and Steven Liday. 2003. "Bargaining by Children." Working paper, University of Oregon.

Harbaugh, William, Kate Krause, Steven Liday, and L. Vesterlund. 2002. "Trust in Children." Working paper, University of Oregon.

Harmon-Jones, Eddie, and Judson Mills, eds. 1999. *Cognitive Dissonance: Progress on a Pivotal Theory in Social Psychology.* Washington, DC: American Psychological Association.

Harvey, J. 2001. "The Trust Paradox: A Survey of Economic Inquiries into the Nature of Trust and Trustworthiness." Mimeo. University of Missouri.

Hawley, Joshua D. 2004. "Changing Returns to Education in Times of Prosperity and Crisis, Thailand 1985–1998." *Economics of Education Review* 23 no. 3: 273–86.

Heckman, James J. 1998. "Detecting Discrimination." *Journal of Economic Perspectives* 12 no. 2: 101–16.

Heckman, James, and Peter Siegelman. 1993. "The Urban Institute Audit Studies: Their Methods and Findings." In *Clear and Convincing Evidence: Measurement of Discrimination in America,* edited by Michael Fix and Raymond J. Struyk, 187–258. Washington, DC: Urban Institute Press.

Held, David, Anthony McGraw, David Goldblatt, and Jonathan Perraton. 1999. *Global Transformations: Politics, Economics and Culture.* Chicago: Stanford University Press.

Hendrickx, J. 2000. "Special Restriction in Multinomial Logistic Regression." *Stata Technical Bulletin* no. 56: 18–26.

Henriques, Ricardo. 2001. "Desigualdade Racial no Brasil: Evolução das Condições de Vida na Década de 90." *Texto para Discussão*, no. 807, Ipea.

Higuchi, Yoshio. 1991. "Joshi no gakurekibetsu syuugyou keireki to chingin kouzou" [Female Wage Structure and Work History across Education]. In *Nihon keizai to syugyou Koudou [Japanese Economy and Labor Participation]*, ch. 8. Tokyo: Toyo Keizai Shiposha.

Hills, John, Julian Le Grand, and David Piachaud. 2002. *Understanding Social Exclusion.* New York: Oxford University Press.

Hoff, K., and P. Pandey. 2003. "Why Are Social Inequalities So Durable? An Experimental Test of the Effects of Indian Caste on Performance." Discussion paper, World Bank and Pennsylvania State University.

Hoffman, Elizabeth, Kevin McCabe, Keith Shachat, and Vernon Smith. 1996. "Social Distance and Other-Regarding Behaviour in Dictator Games." *American Economic Review* 86: 653–60.

———. 2004. "Preference, Property Rights and Anonymity in Bargaining Games." *Games and Economic Behaviour* 7: 346–80.

Holzer, Harry. 1999. *What Employers Want: Job Prospects for Less-Educated Workers.* New York: Russell Sage Foundation.

Hook, J. and T.D. Cook. 1975. "Equity Theory and the Cognitive Ability of Children." *Psychological Bulletin* 86: 429–45.

Horvath, Francis W. 1982. "Forgotten Unemployment: Recall Bias in Retrospective Data." *Monthly Labor Review* 105 no. 3: 40–44.

Hossler, D., Braxton, J. M., and Coopersmith, G. 1989. "Understanding Student College Choice." In *Higher Education: Handbook of Theory and Research*, edited by J. C. Smart, vol. 5. New York: Agathon Press.

Houseman, Susan N., and Katharine G. Abraham. 1993. "Female Workers as a Buffer in the Japanese Economy." *American Economic Review* 83 no. 2: 45–51.

Indian Labour Bureau. Various years. *Indian Labour Statistics.* Labour Bureau, Ministry of Labour, Government of India.

Jacobsen, Joyce P. 1998. *The Economics of Gender.* 2nd ed. Basingstoke: Blackwell.

Japanese Ministry of Education, Culture, Sports, Science and Technology. 2002–2006 (every year). *Annual Report on the Basic School Survey* [Gakko kihon chosa hokokusho].

Japanese Ministry of Education, Science and Culture. 1956–2001 (every year). *Annual Report on the Basic School Survey* [Gakko kihon chosa hokokusho].

Japanese Ministry of Health, Labour and Welfare. Basic Survey on Wage Structure. http://www.mhlw.go.jp/english/database/db-l/index.html

Japanese Ministry of Internal Affairs and Communications, Statistics Bureau. Labour Force Survey. http://www.stat.go.jp/english/data/roudou/index.htm

Jencks, Christopher, and Meredith Phillips. 1998. *The Black-White Test Score Gap.* Washington, DC: Brookings Institution Press.

Jodhka, Surinder S. 2002. *Community and Identities: Contemporary Discourses on Culture and Politics in India.* Thousand Oaks, CA: Sage.

Jodhka, Surinder, and Katherine Newman. In press. "In the Name of Globalization: Meritocracy, Productivity and the Hidden Language Of Caste in the Employment

Process." In *Blocked by Caste*, eds. Katherine Newman and Sukhadeo Thorat. Delhi: Oxford University Press.

Johnes, Geraint, and Yasuhide Tanaka. 2008. "Changes in Gender Wage Discrimination in the 1990s: A Tale of Three Very Different Economies." *Japan and the World Economy* 20 no. 1: 97–113.

Jones, James. 1972. *Prejudice and Racism*. Reading, MA: Addison-Wesley.

Jowell, R., and Prescott-Clarke, P. 1970. "Racial Discrimination and White-Collar Workers in Britain." *Race* 11: 397–417.

Kallaway, Peter. 2002. *The History of Education under Apartheid 1948–1994*. New York: Peter Lewis.

Kanter, Rosabeth. 1977. *Men and Women of the Corporation*. New York: Basic Books.

Kawashima, Yoko, and Toshiaki Tachibanaki. 1986. "The Effect of Discrimination and of Industry Segmentation on Japanese Wage Differentials in Relation to Education." *International Journal of Industrial Organization* 4: 43–68.

Keio University. Japan Household Panel Survey. http://www.pdrc.keio.ac.jp/en/open/about-panel.html

Kessler, Ronald C., Kristin D. Mickelson, and David R. Williams. 1990. "The Prevalence, Distribution, and Mental Health Correlates of Perceived Discrimination in the United States." *Journal of Health and Social Behavior* 40 no. 3: 208–30.

Kijima, Yoko. 2006. "Why Did Wage Inequality Increase? Evidence from Urban India 1983–89." *Journal of Development Economics* 81: 91–117.

Kimura, Kunihiro. 2000. "Rodo shijo no kozo to yuhaigu josei no ishiki" [Structure of Labor Market and Social Consciousness of Married Women in Japan]. In *Jenda, shijo, kazoku* (Nihon no kaiso shisutemu 4) [*Gender, Market, and Family* (Stratification System in Japan 4)], edited by Kazuo Seiyama, 177–92. Tokyo: University of Tokyo Press.

———. 2007. "Education, Employment and Gender Ideology." In *Gender and Career in Japan*, edited by Atsuko Suzuki, 84–109. Melbourne: Trans Pacific Press.

Kimura, Masakazu. 2005. "*KHPS no Hyouhon tokusei, Kaitousya tokusei*" [Sample Characteristics of KHPS]. In *Dynamism of Japanese Household 1* [*Nihonnno Kakeikoudouno Dainamizumu*], edited byYoshio Higuchi, ch. 1. Tokyo: Keio University Press.

Kinder, Donald R., and David O. Sears. 1981. "Prejudice and Politics: Symbolic Racism Versus Racial Threats to the Good Life." *Journal of Personality and Social Psychology* 40: 414–31.

King, Kenneth, and McGrath, Simon. 2002. *Globalization, Enterprise and Knowledge*. Oxford: Symposium Books.

Kingdon, G. G. 1998. "Does the Labour Market Explain Lower Female Schooling in India?" *Journal of Development Studies* 35 no. 1: 39–65.

Kirshenmann, Joleen, and Kathryn Neckerman. 1991. "'We'd Love to Hire Them, But…': The Meaning of Race for Employers." In *The Urban Underclass*, edited by Christopher Jencks and Paul Peterson, 203–34. Washington, DC: Brookings Institution.

Knowles, L. L., and Kenneth Prewitt, eds. 1969. *Institutional Racism in America*. Englewood Cliffs, NJ: Prentice-Hall.

Kraak, A. 2003. "HRD and the Skills Crisis." In *Human Resources Development Review 2003: Education, Employment and Skills in South Africa*, edited by Human Sciences Research Council, 660–87. Cape Town: HSRC Press.

Kramer, Roderick M. 1999. "Trust and Distrust in Organisations: Emerging Perspectives, Enduring Questions." *Annual Review of Psychology* 50: 569–98.

Kutner, Bernard, Carol Wilkins, and Penny Rechtman Yarrow. 1952. "Verbal Attitudes and Overt Behavior Involving Racial Prejudice." *Journal of Abnormal Social Psychology* 47: 649–52.

Lackshmanasamy, T., and S. Mahdeswaran. 1995. "Caste Discrimination: Evidence from Indian Scientific and Technical Labour Market." *Indian Journal of Social Sciences* 8 no. 1: 59–77.

Lahey, Joanna. 2005. "Age, Women, and Hiring: An Experimental Study." Working paper 11435, National Bureau of Economic Research.

LaPiere, Richard T. 1934. "Attitudes vs. Actions." *Social Forces* 13: 230–37.

Lareau, Annette. 2003. *Unequal Childhoods: Race, Class, and Family Life.* Berkeley: University of California Press.

Leibbrandt, M., L. Poswell, P. Naidoo, and M. Welch. 2006. "Measuring Recent Changes in South African Inequality and Poverty Using 1996 and 2001 Census Data." In *Poverty and Policy in Post-apartheid South Africa*, edited by Haroon Bhorat and Ravi Kanbur. Cape Town, South Africa: HSRC Press.

Logan, J. A. 1983. "A Multivariate Model for Mobility Tables." *American Journal of Sociology* 89 no. 2: 324–49.

Loury, Glenn. 2002. *The Anatomy of Racial Inequality.* Cambridge: Harvard University Press.

Madheswaran, S. 1996. "Econometric Analyses of Labour Market for Scientists in India." PhD dissertation, University of Madras.

———. 2004. "Caste Discrimination in the Indian Labour Market: An Econometric Analysis." Mimeo. Institute for Social and Economic Change, Bangalore.

Manning, Patrick. 2005. *Migration in World History.* New York: Routledge.

Mansbridge, J. 1999. "Altruistic Trust." In *Democracy and Trust*, edited by Mark E. Warren, 290–309. Cambridge: Cambridge University Press.

Marais, Hein. 1998. *South Africa: Limits to Change.* London: Zed Books.

Mare, Robert. 1980. "Social Background and School Continuation Decisions." *Journal of the American Statistical Association* 75 (June): 295–305.

———. 1981. "Change and Stability in Educational Stratification." *American Sociological Review* 46: 72–87.

Marwell, Gerald, and Ruth E. Ames. 1981. "Economists Free Ride, Does Anyone Else?" *Journal of Public Economics* 15 no. 3: 295–310.

Massey, Douglas S. 2007. *Categorically Unequal: The American Stratification System.* New York: Russell Sage.

Massey, Douglas, and Nancy Denton. 1993. *American Apartheid: Segregation and the Making of the Underclass.* Cambridge MA: Harvard University Press.

Massey, Douglas, and Garvey Lundy. 2001. "The Use of Black English and Racial Discrimination in Urban Labor Markets: New Methods and Findings." *Urban Affairs Review* 36: 452–69.

Matsuura, Katsumi, and Yukiko Shigeno. 2005. "Daitoshikenni okeru ikujito josei no shugyo" ["Female Childbearing and Labor Participation in Metropolitan Area]. *Kaikei kensa kenkyu [Government Auditing Review]* 32: 181–213.

McConahey, J. B. 1986. "Modern Racism, Ambivalence, and the Modern Racism Scale." In *Prejudice, Discrimination, and Racism*, edited by John F. Dovidio and Samuel L. Gaertner. Orlando: Academic Press.

Mead, Lawrence. 2001. *Beyond Entitlement: The Social Obligations of Citizenship*. New York: Free Press.

Mendelsohn, Oliver, and Marika Vicziany. 1998. *The Untouchables: Subordination, Poverty, and the State in Modern India*. Cambridge: Cambridge University Press.

Merton, Robert K. 1949. *Social Theory and Social Structure*. Reprint, enlarged ed., New York: Free Press, 1968.

Messick, D., and M. Brewer. 1983. "Solving Social Dilemmas: A Review." In *Review of Personality and Social Psychology*, vol. 4, edited by L. Wheeler, 11–44. Beverly Hills, CA: Sage.

Meth, Charles. 2004. "Ideology and Social Policy: 'Handouts' and the Spectre of 'Dependency.'" *Transformation* 56: 1–30.

Mincer, Jacob. 1974. *Schooling, Experience and Earnings*. New York: Columbia University Press.

———. 1985. "Inter-country Comparisons of Labor Force Trends and of Related Developments: An Overview." *Journal of Labor Economics* 3 no. 1: 1–32.

Mincer, Jacob, and Yoshio Higuchi. 1988. "Wage Structures and Labor Turnover in the United States and Japan." *Journal of the Japanese and International Economies* 2: 97–133.

Mincer, Jacob, and Haim Ofek. 1982. "Interrupted Work Careers: Depreciation and Restoration of Human Capital." *Journal of Human Resources* 17: 3–24.

Mitchell, Gregory, and Philip E. Tetlock. 2006. "Antidiscrimination Law and the Perils of Mindreading." *Ohio State Law Journal* 67: 1023–1121.

Miyoshi, Koyo. 2008. "Male-Female Wage Differentials in Japan." *Japan and the World Economy* 20 no. 4: 479–96.

Moely, B. E., and Skarin, K. W. S. 1979. "Sex-Differences in Competition-Cooperation Behaviour of Children at Two Age Levels." *Sex Roles* 5 no. 3: 329–42.

Mohanty, Mritiunjoy. 2006. "Social Inequality, Labour Market Dynamics and the Need for Expanding Reservations." *Economic and Political Weekly* 41 no. 35 (September 2).

Moleke, P. 2005. *Finding Work: Employment Experiences of South African Graduates*. Cape Town: HSRC Press.

Moll, P. 1992. "The Decline of Discrimination against Coloured People in South Africa, 1970–1980." *Journal of Development Economics* 37: 289–307.

———. 1995. "Discrimination Is Declining in South Africa, but Inequality Is Not." Mimeo. Chicago: University of Chicago.

Morgan, Stephen L. 1996. "Trends in Black-White Differences in Educational Expectations, 1980–1992." *Sociology of Education* 69: 308–19.

———. 2005. *On the Edge of Commitment. Educational Attainment and Race in the United States*. Stanford, CA: Stanford University Press.

Moss, Philip, and Chris Tilly. 1996. "'Soft Skills' and Race: An Investigation of Black Men's Employment Problems." *Work and Occupations* 23: 256–76.

———. 2001. *Stories Employers Tell: Race, Skill, and Hiring in America*. New York: Russell Sage Press.

Murray, Charles. 1994. *Losing Ground: American Social Policy, 1950–1980*. New York: Basic Books.

Nagase, Nobuko. 2003. "Danjokan oyobi syuugyou keitai kanno chingin kouzou to chingin kakusa no suikei" [Wage Differentials between Males and Females, or among Work Status]. In *Hitennkeikoyouroudousyano Tayouna Syuugyoukeitai* [*Various Work Status of Non-regular Workers*], ch. 6. Japan Institute for Labour Policy and Training.

National Research Council. 2004. *Measuring Racial Discrimination*. Washington, DC: The National Academies Press.

National Sample Survey Organisation. 2001a. *Differences in Level of Consumption among Socio-economic Groups, 1999–2000*. NSS Report no. 472. New Delhi: Indian Ministry of Statistics and Programme Implementation.

————. 2001b. *Employment and Unemployment among Social Groups in India, 1999–2000*. NSS Report no. 469. New Delhi: Indian Ministry of Statistics and Programme Implementation.

————. 2001c. *Employment and Unemployment Situation in India, NSS 55th Round, 1999–2000—Part I*. New Delhi: Indian Ministry of Statistics and Programme Implementation.

————. 2001d. *Literacy and Levels of Education in India, 1999–2000*. NSS Report no. 473. New Delhi: Indian Ministry of Statistics and Programme Implementation.

Nattrass, Nicoli. 2006. "Trading Off Income and Health: AIDS and the Disability Grant in South Africa." *Journal of Social Policy* 35 no. 1 (January): 3–19.

Neuman, Soshana, and Ronald Oaxaca. 2004. "Wage Decompositions with Selectivity-Corrected Wage Equations: A Methodological Note." *Journal of Economic Inequality* 2: 3–10.

Neumark, David. 1988. "Employers' Discriminatory Behaviour and the Estimation of Wage Discrimination." *Journal of Human Resources* 23: 279–95.

————. 1996. "Sex Discrimination in Restaurant Hiring: An Audit Study." *Quarterly Journal of Economics* 111: 915–41.

Newell, A., and B. Reilly. 1999. "Rates of Return to Educational Qualifications in the Transitional Economies." *Education Economics* 7 no. 1: 67–84.

Newman, Katherine. 1999. *No Shame in My Game: The Working Poor in the Inner City*. New York: Random House.

Nicolaou, K. 2001. "The Link between Macroeconomic Policies, Education Policies and the Education Budget." In *Education and Equity: The Impact of State Policies on South African Education*, edited by Enver Motala and John Pampallis, 53–104. Sandown, South Africa: Heinemann.

Nogueira, Oracy. 1998. *Preconceito de Marca: As Relações Raciais em Itapetininga*. São Paulo, SP, Brasil: EDUSP.

Nowell, C., and Tinkler, S. 1994. "The Influence of Gender on the Provision of a Public Good." *Journal of Economic Behaviour and Organisation* 25 no. 1: 25–36.

Oaxaca, R. L. 1973. "Male-Female Wage Differentials in Urban Labor Markets." *International Economic Review* 14 no. 3: 693–709.

Oaxaca, R. L., and M. R. Ransom. 1994. "On Discrimination and the Decomposition of Wage Differentials." *Journal of Econometrics* 61: 5–21.

OECD, ed. 2002. *Employment Outlook*. Paris: Organization for Economic Co-operation and Development.

————. 2006. *OECD Economic Surveys: Japan*. Paris: Organization for Economic Co-operation and Development.

Ohashi, Isao. 2005. "Wages, Hours of Work and Job Satisfaction of Retirement-Age Workers." *Japanese Economic Review* 56 no. 2: 188–209.

Oliveira, L. E. G., R. M. Porcaro, and T. C. N. A. Costa. 1983. *O Lugar do Negro na Força de Trabalho*. Rio de Janeiro: IBGE.

Oliver, Melvin, and Thomas Shapiro. 1997. *Black Wealth/White Wealth: A New Perspective on Inequalit*y. Reprint, New York: Routledge, 2006.

Orbell, J., R. Dawes, and P. Schwartz-Shea. 1994. "Trust, Social Categories, and Individuals: The Case of Gender." *Motivation and Emotion* 18 no. 2: 109–28.

Orbell, J., A. van de Kragt, and R. Dawes. 1988. "Explaining Discussion Induced Cooperation." *Journal of Personality and Social Psychology* 545: 811–19.

Ortmann, A., and L. Tichy. 1999. "Gender Effects in the Laboratory: Evidence from Prisoners' Dilemma Games." *Journal of Economic Behaviour and Organisation* 39 no. 3: 327–39.

Osório, Rafael G. 2003. "Mobilidade Social sob a Perspectiva da Distribuição de Renda." Master's thesis, Departamento de Sociologia, UnB.

Ott, Bryant, Nikki Blacksmith, and Ken Royal. 2008. "Job Seekers: Personal Connections Still Matter." *Gallup Management Journal*. http://gmj.gallup.com/content/106957/Personal-Connections-Still-Matter.aspx (accessed May 30, 2009).

Oyer, Paul. 2004. "Recall Bias among Displaced Workers." *Economic Letters* 82 no. 3: 397–402.

Pager, Devah. 2003. "The Mark of a Criminal Record." *American Journal of Sociology* 108 no. 5: 937–75.

———. 2007. *Marked: Race, Crime and Finding Work in an Era of Mass Incarceration*. Chicago: University of Chicago Press.

Pager, Devah, and Lincoln Quillian. 2005. "Walking the Talk?: What Employers Say Versus What They Do." *American Sociological Review* 70 no. 3 (June): 355–80.

Papastergiadis, Nikos. 2000. *The Turbulence of Migration: Globalization, Deterritorialization and Hybridity*. Cambridge: Polity Press.

Patwardhan, V., and V. Palshikar. 1992. "Reserved Seats in Medical Education: a Study." *Journal of Education and Social Change* 5: 1–117.

Paulsen, M. 1990. *College Choice: Understanding Student Enrollment Behavior*. Washington, DC: ERIC Clearinghouse on Higher Education and George Washington University.

Perry, Alex. 2003. "India's Great Divide." *Time Asia* 162 no. 5.

Pettigrew, Thomas F. 1967. "Social Evaluation Theory: Convergence and Applications." In *Nebraska Symposium on Motivation* vol. 15, edited by David Levine, 241–311. Lincoln: University of Nebraska Press.

Phelps, Edmund S. 1972. "The Statistical Theory of Racism and Sexism." *American Economic Review* 62 no. 4: 659–61.

Pierson, D. 1945. *Brancos e Pretos na Bahia: Estudo de Contato Racial*. São Paulo, Companhia Editora Nacional. Coleção *Brasiliana*, vol. 241.

Policy Planning and Research Department, Ministry of Labour, Japan. 1966–2001 (every year). *Chingin sensasu: Chingin kozo kihon tokei chosa [Basic Survey on Wage Structure]*.

Posel, D. 2001. "What's in a Name? Racial Categorisations under Apartheid and Their Afterlife." *Transformation* 47: 50–74.

Powers, Daniel, and Yu Xie. 2000. *Statistical Methods for Categorical Data Analysis*. New York: Academic Press.

Quillian, Lincoln. 2006. "New Approaches to Understanding Racial Prejudice and Discrimination." *Annual Review of Sociology* 23: 299–328.

Raudenbusch, Stephen, Anthony Bryk, Yuk Fai Cheong, Richard Congdon, and Mathilda du Toit. 2004. *HLM6: Hierarchical Linear and Nonlinear Modelling.* Lincolnwood, IL: Scientific Software International.

Reimer, C. W. 1983. "Labour Market Discrimination against Hispanic and Black Men." *Review of Economics and Statistics* 65: 570–79.

———. 1985. "A Comparative Analysis of the Wages of Hispanic, Blacks and Non-Hispanic Whites." In *Hispanics in the U.S. Economy,* edited by G. J. Borjas and M. Tienda. New York: Academic Press.

Republic of South Africa. 1995. South African Qualifications Authority Act (Act No. 58 of 1995). Pretoria: Government Printer.

———. 1996. South African Schools Act (Act No. 84 of 1996). Pretoria: Government Printer.

———. 1997. Higher Education Act (Act No. 101 of 1997). Pretoria: Government Printer.

———. 1998. Further Education and Training Act (Act No. 98 of 1998). Pretoria: Government Printer.

———. 2000. Adult Basic Education and Training Act (Act No. 53 of 2000). Pretoria: Government Printer.

———. 2006. Further Education and Training Colleges Act (Act No. 16 of 2006). Pretoria: Government Printer.

Riach, Peter B., and Judith Rich. 1991–1992. "Measuring Discrimination by Direct Experimentation Methods: Seeking Gunsmoke." *Journal of PostKeynesian Economics* 14: 143–50.

———. 2002. "Field Experiments of Discrimination in the Market Place." *Economic Journal* 112 no. 483 (November): 480–518.

Ridley, Stanley, James A. Bayton, and Janice Hamilton Outtz. 1989. "Taxi Service in the District of Columbia: Is It Influenced by Patrons' Race and Destination?" Mimeo. Washington, DC: Washington Lawyers' Committee for Civil Rights under the Law.

Roberts, Ben. 2004. "The Happy Transition? Attitudes to Poverty and Inequality after a Decade of Democracy." In *South African Social Attitudes: Changing Times, Diverse Voices,* edited by Udesh Pillay, Ben Roberts, and Stephen Rule, 101–30. Pretoria: Human Sciences Research Council.

Robinson, W. S. 1950. "Ecological Correlation and the Behavior of Individuals." *American Sociological Review* 15 no. 3: 351–57.

Royster, Deirdre. 2003. *Race and the Invisible Hand: How White Networks Exclude Black Men from Blue-Collar Jobs.* Berkeley: University of California Press.

Runciman, W. G. 1966. *Relative Deprivation and Social Justice: A Study of Attitude to Social Inequality in Twentieth-Century England.* London: Routledge and Kegan Paul.

Saenger, Gerhart, and Emily Gilbert. 1950. "Custom Reactions to the Integration of Negro Sales Personnel." *International Journal of Opinion and Attitude Research* 4: 57–76.

Sagar, H. A., and J. W. Schofield. 1980. "Racial and Behavioral Cues in Black and White Children's Perceptions of Ambiguously Aggressive Acts." *Journal of Personality and Social Psychology* 39: 590–98.

Scarman, Lord Justice. 1981. "The Brixton Disorders 10–12 April 1981." Cmnd 8427. London: Home Office.

Scharleman, J., C. Eckel, A. Kacelnik, and R. Wilson. 2001. "The Value of a Smile: Game Theory with a Human Face." *Journal of Economic Psychology* 22: 617–40.

Schneider, B., and D. Stevenson. 1999. *The Ambitious Generation: America's Teenagers, Motivated but Directionless*. New Haven: Yale University Press.

Schuman, Howard. 1995. "Attitudes." In *Sociological Perspectives on Social Psychology*, edited by Karen Cook, Gary Fine, and James House. Boston: Allyn and Bacon.

Schuman, Howard, and Lawrence Bobo. 1988. "Survey Based experiments in White Racial Attitudes toward Residential Integration." *American Journal of Sociology* 94: 273–99.

Schuman, Howard, Charlottee Steeh, Lawrence Bobo, and Maria Krysan. 1997. *Racial Attitudes in America: Trends and Interpretations*. Cambridge, MA: Harvard University Press.

———. 2001. *Racial Attitudes in America: Trends and Interpretations*, revised edition. Cambridge, MA: Harvard University Press.

Schwab, Stewart. 1986. "Is Statistical Discrimination Efficient?" *American Economic Review* 76 no. 1: 228–34.

Schwartz, Richard, and Jerome Skolnick. 1962. "Two Studies of Legal Stigma." *Social Problems* 10: 133–42.

Scoville, James. 1991. "Towards a Formal Model of a Caste Economy." In *Status Influences in Third World Labor Markets: Caste, Gender, Custom*. New York: De Gruyter.

———. 1996. "Labour Market Underpinnings of a Caste Economy." *American Journal of Economics and Sociology* 55 no. 4: 385–94.

Searle-Chatterjee, Mary, and Ursula Sharma. 1994. *Contextualizing Caste: Post-Dumontian Approaches*. Oxford: Blackwell.

Seekings, Jeremy. 2007a. "The Mutability of Distributive Justice Beliefs in South Africa." *South African Review of Sociology* 38 no. 1 (June): 20–44.

———. 2007b. "'Not a Single White Person Should Be Allowed to Go Under': Swartgevaar and the Origins of South Africa's Welfare State, 1924–1929." *Journal of African History* 48 no. 3 (November): 375–94.

———. 2008a. "The Carnegie Commission and the Backlash against Welfare State-Building in South Africa, 1931–1937." *Journal of Southern African Studies* 34 no. 3 (September): 515–37.

———. 2008b. "The Continuing Salience of Race: Discrimination and Diversity in South Africa." *Journal of Contemporary African Studies* 26 no. 1 (January): 1–26.

———. 2008c. "Deserving Individuals and Groups: The Post-apartheid State's Justification of the Shape of South Africa's System of Social Assistance." *Transformation* 68: 515–37.

———. 2008d. "'Just Deserts': Race, Class and Distributive Justice in Post-apartheid South Africa." *Journal of Southern African Studies* 34 no. 1 (March): 39–60.

Seekings, Jeremy, Tracy Jooste, Mirah Langer, and Brendan Maughan-Brown. 2005. "Inequality and Diversity in Cape Town: An Introduction and User's Guide to the 2005 Cape Area Study." Working paper no. 124, Centre for Social Science Research, University of Cape Town.

Seekings, Jeremy, and Nicoli Nattrass. 2005. *Race, Class and Inequality in South Africa*. New Haven: Yale University Press. Published in South Africa in 2006 by University of KwaZulu-Natal Press.

Selten, Reinhart, and Axel Ockenfels. 1998. "An Experimental Solidarity Game." *Journal of Economic Behavior and Organization* 34 no. 4 (March): 517–39.

Sengupta, Somini, and Hari Kumar. 2006. "Quotas to Aid India's Poor vs. Push for Meritocracy." *New York Times,* May 23. http://select.nytimes.com/search/restricted/article?res=F70C1FFD3B5A0C708EDDAC0894DE404482.

Sharma, Ursula. 1999. *Caste*. London: Open University Press.

Shavit, Y., and H. P. Blossfeld. 1993. *Persistent Inequality: Changing Educational Attainment in Thirteen Countries*. Boulder, CO: Westview.

Silva, Nelson do V. 1988. "Cor e Processo de Realização Socioeconômica." In *Estrutura Social, Mobilidade e Raça,* edited by C. Hasenbalg and N. V. Silva. Rio de Janeiro: Vértice.

———. 2000. "Cor e Mobilidade Ocupacional." In *Mobilidade Social no Brasil,* edited by N. V. Silva and J. Pastore. São Paulo: Makron.

———. 2003. "Expansão Escolar e Estratificação Educacional no Brasil." In *Origens e Destinos: Desigualdades Sociais ao Longo da Vida,* edited by C. Hasenbalg and N. V. Silva. Rio de Janeiro: Topbooks.

Silva, Nelson do V., and A. M. Souza. 1986. "Um Modelo para Análise da Estratificação Educacional no Brasil." *Cadernos de Pesquisa* no. 58: 40–57.

Smith, Sandra. 2003. "Exploring the Efficacy of African Americans' Job Referral Networks." *Ethnic and Racial Studies* 26 no. 6: 1029–45.

Smith, Tom W. 1991. "Ethnic Images. General Social Survey Technical Report, 19." Chicago: National Opinion Research Center, University of Chicago.

———. 2001. *Intergroup Relations in a Diverse America: Data from the 2000 General Social Survey*. New York: American Jewish Committee.

Sniderman, Paul M., and Douglas B. Grob. 1996. "Innovation in Experimental Design in Attitude Surveys." *Annual Review of Sociology* 22: 377–99.

Sniderman, Paul M., and Thomas Piazza. 1993. *The Scar of Race*. Cambridge, MA: Belknap Press.

Soroka, Stuart, Keith Banting, and Richard Johnston. 2006. "Immigration and Redistribution in a Global Era." In *Globalization and Egalitarian Redistribution,* edited by P. Bardhan, S. Bowles, and M. Wallerstein, ch. 10. Oxford: Oxford University Press.

South African Council on Higher Education. 2000. *Towards a New Higher Education Landscape: Meeting the Equity, Quality and Social Development Imperatives of South Africa in the 21st Century*. http://www.che.ac.za/documents/d000009/New_HE_Landscape.pdf (accessed July 1, 2009).

South African Department of Education. 2000. Senior Certificate Examination Database. Pretoria: Department of Education.

———. 2001. *National Plan for Higher Education*. Pretoria: Department of Education.

———. 2002a. "Table 2.12 (2ND ORDER CESM) Headcount of Unduplicated Student Enrolments According to CESM Category of Major(s)/Area of Specialisation and Qualification Type. Institution: Universities." Pretoria: Department of Education, HEMIS database.

————. 2002b. "Table 2.12 (2ND ORDER CESM) Headcount of Unduplicated Student Enrolments According to CESM Category of Major(s)/Area of Specialisation and Qualification Type. Institution: Technikons." Pretoria: Department of Education, HEMIS database.

————. 2004. Senior Certificate Examination Database. Pretoria: Department of Education.

————. 2007a. *The National Policy Framework for Teacher Education and Development in South Africa.* Pretoria: Department of Education.

————. 2007b. "Table 2.12 (2ND ORDER CESM) Headcount of Unduplicated Student Enrolments According to CESM Category of Major(s)/Area of Specialisation and Qualification Type." Pretoria: Department of Education, HEMIS database.

————. 2008. *Education Statistics in South Africa 2006.* Pretoria: Department of Education.

South African Department of Finance. 1996. *Growth, Employment and Redistribution (GEAR): A Macroeconomic Strategy.* Pretoria: Government Printer.

Spence, A. Michael. 1974. *Market Signaling: Information Transfer in Hiring and Related Screening Processes.* Cambridge, MA: Harvard University Press.

Srinivas, M. N., ed. 1996. *Caste: Its Twentieth Century Avatar.* New Delhi: Penguin Books.

Standing, Guy, and Michael Samson. 2003. *A Basic Income Grant for South Africa.* Cape Town: University of Cape Town Press.

STATA Corporation. 2005. *STATA Longitudinal/Panel Data, Reference Manual release 9.* College Station, TX: Author.

Statistical Bureau, Management and Coordination Agency, Japan. 1966–2001 (every year). *Rodoryoku chosa nenpo [Annual Report on the Labour Force Survey].*

Statistical Bureau, Ministry of Internal Affairs and Communications, Japan. 2005–2006 (every year). *Rodoryoku chosa nenpo [Annual Report on the Labour Force Survey].*

Statistical Bureau, Ministry of Public Management, Home Affairs, Posts and Telecommunications, Japan. 2002–2004 (every year). *Rodoryoku chosa nenpo [Annual Report on the Labour Force Surve y].*

Statistics and Information Department, Ministry of Health, Labour and Welfare, Japan. 2002–2006 (every year). *Chingin sensasu: Chingin kozo kihon tokei chosa [Basic Survey on Wage Structure].*

Statistics South Africa. 2001. *Census in Brief.* Report no. 03–02–03 (2001). Pretoria: Statistics South Africa.

————. 2006. *Mid-year Population Estimates, South Africa 2006.* Statistical Release P030. Pretoria: Statistics South Africa.

Steeh, Charlotte, and Maria Krysan. 1996. "Trends: Affirmative Action and the Public, 1970–1995." *Public Opinion Quarterly* 60: 128–58.

Stockard, J., and J. D. P. Van deKragt. 1988. "Gender Roles and Behaviour in Social Dilemmas: Are There Sex Differences in Co-operation and in Its Justification?" *Social Psychology Quarterly* 512: 154–63.

Stockman, Norman, Norman Bonney, and Sheng Xuewen. 1995. *Women's Work in East and West: The Dual Burden of Employment and Family Life.* London: UCL Press.

Stouffer, Samuel A., Edward A. Suchman, Leland C. DeVinney, Shirley A. Star, and Robin M. Williams. 1949. *The American Soldier. Vol. 1: Adjustment during Army Life.* Princeton, NJ: Princeton University Press.

Tajfel, H. 1970. "Experiments in Intergroup Discrimination." *Scientific American* 223: 96–102.

Taylor, D. M., S. C. Wright, F. M. Moghaddam, and R. N. Lalonde. 1990. "The Personal/Group Discrimination Discrepancy: Perceiving My Group, But Not Myself, to Be a Target of Discrimination." *Personality and Social Psychology Bulletin* 16: 254–62.

Telles, E. 2003. *Racismo à Brasileira: Uma Nova Perspectiva Sociológica.* Rio de Janeiro: Relume-Dumará.

Thibodeau, Ruth, and Elliot Aronson. 1992. "Taking a Closer Look: Reasserting the Role of the Self-concept in Dissonance Theory." *Personality and Social Psychology Bulletin* 18 no. 5: 591–602.

Thorat, S. K. 2004. *Caste System in India: Social and Economic Exclusion and Poverty.* New Delhi: India Institute of Dalit Studies.

———. 2005. *Reservation Policy for Private Sector: Why and How.* Pune: Sugava Prakashan.

Thorat, S. K., and Umakant. 2004. *Caste, Race, and Discrimination: Discourses in International Context.* New Delhi: Rawat Publications.

Thorat, S. K., Aryama, and Prasant Negi. 2005. *Reservation and the Private Sector: Quest for Equal Opportunity and Growth.* New Delhi: Rawat Publications.

Topel, Robert. 1991. "Specific Capital, Mobility, and Wages: Wages Rise with Job Seniority." *Journal of Political Economy* 99 no. 1: 145–76.

Turner, Margery, Michael Fix, and Raymond Struyk. 1991. *Opportunities Denied, Opportunities Diminished: Racial Discrimination in Hiring.* Washington, DC: Urban Institute Press.

Turner, Margery Austin, and Felicity Skidmore, eds. 1999. *Mortgage Lending Discrimination: A Review of Existing Evidence.* Washington, DC: Urban Institute.

Umino, Michio, and Yuriko Saito. 1990. "Fukoheikan to manzokukan" [A Sense of Unfairness and Satisfaction]. In *Kaiso ishiki no dotai [Dynamic of Stratification Consciousness]*, edited by Junsuke Hara, 97–123. Tokyo: University of Tokyo Press.

Union of South Africa. 1949. Immorality Act (Act No. 21 of 1949). Pretoria: Government Printer.

———. 1950. Group Areas Act (Act No. 41 of 1950). Pretoria: Government Printer.

———. 1952. Natives Laws Amendment Act. Pretoria: Government Printer.

———. 1953a. Bantu Education Act (Act No. 47 of 1953). Pretoria: Government Printer.

———. 1953b. Reservation of Separate Amenities Act (Act No. 49 of 1953). Pretoria: Government Printer.

United Nations Development Programme. 2008. *Human Development Report 2007/2008 (Fighting Climate Change: Human Solidarity in a Divided World).* New York: Author.

U.S. Council of Economic Advisers. 2007. "Immigration's Economic Impact." CEA White Papers, June 20. http://georgewbush-whitehouse.archives.gov/cea/cea_immigration_062007.html (accessed July 1, 2009).

Van der Merwe, W., and Burns, J. 2008. "What's in a Name? Racial Identity and Altruism in Post-apartheid South Africa." *South African Journal of Economics* 76 no. 2 (June).

Wagley, C. 1952. *Race and Class in Rural Brazil.* Paris: UNESCO.

Walker, Andrew. 2007. "India's Economy 'Nears $1 Trillion.'" BBC News, February 6. http://news.bbc.co.uk/2/hi/business/6334305.stm.

Walker, Iain, and Heather J. Smith, eds. 2002. *Relative Deprivation: Specification, Development and Integration.* Cambridge: Cambridge University Press.

Weber, Max. 1968. *Economy and Society,* edited by Guenther Roth and Claus Wittich. New York: Bedminister Press.

Weisskopf, Thomas E. 2003. "Globalization and Affirmative Action." *Economic and Political Weekly* (Bombay, India) 38 no. 27: 2818–19.

———. 2004a. *Affirmative Action in the United States and India: A Comparative Perspective.* London: Routledge.

———. 2004b. "The Impact of Reservation on Admissions to Higher Education in India." *Economic and Political Weekly,* September 25.

———. 2006. "Is Positive Discrimination a Good Way to Aid Disadvantaged Communities?" *Economic and Political Weekly* (Bombay, India) 41 no. 8: 717–26.

West, C. 1994. *Race Matters.* New York: Vintage Books.

Western, John. 1991. *Outcast Cape Town.* Minneapolis: University of Minnesota Press.

Wienk, Ronald E., Clifford Reid, John Simonson, and Frederick Espers. 1979. *Measuring Discrimination in American Housing Markets.* Washington, DC: U.S. Department of Housing and Urban Development.

William T. Grant Foundation. "The Forgotten Half." *The Phi Delta Kappan* 70 no. 4.

Wilson, William Julius. 1996. *When Work Disappears: The World of the New Urban Poor.* New York: Vintage Books.

Winship, C., and R. Mare. 1992. "Models for Sample Selection Bias." *Annual Review of Sociology* 18: 327–50.

Wit, Arjaan, Henk Wilkie, and Harmen Oppewal. 1992. "Fairness in Asymmetrical Social Dilemmas" in W. Liebrand, D. Messick and Henk Wilkie,eds. *Social Dilemmas.* Oxford: Pergamon Press, 183–97.

Xie, Yu. 1992. "The Long-Multiplicative Layer Effect Model for Comparing Mobility Tables." *American Sociological Review* 16: 159–83.

Yinger, John. 1995. *Closed Doors, Opportunities Lost.* New York: Russell Sage Foundation.

Yonemura, Chiyo. 1998. "Shufu de aru koto, hataraku koto to kaiso ishiki" [Gender, Marriage and Class Identification]. In *Kaiso to kekkon, kazoku* [*Marriage, Family and Stratification*], edited by Hideki Watanabe and Kiyoshi Shida, 181–98. Tokyo: Study Group for Social Stratification and Social Mobility Survey.

Index